WOMEN'S
EXPERIENCES IN THE
HOLOCAUST

This book was written in loving memory of my mother Leona Grunwald (1913–1991) whose experiences conclude this book. Her resilience and fortitude both during the Holocaust and throughout a difficult and possibly unfulfilled life have always been an example to me.

The book is dedicated to my beloved grandchildren James Harry, Sophie Leona Anna and Ava Madeleine: their very existence is testimony to Leona's courage.

AGNES GRUNWALD-SPIER

WOMEN'S
EXPERIENCES IN THE
HOLOCAUST
IN THEIR OWN WORDS

AMBERLEY

First published 2018

Amberley Publishing
The Hill, Stroud
Gloucestershire, GL5 4EP

www.amberley-books.com

British Library Cataloguing in Publication Data.
A catalogue record for this book is available from the British Library.

ISBN 978 1 4456 7147 5 (hardback)
ISBN 978 1 4456 7148 2 (ebook)

Typesetting and Origination by Amberley Publishing.
Printed in the UK.

Contents

Acknowledgements

Firstly, I am grateful to Jon Jackson and his team at Amberley Publishing for commissioning this book and giving me an opportunity to write about a topic I had toyed with for some time. Shaun Barrington and Hazel Kayes have also been a pleasure to work with.

The publication of my previous books either coincided with a hip operation or the birth of grandchildren. This one has managed both with the lovely, jolly Ava Madeleine arriving in March 2017 and my new right hip in May. As before the staff at the British Library went out of their way to help me with my research and also carried books around and helped with photocopying. At the Wiener Library, Howard Falksohn and Verena Donig have been particularly helpful and Ben Barkow has been supportive, as ever. Without their help the task would have been much harder and taken so much longer.

I would also like to thank the institutions who helped me with information, documents and photographs – in particular the Ghetto Fighters' House in Israel, Yad Vashem in Jerusalem, the Imperial War Museum in London, the USHMM in Washington and the Leo Baeck Institute in New York. I would also like to thank Hildegard Abraham for the translation from Edith Erbrich's book and Keith Posner for translating Rosina Sorani's diary. I thank all those who gave permission to use pictures and extracts and if anyone has not been credited correctly I apologise. Any such omissions will be rectified on reprint.

A particular debt is owed to all the women and men who told me their stories and gave or lent me their books and memoirs. As the title indicates, my intention was that their stories should be presented in their own words. Where they had left no writings another members of the family told me the story, so it could be included.

I could have written the whole book about women in the camps, but I wanted to give an idea of the breadth of experience Jewish women suffered during the Holocaust. I wrote about quite a few mothers partly because so many women had to cope with motherhood during the Holocaust, but also in memory of my own mother, Leona Grunwald, who brought me safely though it all even though I was only six months old when we were liberated from the Budapest Ghetto. Additionally, perhaps we should ponder whether we would have had the courage to be a parachutist, *kasharit* or partisan?

As ever if there are errors, I apologise, but I hope I have done these remarkable women justice and ensured their stories are remembered with pride. So many of them died young without the chance to write a memoir or autobiography. It has been an honour to tell their stories, so that they and their courage will never be forgotten and in the hope that the canard of Jews going like lambs to the slaughter may become a thing of the past.

Agnes Grunwald-Spier

Currency Equivalents, 1940 to 2017

Thanks to Dan Spier

Currency	1940 £ equivalent	1940 $ equivalent	2017 £ equivalent	2017 $ equivalent
Reichsmark (Germany)	9.3p	40 cents	£5.20	$6.80
Crown (Czech)	1.4p	6 cents	78p	$1.02
Zloty (Poland)	4.2p	18 cents	£2.34	$3.06
GBPUSD	23p	$4.30	76p	$1.31

Introduction

'Why write about women only?' My son Ben asked me. 'Surely everyone had a dreadful time?' 'Yes,' I said, 'but women had a different sort of dreadful time because of their gender.'

Ruth Bondy, a survivor of Theresienstadt and Birkenau, also pondered this issue, before writing about the topic:

> Zyklon B did not differentiate between men and women; the same death swept them all away. Because the same fate awaited all Jews. I approached the writing of this chapter with grave reservations; why should I focus on women? Any division of the Holocaust and its sufferers according to gender seemed offensive to me. The issue of gender seemed to belong to another generation, another era. But I did not want the story of the women of Theresienstadt to be left out. So I undertook this task in the name of the women of Theresienstadt and began to examine, for myself, in what way the lives of women in the ghetto differed from the lives of men, and how one could explain this distinction, if explanation is possible.[1]

Speaking about Gisi Fleischmann, the Slovakian hero, the Israeli filmmaker Natasha Dudinski said: 'I'm not sure why her story is not better known. Maybe it's because she was from a small country. Or maybe it was because it involved bribery. Or maybe it was because she was a woman. Women in history are often forgotten.'[2]

---

1 Ruth Bondy, 'Women in Theresienstadt and the Family Camp in Birkenau', in *Women in the Holocaust*, edited by Dalia Ofer and Lenore J. Weitzman (New York: Yale UP, 1998) p.311

2 Renee Ghert-Zand, 'New documentary brings forgotten Holocaust heroine back to life' in *Times of Israel*, 27 January 2014, accessed 23 January 2017 wwwtimesofisrael.com

Emmanuel Ringelblum, the most famous recorder of the iniquities of the Nazis in the Warsaw Ghetto, acknowledged the unique role of women in his *Journal*:

> The historian of the future will have to devote a fitting chapter to the role of the Jewish woman during the war. It is thanks to the courage and endurance of our women that thousands of families have been able to endure these bitter times. Recently there has been an interesting development: In some House Committees women are coming forward to replace the men, who fall out exhausted. There are some House Committees whose entire direction is in the hands of women. Relief particularly needs fresh, not worn-out personnel; it is very important there to have a strong reserve.[3]

Ringelblum was as good as his word and at the end of 1941 he asked Cecilya Słapakowa, a translator and journalist, to undertake a research project on Jewish women in Warsaw since the start of the war. It was called 'Two and a Half Years of Nazi Occupation: One Year of Ghetto Life'. Accordingly in the period December 1941 to June 1942 she interviewed sixteen women from different backgrounds. She asked them about their lives before the war and since the occupation. She also asked about how they coped with increasing poverty, hunger, illness and the growing dangers. This was a unique survey looking at women's situations interviewed and assessed by a woman.

Mary Felstiner, who wrote about the Jewish artist Charlotte Salomon, questioned the choices made on the ramp at Auschwitz. Salomon was aged 26 and 4 months pregnant when she was gassed at Auschwitz. Her husband was killed the following January. Felstiner claims women were disproportionately chosen for death:

> Once we see that women did not die of inborn physical frailty – for they lasted longer than men in the Lodz and Warsaw ghettos – then the issue becomes clear. Along the stations toward extinction, from arrest through transport to selection, each gender lived its own journey. It was the weighting of each stage of the Final Solution against women that counted at the end.[4]

Felstiner refers to women's physical strength and this was validated in recent research from Israel. In July 2017, Siegal Sadetzki's team found that Holocaust survivors who were in Nazi-occupied countries 'were subjected to prolonged severe and intensive stressors', which are associated with cancer risk. This impacted on their risk for all cancers but particularly a 37% increased risk of lung cancer and a 12% risk for colorectal cancer. Men had a greater risk for

---

3 Emmanuel Ringelblum, *The Journal,* edited by Jacob Sloan (New York: McGraw-Hill, 1958) p.294

4 Mary Felstiner, *To Paint Her Life: Charlotte Salomon in the Nazi Era* (New York: HarperCollins, 1994) p.205.

all cancer and colorectal cancer than women. What was remarkable was that there was no increased risk for breast cancer or gynaecologic cancers – what we might call 'women's cancers'.[5]

Felstiner explains at length how women's gender let them down at the selection ramp – 'In that crucial moment on the ramp, one sex was chosen disproportionately for death.' One major issue for the Nazis was to stop the Jews from breeding and therefore young women were a particular target. Pregnant women or women with children were condemned.

As early as 8 September 1934, Hitler told the National Socialist Women's League – the faithful Nazi women – that it was their role to produce babies: 'What the man gives in courage on the battlefield, the woman gives in eternal self-sacrifice, in eternal pain and suffering. Every child that a woman brings into the world is a battle, a battle waged for the existence of her people.'[6]

He claimed 'emancipation of women' was invented by Jewish intellectuals. This might have come as a surprise to most Jewish women of the 1930s whose role was in many respects perceived as the same as that of the Nazi women. The '3 Ks' were originally defined by Kaiser Wilhelm II in the nineteenth century as *Kirche, Küche, Kinder* – Church, Kitchen, Children. It appears that the women's movement was always weak in Germany. During the Weimar Republic (1919–33) women did gain some rights, such as to secondary education and the right to vote. There were even 111 women in the Reichstag, but this all ceased after Hitler came to power. So as the Nazi women suffered from what Kaplan called 'reaffirmed male privilege', the Jewish women took on

> ...new roles as breadwinners, family protectors, and defenders of businesses or practices. Gender roles in Jewish families shifted because devastating economic, social, and emotional realities forced families to embrace strategies that they would never have entertained in ordinary times. The Nazis essentially destroyed the patriarchal structure of the Jewish family, leaving a void ato be filled by women.[7]

Men's position was extraordinary. Deprived of their jobs, office, income and dignity they had nowhere to go during the day and yet they were fearful of going out. They could be beaten up or rounded up for slave labour. So they stayed at home getting depressed.

> Jewish men, especially those who were most visible because of their beards and traditional clothing, were immediately targeted for beatings,

---

5 Laura Cowen, 'Holocaust survivors at increased risk for cancer', in *Medicine Matters* – Oncology 25 July 2017, accessed 27 October 2017, https://oncology.medicinematters.com/epidemiology/risk-factors/holocaust-survivors-at-increased-risk-for-cancer/13323424

6 Jeremy Noakes and Geoffrey Pridham, eds., *Nazism, 1919–1945, Vol.2: State, Economy and Society 1933–1939* (Exeter: University of Exeter Press, 2000) pp.255–6

7 Kaplan p.59

humiliation, harassment, arrest and execution. Many were assaulted and had their beards ripped off, mocked and jeered on the streets and taken away for harsh forced labour. It is therefore not surprising that many Jewish men were simply afraid to leave their homes during the day, and they increasingly relied on their wives to deal with the world outside. As a result, their wives began to take over many of their husbands' former roles.[8]

Emmanuel Ringelblum wrote in his diary

(The) men don't go out...
She stands on the long line (for bread)...
When there is need to go to the Gestapo, the daughter or wife goes...
The women are everywhere...
(Women) who never thought of working are now performing the most difficult physical work.[9]

There is a clear trajectory from Hitler's exhortation to Nazi women to have babies, through the Wannsee Conference in January 1942 to the selections at the ramps. The minutes of Wannsee recorded:

Under proper guidance, in the course of the final solution the Jews are to be allocated for appropriate labor in the East. Able-bodied Jews, separated according to sex, will be taken in large work columns to these areas for work on roads, in the course of which action doubtless a large portion will be eliminated by natural causes.

The possible final remnant will, since it will undoubtedly consist of the most resistant portion, have to be treated accordingly, because it is the product of natural selection and would, if released, act as the seed of a new Jewish revival (see the experience of history).[10]

Himmler told his senior SS staff on 4 October 1943:

Amongst ourselves, for once, it shall be said quite openly, but we will never speak about it in public ... I am referring here to the evacuation of the Jews, the extermination of the Jewish people ... Most of you men know what it is like to see 100 corpses side by side, or 500 or 1,000. To have stood fast through this and except for cases of human weakness – to have stayed decent: that has made us hard ... We had the moral right, we

---

8 Leonore J. Weitzman, *Women in the Holocaust*, Talk for The Holocaust and the UN Outreach Programme, 20 February 2011, p.55, http://www.un.org/en/holocaustremembrance/docs/pdf/chapter5.pdf accessed 7 February 2017.
9 Emanuel Ringelblum, *Diary and Notes from the War Period: Warsaw Ghetto* (Hebrew) Jerusalem: Yad Vashem, 1992) pp.51–2
10 http://holocaust.umd.umich.edu/news/uploads/WanseeProtocols.pdf p.6

had the duty towards our people, to destroy this people that wanted to destroy us.[11]

The Auschwitz Kommandant, Rudolf Höss, admitted at his trial that 'there were always more men fit for labour than women'. Himmler had told him 'to deprive Jewry of its biological reserves' and 'to obliterate the biological basis of Jewry'. At his trial the answer to all these questions was the same – in other words children below 15 were exterminated? Just because of Himmler's order? And because they were dangerous to the German people? The answer to each was 'Yes'.

A survivor of the ramp selections said: 'One understood quickly that it concerned separating children, old people, sick people, from the robust and the young, but one imagined that the fate of the first group would be *easier*, more humane.'[12]

Richard Breitman has reported Himmler's secret meeting with Höss, who was an old chum from 1921–22. Whilst there was confusion in Höss's evidence on the dates, Breitman believes the meeting occurred during 13–15 July 1941 and Höss was summoned to Berlin for a secret, private meeting at which no one else was present. He was told:

> The Führer has ordered that the Jewish question be solved once and for all and that we, the SS, are to implement that order...
>
> You will treat this order as absolutely secret, even from your superiors...
>
> The Jews are the sworn enemies of the German people and must be eradicated. Every Jew that we can lay our hands on is to be destroyed now during the war without exception. If we cannot now obliterate the biological basis of Jewry, the Jews will one day destroy the German people.[13]

Kitty Hart-Moxon was with her mother Rosa Felix in Auschwitz for two years. Rosa's presence was a surprise to other women because she was born in 1890 and was therefore 53 when they arrived at Auschwitz in 1943.[14] When they first arrived one of the Kapos asked Rosa, 'Anyway, what the hell are you doing in this camp old woman? No room here for old people. Why weren't you sent over there?' She jerked her whip in the direction of that distant glow. 'How did you get in?'[15]

Kitty told me that she and her mother were sent to Auschwitz as convicted prisoners. They did not come on a normal Jewish transport and therefore did not experience a 'selection'. This was probably why her mother got through the net. Because of the Nazis' fear of Jews reproducing and thwarting their

---

11 Felstiner p.209
12 Felstiner p.208
13 Richard Breitman, *The Architect of Genocide: Himmler and The Final Situation* (London: Bodley Head, 1991) p.189
14 Kitty Hart-Moxon emails to author 20 October 2017.
15 Kitty Hart-Moxon, *Return to Auschwitz* (Newark: Quillo, 2007) pp.70–1

extermination policy, only female teenagers were permitted to live. Women who were pregnant or had children were doomed. Women also lacked skills which the men had, as carpenters etc.[16] This was why there were more men permitted to live in the camps because they could work for the Nazis.

George Clare né Klaar described the reversal in his parents' relationship (Stella and Ernst) when they were confined to St. Pierreville in the Ardèche for eighteen months. He wrote of his father's dependence on his wife and how she had changed:

The change began virtually the moment the ecstatic Nazi hordes swept up the Nussdorferstrasse. She, who most of her life had accepted Father's guidance, suddenly began to display enormous strength of character. Her headaches, her frequent tears, her other complaints, practically disappeared overnight. That spiralling hairline in her eye went, never to return. She, who had always tapped for every kerbstone with the toecap of her shoe, claiming that even with her glasses she could not see that far down, suddenly walked with sure steps through the streets of Vienna.

In spite of their grim existence in France, the short time, just over a year and a half, Mother and Father spent in St. Pierreville was not unhappy for her. It was the only time in their whole marriage Father was completely hers. There was no bank, no Herr Direktor Fischer, no Fraulein Blankenberg, no Grandmother Julie, no sister, no brothers and no son. In this remote village to which the France of Pétain and Laval had assigned them – they were not voluntarily in St. Pierreville – Stella at last had that total unity of soul and body with her husband she had always longed for, probably without ever allowing herself to be aware of it, but had never attained during their years of good fortune. Now, in misfortune, she had Ernst, her man, totally to herself.

I think Father sensed what gave Mother that indomitable physical and spiritual fortitude he so much admired.

In a letter his father sent him dated 23 January 1942 he wrote:

In the evening, when everything is so quiet here that even the mice, frequent visitors of ours, hold their breath, Mother takes a volume of Goethe or some French author from the shelf and refreshes her mind and spirit. Her constant work does not permit her to do this during the day. She is a great and true human being. Had she had the good fortune of meeting Goethe, or rather, had he had the good fortune of meeting her, he would mostly certainly have said, and with greater justification: '*voilà une femme*'.

---

16 Kitty Hart-Moxon, telephone conversation with author 22 October 2017.

Clare then comments: 'This "*Voilà une femme*". – "There is a true woman" – not as Father would have called her in Vienna, "a good wife and mother", seems to me to show how much more clearly he now recognised her qualities, had penetrated the surface of their relationship.' His mother had written underneath his praise: 'If it were at all possible to blush in this ice cold weather, I would, I am merely doing my duty and accept things as they are.'[17] Whilst in some cases the women's new roles caused stress, mostly the men appreciated the initiative of their women. Edith Bick wrote: 'In Hitler times … I had to take over, which I never did before. Never.' Her husband 'didn't like it [but] he not only accepted it, he was thankful.'[18]

Another woman struggled as her husband sank into a deep depression. 'He stopped eating, as he said no one had the right to eat when he did not work and became … despondent … He feared we would all starve … and all his self-assurance was gone … These were terrible days for me, added to all the other troubles, and forever trying to keep my chin up for the children's sake.'

Gabriele Tergit [Elise Hirschmann, 1894–1982] was herself a journalist in Germany from 1920 until the family left for London in 1938. She contributed to the 1935 Nobel Peace Prize winner Carl Ossietzky's journal *Die Weltbühne*. She wrote an early review of Jewish refugees from central Europe in 1951. She commented on the impact of the role reversal on family life:

> It was much easier for the women to find work. The highly specialised men seemed suddenly to be worthless, and the sad psychological fact is that whatever may happen later will never eradicate the sense of frustration and bitterness once it takes root in the individual's heart. The women could take on their ancient jobs, looking after the young, the old, the sick, cooking and mending. The woman as breadwinner however makes married life very difficult. Women off to factory work or trying to sell their handicraft to the buyers of the great stores, men brooding in depressing rooms – only a strong moral tradition prevented the disruption of married life. Looking for a job in middle age is never easy, but looking for a job when one does not even know exactly how to write a letter and is dependent on one's wife's work or charity plays havoc with the personality of all but the most insensitive. In many cases, though, husbands, of course, found great comfort and inspiration in their wives' indomitable physical and spiritual fortitude. The writer Martin Beradt has told the story of the refugee lawyer who goes secretly to his trunk, puts on his gown, stands before the mirror and addresses an imaginary jury.[19]

---

17 George Clare, *Last Waltz in Vienna* (Basingstoke: Pan Books, 2007) pp.214–5
18 Kaplan p.61
19 Gabriele Tergit, 'How They Resettled' in *Britain's New Citizens*, AJR booklet 1952, p.62

Martin Beradt (1881–1949) was a German lawyer whose books were burnt by the Nazis and was expelled from the Bar Association in 1933 because he was a Jew. He went to the US in 1939.

Ofer and Weitzman wrote in their seminal book *Women in the Holocaust*:

> Before the war Jewish men and women in both Eastern and Western Europe lived in gender-specific worlds which endowed them with different spheres of knowledge, expertise, social networks and opportunities with which they faced the Nazi onslaught. In the 1920s and 1930s most Jews lived according to gender patterns all over Europe. So married men were responsible for the economic support of their families and the women even if they knew a trade or helped with the family business, were responsible for their homes, families and children. This meant that the women were generally excluded from the worlds of business, higher education and politics. It also meant they were less likely to have connections in the non-Jewish world who would aid them when things became so difficult.

It was my original intention to write the book in two parts: one part dealing with women undertaking traditional roles and the other with non-traditional roles. This did not really work because many women multi-tasked and did both. When I read that one of the parachutists, Haviva Reik, wrote in her letters of her longing to have a family and babies, I abandoned that approach. I hope the final categories work and make the book of interest whilst doing justice to these courageous and remarkable women.

Gender Differences in Theresienstadt

Ruth Bondy

I came across Ruth Bondy when I first started my research for this book. I found her comments based on her personal experiences helpful and particularly her observations about women adapting their camp uniforms within twenty-four hours.

Ruth Bondy was born in Prague in 1923 to a large Jewish-Zionist family, most of whom were murdered in the Holocaust. Her father Yoseph was a bank executive who died in Dachau on 5 February 1945 and her mother Frantzi died of blood poisoning in Theresienstadt in November 1942. She later wrote: 'Four of us came back from the Holocaust: Grandma Herman, my cousin Otta, my sister Dita and me. Twenty-five were wiped out ... Statistically speaking – a lucky family. After all, someone survived to tell its story.'[20]

She grew up in the democratic Czechoslovakia that followed World War I. Like all her contemporaries she received a broad education in a wide range of subjects, which included journalism and the rich corpus of Czech literature. She lived a full social life with both Jewish and non-Jewish friends. Like most young Zionists, she belonged to a youth group, *Noar Zihyyoni Lohem* (Zionist Fighting Youth), known as *NeZaH*. The young Zionists from various groups were sent for *hakhsharah* (agricultural training) in preparation for going to Palestine (now Israel). However, the invasion of Prague by the Germans on 15 March 1939 meant the Czech Jews had other issues to deal with rather than their Zionist plans.

The Germans started building a ghetto in Terezín, known as Theresienstadt in German, in October 1941. The young Zionists were made to prepare the ghetto for the Jews. Ruth was 19 when she arrived there. Because of her training Ruth Bondy worked in a vegetable garden with other young Zionists. She also participated in the educational facilities that developed in the ghetto.

In December 1943 Bondy was part of a transport sent to Auschwitz-Birkenau, which included many of her chums. They were placed in a special

---

20 Ruth Bondy, *Whole Fragments* p.29, cited in *Women in The Holocaust*.

section of Birkenau (B2b) for the Jews of Theresienstadt. Men, women and children were all together, there were no *selektion* and prisoners' heads were not shaved. However, they were still tattooed on their arms. Ruth Bondy was 72430. After the war in Israel she had the number removed by a doctor. She wrote:

> ... Here in Israel, the Jews also asked me: How is it that you survived? What did you have to do to stay alive? And in their eyes, a flicker of suspicion: Kapo? Whore? This was one of the reasons why I decided, in my second year in Israel, to remove the Auschwitz inmate number from my arm...

In July 1944, Bondy was moved with a group of women prisoners to Hamburg and having survived typhus she was eventually liberated aged 22. In December 1948 she arrived in Haifa to join the fight in the Israeli War of Independence. In 1954 she married a fellow journalist and has a daughter, also a journalist.

She describes the lives of the Czech Jews:

> In normal times the man had been the provider of the family: married women, even those who had learned a profession or a trade while single, were housewives or worked on the family business; very few were employed...
>
> During the two and a half years before they were sent to Terezín, both men and women underwent profound crises, but for opposite reasons. The men lost their jobs and with them their economic security and their status: compelled to be idle or to work in forced-labour squads, shovelling snow or building roads, they felt degraded. The women, by contrast, had to cope with a new and growing burden of work: most Jewish families in Prague had been middle class and had employed Czech household help. By the spring of 1939, Jews could no longer afford to employ 'Aryans' – and were forbidden to do so in any case. Now the women of the house had to stoke the coal fires, wash the clothes, prepare the meals from the scarce rations available for Jews, and knit and sew clothes for the family by recycling old material.
>
> It was even harder for the women to say goodbye to their homes and their lovingly cared-for furnishings. The leave-taking often took place in two stages: first the family moved into a single room in a flat shared with several other Jewish families; then after October 1941, when the first transports left for the Lodz ghetto, came the drastic reduction of all possessions. Each person was allowed to take only fifty kilograms of food, clothing, and other goods, on the transport. In preparation for the unknown, the women baked rusks, fried flour in fat, boiled milk and sugar to paste, changed white sheets for coloured, and endlessly weighed and pondered what was the most important to take. Many, in disregard of the strict prohibition, gave some of their possessions for safekeeping to Aryan friends (or those who seemed to be friends); others purposely

damaged or destroyed what was left behind. Yet, many a woman tidied her flat before leaving, out of habit and hope.

Bondy emphasises the different perspective of the married women:

The trauma of leaving home, with its beloved possessions, went deeper in married women and persisted in the ghetto; while sitting with other women, peeling potatoes or splitting mica, they would talk again and again about what they had had to leave behind. Sometimes they held on to a remnant from the past – a pocket watch, an ivory brooch – as if it were a thread that would lead them back home. The women often tried to cling to such a souvenir even during further deportations, until they stood naked.

She also describes women's attempts at improving their environment:

Women, more than men, tried to convert their place on the three-tiered bunks into a surrogate home, by covering the mattress with a coloured sheet, hanging photographs on the back wall, or laying a napkin on the plank that housed their possessions. Leaving the ghetto on the way to the forbidding East meant losing a home again.

The number of people in Terezín altered each month, even each week as different transports arrived and others left for 'the East'. However, from May 1942, when transports of elderly people began arriving from Germany and Austria, there were always more women. This was partly because elderly women had a longer life span than men, but also because men were sent off to separate labour camps. On 31 January 1944 women made up 60% of the inhabitants and the average age was fifty. In the camp, women's jobs were the traditional ones of cleaners, nurses, nannies, teachers, clerks, laundresses and seamstresses.

In April 1942 about 1,000 women were sent to the forests of Křivoklát for six weeks to plant saplings. This was the only female labour unit to leave the ghetto, and it did so over the protests of some of the husbands. When the first order for women to work in the central carpentry shop was placed, the idea of the women doing 'men's jobs' was not well received, but two regular units – one for carrying planks, and one for constructing bunks – emerged. All the heavy manual jobs – loading, transporting, building, water and sewage engineering – were done by men. When ghetto currency was introduced in May 1943, in preparation for the visit of the International Red Cross, the salaries of women were on average 30 per cent lower that the salaries of men. (The 'money' had only nominal value; the real means of exchange were food and cigarettes.)

The division of labour between the sexes reflected not only the Jewish past but the German present: the SS command in Theresienstadt was composed of men; women held only clerical jobs. The only uniformed German women seen in the ghetto were the *berushky* (ladybirds, in ghetto parlance) who searched the women's rooms for such contraband as money, cigarettes, medicines, flashlights or electric appliances. They came from the nearby town of Leimeritz and were at the bottom of the German hierarchy. Some were even punished for stealing from the ghetto inmates.[21]

Everything was regulated:

According to a ruling published in the *Tagesbefehle* (the daily orders), women had to cut their hair short and men's hair could be no longer than three millimetres. But this order and another forbidding the use of lipstick were never seriously implemented. Anyone who had managed to save such a precious possession as makeup used it sparingly, saving it for meetings with her beloved. The women wore their own clothes brought from home, even when they became too big or shabby with time. As long as the women kept their mental and physical strength, they paid attention to their appearance...

As in all concentration camps, most of the women in the ghetto stopped menstruating, at least for a time, because of undernourishment and mental shock; others suffered irregular periods. Contrary to the view that the cessation of menstruation led to depression and worries about future fertility, in my own experience and observation it was generally received with relief. No sanitary napkins or cotton wool was available, and cotton napkins and folded pieces of linen absorbed poorly, chafed, and were hard to wash. But the disappearance of menstruation made it difficult to know when one was pregnant.

I wrote of the prohibition of pregnancy for Jewish women in *Who Betrayed the Jews?*. The dates seemed to vary from ghetto to ghetto; at Theresienstadt:

At first women who had arrived pregnant were allowed to give birth, but in July 1943 an order for compulsory abortion was issued. The parents had to agree to the abortion in writing. The heads of the living quarters, the *Zimmeraelteste*, were asked to report any case of pregnancy known to them. Babies born henceforth were sent with their parents on the next transport to the East. 'They kill babies in their mothers' womb,' wrote Egon 'Gonda' Redlich, the head of the youth department, in his diary. After a Jewish obstetrician had saved the wife and newborn child of an SS man from death, Gonda's wife, Gerti, and several other pregnant Jewish women were allowed to continue their pregnancies, and on March 16, 1944, Gerti bore a healthy son.[22]

---

21 Bondy p.313
22 Bondy pp.314–5

When Gonda, his wife and the baby were included in a September 1944 transport to the East, they acquired a baby carriage for the journey, which took them straight to the gas chambers of Birkenau. Some pregnant women preferred to be sent to the East than agree to an abortion. Something like 230 babies were born in the ghetto of Theresienstadt; about 25 survived. (One of them, Dr Michael Wiener, was chief of the medical corps of the Israeli Army until 1994.)

Terezín had a home for babies and toddlers who were mostly orphans and children arriving alone. It also housed mothers who had to leave their Mischling children with their non-Jewish spouses. One of these, Fisherova, managed to feed some of the weakest babies, despite the insufficient nourishment, for almost two years, thus saving their lives. Gonda's diary tells of a nursing mother, suffering from an excess of milk, who preferred to give it to her husband than to a motherless infant. The orphans were always hungrier than children with mothers, as the mothers always managed to get extra food for their children, often at the expense of their own health.

Food was an issue for all the persecuted Jews.

Most girls and young women avoided speaking of food while hungry, but former housewives would 'cook' for hours, telling each other how they used to prepare mushroom sauce with cream or debating the preferred number of eggs for dumplings. Some would even write down recipes, whose ingredients seemed like greetings from another world. In addition to the memories, an entire cooking industry existed in Theresienstadt. The common kitchens in the barracks supplied a black fluid in the morning and a thin greyish soup and two or three boiled potatoes, often rotten, at noon. The evening bread ration was distributed in the living quarters. All this saved the inhabitants of Theresienstadt from the maddening hunger that existed in the ghettos of Poland and ensured minimal nutrition for everybody, but the rations were not enough to give them a feeling of satiety. In the women's barracks and dormitories there were in addition to the communal kitchens, 'warming kitchens', stoves heated by coal, where women were allowed to place small pots, mostly of soup made out of their dwindling food supplies brought from home, potatoes stolen during sorting or peeling, or stalks left in the vegetable gardens after the produce had been delivered to the German command. For birthdays, dark, bitter bread was soaked in black 'coffee' with some sugar, margarine, and jam added; at least in its brown colour, this concoction resembled chocolate cake.[23]

The sexes reacted to their incarceration differently. Some Jewish men felt themselves superior to the Jewish women in coping with ghetto conditions. For example, Fritz Wohlgemut, head of the food distribution service (*Menagendienst*) in the Hamburg barracks, writes: 'Women are not used to keeping discipline and therefore it is often up to the *Menagendienst* to

---

23 Bondy pp.316–7

educate them, to make it clear to the women that they cannot come to get their food whenever they like, but only when it is it the turn of their room.' The men, however, were dependent on the women for comfort. The women's living space was usually the daily late-afternoon meeting place. The women prepared the additional food, if there was any, darned the men's worn clothing, washed their linen and stockings (usually in cold water and without soap) and searched for fleas and lice. Generally, men, with the same rations, suffered more from hunger and women more from filth, bedbugs, and fleas, which became the eleventh plague of Terezín because of the terrible overcrowding (as many as 60,000 Jews lived in Terezín, where 7,000 people had lived before the war). The bugs resisted all efforts to keep the rooms clean, to air the bedding, to disinfect. All the women's memoirs about ghetto Theresienstadt describe the war against dirt and insects. In the heat of the summer, when the bedbugs were especially agile, many women slept on the ground in the yards. In some rooms, the old women had to wash from head to toe every day supervising each other, and the rooms were swept every morning. The bread was transported on former hearses, and brought in by workers with dirty hands and stained coats. Hedwig Ems, who arrived in Theresienstadt at the age of 71, always wiped her ration of bread with a napkin, at least symbolically cleaning it.[24]

Bondy went on to describe their move to Birkenau:

We have now come to the last chapter, the family camp B/2/b in Birkenau, where 17,500 inmates of Theresienstadt were sent between September 1943 and July 1944. This was the only Jewish family camp in the vast complex of Auschwitz-Birkenau. Although men and women lived in separate barracks. They could meet for a few minutes while walking the camp road to the latrines, or they could meet clandestinely for a moment in the barracks. Here, at Birkenau, only a day after their arrival, the differences between the sexes was already striking. The men, in hats with cut-off brims and in trousers and coats thrown to them at random – too short, too long, too wide, too small – looked like sad black storks. The women, also wearing garments that had been distributed to them at random, had somehow succeeded in only twenty-four hours in adjusting them to their bodies and sewing up the holes, using needles made out of wooden splinters and threads pulled out of the one blanket allocated to them.[25] Some of them learned to iron shirts with bricks heated in the stove. They carried the heavy wooden soup barrels, three women on each side, for the privilege of scraping whatever stuck to the sides and bottom after distribution – most of it for their children, husbands, or brothers. In the same conditions, with the same scarce nourishment, they could bear hunger more easily, and deteriorated more slowly than the men.

---

24 Bondy p.318
25 Bondy p.323

Nobody knew for certain the reason for the family camp's existence – why there had been no selection on arrival (as in all the other transports), why the prisoners' hair was not shaved, why they were not taken outside for work. It was assumed that the special treatment was connected with the planned visit of an International Red Cross delegation Theresienstadt and some other camp and that they would be kept alive until the end of the war. The SS even allowed Fredy Hirsch, a sports teacher from Aachen, to open a children's home in B/2/b. But exactly six months after their arrival, all 3,800 of those who had survived from the first transport (about 20 per cent had died of cold, hunger or disease) were gassed during one night, without any selection. Those who had arrived three months later knew the same fate awaited them in June 1944. Because of the heavy bombing attacks on Germany by the Allies, the Nazis needed working hands, so a selection was held by Dr. Mengele and his helpers in the family camp in late June. Mothers of children were allowed to present themselves for selection. But after a six-month stay in Birkenau they knew that this meant leaving their children to face death alone. Only two of about six hundred mothers of young children appeared for selection; all the others decided to stay with their children to the end. Mothers of girls under the allowed age of sixteen tried to pass them off as older and were determined to stay with them if they failed. Girls of the right age tried to spruce up their mothers to make them look younger and healthier so they could pass. One young woman sedated her small baby and tried to smuggle him out wrapped in a bundle. But the baby's cry gave her away.

I worked in the children's block, taking care of a group of five-and six-year-olds. Some of their mothers came to me before the selection to ask my advice – what would I do? I tried not to give them a straight answer: 'How could I know? I don't have a child of my own.' But after they persisted, I said: 'I think if I had a small child I would stay with him.' They nodded: their decision was the same; they just wanted my approval. For years the heavy burden of responsibility weighed on me: the mothers were young, they could have survived and begun new families. But after my daughter was born, I was reassured: I would not have left her alone when she most needed my embrace.[26]

---

26 Bondy pp.324–5

Mothers and Families

Leny Jacobs

The story of Leny Jacobs personifies so much of what I have tried to bring to the reader that it seems appropriate to give her story here in the section about mothers. The background appeared in Who Betrayed the Jews? *However the letter Leny wrote was not included and it is here. I am grateful to Professor Dan Michman for sending me this family story – Leny was his aunt, murdered before he was born.*

Leny Jacobs (née Melkman) was a pregnant young Jewish woman in Amsterdam when she wrote to a non-Jewish friend, Theo Westerhof, on 19 October 1942. Theo kept the letter and it only came to light when he died in 1991. His son was determined to try to find the family of the writer so he could return the letter. The person he found was Ada – the child Leny had been carrying when she wrote it.

Leny was born on 29 September 1910. When she finished her medical studies in 1936 she joined the Faculty for Pedagogy in Amsterdam. Theo Westerhof was the Secretary and they must have become friendly as they were of a similar age and both had two children. In the letter Leny explained that she could not speak to Theo adequately on the telephone about going into hiding. She was concerned about going into hiding herself as she was pregnant and sending her children into hiding whilst she was still around to care for them herself. She was surprisingly realistic about the future:

> The Jews are to be eradicated and it is such foolishness to think that you will be the only one or one of the few who will not be eradicated. And yet you have to believe in that nonsense because it is the only way to keep one's spirits up. The possibility of winning the race against the end of the war seems to become smaller by the day.

In the end, after the birth of her baby, Ada, Leny and her three children all went into hiding in different places. Her husband Jo, who was 34 at the time, stayed in post as Head of the Amsterdam Jewish Council's Medical Services. On 29 September 1943, the entire Jewish Council – including Jo – was rounded up and sent to Westerbork. He was killed on 26 February 1945 in Kommando Ebensee, an annex of Mauthausen Concentration Camp in Austria. Leny was arrested in January 1944, a year after the birth of Ada, and sent to Westerbork. She was sent to Auschwitz and killed on 28 January 1944. She was 33 years old. The three children all survived. Leny's brother and his wife took the two older ones, Bram and Poortje, to Israel in 1957. Jo's sister Gonnie brought Ada up and took her to Israel in 1955. It was because Ada had registered her parents' fate with the Dutch Jewish Community Memorial (*Joodsmonument. nl*) that the Westerhof family could find her and ultimately pass the letter to Ada in late 2010. Ada replied that that she had never known her parents and just had a few pictures of them. Her sister Tsipora also wrote how touched they were by their mother's letter.

Their cousin Dan Michman, who is the Chief Historian at Yad Vashem, arranged for the letter to be donated to the museum. He commented that he

... appreciated the universal value of his Aunt's letter. He considers her exemplary in the intimation of her poignant motherly feelings. More, he indicates that Lenny was, already, then and much earlier than the general public, painfully aware that the purpose of the Germans was the total eradication of all Jews.

Here is the letter:

19 October 1942.

Dear Mr. Westerhof

What I wanted to tell you, and what I could not adequately do over the phone, is that if and when we have to leave, we will most likely take our children along. I had an address where I could possibly find shelter for Poortje but that would mean that we would have to bring her right now and that we would have to go into hiding as well. It is impossible to do that as we are expecting a baby. Going into hiding is in itself already quite a job and with an "illegal" child to boot it becomes very complicated. If you were to find an address where you'll be taken in and your presence becomes too troublesome for your hosts, then the problem arises where to go next. I have already seen such a situation.

We could possibly find shelter for the children with Miss G. but it seems that the people who want the children want them right away too. And I cannot do that. I cannot bring myself to part with my children while I may still have some months left to stay at home. Our neighbours would surely notice that Poortje, remarkably pretty as she is, would no longer be around.

As one cannot trust most people, this would create an unacceptable risk. I know of parents who were deported to Germany because their children were no longer at home.

Now we may have an opportunity that, when we are being picked up, we can secretly leave the children at home and leave them in the care of good friends who can then place them in hiding. The possibility for this to happen is moot. Homes are immediately secured and sealed right away after the residents' departure. We have actually experienced that ourselves. We were taken one evening to the Gestapo Headquarters but, fortunately, were released. We were back home again at 6.30 in the morning. It was an awful experience and it is a happy circumstance that we can still talk about it here in Amsterdam. (...) I was so incredibly worried about the children. We had notified our neighbors, but it was still horrible to think that I would never see them again or how they would end up in the care of others. If I do not know with absolute certainty that they are being looked after properly, I cannot leave them.

It is perhaps easy, theoretically, to figure out what is best for them, or what the best chance of survival might be. And may be that is not as simple as it seems, but the practical side is so much more complex. I know of a couple of kids who were left behind by their parents and who were shunted from one family to the next. You must have experienced that yourself to really know what it means to have to "abandon" your children. My children are too young and I cannot do it. Unless I know that this is the best option for them.

In the meantime we have received our deferment stamp. We had emptied our back-packs already, but I am going to pack them again now that Mr. Bole and the Chief Rabbi have been taken into custody. Their stamp has been nullified with a second stamp "INVALID". That is the intrinsic value of this stamp business. People want to believe in it, even if it is a sham! The Jews are to be eradicated and it is such foolishness to think that you will be the only one or one of the few who will not be eradicated.

And yet you have to believe in that nonsense because it is the only way to keep one's spirits up. The possibility of winning the race against the end of the war seems to become smaller by the day.

I am so surprised that the Nutsseminarium, my good old school, is still alive and well...I would have liked very much to have paid a visit to professor Langeveld. That is now impossible for me. I owe him a lot. When others, ever so presumptuous in thinking that only they had the right to show us the way to conduct our lives, had disappointed me greatly, it was professor L. who, with his independent judgment, brought true spiritual relief to me. (...) Hence my special affection for him. Please give him my most cordial greetings.
With best wishes,
Leny Jacobs-Melkman

Anka Bergman – Eva Clark's Mother

I first met Eva Clarke in November 2008, when we both spoke about the Holocaust to schoolchildren for a project called Valleys Kids in the Rhondda. I heard her mother's remarkable story then and am delighted to include it here. The pupils were very responsive and I was touched when some of the boys shyly asked if they could have a photo with us.

Eva Clarke's birth certificate states she was born on 29 April 1945 in Mauthausen concentration camp to Anna Karderowa and Bernd Nathan – both Jews. The SS abandoned the camp on 3 May 1945 and the US troops arrived on 5 May. That makes Eva one of the youngest Holocaust survivors.

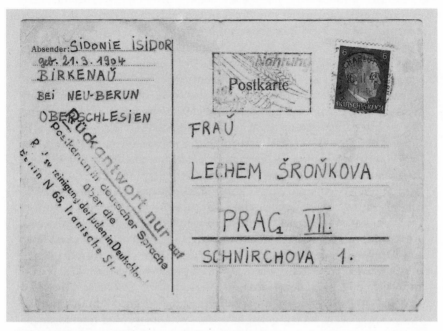

Above and below: Zdena's postcard from Auschwitz.

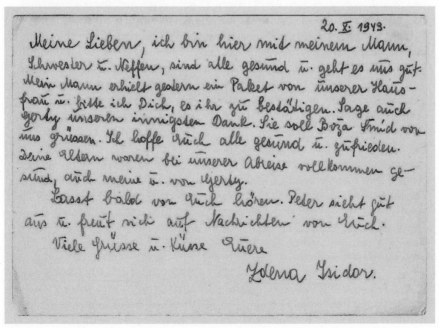

Eva told me that she married Malcolm Clarke in Cardiff in January 1968. He was a research fellow at Fitzwilliam College in Cambridge at the time but in August he was invited to set up a Shipping Law course by the University of Singapore Law Faculty and so they lived there for eighteen months.[27] 'When first married, living in Singapore and feeling the distance from my mother for the first time (although not homesick), I asked her to write down an account of her wartime experiences and she then wrote me a letter.' That letter from Cardiff in October 1971 is reproduced below.[28]

My Darling Daughter
I got married to your Father on 15 May 1940. The Second World War was 6 month old, but Hitler had reigned over Czechoslovakia practically from the Munich agreement (October 1938). Even then we did not realise the deadly danger we were in. In September 1941 Heidrich arrived in Prague as Reichsprotector (vice-ruler for Hitler). Very soon after his arrival the transports to the East started. All Jews had to register with the German Authorities, give them information about all their possessions, money, jewelry, houses etc. The first five transports, each consisted of 1000 Jews, left for Poland (Lodz) in October 1941. In one of them was Daddy's (Karel Bergman) sister and her family. None of them returned. After a lull of a few weeks, 2000 young able bodied men were called up to go to Terezín and build a Ghetto for the rest of the Jews in Bohemia and Moravia. Your father [Bernd Nathan] was among them and left on 28 November 1941. I followed on 14 December. Terezín used to be a garrison town and was well suited to the purpose the Germans wanted it for. There were several huge barracks, where we were housed at the beginning. Men in separate ones from the women. At that time, there were still civilians there, who were slowly rehoused somewhere else. By the summer of 42 it had become a Ghetto, with Jewish authorities, police, hospitals, autonomous as it suited the Germans, who had their headquarters outside the city walls. Your Father and I and about 3000 young people in similar circumstances were the so called pioneers and took it all in good spirit, until the first executions started. Somebody smuggled a letter out, was caught and executed. There were about six punishments like this and it made us realise that it will not be easy to survive.

Meanwhile there started an avalanche of transports from Bohemia, Moravia, Austria, Germany, Holland, mostly old people, who started to die like flies because of malnutrition, bad housing, lack of washing facilities – it was fatal for old people. Everybody who could, stole. At one time I had to feed about fifteen people, my parents, sisters, Peter, aunt and uncle, your Father's Father and the lady who took care of him (he was blinded in the First World War, had the highest German

---

27 Eva Clarke, email to author, 9 September 2017 21.00
28 Eva Clarke, copy of letter from Anka Bergman, received by author 8 September 2017.

decoration – *Eisernes Kreuz erster Klasse*)[29] then your Father's Mother and her husband – it was jolly. Thousands of people arrived in Terezín, only to be sent in a few days further east. At that time we did not know the destination. Thousands came, thousands died, thousands went off. 1942 came and went, 1943 carried on in the same way until September, when 5000 people were sent East, among them my two sisters and Peter [Zdena and Ruze; Peter was Ruze's 8 year old son].[30] Meanwhile I became pregnant and your Father and I were forced by the Germans to sign a document to the effect that after the baby had been born, they will destroy it. We and five other couples signed. For some unknown reason we were pardoned, but that was some time later December came and my parents went East – no need to tell you I never saw them again. February 1944 came and my son was born. We called him George, but the Germans did not allow us ordinary names, we had to use a Jewish one. We chose Dan. When he was two month old, he died of pneumonia. I did not know then that his death saved your and my life.

Summer 1944 came, the war news, which the Czech gendarmes smuggled inside the Ghetto was good, the Allies moving across France and we thought that we had won. Quite deliberately we started another baby. That was in July. By then we lived in a hay loft, which we adapted for our use very prettily, by 'we' I mean your Father and I, until then we lived separately in various barracks. Came September and the devastating news that everybody will have to go East. Again your Father was among the first 5000. And I volunteered to follow him. He left on 28 September and I on 1 October. I never saw him again.

Our first stop was Dresden which made us think we would be staying somewhere in Germany. But from there we turned East and slowly, but surely it dawned on us that we were heading for Auschwitz. After an interminable journey we arrived. The train stopped at a ramp, everybody had to get out and leave all the luggage behind. Long before the train stopped, we saw huge chimneys spouting flame and smoke, we did not know then, what it meant, but the impression was gruesome. As soon as we got out of the train, a sickly smell hit us but still it did not mean anything. The SS started shouting and hitting everybody who came their way, we had to line up in front of a higher ranking SS officer (the infamous Dr. Mengele, which we found out later) who directed some of the people to one side, some to the other, it seemed quite senseless at that time, it was not though.

The very young and old ones were destined for the gas chamber and the able bodied ones survived for the moment and were to be sent to Germany to various factories. But of course we knew none of that. We were herded in some sort of building, had to take all clothes and underwear off, leave it all in a heap and proceed to the next building stark naked, the Germans milling around and the temperature nearing

---

29 Iron Cross, First Class.
30 Eva Clarke, email to author 11 September 2017.

32 F [freezing]. There our hair was shaved off, we had a shower, no soap, no towel and to the next building where we were given clogs and some old rags to wear. By then we were so frightened and confused and everything became a ghastly nightmare, which unfortunately was true. We were marched off to a barracks, where there were huge wooden bunks without anything on them. There would have been room for about six people on one bunk, there had to be 12 of us to share it. They brought some soup in, but did not give us any spoons to eat it with and only one plate for two people. But fortunately we were so stunned by all these goings-on that nobody was hungry, for the time being anyway. Next morning there was a roll call at about 4a.m., we had to stand for hours, many people fainted, I among them, due partly exhaustion, partly to my being pregnant. There was one separate building serving as latrines. There were about fifty seats there, without any partitions and the Germans were prodding everybody with long poles to make you hurry up. Practically everybody had dysentery, I leave it to your imagination, what it looked like and how it smelled. Before you got there, you had to wade through acres of mud and all the time above you the towering chimneys spilling flames. A real inferno.

Slowly we started to understand what was going on, the Kapos (Kamp Polizei – camp police) who were internees like us, only had been there for some time and got this better job, some of them were all right, but some were worse than the Germans, dropped a word and a word there, we put two and two together and suddenly we knew. The people who were sent to the other side, had been gassed within minutes of our arrival. My parents, sisters, Peter and everybody who preceded us here, ended in the gas chamber. We were lucky that the Germans did not have enough workers at their disposal and had to use us as slave labour. Every now and then we were chased out, had to strip and go through a selection. Had they found out I was pregnant, I would not be here today to write about it. On this way we spent 10 days. On the tenth day we had to go through another selection and I overheard Dr. Mengele saying when we passed him stark naked as usual – *Diesmal sehr gutes Material* – This time a very good quality – like cattle being sent to the slaughterhouse. After this last selection we never returned to our barracks, but were brought to the station, still completely naked, were given some rags to wear, put on a goods train in locked waggons and sent away. We were thrilled because we knew it could not be worse. After about 48 hours the train stopped and we left our waggons, half-starved and terribly thirsty, but nevertheless alive. We were in Freiberg, Saxony, practically at the other side of the frontier between Germany and Czechoslovakia, not far from Dresden. We were marched to a huge factory where we started working forthwith. Till the end we never found out, what we were doing, it was after the end of the war, when it became clear to us that we were manufacturing V–1s. For the time being we were more than pleased to be able to work in a heated place, had some little food and a bunk for oneself. We worked 14 hours a day, the SS kept bothering us, but there was not a gas chamber in sight and that was all that mattered.

In January they found out I was pregnant, but by then it was too late for me to be sent back to Auschwitz, the Russians got there on 18 Jan. and that saved our lives. At the beginning of April we had to evacuate Freiberg, the Americans were getting much too near, again they put us in goods waggons, but this time they were open to the sky, otherwise locked, we were squeezed in like sardines, it was cold, it rained, we had hardly any food, we could not wash and I was nearing the end of my pregnancy. At one time we were standing at a siding for about a fortnight. That was inside Czechoslovakia. Suddenly we got moving again, in a southerly direction, crossed the Austrian frontier and were heading towards Mauthausen, where we arrived towards the evening on Sunday, 29 April. When I saw the name 'Mauthausen' on the station, I got so frightened that I started labour. Mauthausen was in the same category as Auschwitz. Gas chambers, selections – in short an extermination camp., When we got off the train, those who could walk were marched off, and the few of us who could not, were put on a cart and driven to the fortress. After arrival there, I was put on a different cart with other women, who were all dying of typhoid fever. Lice were crawling all over the place, the poor women were unconscious, were leaning on me, lying across my legs, I was sitting up and my baby started to come.

It was a beautiful cold evening, the sun was just going down and suddenly my Baby was here. It did not move, it did not cry and frankly I could not care less. At that moment we arrived in the camp hospital, they called a doctor, who happened to be chief obstetrician of a Belgrade Hospital, himself an internee, he cut off the baby, he smacked its bottom, it started to cry and he told me, 'It's a boy.' Somebody wrapped it in paper and suddenly I was terribly happy. By then the Germans were more frightened than we were, the Americans were only a few miles away, the gas chamber had been blown up only a day before and the Germans tried to make up to us. They brought me so much food that that could have killed me. But it did not, after three days we were liberated and the nightmare was over. At that time I asked the nurse who looked after us to give my little boy a bath. She looked at me as if I had gone mad and said that I had a girl. I got quite frantic, called the doctor and he confirmed that I had a little girl. Apparently it is quite common that such a mistake can happen with babies who are premature or very small. You weighed 3 pounds and 15 stone [sic – must be ounces].

That is how we arrived in Prague, when you were three weeks old. I took us to my cousin, whom I presumed to be there, because of her being married to a Gentile. We came for three days and stayed for 3½ years. They gave us a home and a new start in life. I found out later that your Father was shot dead on the evacuation of Auschwitz on 18 January, he worked somewhere nearby in a coal mine. In February

1948, Daddy and I got married and in September of the same year we left Czechoslovakia to settle in GB.

Mummy (Anka Bergman)

After I had read Anka's letter I had several questions for Eva especially about Anka's sisters who were deported in September 1943. I was told they were Zdena (Sidonie) and Ruze and Peter was Ruze's eight-year-old blond blue-eyed son. Eva also sent me copies of the postcard her Aunt Zdena was forced to send from Auschwitz, dated 20 October 1943. Of the many which were sent, Eva speculated how many contained a code word. Instead of putting her cousin's real name, Olga, in the address, she wrote 'Lechem Šroňkova'. *Lechem* is the Hebrew for bread, so she was telling the family they were hungry. Her cousin understood and sent a parcel but the contents were stolen long before it arrived. Eva added 'even before the postcard was sent, they'd all been sent to the gas chambers'.[31] The translation of the card is below:

My Dear Ones
I am here with my husband, my sister & my nephew; all are well & in good health.
My husband received a parcel yesterday from our housekeeper & I would ask you to confirm this to her. Please also thank Gerdy. Could she greet Birza Smid for us. I hope you're well & happy. Your parents were very well at the time of our departure. Write soon. Peter looks well & looks forward to receiving news from you.
Greetings & kisses. Your Zdena Isidor.

The depth of the tragedy of Ruze and her son was detailed in *Born Survivors*.

Others given a similar *Dutchlassschein* or special exit permit did leave, but they were in the minority. Among them was Tom Mautner, the husband of Anka's sister Ruzena, who seized the chance to flee to England on one of the last trains to London. He'd pleaded with Ruzena to go with him and bring their son Peter but she'd refused to leave her home and family. 'It was so much nicer to stay there than go to England so she stayed, and she paid dearly for it,' Anka said sadly.[32] So did young Peter.

Anka was born on 20 April 1917 in a small Czech town. Although her family was Jewish, they were not observant and ate pork. As a young woman she moved to Prague in 1936 and attended the Charles University to study Law. Following the German invasion, student demonstrations were crushed and nine student leaders were executed. 1,200 professors and students were rounded up and sent to camps and universities were closed. The imposition of the Nuremberg Laws, brought greater restrictions. The Anka's family car was

---

31 Eva Clarke, email to author, 11 Sept 2017.
32 Wendy Holden, *Born Survivors* (London: Sphere, 2015) p.78

taken as was the family business with her parents thrown out of their home. The family's assets were then frozen so they couldn't withdraw more than 1,500 crowns a week from their own bank account. Their citizenship was taken away and were only permitted in segregated parts of restaurants and a few hotels. In Prague, Jews were banned from the public baths, swimming pools and the popular cafes along the River Vltava. Forced to the back of the trams, they were also prevented from owning bicycles, cars or wireless radios.

However the measure that really upset Anka was being banned from the cinema – it was an unnecessary torment to someone who loved it. When she really wanted to see a particular film, she decided to go without telling anyone – she later admitted she was 'a complete fool'. She was right in the middle of the cinema, halfway through the film when it flickered to a stop. The lights came on and members of the Gestapo burst in to check everyone's ID row by row. As they came closer she froze in her seat wondering what would happen when they saw the 'J' on her documents. She toyed with making a run for it but decided that was a mistake. Suddenly the Gestapo abandoned their inspection just at the row in front of hers. She waited until the end of the film before leaving. Her friends were shocked, saying, 'They could have shot you.' Ironically, she could never remember the name of the film.

Anne-Marie Lever – Annick's Story

I met Annick through a friend, Gillian Keve, who said Annick's mother was still recovering from giving birth to her when she was deported by the Nazis and died. Annick had written her story and it was expanded following a meeting on 2 May 2017 with her and her husband at my home.

My name is Annick. I was born in France on 23 November 1943 during the last World War. When I was 11 years old I went out with a friend to buy some milk in Saujon. Suddenly I found myself with a rope around my neck. Some teenage boys were pulling it and calling me "dirty Jew". Everybody in the small town knew my story. I had no idea what they meant because I did not know then that I was Jewish. I was only a baby when the story I am about to tell you took place. I can tell the story not from my own memories, but because I heard it many times from the family who brought me up.

I was told my 'mother' was not my real mother – I called her *Maman*. Her marriage was rocky and her husband left for a while. He came back drunk one evening with a hunting rifle and wanted to shoot her. I was only six years old and went between them and said you will not kill my mummy. He pushed me aside and said 'She is not your Mummy.' That was the first time I heard that. I was ill afterwards with jaundice caused by the fear. I never talked about it. I think I was scared to know the truth. I had photos of my mother and aunt in my bedroom, but I was never told who they were and never asked. She was always a real mother to me. I called her husband 'Uncle'. As a little girl I used to say that my mother

Above: Auschwitz staff. Liliane was killed on the way there. (Courtesy Iga Bunalska, Auschwitz Study Group)

Below: Liliane Foks's diary. (Courtesy Annick Lever)

Above and below: Liliane and Marcelle, Annick's mother and aunt. Liliane is on the right above and the left below. (Courtesy Annick Lever)

slept with my uncle. She loved me very much. Her grandchildren called her Mimi, so then everyone else called her Mimi. She died in 1992.

My birth mother was Liliane Foks who was born on 4 March 1919 and died on or after 10 February 1944 en route to Auschwitz. My father, Roger Albert Xavier, was born on 31 March 1902 and died on 18 July 1988. He was not Jewish.

My maternal grandfather was born in Belgium (1874) and my grandmother in Holland (1887). They had three daughters. After my first aunt Henriette, was born in Belgium, they moved to Paris. Marcelle, my other aunt and my mother were both born in Paris. They all acquired French nationality in 1931. In the summer of 1939 they came to the south west of France. Sadly enough war was declared and they were never able to go back to their apartment in Paris, except for my grandfather who went to collect whatever he was able to bring back with him.

Henriette was married to Karl van Dam, a Dutchman and lived in Amsterdam with her two children. Jacques Van Dam, now dead, and Helene Van Dam, now married to Nico Kamp and living in Amsterdam. When war was declared the family in France was very concerned about them. The invasion of Holland was in May 1940. I am pleased to say that they all survived and had themselves quite a story to tell.

I have all this information because about 30 years ago I was given some diaries which belonged to my mother. They cover the last three years of her life from January 1942 to 22 January 1944. I also learned, as I was reading them, that when she found out she was pregnant, my father really wanted a boy. They were going to call him Alain. What a coincidence my husband's name is Allen. I knew my husband long before I read the diaries.

My aunt and my mother were both young women when they arrived on holidays. My aunt Marcelle was 22 and my mother 20. I have been told many a time that they were two very beautiful women. ... They soon found husbands. My grandparents were not very religious, but in those days mixed marriages were not very well accepted, but in the circumstances they agreed that their daughters could marry outside their religion.

Marcelle had a daughter, Marie-Claire, she was born at the beginning of 1943 and at the end of 1943, I was born, not exactly the boy my father expected.

In 1940 life became very difficult for the Jewish population in France and my grandfather had to go to the town hall to register in October 1940. In December they had to declare all their possessions. Their misery did not stop there as in May 1941 their ID cards had to be stamped with the word "JEW" across, as elsewhere in Nazi-occupied Europe. From 7 June 1942 came the yellow star. From the age of 7 you were not allowed outside without wearing the yellow star. The worst was that they had to pay for it with their textile coupons.

As we all know it did not stop there. In July 1942 a curfew was imposed from 19.30 until the morning (time not known). During this period the family was living in Royan, on the coast, where they had originally come on holiday. In 1943 they all had to leave the coast on

30 January as Jews were no longer permitted to live by the sea. My father's uncle lived in a small village called Thenac. The whole family moved there. My parents lived with the uncle and the rest of the family lived in rented accommodation. I was born in this little village.

On 30 January 1944 the family was invited to spend the day at the home of some friends in Saintes, a town near the little village where they lived. They were so happy to get away from their misery for a day. When the time came to go home my father's van would not start. They were very concerned because of the babies (my cousin and me). Petrol was very scarce and this van was operated by a wood gas generator. After a while the engine started. They arrived back in Thenac at midnight, to find the police waiting for them. We were to be taken to a prison straight away. My father talked the police into waiting until the morning. They agreed but left a policeman to guard us. At the first hour of the day we all went to La Rochelle, the main town of the department, where a school had been converted into a prison.

My parents had some very good friends who lived in Saujon. That is the little town where I was brought up. My mother had asked the friend, Andrée Castex, if anything was to happen to her, would she take care of me until she came back? My mother had a premonition that something was about to happen. My father had a good friend as a result of Mimi's father-in-law and Annick's paternal grandfather both being from the Basque country and had come to the area a long time ago looking for work. My father was godfather to Mimi's third child who died as a baby in May 1943 – aged about a year and half. His sister Claudie, who was eleven at the time said she remembers her mother and my mother going into a room together and Mimi coming back crying and she thinks that was when she asked her to look after me.

My family's home was in Thénac, having been forced to move from Royan. My birth was quite straightforward at 8.15pm with a doctor present according to Liliane's diary. They were very beautiful girls – my mother and aunt were dancers – they went to a famous dance school – Madame Irene Popard. The sisters were very close.

After our arrest, my father, who was not Jewish, was freed. He drove straight to his friends to tell them what had happened. They all drove back to the prison. They were able to smuggle my cousin and me out. That was not all. When we were all in the prison another woman realised what was happening. She came to my parents' friend and asked her if she would also take her two children (a boy of 9 and a girl of 6). The friend said she could not. The lady answered, "If you had a mother's heart you would not refuse." However she would have been unaware that only 8 months previously this friend had lost a little boy through illness. So they all walked out of the prison together. The friends, my father, we two babies and the two children.

The same evening the police were at the friend's house saying that if they did not take the children back to the prison they would all be arrested. I was told that they spent a long and difficult night but in the morning they drove the children back to La Rochelle. They, the brother and sister, had to go to the station where the train was waiting for them to go to Drancy and then on to Auschwitz. Those two children, the mother and the father all survived. I met them after the war when I was much older and heard their story many times.

My father was a cattle dealer. He had wanted to be a vet and lived in the same town in his own house. I called Mimi's husband "Uncle". When I was 17 and just before going to Holland to see my aunt my father took me out for lunch. He gave me my mother's wedding and engagement rings and spoke about her for the first time. He told me that he spent the night with her in prison as he had bribed the French police. My cousin Marie-Claire went to Royan where her father had three sisters who brought her up. Her mother was Marcelle.My father was in the French resistance He was able to provide my aunt and my mother with some fake identity cards. With money he bribed someone at the prison, a back door was left open, my aunt and my mother were able to get out. However they felt they could not leave their parents behind and went back to the prison after just a few hours on the outside. They left La Rochelle for Drancy (the main transit camp in France) near Paris on 2 February with their parents. On 10 February they boarded a train made up of cattle wagons and were taken to Auschwitz on transport 68.

For many years I thought that maybe my mother was not dead. The official papers always said: "presumed dead". Then one day, one of her cousins told me that just after the war a woman came looking for the family. She had also travelled on transport 68. She wanted to tell us that my mother had died on the way to Auschwitz, but I had never found out why. Later, however, the local village (Thenac) put the names of my family on the Cenotaph alongside the names of the fallen French soldiers.

I only heard in April 2016 what really happened to her. Apparently the woman told the family she went mad en route to Auschwitz and was shot and killed by the SS. Her sister is recorded as dying at Auschwitz. My mother was not well when they were transported to Drancy on 2 February 1944 and she was offered a stay at a hospital in La Rochelle with me, but she refused.

Now the part of the story I remember. When I was 17, a letter came from Holland. My aunt who had survived in Amsterdam wanted to have contact with me. For the first and only time my father talked to me about my mother. It was very difficult for him. He told me that my mother had asked him never to marry again. He was 38 when they had married and my mother was only 22. Sadly they were only together for 2 years. Within a few months of receiving my aunt's letter I was on the plane to Amsterdam. What was strange for me is, the moment I found my family in Holland I felt at home. As I was growing up I was always told that I was different. I should mention that I was brought up as a Catholic, not very religious, but until I went to Amsterdam I had never eaten meat on a Friday. I arrived on a Thursday and on Friday night I had to eat chicken soup. It was difficult at first. I stayed for about 2 months and then went back to Saujon and went to work on the Isle d'Oleron at a special children's hospital in 1961.

A few years later, my Dutch family decided that I should learn more about my Jewish roots and also maybe learn English properly. They arranged for me to stay with a wonderful Jewish family in Bristol as their au pair. I arrived in August 1963 and in September I went to the synagogue for the first time in my life. It was the Jewish New Year. I was 19 and I met my future husband there. We were married on 26 October 1967. My family had succeeded regarding the Jewish side of the story, but as you can probably see I have never quite mastered the language.

We had 2 boys, Antoine who was born on 27/6/70 and Pierre who was born on 25/02/73, and now we have 5 granddaughters.

Before I conclude, I would like to point out to you that the dates and facts that I have given are very accurate. I am fortunate to have in my possession photocopies of documents brought to me by a historian. They were discovered in the loft of a police station in the town where the prison was.

Finally I did check my mother's diaries for anything to do with the war and what was happening to the Jews at Agnes' request. Unfortunately most of the entries were fairly mundane, with no particular interest to the larger story. However just weeks after my birth, on 31 December 1943, New Year's Eve, she wrote (translated from the French):

Last day of a year full of anguish and momentous events. If only 1944 could lead us to the end of our nightmare. May the almighty protect us. May He bless those who are dear to us.

Normal working Friday. Washed myself and washed my hair. Evening – some New Year's Eve celebration! – just a glass of schnapps with grapes. Home very late. To everyone – adieu 1943.[33]

Edith Erbrich

I came across Edith Erbrich's story quite early in my research for this book. I read about a small girl studying her mother's face so that she would remember how she looked as they set off for deportation. Edith and her older sister Hella, born in 1933, were being deported with their Jewish father Norbert Bär, but their Catholic mother Susanna was forced to stay behind. So this also aroused my interest, as I had written at length about Mischlings *in* Who Betrayed the Jews?

Edith Bär was born in Frankfurt on 28 October 1937. She was classified as a *Mischling*, being of 'mixed blood', as her father had Jewish parents whilst her mother was from a Catholic family. Edith, aged two, had an identity

---

33 Annick Lever, email to author 9 May 2017.

Edith Erbrich (right) and author, 6 October 2017, in Edith's flat.

card which displayed the obligatory 'J' and the middle name Sara, given to every female Jew. Also mentioned are the deformities on her hands, a genetic handicap passed down from her paternal grandfather's side.[34]

Her grandmother came from Warsaw as a young Jewish woman but her grandfather's family had come from Switzerland in the late nineteenth century. Norbert, born in 1909, was their youngest child and worked in a leather goods business. As a Jew he lost his job in 1933, which unfortunately was the year he had got married and Hella, his first daughter, was born. His wife, Susanna née Henz, was *Aryan* and they lived in a 'privileged mixed marriage' which meant that the Jewish partner was exempt from deportation. I asked Edith how they met. She said Norbert and his parents lived above a café where Susanna was a waitress.

In the early 1930s, about 10,000 Jews, a third of Frankfurt's Jews, lived in the east end. They were just under 20 per cent of that district's population and consequently it was called the 'Jewish quarter'. From 1939 on the city authorities compulsorily acquired Jewish institutions such as schools, hospitals, orphanages, synagogues and social welfare organisations in the area at knock-down prices. Edith was too young to remember this but later

---

34 Most of this information comes from an English précis of Edith Erbrich's book *I've not Forgotten How to Laugh*, published only in German. It is supplemented by information from my meeting with Edith on 6 October 2017 at her home and http://db.yadvashem.org/deportation/transportDetails. html?language=en&itemId=5092428

learned from history books that Jewish factory owners and merchants had settled in the area in the late nineteenth century. With the introduction of *Aryanization,* Jews were forced out of the retail and market trades. Edith thinks this exclusion of Jews from economic and public life was carried out more brutally in Frankfurt than elsewhere in the Reich.

Edith wrote many 'old Frankfurters' who 'had never been against the Jews' told her, 'We did not know anything about what went on; we were never aware of these actions.' They were lying, because in April 1939, 400 flats became *Judenfrei.* Those evicted were herded into 275 'Jew houses', creating a virtual ghetto visible to everyone. This inhuman resettlement policy coincided with further restrictions: in 1940 all radios had to be handed in, Jews were no longer given clothing ration cards, groceries could only be bought in certain shops between 4 and 5 pm and telephone lines were cut. From 1941 forced labour was introduced, Jews aged six plus had to wear the yellow star and public telephones were out of bounds. Jews were forbidden to buy newspapers and magazines, to visit 'Aryan' barbers or to keep pets. Eventually, ration cards for meat and milk were withheld.

Without work since 1933, Norbert could hardly provide for his family and had to do odd jobs. He worked for Jewish welfare, cleaning or doing shop work. This work was illegal for Jews and therefore was often done at night. Despite his handicap, he was skilful in all sorts of practical jobs. Edith herself was also brought up to use her hands as best she could and not to expect help from others.

Susanna, besides being a housewife, worked as a cleaner for extra income. Some friends secretly helped the family with food when possible. She suffered as a result of her marriage and ration cards for clothing that were an entitlement for a German of 'pure blood' were withheld. The Gestapo tried to persuade her to give up her 'privileged marriage' status by divorcing Norbert. When she complained to the official in charge of ration cards he said, 'You should not have married that Jew; go and get a divorce!' A file note mentions that Bär had 'misbehaved' at the particular office and was, therefore, given 21 days' 'coercive detention'. One of the Gestapo interrogators commented, 'I don't know why so much fuss is made about the Jews. They'll all be gassed anyway.' However, Susanna loyally stayed with her husband and family. Edith told me her mother was imprisoned in Hammelsgasse Prison in Frankfurt – a Gestapo prison. Her mother never spoke of it. Edith said a former inmate, Hans Schwerdt, who at the time of writing is 104, told her, 'It is good you don't know.' Apparently, prisoners were hung up be their feet until they agreed to the Gestapo's demands or died.[35]

Things got progressively worse and Edith and her sister Hella were increasingly isolated as unlike their 'Aryan' friends they could not go to school. Jewish children and *mischlinge* were excluded. Their father had to work for the municipal burial authority: prepare graves, retrieve corpses from under the ruins and take them to the cemetery. Mother was a forced labourer for Bigoform – a pharmaceutical factory that made pills, syringe needles and

---

35 Interview with Edith Erbrich in Langen on 6 October 2017.

bandages. The girls were left on their own. One day they played with their dolls outside. An 'Aryan' neighbour chased them away saying, 'You Jewish brats, get out of the garden!' so they hardly dared to leave the flat. However, sometimes they removed their yellow star – a highly dangerous thing to do – and collected bits of coal that sympathetic lorry drivers dropped for them from their loads. Edith calls them her 'silent heroes'.

In the spring of 1943 Frankfurt was declared *Judenrein*. Of 15,000 members of the Jewish community (1941) there were 495 left, plus several hundred people of mixed background. Hella, being older, suffered terrible anxiety attacks, fearing their father would be taken away at any moment as she overheard their parents talking about deportations.

One day Edith was attracted to a troupe of 'midgets' working for a circus nearby. They let her look around their wagon where everything was small as if made for Edith. Her father got her back and for the only time gave her a good hiding! She alone in the family did not understand the dangers of those times. In 1939, her unmarried Aunt Fanny, a seamstress, managed to emigrate to Argentina on the last boat. Edith had been very fond of her grandparents, who were deported to Theresienstadt in 1942. They had been duped into signing a contract for bed and board in a so-called old-age home in Theresienstadt and giving away all their possessions. Her grandfather died only three days after arrival. Of the 1,378 members on that transport, 326 were taken to extermination camps and killed. Only 105 lived to be liberated on 8 May 1945, including Edith's grandmother.

The days and nights when the bombs were raining down were the worst. Everyone wearing the yellow star was forbidden to enter the air-raid shelters or take part in civil air defence exercises. The children left 'home alone' were terrified. Sometimes their mothers' bosses let them come home during a raid to see them. When they had to take refuge alone in the cellar they could not wait to see their parents again in the evening. Having to get up at night was hard – Edith was too tired and Hella dragged her to safety. They had to go to their own cellar, as the 'Jewish brats' were not permitted to enter the general bunker.

Over half a million inhabitants had to run to the air-raid shelters only to be ordered right back to work! Leaflets rained down on the city warning of continued bombardments, day and night, trying to wear down the population – 'you know that you have no chance'. On 4 October 1943 Frankfurt was hit with a two-hour relentless air attack and a similar raid in March 1944 destroyed the Bärs' flat. Residents were buried under the ruins but survived. Edith's father and a neighbour dug a way out of the cellar into the street.

In early February 1945 Norbert Bär received deportation 'call-up papers' for himself and Edith, then 7 years old, telling them to report to the railway station. He broke down in tears but his wife comforted him, 'We'll manage. You do have a family!' Hella's papers came two days later. Norbert only knew their destination was Theresienstadt because Susanna was told when she asked the *Judenrät* to keep her husband in Frankfurt and from the postcard his mother had sent after being taken away.

By that time 10,000 Frankfurt Jews had already been deported to Eastern Europe. Their possessions were stolen and auctioned off. *Aryans* taunted them en route, apparently relishing the deportees' misfortune, shouting, 'We are glad to be rid of you!' It appears the local Gestapo were more zealous than, say, those in Berlin to rid their area of the Jewish population, even as late as February 1945. We should remember by this date my mother and I had been liberated from the Budapest Ghetto on 18 January 1945 and Auschwitz was liberated on 27 January 1945.

Apparently, in October 1944, Himmler ordered the transport of *Mischlinge* Grade 1 and Jewish spouses for slave labour and the RSHA implemented this from January 1945. This was how the Frankfurt office of the RV sent out to all Jews with non-Jewish spouses:

You are required to report on Wednesday, 14.2.1945, at 2.00pm, to the Ostbahnhof, at the compound in front of the Grossmarkthalle (eastern side). You may bring luggage of regular size. Work clothes [...] strong shoes, warm underwear, socks [...] and eating utensils should be brought. The trip is liable to last three days. Therefore, you are asked to bring enough food for four or five days [...].

To encourage the deportees to do as they were told, the following was added in boldface: 'This summons shall not be considered similar to other transports summonses that were implemented in the past.'[36] When I met Edith on 6 October 2017 in her home in Langen, I asked how her mother learnt she could not accompany her husband and daughters. Edith said she was told in an office and was very upset. Edith told me that as they walked to the collection point at the *Grossmarkthalle* (wholesale market hall) she kept stumbling because she was watching her mother's face so she could remember her. The girls were only told that morning that their mother was staying behind. Edith saw her heavily pregnant mother was crying.

Over 300 Jews were deported that day from Frankfurt and en route other transports were added, so when they arrived at Theresienstadt four days later, there were about 600 Jews. Norbert had taken 9 franked postcards which he threw out of the window of the train with brave and hopeful messages (we are okay, stay strong! see you soon again!, etc.) for Susanna. Amazingly 8 of them reached her, posted by more of Edith's silent heroes! (Many other cards 'posted' in the same way from other trains also arrived at their destination.) Yad Vashem records Edith testifying:

I still remember how we marched from the *Uhlandstrasse* to the *Grossmarkthalle*. The street was black from the sheer number of people ... The SS knew exactly which people were to be deported. I held my mother's hand and stared at her because I wanted to remember her face.

---

36 Yad Vashem, *Transports to Extinction*, http://db.yadvashem.org/deportation/transportDetails.html accessed 8 October 2017.

She wanted to join the transport voluntarily but [as a non-Jew] was not allowed to. At the *Grossmarkthalle* everything happened very quickly. The cattle cars were ready. We had to get aboard, 30–40 people per car. There was no straw in the car and the wooden benches were bare. The doors were sealed; the bolt was thrown across them [...]. It was evening. The people were in a state of shock; some of them wept. The door was opened and an SS man shouted, 'Pick up the two children [Edith and her sister] high! Their mother wants to see them one more time!' I saw my mother crying [...]. Through the slats we could see the train moving. It was February and it was cold. We froze in the cold and huddled together [...]. Those who didn't survive were simply 'gotten rid of' and thrown down the slope, over and done with. The next stop was Theresienstadt.[37]

The entrance gate said 'Arbeit Macht Frei' as at Auschwitz. The girls were separated from their father. Their few possessions were taken away and their hair cut off. Even so they became infected by lice and were deloused. Everything was scary – Edith had a dark premonition when she had to shower as she remembered what her parents used to say. She fainted and panicked until she was reunited with Hella, who constantly told her not to scream or cry in case they were separated.

As Edith had never been to school she was scared of the camp school timetable. They were taught to read and write and learnt poems by heart. Once a week they were allowed to walk with their father who begged them to stay strong. The food was poor – watery soup with an ounce of horse meat; bread came twice a week but no vegetables, fruit or dairy products. They were always hungry.

In March Hella, like all children aged over 10, had to work. She had to dig up potatoes and put them in sacks, also weeding and digging holes in the ground. Her group was promised a train full of sweets but instead, the next day a train arrived with corpses, which the youngsters had to move. On 6 April 1945 a Red Cross delegation came. Her group was dressed up and had to stage a play. The tables were laid with real cakes and sweets, but the children had told to decline saying they were 'not hungry'. The Red Cross delegation failed to observe the children's true condition.

Edith developed a high temperature and was relieved to go to the children's sick bay. Hella was elsewhere, away from Edith. Once a week they still met their father but did not hear anything from their mother. Edith suffered terrible nightmares. She was moved three times and luckily ended up opposite her father's window. Hugo and Leo, friends of Norbert, became like members of the family. Norbert managed to find his mother but the once portly woman had aged and become so bent over that Edith hardly recognised her. She never dared to ask what had happened to Grandpa.

During the night of 7 May 1945, Edith was woken by terrible screaming and shots fired outside. She saw the people who had bullied and harassed

---

37 Yad Vashem, *Transports to Extinction: Transport XII/10 from Frankfurt 14/02/1945* accessed 8 October 2017

them taken prisoner and driven off in lorries. Her father and sister appeared in the doorway: 'We are free!' Edith believed they would be able to return home at last. She did not understand how her father had stayed so positive. She believes he knew that in February and April 1945 some prisoners had been sent to Switzerland and Denmark. The SS burnt files and Himmler had been negotiating with the Red Cross to take over the camp, which happened on 3 May. Two days later the SS left – three days before the Red Army arrived.

They were quarantined in Theresienstadt for several weeks because of a typhus epidemic brought by inmates from camps like Auschwitz and Bergen-Belsen. On 7 June, finally having the required documents, they were free to leave. Norbert had read in Gestapo documents that they were scheduled to be gassed in Auschwitz on 9 May. A gas chamber was even being built in Theresienstadt but was not completed. Their journey home, with father's friends, was with a handcart. It was slow and difficult along the broken roads and they stopped briefly at a liberated women's camp in Saxony and an American military camp, enjoying welcome rations. When they finally got back to Frankfurt Edith was overjoyed to be with her mother. They also met their little brother, Norbert who was born on 10 May.

I asked Edith what happened to their mother whilst they were away. Edith said her mother often went to talk to the nuns in the Convent near their home and prayed with them. In 2016 Edith spoke in a church near Cologne when an elderly nun told her she had been in that convent which was now closed. Edith said she did not know how Susanna managed for food and what rations she had. She had no friends to talk to at that time and Edith assumes she had gone to hospital to have her brother.

Soon Norbert found a larger flat for his family of five and also a job with the municipal utilities where he stayed until his retirement in 1973. Frankfurt lay under mountains of rubble, with essential services and facilities disrupted. People were being injured or killed by unexploded bombs and mines daily. There was no psychological care for people who had survived the war and/or the Holocaust. The only person Edith was able to share her horrible memories with was Hella. Their parents did not wish to look back and were very resilient people, mainly concerned with their children's future.

In 1946 the girls started proper school but Edith told me she found it difficult to adjust. Fortunately she had a very understanding teacher who helped her settle into school routine. She was a popular but mischievous girl. After their grandmother's death in 1950, the family gradually lost their Judaism and stopped celebrating Jewish festivals with traditional food. Both her parents are buried in a Christian cemetery as mixed couples could not be buried in the Jewish graveyard.

After leaving school Hella trained as a seamstress and Edith was apprenticed as a clerk with a Frankfurt daily newspaper. Germany and certainly Frankfurt, as an industrial, commercial and financial centre, was booming and the girls' future seemed secure. She enjoyed the working at a busy newspaper with a good social scene. During the last year of her apprenticeship she met Willi, a Post Office clerk. Although initially reluctant, she soon warmed to him and they had fun. They loved going to football matches and went camping with Hella and her husband Walter.

Edith and Willi married in a registry office in February 1962. Edith left the Jewish community and they had a Christian (protestant) ceremony a year later. Edith thought she might be pregnant and feared having a Jewish child, in case the Nazis returned. In fact, she never had a child. At this time Eichmann, whom Edith herself had seen in Theresienstadt, was being tried and executed in Jerusalem. In Frankfurt, Fritz Bauer – himself Jewish – initiated the Auschwitz trials, which forced the Germans to confront their past.

Edith never spoke to neighbours and colleagues about her past. The young couple moved to a new satellite town south of Frankfurt but Edith was very unhappy – it was a sleepy, boring place. Willi liked it there, but tragically after only 5 years of married life, he died "of a hole in the lung" bringing a happy marriage to a premature end.

Edith had several office jobs until she joined her father's employer, the municipal utilities, in 1972. She stayed there until she retired 26 years later in 1997. Neo-Nazis became active in local politics in the 1970s and 1980s but Edith did not engage. She also kept out of debates about Rainer Werner Fassbinder's highly controversial play which many regarded as antisemitic. At this time her father had a heart operation and her mother was developing dementia. They died in 1987 and 1990 respectively leaving Edith feeling quite bereft.

Fifty years after liberation, the sisters returned to Theresienstadt. After long hesitation, they felt they had to revisit the past, in spite of the pain it would cause. A Czech professor, a former inmate, guided them around the former camp some of which they recognized. They found the mass grave where their grandfather was buried. Although difficult, Edith felt that the visit and sharing memories with Hella gave them some closure and as a result she was able to discuss her experiences and feelings better. Her motto is: 'The Nazis wanted to rob us of everything, to make us into human beings without any feelings. In our case they did not succeed.'

Aged 60, Edith retired and spent four months visiting friends in Australia. Whilst she was away, an exhibition focusing on "Children in Theresienstadt" was staged in Frankfurt. On her return she contacted the curator and during a long conversation the dam burst: she couldn't stop telling her story! She wanted to thank those who helped the family with acts of kindness – the men with the coal lorries, the people who mailed the postcards to her mother and the others. It led her to write the family's story and changed her life. She was interviewed by radio, TV and newspapers and was involved in staging exhibitions and in many documentaries. Even in her town of Langen she gave talks, staged exhibitions, worked as a guide and engaged in the local Stoplerstein (stumbling stone) initiative. She participated in torchlight processions commemorating *Kristallnacht*.

Since 2001 Edith has told her story to 25,000 pupils and young people in 150 schools and youth centres all over Germany. Even the teachers are amazed by the students' interest even though they have studied Germany's recent history, seen documentaries and many have visited concentration camp memorial sites. But listening to a real witness of that dark period is a unique experience for them and they have a lot of questions for Edith. She has received hundreds of letters thanking her and telling her of their horror, tears and "goose bumps" at her story. Some letters include drawings of flowers begging her to come back.

On the 98th anniversary of Norbert's birthday in 2007, Edith received the greatest honour of the Federal Republic of Germany at the Bellevue Palace in Berlin – the official residence of the President. When the national anthem was played, everyone present rose to their feet, and Edith could not hold back her tears!

Every year she now takes a group of young people from Mainz University to Theresienstadt, on the 8 May which is the anniversary of the camp's liberation. This is for her a day of celebration, joy and gratitude. Many people find it hard to believe that she has such a positive attitude to life after her terrible experiences. In 2011 she finally received her grandfather's death certificate from the Theresienstadt archive which confirmed his fate. A "Stolperstein" has been placed outside his final address in Frankfurt.

I asked Edith about the impact of her experiences on her life. She told me:

> My mother felt it was important to live a 'normal life' and that meant not complaining about her imprisonment. Up to receiving my pension I never spoke about the deportation and never complained about anything. I worked in an office and only my boss knew about it from my file. I feel the fact that I could talk to Hella lessened the impact. I always tell people 'Keep your eyes and ears open – so that never again will such things happen.'

Sophie Urman – Jerzyk's Mother

I heard the tragic story of his young cousin's suicide from Anthony Rudolf in the 1990s. When I was planning the book I approached him and discovered he now had more information as Sophie Urman's diary and other writing had come to light recently. The piece below was written in English around 1985.

'A Wound Which He Doesn't Heal'[38]

Again, I am writing about the Second World War, I usually try to avoid this painful the theme but as memories fade away with time, I would like to preserve them for my family in the United States. Thank God they didn't experience the war on their own skin. They always ask me how such impossible things could have happened.

I would like to dedicate this composition to my son, who died during the Holocaust.

---

38 Sophie Urman, in *Jerzyk,* Ed. Anthony Rudolf (Bristol: Shearsman Books, 2017) pp.64–9

Jerzyk aged 7 or 8 in 1939/40. His initials on his pullover JU are accidentally the first two letters of the German word for Jew. (Courtesy Anthony Rudolf)

Jerzyk grew up in excellent pre-war conditions. He was a lovely, well developed, and cheerful child with big blue eyes and a brilliant intelligence. He loved me as I loved him and although he was always ready to share things with other children, he would never let them touch toys made by me. 'Don't touch it, my mummy made it for me,' was his usual warning. Later at school he was always top of his class, affectionate and helpful to his friends who admired him as their leader. Even older boys came to him for advice on difficult matters (stamps, books, etc.).

He showed an unusually brave and noble character during the war, when he had to adapt himself to all kinds of situations in order to save his and his family's lives.

In 1941, when the Germans invaded our part of Poland they started with a so-called *Aktion*, which meant that Gestapo soldiers went from home to home looking for Jews who they sorted into groups and led to a square or a cemetery. Here they were ordered to dig graves for themselves and then were shot to death.

During the first *Aktion* my son and I were at home. My husband had been called to a patient and couldn't get back. A neighbour knocked on the door and said that the Germans were taking Jews somewhere. I went with Jerzyk to a Polish neighbour on the third floor and asked her to hide us. She put us in her bedroom beneath a lot of pillows and covers. We stayed there for about an hour in horrible fear. The child said he was choking. I had the same feeling, but I asked him to endure because our lives were in danger. The Germans with a big dog checked the entire building and when they began approaching our neighbour's apartment the woman got scared and shouted: 'Go away from here, I don't want to hide dirty Jews.' I begged her, kissed her hands, and asked her to keep my son only. He could play with her children and nobody would recognise him because he didn't look Jewish. But she kept shouting 'out, out'. I took Jerzyk by the hand and we went down the steps to our apartment on the first floor. On the way we passed the Germans who were going upstairs and in their fervour they didn't notice us. We entered our apartment, I closed the door and we sat there in darkness until early morning when my husband returned. On his way home he met people who had spent the whole night in graves among the dead bodies, waiting to be shot. Now, half crazy, they tried to return to their homes.

Aktionen took place from time to time under different pretexts. During one of them they hanged the most prominent people in the ghetto on the lamp posts of the main street and left their bodies there for a whole week. When we went to receive our weekly bread ration (300g) we had to pass by this macabre sight because there was no other route. No wonder children who grew up in such circumstances very quickly became serious and mature. My son was very quiet, read widely, and wrote a great deal on pieces of paper which he collected together. His only friend was our cat Maciek who followed us to the ghetto and remained with us. Maciek had no food problems, the ghetto was full of rats.

There were different *Aktionen* for men, children and old people. One morning the Germans decided to reduce the ghetto and organised a general *Aktion* for whole families. As we passed the Jewish hospital we saw all the patients, doctors and nurses dead in the yard. It's not easy to forget such a sight. The Germans took some of us to an old school which served as a collection point from which Jews were sent to concentration camps. We spent a whole day there. In the evening some of us were told we could go home because we were still needed by the Germans. These included two doctors, a pharmacist, and a social worker, as well as their families. It was a trick. When we came out of the school, they told us, they told us to stand in the line destined for Bełżec. My husband and Jerzyk and I stood there for a while but took advantage of the moment when the guards changed and then ran like mad in the darkness. I shan't describe the details of our return home. Everything had been burned down. We were homeless again. We made several other moves before it was possible to escape to Drohobycz. Here began the second part of our experiences.

We were again dependent on the mercy of good or bad people and felt like a hunted dogs. We changed quarters and finally landed in half of a small house. The apartment belonged to my brother-in-law Artur's former Polish housekeeper, Hela, who agreed to take us in – in return for heavy payment, obviously. She told all our neighbours that I was a friend who had come to stay with her. Of course nobody was told that four other people were in hiding. I had 'proper papers' and could move about more freely. My physical features also made this possible.

My new landlady was very religious and insisted that I accept and follow her way of life. I had to go to church twice daily and learned by heart Catholic prayers, the Christianised names of my patents and forefathers, as well as a lot of other things, including customs and special greetings associated with holidays. She wanted to convert me into a decent Polish girl in order to save a sinner's soul. I did everything she want so I could protect and care for my son, my husband, my brother-in-law Emil, and my mother-in-law.

They could not go out. Practically speaking they did not exist. They almost could not move or speak for fear of being noticed by our neighbours. They read and listened to the radio news, which worsened every time. Jerzyk continued with his schemes and drawings and plans. He once said that he would not let the Germans take him alive because he knew the hiding places of our friends and other secrets and he thought that being a child he wouldn't be able to withstand their tortures and would have to tell them everything. Through the heavy curtain he watched Polish children playing in the yard and looked at me with his big blue eyes without saying a word, but I saw that he was suffering enormously. He did not go outside for about three or four months. I promised to take him out.

After a long cold winter, spring came and with it a tiny hope for something better. One night I opened the door to the little garden in front of our house and let Jerzy crawl into it. He bent his head to the ground and sniffed the earth like an animal. 'Mummy, do you know how beautiful the earth smells?' The garden had jasmine and lilac bushes, then in full blossom, but I could not allow my poor child to stand or even sit up and raise his head. I couldn't reply because my heart was as if in a clamp and heavy tears ran down my cheeks. After a while we went inside and he told everyone he was in paradise. It was his first and last outing.

People must have noticed that something unusual was going on in our house. Maybe we brought too much food from the market or fetched too many pails of water from the well in the yard. Someone sent for the German police who came in the evening and started to hit my husband and the others bitterly. They thought I was a Pole who had hidden Jews, so I wasn't spared. They rummaged around in order to find treasures (money or jewellery) and were angry when they couldn't find anything. We were as poor as church mice by this time.

Suddenly I noticed Jerzy was tumbling over. He was very pale and I thought it was a reaction caused by fear. We put him to bed and when I wanted to bring him a glass of water he grasped my hand and said only: 'Mummy I took the cyanide.' Those were his last words. I thought that I was going mad, I became a wild animal. I ran into the street and instinctively ran into to the special camp for Jews, where my brother in law Artur lived. The Germans had also left a few doctors alive who were needed to take care of the German refinery staff. They had to watch out that an epidemic did not start up in the camp. I approached the guards and shouted: 'Give me a doctor, give me a doctor.' There must have been something terrible in my eyes because they let me in without checking my identity and even told me where to find a doctor.

The doctor was by chance a friend of Artur. He agreed to help and on our way home I told him the whole truth, who I was, and under what circumstances I was living. When we arrived the policemen had already left the place. They were somehow embarrassed by the unexpected situation. They had taken our clothes, food, even pillows and blankets with them, and send they did not take is because they would return in a week and expected us to prepare 100,000 zlotys for them, a huge sum of money. We approached the child, who was already unconscious. The doctor had no appropriate medication. I don't remember exactly but I think he cut the veins on both wrists in order to lessen the amount of poison flowing through his blood. I cannot explain today what he really did, but I remember that something of this kind took place.

To our great sorrow it was too late. The child could not be saved. The doctor returned to the camp. I knelt beside the bed, holding the hand of my child, perplexed at the inhuman pains and slow pace of death of the child of my flesh and blood. I don't remember any more how long I remained in this position. I held my son until his body began to grow cold and stiff, and the pulse stopped beating. It was nine o'clock in the evening.

We acted as if in a bad, macabre dream. It was after midnight when we decided to bury Jerzyk in a shed in the backyard, where no one would notice. We had no tools and dug the grave in the firm and frozen ground with kitchen knives and spoons. The moon was shining and the white snow reflected its light, therefore we could see what we were doing. After about two hours the grave was deep enough to cover his body. We wrapped Jerzyk in a sheet over his clothes his clothes and I put a little pillow under his head. We spread earth on him, this time with our hands. By the time we had finished it was almost day. I closed the door of the shed and we returned to the house. Both of us were paralysed. Later I would cry often, but at the time I was like a stone. I couldn't speak or move and the family left me alone. I took no food for several days.

After a week the same Germans came again. This time they were accompanied by two Ukrainian agents. They asked for the money and when we said we had none they got furious and hit us again. I told them that they could do with us whatever they wanted, for life without our child had no more value.

They looked at us and it seemed that even bandits could have some human feelings. They robbed us of the rest of our poor possessions, but when I wanted to give them the golden 'Holy Virgin' pendant which I wore on a chain, one of them said: 'We are religious people and do not take holy objects. It seems as though the war will be coming to an end in the very near future and we have decided to leave you to your fate. You Jews have suffered enough.' Our rescue was paid for with the life of our son. But life went on and to our shame we hadn't enough strength to put an end to it in order to follow our child.

I will briefly describe what happened afterwards. Every day I went to the shed with an empty pail under the pretext of filling it with rain water, which was stored there in a big container. We had placed the container on the grave – which I checked constantly, praying that people would not discover it. After about a month Hela took us to the house of her friend Zajączkowski where I lived openly in an attic room. Unknown to the owner Izydor lived in hiding above me under the roof. My mother-in-law remained at Hela's.

After eight months of continued suffering and fear it was clear that the war was almost over. Russians defeated the Germans and annexed our part of Poland, calling it West Ukraine. Life returned to normal, even for the Jews. We had more freedom, our food rations were larger, and everyone had work in his own profession. The first thing we did was to sell my last cardigan and my husband's cigarette lighter (things of great value at that time). With the money we bought an oblong case in which we put the body of our dear son. I would not want my worst enemy to see the body of a child buried for so many months without a coffin. Good people helped us to bury Jerzyk in the Jewish cemetery in August 1944. With the money we earned at work we ordered a simple tombstone for his grave. We found his diary among the books he treasured.

We spent about a year in Drohobycz, then, after the war, we got permission to emigrate to Silesia, My husband, who is a gynaecologist, worked again at a hospital, and so did I – as a surgical nurse. Meanwhile I became pregnant and gave birth to a daughter. This was the immediate post-war period. There were curfews at night and it was impossible to reach a hospital because of shooting in the street. I was sitting in the living room around 10 pm, mending my husband's socks. Suddenly I felt strong pains and understood that the time had come. Between contractions I went to the kitchen, boiled a lot of water, prepared the bed, put a blanket and some nappies on the table. Afterwards I placed myself in an appropriate position on the bed.

My husband was terribly worried, for he had no instruments of his own. We had no medication, no syringes. All we had at our disposal were boiled water, a new piece of soap, and a clean towel. I spent the night in terrible pain and asked my husband if I could scream. Until then I restrained myself because I didn't want to annoy him. He replied that of course I could yell if it would give me some relief. I screamed like mad and after superhuman efforts I gave birth to a baby girl [Irit]. We embraced each other and cried with joy that we had an aim in life again.

Jerzy Feliks Urman, Jerzyk, was born on 9 April 1932 in Poland. It was called East Galicia but is now western Ukraine. He kept a diary with full entries and fragments during the German occupation from 10 September until 12 November 1943, the day before he died. He was in hiding with his parents

Sophie and Izydor Urman, Emil Urman (paternal uncle) and Hermina Vogel Urman (paternal grandmother). They were in Drohobycz (now Drohobych). Another paternal uncle was Artur.

Anthony Rudolf is a second cousin, once removed, of Jerzyk's. He has written:

> It is clear from all the literature that East Galicia, Jerzyk's homeland, hosted more enthusiastic collaboration by the local population (against Jews and also Poles) than anywhere else in Europe. It also hosted some of the cruellest *Aktionen* and sadistic killings.[39]

Jerzyk killed himself with cyanide when he was eleven and a half. He is the only child suicide in Yad Vashem's records and of course, just one of the 1.5 million Jewish children who died in the Holocaust.

Rudolf writes about the short diary that was found after his death:

> ... I regard the keeping of Jerzyk's diary and the manner of his death as acts of resistance, resistance of the noblest and most tragic kind. Although Jerzyk was precocious, clear-sighted and sharp-witted, the diary is not a work of literature... It is an intelligent child's truthful account of experiences and states such as threat and rumour, nervous energy and fear, pain and insight. He kept the diary, he said, because he wanted people afterwards to know what happened.

Apparently people criticised Sophie for letting Jerzyk have the cyanide pill with him. Rudolf explains the circumstances that led to that decision.

> Some time between April and August 1942, when they were living in the Stanisławów ghetto – where only the cat enjoyed himself, thanks to ghetto rats and milk supplied by the guards – the boy had witnessed an atrocity: a child's eye was gouged out with a red-hot wire because he had been caught smuggling. The boy had also seen members of the *Judenrät* hanging from a pole. Jerzyk, then aged ten and already in some respects a man, refused to go into hiding without promise of his own portion of cyanide: he was afraid that if caught he would give away, under torture, information such as the hiding places of friends.

Izydor died in September 1992 and Sophie in March 2002. Their daughter Irit now lives in Miami. She is a musician and composer and became a grandmother earlier in 2017.[40]

---

39 Anthony Rudolf, 'New Introduction' (2016) in *Jerzyk*, p.15.
40 Anthony Rudolf, emails to author 20 and 21 October 2017.

Miracle on Dan Bus #4

I came across this story on the internet. I have included it because so many of the stories in this book are tragic and this has delayed joy. Esor Ben-Sorek is a retired professor of Hebrew, Biblical literature & history of Israel. He is very proud of being an Israeli citizen. The story was published in The Times of Israel *on 27 March 2016.*

It was a very hot day in July 1951. I was in Tel Aviv and too hot to walk. I boarded Dan bus #4 on the corner of Ben Yehuda and Gordon streets.

The bus was very crowded and there was no available seat. I had to stand next to a Yemenite woman holding a live chicken under her apron.

People were chatting, discussing with fervor the day's news, each one offering a personal description of the political situation, everyone with a different opinion. As is common in Israel, every person holds himself to be the authentic source of "inside" information. This one said "I have a cousin in the police force and he told me…" Another replied, "that doesn't make any sense. My neighbor's son is in the army and he was telling us…" And from the rear of the bus, a passenger shouted "who cares? Nothing will change soon".

At each bus stop some passengers alighted and new passengers boarded. Now there were a few empty seats and I grabbed one in the middle of the bus.

As we approached another bus stop (I can't remember which corner), three or four new passengers boarded. One elderly lady stepped up to the coin box next to the driver and deposited a few coins.

Suddenly, looking at the bus driver she gave a loud shriek. "Moishele, Moishele, Moishele mein kind."

The driver jammed on the brakes, looked at the elderly woman and cried, "Mama, Mama, is it you Mama?"

Both were Holocaust survivors from Poland and each one thought the other one was dead.

Jumping up from his seat, the driver embraced his long-lost and presumed dead mother and both hugged and hugged and both wept bitter tears of joy.

All the passengers clapped hands. Several were weeping from the joy of seeing mother and son re-united. One passenger jumped off the bus and hailed the next approaching bus. He shared the news with the new driver and requested him to notify the Dan bus company to send a relief driver.

None of us left the bus. A relief driver appeared about half an hour later. Passengers sitting in the row behind the driver got up and gave the seats to the mother and son, still clutching one another and weeping with heart-wrenching sobs.

At some point, our original driver and his mother left the bus while all of us clapped hands and the Yiddish-speaking passengers shouted "Mazal tov. Mazal tov. Tzu gezunt. A sach nachas".

I never knew where they were going. Probably to the driver's home so his mother could meet his wife and her new grandchild.

All of us were so filled with emotion that it was difficult to contain ourselves. There was not a dry eye among our passengers.

It was a hot July day in 1951. But I will never forget the miracle on Dan bus #4 on that very happy day.

Camp Sisters

I interviewed Kitty Hart-Moxon on 19 June 2013 for my previous book, after I heard her say she had been both helped and betrayed. When I came to research this book, I remembered her telling me that women in Auschwitz created substitute families which provided support to help them survive the camp. I went back to see her in February 2017 and she lent me her book Return to Auschwitz.

Kitty, who was in Auschwitz for two years, has written that women coped better in the camps:

> This seems to be because of the way in which women responded to their predicament. Whereas the men tried to work through their own individual problems, the women formed little families for mutual support. ... If it is appropriate, I would suggest that there was a bonding among the women similar to that found in the animal kingdom. Maybe it was altruism, but I rather think it was a matter of survival. However, also similar to the animal kingdom, the men tended to be less community-minded and led largely solitary existences. To be alone in Auschwitz was to really risk your life. Without someone to help you out from time to time, it was virtually impossible to survive for long.[41]

Later she adds:

> Little 'families' formed within a block: three or four friends would stick together and organize things together. One acquired some bread, another found a handkerchief or a pencil and some scraps of paper, another a mug of water. Members of a group helped each other and defied the rest. Outside the family there had to be bribery; within there was love and mutual help.[42]

Brana (Bonnie) Gurewitsch interviewed 25 women survivors who were mothers, sisters or resisters for her 1998 book. She wrote:

> One reaction that seems to be uniquely feminine, however, is the tendency of women to form close long-lasting relationships that became

---

41 Kitty Hart-Moxon, *Return to Auschwitz* (Newark: Quill, 2007) p.72
42 P.81–2

a source of mutual assistance and strength. The *Lager Schwestern* (camp sisters), coined by the women in the camps. The term in unique to women. A parallel term, describing male friendships as 'brotherly' does not exist for men, indicating that whereas men may have been loyal to family members or friends, they did not perceive the relationship either as 'brotherly' or unique to the camp experience.[43]

Sometimes these women were real relatives – mothers and daughters, sisters or cousins – and sometimes they were pre-war close friends. But many of the camp sisters met and bonded in the camps, forming 'little families'. Perhaps one of the most unusual was the 'Kaufering' group. Somewhat bizarrely: in the winter of 1944–45 the Nazis collected together seven pregnant women from various labour camps and took them to Landsberg to the Kaufering I camp where they were able to give birth and keep their babies.

These seven women, strangers to each other, helped each other recuperate, a stronger woman nursing the weaker women's babies, and physically and morally supported each other. All seven women and babies survived and were liberated after a death march to Dachau. Some of these women are still in touch with each other.

Miriam Rosenthal was one of those women and I wrote about her and her son Leslie in my earlier book. Her son was much admired by the Nazis as he had an Aryan look.[44]

Tilly Stimler was separated from her mother and older sister on the Auschwitz platform and from her remaining sister at a subsequent selection. Totally alone, without the support of family, she was adopted first by two other girls and then by a girl from her hometown with whom she stayed throughout her experiences. These camp sisters shared their food and plotted how to stay together until and after liberation.[45]

Joyce Parkey emphasised the significance of physical support particularly with sharing food and caring for anyone who became ill:

Survivors speak of the care that went into dividing food absolutely equally among their groups because 'these are hungry people; everyone must receive exactly the same portions.' Not that there was much to divide but an occasional piece of meat or vegetable discovered in the soup, extra bread acquired in a bartered transaction, or a gift from a prisoner in a better work detail could provide much needed nourishment.

---

43 Brana Gurewitsch, *Mothers, Sisters, Resisters: Oral Histories of Women Who Survived the Holocaust* (Tuscaloosa: University of Alabama Press, 1998) p.xviii – xix

44 See *Who Betrayed the Jews?* pp.464–547

45 Brana p.98

By banding together, the odds increased that one of these sources of food materialised. There was also a special need for protection when a woman became ill or injured. To begin with, any evidence of illness or injury, such as faecal matter or blood, needed to be cleaned up because if the kapo, prisoner in charge, suspected someone was sick, she would send the woman to the infirmary, and the infirmary meant almost certain death. Also, any weakness or disease shown before the SS meant selection and subsequent death. Something as trivial as scabies was now a life-threatening illness and must be covered up or salve bartered for to heal it. Someone too ill to keep up with the work demands placed upon the prisoners must be compensated for and protected, including being propped up at roll call if unable to stand. Irene Csillag speaks of even engaging in a form of physical therapy with her sister who had fallen so ill she could barely walk. Irene would take her out of their bunk twice a day and put one foot in front of each other until she could manage on her own again. Sara Bernstein's camp sister lost her glasses during a beating by a kapo. She was unable to see without them; so from then on one or more of the camp family stayed by her side. More than one prisoner recounts feeling unable to keep going, especially on the death marches away from the camps and the advancing Allies, and only the other members of her lager family urging her on, physically pulling on her each step of the way, or making her promise to keep trying, kept her from dying. Rena Gelissen, became gravely ill on the march out of Auschwitz, extremely weak and ready to die, but her sister Danka and their friend Janka wouldn't let her give up so they each took one of her elbows until she was able to walk again on her own. Had these women not had camp sisters by their sides to physically provide for them, they could not have survived.[46]

Isabella Katz was deported from Hungary to Auschwitz the day after her 23rd birthday, on 29 May 1944. She too wrote about her 'sisters':

To have sisters still alive, not to be alone, was a blessing too, but fraught with tests daily, hourly: when this day ends will there still be four of us?

If you are sisterless, you do not have the pressure, the absolute responsibility to end the day alive. How many times did that responsibility keep us alive? I cannot tell. I can only say that many times when I was caught in a selection, I knew I had to get back to my sisters, even when I was too tired to fight my way back, when going the way of the smoke would have been easier, when I wanted to, when it almost seemed desirable. But at those times, I knew also that my sisters, aware that I was caught up in a selection not only wanted me to get back. The burden to live up to that expectation was mine, and it was awesome.

---

46 Joyce Parkey, *Camp Sisters: Women and the Holocaust*, VCU Menorah Review Summer/Fall 2007,No: 67 accessed 23 October 2017, http://www.menorahreview.org/article.aspx?id=57

Does staying alive not only for yourself, but also because someone else expects you to, double the life force? Perhaps. Perhaps.[47]

Kitty referred to one of her families which consisted of Isa, Jola, 'Ruda' (Ginger) and Kitty when she was working in the *Kanada* section. The 'family' split themselves so that two of them worked sorting clothes and the others spent their time sorting the food. 'This way we could organize most effectively on one another's behalf.' She wrote that she had assumed that all the girls had been killed, but the publication of the book led Isa, with whom she had shared a bunk, to get in touch after fifty years. She had gone to Palestine and changed her name to Batsheba. Life was still a struggle and Batsheba had to integrate herself into a new life in a new country. She worked hard to become a child psychologist but then her husband died young leaving her with small children. 'She never re-married, but has a beautiful family and a successful career behind her.'[48]

One day Kitty discovered that the long hut in which they sorted belonging, had an extension used by the SS men and women:

I discovered this one night when I had finished my quota and slunk away without being noticed for a quiet nap behind a load of jumble. Even if you had finished the work, and finished satisfactorily, you were not allowed to go back to the block to sleep; but with more than 100 girls in that one room, you could easily disappear. In our own little 'family' we worked it turn and turn around, with one of us resting while the others looked busy and lulled suspicion.[49]

Other writers discuss the concept of the surrogate family. Myra Goldenberg who examined three memoirs written by women held in Auschwitz commented:

The three memoirs I have discussed also illustrate the importance of connectedness, nurturance, and caregiving in women's memoirs. Social bonding, the formation of groups of two or more, encouraged women to struggle to survive. These groups functioned as surrogate families that took on the responsibility of gathering food, 'organizing' necessities, building hope, and sustaining life in any way possible. In both Cecilie Klein's and Judith Issacson's narratives, natural family bonds are intensified as sisters pledge to care for each other, whereas Sara Nomberg-Przytyk forms a surrogate family with her prewar political friends. When she finds herself alone in the next camp, she adopts a camp sister to improve their chances for survival.

---

47 Isabella Leitner, *Fragments of Isabella: A Memoir of Auschwitz* (Ty Crowell Co, 1978)
48 P.52
49 P.158

Although political and family affiliations were the stimuli for these supportive relationships, virtually all women, as revealed in scores of memoirs, formed surrogate families because, as one German-Jewish survivor of Auschwitz explained, it was 'the best way to survive. You needed others who helped you with food or clothing or just advice or sympathy to surmount all the hardship you encountered during all those many months and years of incarceration.' Lucie Adelsberger, for example, was adopted as a 'camp mother' by two teenage girls who tried to provide her with clothes and food whenever they could. As she noted, 'There were many families like this and everyone... felt responsible for one another, often putting their own lives in jeopardy by denying themselves the very morsel of bread they needed for their own survival.' Even for those who did not survive, the 'friendship and love of a camp family eased the horror of their miserable end.

Such bonding was not exclusive to women, but it is difficult to find consistent evidence of men's caring about one another to the extent that women did. Elie Cohen found that comradeship was 'occasional' if not rare, among men, and was conspicuous by its absence. Although he points out nothing could ever guarantee survival in a death camp, 'lone wolf' behaviour could almost guarantee death.

Women memoirists even used bonding imagery to narrate and to understand their experiences. For example, Giuliana Tedeschi's attitude towards survival is reflected in her metaphor:

> Prison life [in Auschwitz-Birkenau] is like a piece of knitting whose stitches are strong as long as they remain woven together; but if the woollen strand breaks, the invisible stitch that comes undone slips off among the others and is lost.

The women often describe extraordinary caring of one woman for another, and they even recount the 'feminization' of male prisoners, 'men who had to learn to trust and share in the manner of women.' Men, many survivors assert, 'had to learn behaviours that women already knew'.

Sarah Nomberg-Przytyk (born 1915) was a committed Communist. Arriving at Auschwitz in August 1943 she was so devastated by

> ...the humiliating process of being shaved, she felt so dehumanized, and so deeply depressed, that she prepared a noose with which to hang herself. A political comrade from the Bialystok ghetto, however, found her and provided the bread, warm sweater and boots that restored her physically; no less important, the other woman offered friendship. She fell asleep with 'hope in [her] heart...and began to thaw from inner warmth.'[50]

---

50 Myra Goldenberg, 'Memoirs of Auschwitz Survivors', in *Women in the Holocaust*, p.328

Jews in Hiding

Jacoba and Abraham Obstfeld – Henri Obstfeld's Parents

Henri's story, as a hidden child in the Netherlands, was told in my first book. He told me the story of his parents' experiences on 17 March 2017. It is important because it is hard to envisage the tedium of being confined for so long.

Henri's parents Jacoba (née Vet) and Abraham Obstfeld lived in Amsterdam. When life became dangerous for Jews they and his Aunt Nettie and Uncle Simon (Henri's father's brother) and Mr. Elkeles went into hiding together. Henri doesn't know anything about Mr. Elkeles. Henri's father and Uncle came from Krakow around 1910. After spending some years in Vienna, they arrived in Amsterdam in 1927. They ran a slipper factory together in Amsterdam – the SOA slipper & leather goods factory. It had been started by their father Selig in 1931

Above and opposite: Pages from Abraham Obstfeld's books sent to his son Henri. (Courtesy Imperial War Museum)

They went into hiding during the second half of 1942. They had false documents which Henri still has, in the names of Hendrik Oom and Berendina de Groodt. They came out of hiding at the end of April or early May 1945.

The factory was left unattended for the two-and-a-half years they were in hiding but their flat next door had been occupied by someone. Abraham had kept the keys to the factory with him all the time they were hidden, and unlocked the front door on their return. The Obstfeld family lived in the factory with Henri. They managed to get beds. Several pre-war workers eventually returned to work.

The danger they were in is exemplified by the six pink slips Henri has which were sent to his parents between 1949 and 1953 by the Dutch Ministry of Justice detailing the fate of their parents and other relatives at Auschwitz and Sobibor.

The Obstfelds hid in a loft above an infants' school in Haarlem. A rather eccentric woman ran the school and hid them for money which she used to feed her six dogs and numerous cats. She also lived on site. The Resistance (*Ondergrondse*) knew about them and also Dr. H.A.L. Trampusch and a Mr Zegwaard, who was a Catholic. A daughter became a nun and he was honoured by the Pope. Presumably they brought food and other necessities. Trampusch was Austrian with a Jewish wife – he was a lecturer at Amsterdam University on Axolotls – Mexican salamanders. He was recognised as Righteous Amongst the Nations. He spoke German (his mother tongue) and he had acquired a German army uniform. Right at the end of the war he managed to get into the Royal Palace in Amsterdam and could fire from there at the next door building, which was a German officers' club. It appears he phoned the club and demanded the officers surrender otherwise he would shoot them.

Abraham was used to running his factory and found being in hiding very irksome because he was confined to the loft and in all the time they were there he only went out once with his wife. They were recognised as Jews even though his mother was blond. So it was too dangerous to go out again.

After a while Jacoba suggested to him that he could make some little books for their son, Henri. They could contain the children rhymes which they heard from the children downstairs in the school. Jacoba being Dutch was familiar with them anyhow. Abraham had been trained as a shoe designer in Vienna and therefore had drawing skills. Henri's grandfather was also good at design and drawing and Henri has three of his pictures in his home. There are seven books in total – one from 1943, one from 1945 and the rest from 1944. The books had 12 sheets of paper sewn together by hand, presumably by Jacoba or Abraham.

The books were sent by normal post to Henri where he was being hidden – he remembers his foster father reading from them to him before he went to bed. Henri had no idea that the books came from his father as his parents were never mentioned whilst he was being hidden. The required paper and card were readily available in the school and they helped themselves. The brothers used to creep down and decorate the blackboards for the children with pictures appropriate to the season. Henri's cousin Herman, who is 9 months older, also has similar books with somewhat different contents. Henri only discovered this 5 years ago. Simon obviously copied Jacoba's suggestion for Herman. The colours are still very bright and one dating from 1943 is bound with an old newspaper.

They have been displayed by the Imperial War Museum in London (No. 723). Henri commented to me: 'These books must have kept my father occupied during the time they could not move around whilst the children were in the building.'

Henri's parents stayed in Amsterdam after the war. His father died in 1962 and his mother in 2014. Henri came to London in January 1961. His story is told in my earlier book *The Other Schindlers* and in *We Remember*.[51]

Else Pintus (1893–1975)

I wrote about Else Pintus in The Other Schindlers. *She had a horrendous experience being incarcerated in an attic room in Chmielno, Poland for over two years by the courageous Stenzel family. When I heard about the Obstfelds' tedium in hiding, I went back to Else Pintus, but found her experience was somewhat different.*

The Stenzels ran a boarding house, and during the time Else was in their attic they had Nazis resident and other people who would have been horrified to know the Stenzels were hiding a Jewish woman in the house and would have betrayed them all. The Stenzels had six children. The three girls are mentioned regularly by Else. They are Trude (Gertruda), the eldest daughter, Regina, the middle daughter, and Dorota (Thea), the youngest. Dorota was still alive when Doris Stiefel visited Poland in 1992. At that time she was still living in the family home where Else was hidden and as she had been a young girl at the time she remembered those days. The Stenzels also had three sons, Josef, Konrad and Franciszek. All three were drafted into the German armed forces. They were not around when Else was hidden there so are not mentioned. The youngest son, Franciszek, died of wounds. The husband of Trude apparently escaped to England and fought (with the Free Poles?) against the 'enemy' (the Germans?) for independence.[52]

When I heard about Henri Obstfeld's parents being confined indoors for months on end without the opportunity to go outside for fear of being picked up by Nazis in the street, I remembered Else. I hadn't looked at her memoir since 2009 and wondered what she had to say about the tedium of her confinement.

The first reference of interest was when she first moved in with the Stenzels on 14 December 1942. It was originally planned that she would move on

---

51 Henri Obstfeld, 'A Bridge Too Far' in *We Remember* (Leicester: Matador, 2011) pp.113–124.
52 Doris Stiefel, email to author 9 July 2017.

in the summer but in fact she stayed until March 1945 – two and a quarter years. She wrote:

> With the arrival of many summer guests, I was put up in an attic room way up under the low cardboard-thin roof, the place approximately 3 meters long, 2 meters wide – where they stored junk. In the summer it was hot like an oven, in the winter, icy cold. In the winter my breath froze the bed to my nose. So in this chamber facing the street, I was housed. On the street I could see and hear acquaintances. The window I dared open only a tiny crack. I was afraid that I would be seen from the street and recognized. Would I ever walk that street again, as a free person? Often I despaired of it. How often I was reminded of the song, 'Freedom, it is mine'. One had sung it at school without understanding its meaning. Now I knew what it meant to be free. Stenzels brought the food up to me; but had to make sure that neither the maid not the children noticed it. For me, the worst and most embarrassing was the toilet arrangement. A bucket for the night was placed in the hallway at the window next to my door, ostensibly for Regina, who also lived upstairs. In the morning the children had to bring it down.
>
> Stenzels get the first summer guests-in the room next to my chamber, the walls so thin that the slightest sound can be heard. High school teacher Neumann with wife and child, from Langfuhr, were my neighbors; from the conversation I can tell – fanatic Nazis. I had asked Stenzels for some work and they brought me sewing, mending, knitting; Regina, too, always had something to be done for the child. Now I had to be careful that the scissors or something else didn't fall on the floor or that I didn't reveal my presence in the room in some other way. I had asked Stenzels to bring me food only once a day so it would be less likely to be noticed. Mrs. Stenzel would then bring me a fresh loaf of bread, butter and cold cuts, and a pot of coffee. Work I had aplenty. During the canning [bottling] season, I pitted cherries by the ton for Stenzels, Regina and Trude, the oldest daughter, cleaned strawberries, sliced tons of beans and so on.[53]

Else described the comings and goings of the guests in the house. Those that could be trusted were told of her presence, such as the pregnant niece who came to stay until her baby was delivered. Others were a danger to them all:

> The worst of it, Mrs. Stenzel's two married nieces from Berlin, where they had been bombed out, come with their children. The one has two children, 6 and 3 years old, and the other, one child, 6 weeks old. They are to stay for the duration of the war – fanatic Nazi women – Under no

---

53 Else Pintus, *The Diary of Else Pintus: The Story of a Holocaust Survivor*, unpublished memoir c. 1948, p.44, translated from the original German by Doris Stiefel of Seattle in 1998. Doris' father, Richard Pintus, was one of Else's first cousins.

circumstances must they find out about me. They are inquisitive about what was in the room next to them. Often they try the doorknob, rattle the door, spy though the keyhole and cuss at Regina – I had to cover the keyhole and all the cracks. Stenzels warned me whatever I did, not to reveal myself. The Berlin children were all over the place. To bring food up to me was very difficult. Even worse was the toilet business. In the oppressive heat, under the cardboard-thin roof, I didn't take a drop of liquid, suppressed my thirst, just to dry up my bladder. I couldn't fall asleep at night for fear that I might give myself away as I slept; I was afraid I might sigh. The women had no common ground politically with Stenzels. And on top of it, during bad weather they stayed upstairs the whole day. It was just awful. I had to suppress even the slightest sound. And in spite of it all, these females were to catch sight of me one time!

Regina's son got sick. Late at night, thinking that the women were asleep, Regina comes to get me to sit with him. She, wearing noisy shoes, I in stocking feet next to her. At that, in the darkness, the women get up, peek through the glass door and see me. Luckily they didn't recognize me. Downstairs the next morning, they relate that Regina was hiding a woman in the room next to them. Now things got nasty. Hastily I had to disappear from the chamber into Regina's bedroom. While the women were downstairs at breakfast, all traces of my presence had to be removed from the room. Bed, everything was cleaned out. Then they were told all kinds of stories – it was an aunt of Regina's husband, the husband drunk and wanted to beat her up (it was true that there just been a distribution of the liquor ration). So she ran away in robe and stocking feet (me) to Regina, had to hide, etc. Regina was afraid the husband might look for her and hid the aunt in the chamber. Such were the stories told the women. As if unintentionally, Regina let them peek into the chamber so they could convince themselves that there was nobody there. Well, anyway they didn't get along; the bomb attacks on Berlin had let up and the parents came, thank God, to pick up their daughters and they all departed. I could retreat back into the chamber.[54]

After further changes in visitors, the next major crisis was when

...Chmielno was declared a summer resort and tourism was to be promoted. With State funds there was construction going on everywhere. Again, very bad. At Stenzels' ten rooms were reconstructed and renovated: building, remodelling all over the place, plumbing, the entire upstairs. The whole house was swarming with carpenters, masons, plumbers and painters, including, of course, people I knew. Upstairs they put in a bathroom and toilet, which unfortunately I couldn't use because the long hallway would have been too dangerous. The workmen constantly try my door. 'Every place we've been into, but this one is always locked – this must be where they keep the bacon!' All we

---

54 Pintus p.44–45

needed was for the police to hear this, or that they might pick the lock. Again Stenzel's had trouble with this mass of people around, to get the midday meal to me....

One time a policeman comes upstairs, looks over the construction, tries my door – 'What's in here?' Stenzel: 'Laundry, baskets, old stuff my wife keeps.' Towards the end I had to disappear again from the chamber because they were painting all the windows. This time too passed. The construction is completed, thank God. At that time there was building going on all over Chmielno. The District Commander of Danzig [Gdansk] Gauleiter Albert Forster, known as a protégé of Hitler's, comes to Chmielno to inspect the buildings. (He recently was convicted in Danzig.) My fear was that they might be afraid of an assault and that there'd be a house search in the houses he would visit but that didn't happen. Gauleiter Forster comes into Stenzel's house, looks over everything – while I sit locked into my attic chamber. Later I could have paid Gauleiter Forster a return visit – after the war. He was sitting in jail then, for the many crimes that he had chalked up – but why did I have to sit in hiding these 2½ years? Now I have my golden freedom and he has to sit.

Else wrote of the Gestapo making arrests at night and 'people are pulled from their beds'. She wrote:

Whenever I heard a car at night, I got up, got fully dressed, so that if they caught me I would, if at all possible shield Stenzels. I could not have been saved. I would have said I had just arrived. It turned out later that cars full of Gestapo, mostly in the company of females, had gone to Skrypkowski's to gorge themselves on food and booze.[55]

Later she wrote about Regina, the second daughter, whose husband Anton Plichta died in March 1944 in tragic circumstances. Else worried that the police might come to search the house especially as Regina was known to have shady business dealings. 'She had squirreled away a whole warehouse-load of stuff. There were 100 terry cloth towels alone that I counted.' Three weeks later Regina gave birth to her second child.

Following Anton's death, Regina had me work entirely for her. Next to Regina's kitchen was a closet where I could disappear if need be. And so began a period of time for me that I would just as soon draw a curtain over. But then, you might as well know everything. In any case, in my entire life I didn't get as much abuse as I did in my year with Regina. She pestered me with work day and night, chased me from one job to another. I took care of the two children and the household: washed, scrubbed, cooked, ironed, sewed, just everything, often needless work, just to harass me. Even the bottom of the laundry kettles I had to scrub.

---

55 Pintus p.46

Ten jobs at once, even Mrs. Friedmann was like gold in comparison. There was nothing I could do right for her, constantly chewed me out.

Regina would get me up between 5 and 6 o'clock in the morning, to cook cereal for the children. The oatmeal I had to weigh out on the letter scale, the milk had to be measured and cooked with a timer on the electric stove. Never was it good enough for her – one time too thick, another time too thin. Then the lady got up. I polished her shoes, pressed her widow's veil, brushed her coat; then the lady went to church. In the meantime I had to clean the apartment, set the coffee table with her best Rosenthal china, and prepare breakfast. Heaven forbid if one of the children in the meantime messed up and I didn't quite finish my work. There would be fireworks immediately. Breakfast I had with her. At noon Stenzels would send up a meal for me. Then I had to wash a big tub full of diapers [nappies] and other laundry for both children. The boy was not being trained to stay clean. She wouldn't want to distress the poor child; after all what was I for. From the constant laundry and the poor wartime detergent my hands were raw and cut. They were extremely painful. I had to wash all the laundry.

In the evening the children were served pudding with syrup. I placed a saucer next to it so the syrup wouldn't leave a mark. She takes it away, I could wash the table linen. The muslin diapers I had to darn. I said one time what a waste of thread! That was too much. She guessed I was just too lazy to work. No matter that there were dozens of new ones lying there. The boy drank only carrot juice. The carrots I had to grate and press out.

In the meantime the aunt picked up the two children; didn't want them tyrannized any more by Regina. Now she had me; such a permanent slave she could put to good use. She always said as far as she was concerned the war could last another ten years. After all, I had food and drink and was doing all right. When the boy messed himself up he was brought up to me, and after a while was picked up, clean. But nothing I could do was right for her, even when I made the utmost effort. The children's bedding with much lace and ruffles that was so tiresome to press, was carelessly crumpled together in the wardrobe so that it had to be pressed again before use. She neither spared nor appreciated work. From early in the morning 3–4 o'clock, she chased after me and pestered me.

Mrs. Stenzel and Thea often stepped in on my behalf, but with this female even the devil couldn't deal. The person who could satisfy Regina had not yet been created. Mrs. Nagorski, Mr. Stenzel's sister, about whom I will write more, was often in tears when she heard how Regina treated me. She wanted to tell Mrs. Stenzel but I held her back. In situations like mine, I could not come with complaints … In any case, it was a terrible time. Whenever I heard her coming up the stairs I trembled in fear. What have I not done right now?

The children's appearance was always spic and span. People wondered how she managed it when she was always seen going somewhere. She had excuses for everything. She did everything at night when the children were asleep. We had arranged that whenever she had company upstairs she would talk loudly and awkwardly unlock the corridor door. So that I would always have time to put down the child and disappear into my chamber. The people wondered about the child lying there, her bottle next to her. She always had excuses. Mama had just been there, and had to go to the bathroom quickly. But one time she comes up and there the boy is sitting on the john; another time he comes in his undershirt to meet her. They were surprised that she would leave the children like that in the locked apartment. Excuses for everything.

It was a terrible time for me. That she didn't beat me up was a miracle. Threats to sock me a few were made often. There were times when I thought I couldn't bear life any longer. And better to make an end to the horror than to have horror without end. I had the bottle from the doctor with me. But then the newspapers that Stenzels brought me daily gave me courage to hang on. The ongoing withdrawal on strategic, retreat movements, the second landing; one only had to look at a map and one could tell what was going on, that the beasts couldn't get any place any more.

Later after the war she [Frieda – a non-Jewish school friend of Else] worked temporarily for a short time for Regina. She too got her share of Regina. In tears she would always come back to me and blame me for not telling her what a beast Regina was. For God's sake, what I must have suffered though, powerless against this bitch. Frieda said she had been around in the world but had never encountered such a mean beast of a person. Frieda had lost the roof over her head and Regina had thought she had found a new slave to take my place. But Frieda had the golden blessing of freedom, and soon moved out. Well I want to spare you some details. Let me tell you one thing. If I had not seen from the newspapers that the Russians were approaching ever closer, if the Nagorskis wouldn't have been so comforting to me, and if I wouldn't have had such a strong will to live, I would have collapsed at the very end because of Regina.[56]

The Russians liberated the area on 10 March 1945. However it was not until 25 March that Else finally left the attic room where she had lived since December 1942. She discovered she was the only Jew to have survived in the Kartuzy region. She told her brothers, 'Of the Jews we had once known, no one is left here.' Else moved to Berlin after the war and died in an old people's home in 1975.[57] In gratitude to the courageous Stenzels, for hiding her and saving her life, she left her property to them when she died.

---

56 Pintus pp.47–48
57 Agnes Grunwald-Spier, *The Other Schindlers* (Stroud: The History Press, 2011) pp.157–162, 235–7

Ruth Abraham – 'In Hiding'

Ruth Abraham appears twice in this book. I first came across her when I was researching women rescuing men after Kristallnacht. *Then I discovered she had gone into hiding in Berlin with the help of an Aryan woman. After thinking her memoirs were only available in German, I found an English version.*

In the book, edited posthumously by her daughter Reha and husband Al Sokolow, Ruth describes what happened to her after war broke out. She and her husband had tried to leave. In 1939 they went to the port of Hamburg to try to find an escape route with a visa to Russia. Their hopes of leaving by the popular route Russia to Shanghai were dashed and they were out of luck.

I believe this book is unique – certainly I have not seen anything similar. It is in effect the story of three women – Ruth a persecuted Jew, Maria an ordinary German and the Jewish baby Reha who survived because of Ruth and Maria's joint efforts. Ruth's original story has been interspersed with chapters telling Maria's version based on Reha's interviews with Maria in Berlin in 1998. Maria Nickel, with her husband Willi, saved Ruth and her family. She was a simple woman who had worked with Jews as a young woman. She had two children and lived on Heimstrasse 10, around the corner from Willibald-Alexis-Strasse, in a sixth-floor walk-up apartment. She was too poor to have a phone. Her husband Willi was a 'war essential' truck driver.

In March 1941 forced labour was introduced. Jews aged fifteen to sixty-five were drafted and had to obey orders over work for which they were paid around 12 Reichsmarks per week. They had to pay tax on it.

In September 1941, we were forced to buy and sew a big yellow Star of David, with the word 'Jew' written on it, onto all our clothing to make it easy for us to be recognized as Jews.

I already had a plan to use my reversible coat. I sewed the Star on only one side of the coat so when I went to work I was a Jew, and that was the side I showed to the world. But sometimes, I would need to pass as a Gentile. Then, all I had to do was wear the coat inside out...

I was lucky with my forced labor assignment, working for a company that made aspirin for the German army. My boss was a good, man willing to risk his own safety for his workers. I worked about ten hours a day. I had to wake up at 5.30 every morning, take a 45-minute trolley ride across town, and then walk another fifteen minutes up a steep hill. But the long hours of work, the long commute, the curfews at night, and the few short hours a day we were allowed to shop left very little time for me to buy groceries, clean the apartment, and prepare meals.[58]

---

58 Sokolow, Reha and Al, *Defying the Tide* (Jerusalem: Gefen Publishing, 2013). (Original memoir by Ruth Abraham), pp.65–68

Her work was at the Starke pharmaceutical plant in Berlin's Tempelhof district.[59]

Walter's forced labour changed from day to day. He was a strong young man and was given the hardest jobs. 'Sometimes he delivered coal, other times he operated a crane at a construction site.' This meant Ruth never knew where to find him in an emergency.

In the autumn of 1941 Jews began to disappear. At the festival of *Sukkos,* Ruth prepared a basic meal and waited for her bachelor uncle Isidor to join them after going to the synagogue. They waited but he did not come. Eventually they went to the synagogue and in the great commotion were told 'The first transport left.' 'We never saw Uncle Isidor again.'

Later they tried to phone Walter's parents and grandparents who all lived together in Mannheim. No one answered that day nor the next. They were frantic and so Ruth took the train to Mannheim to investigate.

When I arrived, I found their door sealed, taped, and marked with swastikas.

This sight was appalling. It was especially devastating to find Walter's family gone without a word, without a trace. We knew about concentration camps, and we just knew people vanished. First, you heard about it happening to an acquaintance, a friend of a friend, someone you had met once years ago. Then closer and closer it came, until it was your uncle, your in-laws, your parents, your sister, your dearest friend. And, worst of all, you didn't know when it would be your turn.

Amongst them was Julius Abraham, whom Ruth had rescued from Dachau years before (see pages 127–8). The local police were vague, but some time later they heard from the Red Cross that the 2,000 Jewish residents of Mannheim had been sent to Gurs, an internment camp in France. They had no means of contacting them or saving them.

Ruth described how life became progressively more drab with cultural outings banned and 'many Jews committed suicide, and some even killed their own children to prevent them from falling into the hands of the Nazis'. She described how Jews could not listen to the radio and from July 1941 were not allowed telephones. If caught doing so, deportation could result. However some took the risk and Allies' success gave them the courage to carry on.

In her sister Ella's home a scenario was played out that was repeated all over occupied Europe. Her children Helga aged fourteen and Johnny aged twelve were being discussed as Ella's husband Martin refused to let them go on the Kindertransport to safety in England:

Martin felt very confident and secure because he had fought for Germany during World War I and was even awarded a medal.[60]

---

59 Maria Nickel, *The Righteous Among The Nations,* Yad Vashem No: 474
60 I dealt with the predicament of Jewish soldiers who fought in World War I, in *Who Betrayed the Jews?* pp.407–425

But more important, he believed the Germans needed workers like him. He did forced labor for the Siemens Company, which produced electronic equipment for the German army. He thought that he was indispensable to the Nazis. It was a fatal error. The whole family died.

In the midst of this mayhem Ruth decided she wanted a baby. Walter was aghast. 'Yet, I felt compelled to create a Jewish life, even with the horror around me. My desire and need for a child kept me going, it gave me something to live for.' Walter finally agreed and in the spring of 1942 she became pregnant. She and Walter had already agreed never to allow themselves to be taken onto a train – they would hide when they got the notice. They set aside funds to buy supplies on the black market and collected names of Germans who might help them – vital to success in hiding.[61]

At the time I became pregnant, I was still doing forced labor; therefore, I had official papers that allowed me to ride the trolley. But I was not permitted to sit, so I would have to stand for the entire trip. Sometimes as I stood in the trolley wearing my yellow star on my coat, somebody would feel sorry for me and slip an apple or a piece of bread into my bag.

A little luck helps. I worked in a factory that was owned by Herr Starke, who let me hide some important papers and money under the floorboards there in case the Nazis came unexpectedly and I needed to run. He also promised his workers that if he ever knew in advance that the Nazis were coming to take us away, he would warn us first so we could try to escape.

Early in the pregnancy she was confined to bed for six weeks on the advice of an elderly Jewish doctor. It was a risk because of her obligation to her forced labour.

Herr Starke was a remarkable, decent human being. He let me stay home, held my position and didn't report me to the Nazis. I was also fortunate to have my parents close by. My mother, now 62, was working at a munitions factory; but my father at the age of 70, was too old and frail to work. So while I lay in bed, my father took care of me. He prepared meals for me and brought them to my bed. My parents were very happy that I was going to have a baby. A new grandchild was something wonderful to look forward to.

Then, in July 1942, they got a letter ordering them to be ready for a transport two weeks later. We knew that the transport would take them to their deaths. My mother understood.

---

61 Pp.70–77

Her parents were too old to hide – her mother was nearly blind and her father was very frail. Her mother accepted their fate saying: 'I'd rather have an ending with terror than terror without an end.'

Two Stormtroopers arrived with dogs and rifles to escort the frail couple on to the truck and Ruth went with them and sat in the truck with them.

> We embraced, we cried, we prayed. I wanted to hug into them the lifetime of love they had showered upon me. My presence on the truck infuriated the guards. They warned me that I could be transported together with my parents if I wanted to. I was sorely tempted. I could not bear the thought of leaving them. The moment I jumped off, the truck began to roll. I followed behind it, walking like a mourner behind a coffin. Then running for one long city block I raced to keep up, but in vain.

Wretched with the situation, Ruth decided to get to the assembly point at Gross Hamburger Strasse – it was right over the other side of town and she used the trolley illegally but was not discovered and entered the building.

> The room I entered was a scene from hell. Hundreds of people crowded together, children wailing, women nursing, men praying aloud, others babbling to themselves. In the midst of all this, I saw my parents. They were close to the entrance, almost as if they had been waiting for me. We embraced again. My father was in shock. My mother told that just that afternoon the Nazis had come to ask my father about his bank account. They made him sign away everything they had to pay for their trip to Theresienstadt concentration camp near Prague. My mother signalled me with her eyes not to say anything to further upset him.

When it was time, they embraced and together said the prayer *Shema Yisrael*. Ruth then slipped out through the unguarded door she had used to enter. That evening she and Walter sat *shiva* for her parents. They hatched a plan to save themselves and their unborn child.

> The next night, we ignored the curfew and made our way to my parents' apartment. A Nazi swastika seal was already pasted to the door, meaning that the occupants had been taken to their final destination. No one ever touched this seal. It was like a marker on a fresh grave. I carefully peeled it off. Walter opened the door.

> The apartment looked as we had left it the day before, but now it was empty and silent. I thought I would be sick. The furniture and good dishes reminded of the wonderful holiday and Shabbos meals we had had together. But this was no time to be sick. Our plan was to take what we could of my parents' furniture and sell it. We had to concentrate only on surviving and on the baby. This would certainly take money, and selling the furniture would help. The furniture wasn't luxurious, but it was still stylish. Many people in Berlin had been bombed out, and replacing furniture was very difficult, so we were sure to have customers.

We took only the small nicer pieces that could bring in substantial cash. The following night, we snuck back again, and then again. At the end of each night, we'd put back the Nazi seal; the next night, we carefully peeled it off again. There were several friends that Walter had from his furniture business and they, at great risk, helped us each night. One of the friends used a truck to deliver the furniture to people who would sell it on the black market. I, too, managed to carry some light furniture, using a small hand-cart to pull my load. With our hearts pounding and terrified every moment that someone might look out from a window and report us to the Nazis, we rolled my parents' furniture through the streets of Berlin. This might be called a miracle. We sold the furniture without being caught.

This gave them money for bribes and living off the black market when they went into hiding. 'This money from the furniture was my parents' last gift to me. Even though they never knew it, they helped keep us alive.' Perhaps they also had satisfaction knowing those proceeds avoided the Nazis' coffers.

The Nickels had a son, Gerhard, born in July 1935. When Maria Nickel was 18 she had worked for Israel Schmidt und Söhne, the largest real estate company in Berlin. It employed about 50 people, most of whom were Jewish. 'They were very decent and helpful to me, and I grew very close to them. The company paid me well, and I must say that I felt as though I was part of a loving, caring family.'[62] She hated the Nazis and became concerned at what was happening to Jews and her former co-workers. Willi listened to forbidden radio stations and was caught once by a policeman through an open window. He got away with it but was more careful in future.[63]

Realising she couldn't protest against the Nazis but could do other things, one day she was shopping in the Moritzplatz where she heard grapes were available. She bought some as a treat for her family:

… but then I saw some children wearing yellow Jewish stars looking longingly at the grapes in the store window. I knew that grapes and all fresh fruit were forbidden to them. The sight of this upset me very much and made me angry. I looked around to make sure no one was watching me, and as the children passed I quickly gave them my grapes.

Maria told Reha that in November 1942 she was going home and saw women leaving a factory on Willibald-Alexis-Strasse where she lived. She noticed them because they all wore the Jewish yellow star, but there was one who did not look Jewish:

She had very light blond hair, yet she wore the yellow star that all the Jewish people were made to wear. It was easy to see she was pregnant. She looked sick and appeared to be very tired I felt very sorry for

---

62 P.40

63 Pp.78–81. Maria Nickel's story is based on interviews conducted by Reha, Ruth's daughter, in Berlin in 1998.

her...I thought to myself that this could be an opportunity for me to help a Jewish person.[64]

She returned each day at the same time but was careful because of the dangers of contacting Jews. One day she spoke to her and said she wanted to help but Ruth said: 'Go away, you know you are forbidden to speak to me. We are both in danger.' However they went round the corner to Mittenwalder Strasse where no one could watch. Ruth told her she needed to leave her flat because all the Jews were being rounded up in the area.

Maria thought of the nearby Catholic kindergarten where her children had gone and took Ruth there. The nun said they could not take Ruth because a baby would 'endanger all the nuns. I didn't expect this from a nun.' Maria realised she could not rely on anyone else to help her with Ruth. 'It was very dangerous for Gentiles to have any contact with Jews. As soon as we saw a person wearing a Jewish star approach, we were ordered to go out of our way to avoid them, not even look at them.'

It was getting close to Christmas, but food was scarce because of the war. Maria thought she would get some food for Ruth. She took a basketful of food to the factory where she described Ruth to the man in charge. He knew who she meant and went to get Ruth who was surprised to see Maria. She offered to pay Maria for the food but Maria refused, just asking for her address so she could continue helping her. Ruth now trusted her and gave Maria her name and address.[65]

Ruth's version of this event is that when her boss summoned her, she thought the Nazis wanted her. She remembered Maria from their visit to the convent:

She crossed the room and handed me a basket piled high with food: flour, margarine, milk powder, potatoes and rice. 'This was the Christmas ration from the German government to its people. Take it, I can't enjoy Christmas with my family, knowing you don't have enough to eat and are carrying a baby.'

Ruth was amazed both by the generous gift and the risk in coming to see her at the factory. Even her supervisor was amazed at Maria's courage.

Before I could go home, I took most of the food and hid it under the floorboard where I kept my money. I didn't want to attract attention to myself on the trolley or walking down the street. It would appear suspicious for a Jew to be carrying so much food.[66]

A little later Maria called at their home on Paulsborner Strasse, with a bunch of Lilies of the Valley to show she was serious about helping. They told her

---

64 Pp.84–85
65 Pp.86–7
66 Pp.90–1

they were going into hiding after the baby was born and needed identity papers. Maria asked Ruth for a small photo of herself so she could get some papers:

> Scared, with my heart pounding, I went to post office with Ruth's picture and asked for identity papers for myself. I was concerned because even though we both had light blond hair, we really didn't look alike. The official looked at the picture for a long time and said I didn't look like the picture in front of him. I told the official that I was pregnant and that's why I didn't look that sharp. I offered to bring another picture, but he said it wasn't necessary and gave me my new identity papers.

Walter had asked her to get him a military pass and she asked Willi to give him his pass. Willi was terrified and said if the Nazis found out they could shoot him and Maria would be left alone with the children. However Willi did offer to give Walter his driving licence.

It was about a week later that Maria visited them with the two forms of ID and the Abrahams were very grateful. They tried to give her some jewellery which she refused, saying they might need it another time.

Maria visited Ruth often hoping to reassure her as she was anxious about the birth. Maria had offered to keep the baby with her as long as possible. She told them to leave it on the doorstep so she could say it was a foundling.[67]

The Abrahams had been given the name of a man called Jahn who would hide them for a lot of money. In late November 1942, Berlin was being pounded by both the US and Britain. Although there was a cellar in their block Jews were not allowed in the shelter so they stood in the hallway. This distracted them from preparing for the baby's birth but at least they found a very old pram.

On the morning of 19 January 1943, Ruth's sister Ella came to say the Nazis were searching the area and later in the day a German woman came with a message from Ella saying they were all being taken and begging Ruth to leave straight away.[68] They went to her Aunt Marta and Uncle Sally but Ruth started labour pains in the night and Marta told them to leave because it was too dangerous. They went back to their apartment and Ruth asked Walter to fetch her aunt and eventually the doctor came. She had a baby girl which simplified matters because a boy would have required circumcision on the eighth day. Ruth had to stay in bed for three days according to the doctor.

Then at the end of the third day Jahn came to take them to the train station. They gave him the 500 Reichsmarks he asked for and assured him they sedated Reha with wine. Their bags were ready. It was very cold and they wrapped Reha as best they could and put her in the battered pram. Its wheels were squeaky. They worried that 'it would wake the neighbours, who would be suspicious at the sight of three adults and a baby carriage walking late at night, and the sounds would wake up the baby. We were stealing away

---

67 Pp.92–4
68 Pp.97

from a place where we once belonged. This short walk to the train station seemed to take forever.'[69]

When the train came, it was full of soldiers but Jahn cleared their path and the soldiers made room for her to sit. It took four hours to get to Beauleu, the nearest station to Scheiblesburg and Jahn led them to a small cottage with goats and an outhouse at the back. The old woman took the money agreed upon and seemed pleased. Ruth and Walter had mixed feelings:

> How we would manage to live in this hut we did not know, but for the time being we felt quite safe. We were hundreds of miles away from the transport list that may have had our names on it and the Nazis who were searching for more Jews. Who would ever think to look for us here?

They arrived on 22 January 1943 and gradually Ruth realised how primitive the cottage was with no water or electricity and they could hear wolves howling at night. As she visited the outhouse, Ruth feared being eaten by them. They couldn't bathe, or even change their clothes often. Ruth couldn't remember how she coped with Reha's nappies and growth. When it snowed they were stuck in their room.[70] They were on their guard all the time not to betray they were Jews. Their only pleasures were being alive – and their baby.

They were living with an old peasant woman who hardly ever smiled – she had no husband or children. In the time they lived with her no one came to visit Frau Higgnut and they never saw Jahn who bought his eggs from her. She only loved her goats and chickens. She made cheese from the goats' milk and let a few of the eggs hatch into chicks in the spring. Reha smiled and gurgled when she saw them. She gave them extra fresh food – better than they had in Berlin.

One day, with great excitement, she offered them some bacon. It was a special treat but their Judaism prevented them from eating it. They pretended to have a stomach virus but the old woman was amazed. They were worried she would realise the true reason. As the weather improved they walked around with Reha in the pram. Walter found a rusty old bicycle and would cycle around to get some exercise and fresh air.

One morning in June 1943 Ruth woke to a loud noise and immediately felt danger. Walter and Reha were asleep. Through the window she saw motorcycles and two SS men in black shirts. She woke Walter and said 'Pray for Reha. Our end has come.' They pounded heavily on the door and barged in. 'Identity papers! Show us your identity papers!' As they looked at them Ruth sensed the confusion her Aryan looks and Walter's Jewish looks. They weren't sure. Walter handed over Willi's driving licence – the guard demanded 'What is your name? What is your address?'[71]

---

69 Pp.104
70 Pp.109–10
71 Pp.113–116.

Ruth 'felt like all the air had been sucked out of the room. My heart stopped.' She realized Walter had not learnt the information on the ID and neither had she. Not only had they risked their own lives with their foolishness, but they had put the kind Maria and Willi at risk too. The SS told them to stay put as they were going to town going to check the papers.

Frau Higgnut was confused but Walter left on the bike taking all Ruth's hope. Ruth grabbed Reha, put her in the pram and rushed to Herr Schneider, who was a friend, and begged him to take her to the station claiming Reha was sick. He took her and as they arrived she saw Walter there. The train arrived at once – there were only two to Berlin that day. The guard said it was overcrowded and they should wait for the second. Ruth knowing that it might not be safe to wait, pleaded her need to get to the doctor in Berlin. The guard shrugged, directed her to the back of the train saying, 'There is only the cattle car.' It was only 30 to 45 minutes since the SS had arrived. They had got away, but all the way they worried about the Nickels' plight, as a result of their folly.

When they arrived at Berlin's *Schlesischer Bahnhof* it was very busy with soldiers. They had to wait for half an hour for a free phone. They dialled the number at the bakery Maria had given them. She immediately said she knew everything and Ruth knew not to say any more.

Later, Maria said that when Ruth phoned her, they had already been interrogated by the Gestapo. Willi had worried. She told him to say that he always left for work before seven, and did not know what his wife did during the day. She also told him to say they didn't know any Jews. She also told him to drink a lot so they would dismiss him as drunk.[72]

When she was called in, there were six Gestapo men around a large table. She hoped her fear didn't show. They agreed she was Frau Nickel. When they asked: 'Where is the Jew Abraham?' She said 'Jew! Jew! I don't know any Jews. Where we live, there are no Jews.' They repeated the question and she denied knowing him. They then asked how he had her papers. She invented the following story on the spot. She claimed she was sitting in the park when a tall, dark-haired woman sitting next to her said she needed a pram. She said she needed a birth certificate and she asked Maria to help her, so she gave the woman her ration book. The Gestapo believed her, thinking the woman used the ration book to get the ID.

I was released. I was free to go but was harshly warned not to ever think about helping a Jew or to have any contact with one. They lectured me about my responsibilities as a German woman, and if I caused any more trouble they said that they would take my children away from me and put them in a home where they would get a proper German upbringing.

When Willi was called in, Maria was worried, but he stuck to the rehearsed story and was released quickly.

---

72 Pp.117–119

The Abrahams were in Berlin with no ID and nowhere to stay. They tried sleeping in telephone boxes or park benches but it was impossible with Reha. Walter and Ruth lived on the streets, managing to buy some food but often sleeping in the park. They got soaked by rain. They knew they had to separate because a healthy young man should be fighting.[73]

Their former accountant had given Ruth the name of the Dutch Ambassador to Germany. Although she didn't have an appointment he saw her. Only in his sumptuous office did she realise how scruffy and dirty she and Reha were from weeks of hiding and sleeping rough. She started calmly telling him her story but suddenly her fear took over: 'Help me! Help me! I'm living on the streets with this baby. You must help me or I will commit suicide. I will jump out of your window.'

He was a decent man and offered his own apartment nearby, however it was in their old area and she could be recognised and betrayed like her sister Ella. He gave her some ration books for food but didn't know what else he could do. She felt desperate and Reha, only six months old, began to wail. Just then a woman's voice said, 'Wait.' It was his secretary, Mrs. Schott, who had heard her story. 'You can stay with me.'

It was in west Berlin on the sixth floor. When the bombs came they whistled and Reha began to scream, which could betray them. Then one day Ruth saw Reha's face was swollen and a doctor she could trust told Ruth to take Reha to the Charité Hospital. That was too risky because of the need for ID. Her only option was Maria, and they met for the first time since they had left with Jahn in January. Maria met her at the hospital and comforted both Ruth and Reha. She took Reha in to see the doctor, who said Reha would be OK. Mrs. Schott had a friend who would take her to the country to find somewhere.

She said goodbye to Walter again, not knowing if they would see each other again, and he told Reha to 'Remember Papa'. The woman took her to a small town three hours from Berlin but there was nowhere to take her and Reha in. Eventually she found somewhere with a leaky roof, but she saw a copy of *Der Stürmer*, which frightened her. She was so weary she took the room, paying a little more than the man had asked, as she always did.

The man who owned the house was Herr Jonas. His wife was out at work all day. Frau Jonas was addicted to real coffee but there was little available other than the chicory ersatz. Walter was dealing on the black market – he managed to keep Frau Jonas happy sending it by post or bringing it himself on rare visits. 'Who knows? The coffee may have been the main reason I was allowed to remain renting my room.'

She was only allowed to use the cellar kitchen where the animals' food was prepared. She lived on potatoes and vegetables plus pigeons, which are kosher, that she bought from local farmers. Walter and she tried to meet once a month and very occasionally she risked a train journey to Berlin. When Walter came to see her Herr Jonas watched him with suspicion, often commenting whilst reading his *Der Stürmer* that neither Walter nor Reha looked like her. She ignored him.

---

73 Pp.120–8

Next door to her was a Polish prisoner who always seemed to know what was happening. Ruth heard in June 1944 of the Allied landings in Normandy but could not express her delight. By early 1945 you could hear the fear in the voices of the Nazi radio commentators.[74] The Russians were expected and feared. Jonas wanted to flee and take Ruth with them. She worried that Walter would never find her.

Then she heard a crack on her window late at night – the window was broken and she heard 'Ruth! Ruth!' It was Walter – she let him in and they waited in bed. Eventually, she revealed that they were Jewish. 'Jonas and his wife didn't seem surprised. They said that they had suspected something but decided not to do anything about it.'

The tables were turned – Jonas had controlled their lives for two years and now:

> ... Jonas and his wife on their hands and knees, kissing our shoes, were begging us to report them as decent Germans...'We saved you. From the beginning, I always suspected you. Remember, I said that the child looks so different, that your husband looks so different. We felt you must be Jews. But we did not betray you. Now, please, save us!'

Ruth felt pity and embarrassment. Jonas was right – they hadn't betrayed them. Suddenly Russians on horseback arrived with rifles. Ruth showed them they were Jewish with her prayer book, Franz spoke Russian and told them he was a Polish prisoner and the Abrahams were Jews hiding from Hitler. Then they asked about the Jonases – Ruth saw the same terror on their faces she had felt for all those years of hiding. She said they had hidden them, they gave them food and were not Nazis. Franz translated for the Russians. Walter and Ruth gave the Russians their wristwatches and other valuables, which satisfied them.

In all the chaos people were freed, including Franz, and ID was issued saying they were Jews and transport was being provided. Ruth felt too weak to travel. It was too cold and she had a cough but Walter insisted. They were told they could go into German homes and take what they wanted. They found food and something Ruth really wanted, a little red knitted coat that would keep Reha really warm. 'I held it up to Reha. It looked like it had been made for her. I slipped her arms in.'

They travelled in carts and wagons but the men had to walk. Each night they stayed in abandoned German homes.[75] Reha enjoyed the wagon but after stopping in Landsberg, one day Russians took Walter away. She tried everything to get him back, as she had all those years ago when Julius Abraham was in Dachau. One day she collapsed in the street and was seen by a woman doctor who told her she was pregnant.[76] She could not cope with that and asked the doctor to abort the baby, which she did reluctantly because of the lack of facilities. She had to stay overnight with Reha.

---

74 Pp.139–144
75 P.145
76 Pp.151–6

On 12 April 1945 President Roosevelt died and on 30 April Ruth heard the Russians were in Berlin and Hitler had committed suicide. However, without Walter she was depressed and lacking in hope.

One day a beggar appeared at her door:

He was filthy. His body reeked with horrible odours. His breathing was more like wheezing and coughing. He looked like a very sick man. His clothing was torn, tattered, and in many places did not properly cover his body. His hair, falling all over his face and ears, was almost too filthy to describe. He raised his eyes. Some clothing fell away from his head and neck. I gasped. Was this my husband, Walter?

Reha was obviously scared and, starting to cry, said, 'Make him go!' Ruth was both thrilled but revolted by the lice she saw scurrying over him. She realised she had to care for him whatever the risk. She knew his clothing had to be burned. She found some concentrated vinegar in the house and made a solution with water from the well. She poured it over him outside and washed the lice off him. He felt very warm. When the lice were all gone, she took him inside.

There was a Russian military hospital nearby and they took all three of them into quarantine for 30 days because of fear of typhus. He had been freed when someone brought a prayer book and he could read the Hebrew. They also saw he was circumcised. Their quarantine and the war ended at the same time. Russian soldiers took them to Berlin in a truck and they went back to their old neighbourhood. All the Jewish stores and synagogues had disappeared. However, they came to the area where her sister had lived before she left for Philadelphia and her block was still standing in the Oliverplatz. She saw the old caretaker and he told her Anna's apartment was vacant. He gave them the key and helped them find a few mattresses and chairs. They tried to contact Maria without success. There was no transport so they could not get over to see her.

Maria described how they were struggling to find food and had nothing with which to barter.[77] She ignored the requests to meet the Abrahams. 'Why should I go? I didn't want thanks for what I had done. To me, it was what had to be done – nothing special or unusual.' After several requests she took the children to see the Abrahams and they were all pleased to see each other again. Ruth said she had TB and was going to Switzerland soon.

The Abrahams asked what they could do to help and she said Willi had no work. Walter managed to get Willi a job as a driver for the Americans. They also helped them move to a better apartment on a lower floor. Ruth and Maria became very close and Maria dreaded them leaving Germany. They went in spring 1948 but sent food parcels every month. Maria was reluctant to accept the help but 'I was in great need'. Ruth and Maria maintained their friendship in spite of the distance and Maria said: 'Ruth became more than a sister – she was like a mother to me.'

---

77 Pp.157–158

Ruth described how she and Walter joined a small group of Jews who set up a self-help group that provided food, shelter and other needs. They were moved to a former ambassador's beautiful home but they were too hungry to enjoy it. Every day they went to collect a small amount of rations but everyone was desperate for food. In the spring of 1945 when the British began to arrive in Berlin she accosted a group of soldiers and Reha was saying, 'I'm hungry, I'm hungry.' The soldiers gave Ruth all the rations they had with them and she sobbed her thanks. Walter spoke to an American soldier who gave him bars of chocolate and Walter asked him to contact Ruth's sister Anna in Philadelphia and tell her they were alive.

Finally it was all over. They left in May 1948 and went to New York where Walter established a new furniture business with Ruth's help. In 1952 they had a son, John Mark.

Only her mother-in-law Elsa Abraham survived through her knowledge of French. All the other deported relatives were murdered, including Julius Abraham, whom she had rescued from Dachau. He died at Majdanek in September 1943.

After the war, Ruth heard from Josef Müller, whom she had met at Dachau in 1938, when he sent her a beautiful gold enamel wristwatch. A few months later she heard from one of his colleagues that he had committed suicide for fear of being tried for his work at Dachau. She never found out what he had done but he may have helped with Julius' release.

Life is not fair. Maria had a little girl in September 1948 but she contracted German measles, then had meningitis and died in 1956. In the early 1950s on an illegal shopping trip to East Berlin she was caught and imprisoned for four weeks. In 1965, seventeen years after they had last seen her, the Abrahams were delighted to pay for Maria Nickel to attend the wedding of their daughter, the child she helped to save. Her husband Willi died in 1970 and her son Gerhard in 1974.

Judith went to Germany with Reha to celebrate Maria's 90th birthday on 22 May 2000 and she died in January 2001. Walter had died in 1979 and Judith died on 25 August 2003. In all her tribulations she carried with her a silver hairbrush which had belonged to her mother. In 2014 Reha presented it, with other items, to the USHMM.[78]

On 1 December 1970 Maria Nickel was recognized as Righteous Among the Nations by Yad Vashem for rescuing the three members of the Abraham family. Reha has visited the carob tree that Maria had planted as a sapling.

Why a carob tree? Because it is an evergreen that blooms all year round; it is a fruit-bearing tree; and it is not a very tall tree. It characterizes the Righteous. It exemplifies Maria. She was as steadfast and constant as the tree she planted; she was as giving and sustaining as its fruit; and as selfless and modest as its stature. May her memory be a blessing for us all.[79]

---

78 USHMM, Hair Brush donated by Reha Abraham Sokolow, https://collections. ushmm.org/search/catalog/irn114599, 13 June 2017, accessed 27 August 2017.
79 P.169

Domestic Service

Joanna Baron and Others

Domestic service in the UK was the only realistic option for young Jewish women needing to escape Hitler. After I gave a talk in Pinner, north-west London, in January 2013, Brenda Silverman came to tell me about her mother Johanna Stössel, who came from Vienna in 1938 as a domestic. She married her employer and as a result was also able to save her parents and siblings.

In my teens when I was becoming aware of the impact of the Holocaust on my family, I asked my mother, Leona Grunwald, why she had not left Budapest before things got too bad. She said she could only have come as a domestic servant and, in any event, she did not want to leave her family behind. When she suggested leaving, her father's response had been, 'Why should I leave my native land?' He died in Auschwitz in 1944.

Anka Bergman's first serious boyfriend as a young girl in Prague was Leo Wildman. After the *Anschluss* he decided he would go to England to join the British Army, as his father had already been arrested. Although they were quite serious about each other, it never occurred to Anka to go with him, even though she had been offered an opportunity.

Two English ladies came to Prague to offer work to Jewish girls as domestics or in nursing. I applied for a job in nursing and got it. They provided me with a valid visa and exit papers and I could have gone then but ... I procrastinated so long ... I had all the papers in my hand and then war broke out in Europe ... and I couldn't have been happier that I [had] managed to prolong it so long that I couldn't go any more ... How stupid was that?[80]

Johanna Stössel (known in the family as Janka) was born in June 1914 into an orthodox Jewish family. They lived in a small village called Lockenhaus in Burgenland, which was in Hungary at the time, but became Austrian in

---

80 *Born Survivors* p.78

Advertisement for domestic help in the *Jewish Chronicle* 13 May 1938, middle column, third from top. (Courtesy *Jewish Chronicle*)

Joanna Stössel's Austrian passport dated 27 May 1938. (Courtesy Brenda Silverman)

1919. Her parents, Ignatz and Kaethe Stössel, were in business selling fabrics and also had a small farm which met their domestic needs. Johanna was the second of seven children. She attended the local Convent school and learned sewing and allied handicrafts which were useful when she worked in Wiener Neutstadt in the 1930s.

At the time of the Anschluss in March 1938 she was working in Vienna. Her daughter Brenda told me she was 'fortunate to make contact with a lady who was attempting to place girls in domestic positions in England through Wizo'.[81] The lady in question was Luise Fischer and Brenda sent me copies of the correspondence that ensued.

The prospective employer Maurice Baron, was a single man living with his mother in Weybridge and needing domestic help. Both his siblings had died of TB in the mid-1930s, which was the reason they had moved out of London. An advertisement was placed in the *Jewish Chronicle* on 13 May 1938. The first letter from Luise is dated 28 March 1938 and refers to a letter she received but the family do not have a copy. He must have been asking for names of suitable girls. In her reply Luise lists four young women, one of whom was Johanna:

> There is a most nice girl, just of 24 years, out of a little Austrian place and I recommend her highly. Her name is Johanna Stössel. She has not been in a large town till now and she will feel well with you in the little one. She knows all household duties: as her testimonial shows it, and Madam

---

81 Brenda Silverman, *Johanna Baron*, biography received by author 10 May 2013.

your mother will not be disappointed with her. Unfortunately she does not know English language (I am not sure and I will ask for, but I don't suppose her to know). Miss Stössel also is out of a religious home.

…Please let me know what you are thinking about those applicants, and I ask you not to hesitate a longer time to avoid the disagreablement [*sic*] to find those you should like to engaged already fixed up to another household.

Those work is done in honour's sake and no fee to pay but to enclose with your next letter Reply coupons which you get at the post-office.

Yours faithfully. For Bela Fischer

Maurice obviously heeded her advice not to hesitate as on 6 April 1938, another letter came from Luise Fischer, given here verbatim:

Dear Mr. Baron,

Receiving your letter I have at once written to Miss Stössel who came to speak with me just now. I got the same good opinion by speaking with her as I got by her papers and her photo.

Miss Stössel thanks your and Madam your mother very much and she will do everything to fulfil her duties and to satisfy you. She is enjoyed to have got a place in a little town as she is accustomed to live in such a town and she likes it.

Please ask now a permit for Miss Stössel at the Ministry of Labour (Home Office). You will easily learn where is the right place to ask it, the competent place for your town. I can't know it from the distance. This permit is generally and easily given for an applicant who will do household duties like Miss Stössel and it is easilier given for the little town as for the large one.

When you have got the permit, please send it together with the fare-money, which you can take back out of Miss Stössel's wages by instalments. That is the usually way. After staying at your home for a year Miss Stössel can ask for the money for the return. In this way, each of both parts will have paid one travel. You will well understand that Miss Stössel will not return after a year's time. She will be glad to have a good home with you for long time.

The best and most comfortable way to send permit and ticket is to do it with help of Cook's. What ever may be at the time you send the permit and the ticket, Cook's or also the English Consul will get the papers certainly and will promptly deliver up them to Miss Stössel. You may do so by help of the next branch of Cook's in your country or sending directly to 'Cook and Son, Vienna I, Kärtnerring ll' and advising them to deliver up at once, not to me, but to Miss Stössel, whose exact dates are:

Miss Johanna Stössel, born 4 June 1914 at Lockenhaus (Burgenland, Austria) citizen of Austria (or now Germany) residing at present: Lockenhaus.

You needs those dates for the permit.

Do you wish Miss Stössel to wear a servant dress as it is usually in England or are you satisfied with a neat household – and working – dress as she was always wearing till now? Please write at once if you have especially wishes because Miss Stössel is willing to sew the clothes if she has not, waiting at the permit.

I should be grateful to have the references you mentioned. I am not in doubt of your integrity, but you know the times we are living in and I must see to have security when I am asked. Please inform me when you send the permit and ticket to Cook.

Yours faithfully for Bela Fischer. Signature of Luise Fischer.

A month later Maurice Baron received a letter dated 5 May 1938 from the Ministry of Labour in London from a J. Constantine with a heading of 'The Aliens Order 1920'. It tells him that his application for a permit dated 13 April cannot be issued. He has failed to demonstrate that he has made every effort to fill the post recently with 'either a British subject or a foreign person already resident in this country'. He is offered encouragement by being told he can re-apply, if after attempting unsuccessfully to comply, he can demonstrate the efforts he has made.

Accordingly the advertisement was placed in the *Jewish Chronicle* and presumably no one suitable came forward. He did receive a letter from WIZO in London, dated 13 May, saying they had seen his advertisement and asking him if he would accept an Austrian Jewish girl. 'We have a large number of applications from young Jewish girls and women from Austria who want to get out of the country and we are sure that from amongst these we can find the type of girl suitable for the post.'

Anyhow, on 23 May J. Constantine wrote again, saying the additional information he had sent on 17 May enabled them 'to grant the desired permission' and the permit was enclosed. The next day Maurice wrote to Johanna: 'Your permit arrived safely and tomorrow morning D.V. I shall go up to London to Messrs Cook's and make arrangements for your journey. I know this has been a very worrying time for you but I could not get the Permit quicker – the Home office are very strict these days and I was put to a lot of trouble. That however is nothing...' On 25 May, he wrote as promised:

I attach herewith the Permit from the Home Office which should enable you to get the necessary visas from the English Consul. Mrs. Fischer will no doubt advise you what to do in the matter. I have been to Messrs Cook's and arranged for your fare. If you will go to their offices Kartnerring II and disclose your identity they will provide you with a Second Class Ticket to London and also a sleeping berth as you will be coming for some 24 hours by rail to Ostend.

If you catch the train which leaves Vienna about 9.30am you will arrive in London about 4.30pm the following afternoon and I could then meet you and bring you to Weybridge.

Johanna arrived in London at the end of June 1938 according to her daughter.

Love developed fast, because within six weeks Johanna and Maurice were married in Richmond Synagogue on 27 July 1938. Some of the haste was due to the need to get Johanna's parents and younger siblings out of Austria as soon as possible. The older siblings had already gone to Palestine. Maurice could now sponsor these relatives and they all arrived safely. There is a telegram dated 15 February 1939 to Weybridge, stating 'arriving 9 pm Victoria' and underneath someone has written 'Mum and Dad' – I assume that would be Johanna's family.

It looks as though Luise Fischer was sent an invitation to the wedding as the following letter was received. I am grateful to Johanna's son-in-law Warren Silverman for the translation. It was sent from the Jewish Community of Vienna, Emigration Department at 1 Seitenstennengasse 2–4, dated 10 August 1938:

Dear Miss Stössel

I am really glad that I have struck lucky and I have made two people happy; not to forget Mrs. Baron who is also certainly happy to be getting a daughter-in-law.

I cannot unfortunately accept your invitation to the wedding since I will not be so soon in England. Not so soon, for I will not be long also be over here. I must also unfortunately leave my homeland. We have not thought fully about it, as I have been corresponding with you and your beloved. Hopefully, my family and I, as with you, will get to another country.

I wish you all, once again, heartfelt good fortune and salutations.

Luise Fischer

Following my recent contact with the Silvermans, Warren went to the Wiener Library in London and discovered Luise was born on 21 March 1889. She sent her 13-year-old twins Hannah and Raphael to England in September 1938. She came later with a domestic permit as a cook. The twins initially went to a children's school in Deal. Hannah went to the Quaker-run Badminton School in Bristol until July 1941. Luise was unlucky in her employment in domestic service but eventually got a job as a hospital cook in Newark. After schooling Hannah worked at the Hampstead War Nurseries of Anna Freud. Later she worked at the Austrian Centre's Nursery and was reunited with her mother who was then working in an office in London. After the war, Luise went to Palestine where her husband Bela was living. He had fled Vienna and arrived in Mandate Palestine. There, he was taken by the British as a survivor of the 'Patria' tragedy in Haifa Harbour and was interned on Mauritius during the war. Raphael went to Canada after his education was completed. Later, Luise returned to Vienna alone, where she died in 1954.[82]

Once Johanna was a British citizen, she was able to help her family. Her three older siblings, Max, Shmuel and Moshe, got to Palestine, whilst the youngest siblings Romi and Rozhi came to England on the Kindertransport. Her parents and 19-year-old Judith had passports issued on 12 January 1939 and arrived in London not long after, as we see from the telegram. The family were helped by Moshe Hillel Baron and established themselves in the East End of London. After the creation of the state of Israel, they moved there, except for Johanna's father who had been interned on the Isle of Man in 1941 and died in 1942.

By then the couple had two daughters, Deborah and Brenda. Maurice became unwell and in 1955 they moved to Bournemouth. They enjoyed a full and happy life there. Maurice died on 8 March 1975. Johanna died in September 2012, aged 98.

---

82 Warren Silverman, email to author 11 July 2017, 13.59.

Coming to England for domestic work was virtually the only way female refugees fleeing Nazi Germany and Austria could get into England. Women were most likely to receive permits and one in three, or 20,000 of the refugees who came to England before the war, came for that work – the most common form of employment for women before the war. Jillian Davidson wrote of the war 'transplanting these women from their "upstairs" life in Central Europe to their "downstairs" life in England'. She notes the Cambridge Refugee Committee on domestic permits saved 500 women; only two of them had relevant training.

Lore Segal wrote about her parents' experiences with a family called Willoughby. Whilst Mrs Willoughby had little understanding of the travails of the Groszmanns, she had sponsored them on a married-couple visa. This was for a husband and wife working as cook and butler. Mr Groszmann, a former accountant, was a useless butler and was demoted to gardener. Lore Segal describes what happened when his mother was shown the drawing room:

'Ah' my mother cried, 'a piano! It is a Bechstein, no?' and she told Mrs. Willoughby that she had had a Blüthner, which the Nazis had taken, and that she had studied music at the Vienna Academy. 'Oh really?' said Mrs. Willoughby. 'In that case you must come in and play and play sometime when everyone is out.'[83]

Mrs Groszmann was incensed when 'I made them an *Apfelstrudel* and they asked for custard to pour over it'. When she fell down the stairs, Mr Willoughby turned to her husband demanding, 'Tell me the truth! Was it a fight?' Lore commented: 'And so the Willoughbys had put my parents in their place; the refugees belonged to the class of people who eat in the kitchen, sleep on cheap mattresses, and throw their wives down the stairs in an argument.'[84]

Tony Kushner comments that this topic has been avoided in the literature of the refugees from the Nazis. Most women perhaps only did it for a year or so. In the most important period between the Anschluss to the outbreak of war 40,000 refugees arrived, of whom 14,000 were domestic servants. This occurred at a time when there was, of course, a servant shortage in the UK.[85]

Another woman, Marion Smith, wrote to AJR Information about her experiences as a domestic in a 'grand house' as an 'upper-housemaid'. She had to ask the under-housemaid (aged 14) how to turn out a room and prepare the spare rooms for weekend guests. The lady of the house had particularly insisted that she had to wear dirndls with matching aprons when she helped the butler at table at dinner parties. She wrote she felt very stupid in the two outfits her mother had managed to find – but her success enabled her mother to get a domestic permit too, which arrived just in time.[86]

---

83 Jillian Davidson, *German Jewish Women*, in 'Second Chance: Two Centuries of German-Speaking Jews in the UK', Ed. Werner E. Mosse (Tübingen: JCB Mohr, 1991) pp.539–540

84 Lore Segal, *Other People's Houses: A Refugee in England 1938–1948* (London: Bodley Head, 1964) pp.74 and 85

85 Tony Kushner, *Domestic Service*, in 'Second Chance' p.576

86 Marion Smith, *Upper-Housemaid's Tale of Dirndls*, in AJR Information, April 1988, p.13

Careers Disrupted or Destroyed

Margaret (Gretel) Bergman-Lambert

I read about Gretel when she died aged 103 on 25 July 2017 and her obituary was published in The Times. *I had become interested in Jewish Olympians when I wrote a chapter about them in my last book.*

Margaret Bergman-Lambert was known as Gretel and was born on 12 April 1914 in Laupheim, south of Stuttgart. Her father Edwin owned a wig and hair product factory and they lived a comfortable life until the Nazis came to power.

She was an athletic girl with long legs (and large feet!) and hoped to became a PE teacher after university. However the anti-Jewish policies of the Nazis destroyed those options and she left Germany for London where she studied English and joined an athletics club at the college. In 1934 she won the high jump in the British championships.

The Berlin Olympics were looming and the Nazis had promised the Olympic organisers that Jews would be allowed to participate in the Berlin Games. Accordingly Gretel was summoned home to train with the team and compete in the Games, otherwise her family would be in danger. The Americans had threatened to boycott the Games if Jewish athletes were not treated fairly and so the Nazis embarked on a duplicitous charade.[87]

An interview with the *Los Angeles Times*:

> ... she remembers how Nazi authorities forced her to train with the German team, largely because the US Olympic team had threatened to boycott the event if Jewish athletes were forbidden to take part. 'I felt like a prisoner, but my family were told there would be consequences if I didn't go. I was their decoy, a pawn in their political maneuvers. They wanted to use me to show the world that the Nazis were not all that bad after all. I lived in constant fear that they'd find a way to exclude me, by maybe even killing me, and at the same time I was fearful of winning a medal. What would I have done if I'd had to stand on the podium

87 Obituary, Margaret Bergman-Lambert 1914–2017, *The Times*, 28 July 2017.

and stick my arm out in a Hitler salute? The thought turned me into an absolute nervous wreck.'

Bergmann took her place at training camp as the only *Volljuden* (full Jew) on the German team. She is convinced that her anger at the way she was being used drove her to her personal bests. A few weeks before the Games, she participated in a competition at the Adolf Hitler Stadium in Stuttgart setting a German record. 'I was determined to show them that a Jew can do it, and better.'

The American athletes set sail on 15 July 1936 having been assured that Gretel was going to participate.[88] Gretel wrote in her autobiography about the time after she achieved the German record and realised how mendacious the Nazis had been both to her and the US team.

My parents had long ago changed their minds about thinking of me as an oddball for my love of sports. My constant successes had convinced them that there was merit in what I was doing. Now I needed to go home, now it was my time to share with them not only my triumph but also my anxieties. Suddenly I felt that I no longer could bear that heavy burden by myself. I had the urge to spill out everything I had kept inside of me for too long. Ignoring the pleas of my friends to stay overnight in Stuttgart for a victory party, I packed my gear and headed for the railroad station.

During the two hour train ride back to Laupheim, my mind was flip-flopping at an alarming rate. One minute I sat there with a big grin on my face, going over the events of the morning step by step; then my heart started to hammer and a wave of apprehension would replace my happiness. I knew it was an exercise in futility to speculate about what was going to happen, and yet I was unable to stop. When I arrived home it was already night-time. I recreated for my family every detail of my triumphant performance; how convincingly I had defeated the German superman, the repugnant attitude of the officials, how the kindness of a perfect stranger had made me feel so good. My parents and my brothers had a million questions, and I was only too happy to answer them. They, as well as I, viewed my performance as a victory over evil rather than as a victory in a sports event. We went over everything again and again, laughing triumphantly about what I had done to the German mentality, the German womanhood. And yet we had to keep in control; we were afraid that if we got too boisterous, the maid might overhear us. We considered her to be loyal, but one could not take chances. An innocent remark to her boyfriend could bring us a heap of trouble.

Somehow, it seemed as if sharing this experience made us into an even more close-knit family unit. It was an evening never to be forgotten. I decided that it would be quite selfish to spoil this wonderfully warm feeling by revealing my innermost turmoil. Besides, my brother Walter,

---

88 Kate Connolly, 'The saga of Gretel Bergmann, Jewish high jumper', in *Los Angeles Times* 11 November 2009

then ten years old, had enough problems to cope with in his young life and I wanted to shield him from any additional apprehension. At breakfast the next morning, with Walter safely away at school, the dam broke. All my frustrations, all my fears were gushing out of my mouth in torrents. Then the tears came, tears of relief that, at last, I had been able to unburden myself, but mostly they were tears of rage, tears for the years of psychological abuse and for the years of anxiety. It seemed as if I was rambling on for a very long time, but finally the emotional storm exhausted itself, giving my parents and my brother Rudolph a chance to speak. They, too, they said, had great misgivings about how all this was going to end. They talked about how hurtful it had been to sit by helplessly, that they had seen the pain I was trying to hide but that it was their decision not to pry, that they had wanted to respect my desire to keep my feelings to myself. We talked for hours. The more we talked, the more I realized how near-sighted I had been. Instead of being protective, sparing them from what I was going through and being so close-mouthed had made them feel slighted. My brother Rudolph, with whom I used to discuss everything, came right out and called me a stupid fool and a moron (which is a very gentle translation of what he really said). It made us all laugh, breaking the tension. Although nothing in our power could change my situation one iota, I felt that with the aid of my family, I would be able to endure whatever was to come.

And now there was nothing left to do but wait. Every day I sat on the stoop in front of the house, waiting for the mailman. One day a letter arrived, addressed to 'The Bergmann Family, parents of the high jumper'. The envelope contained a series of photographs, taken by Erich Scriba under such trying circumstances, and a few words wishing me luck. I was touched to tears.

Two weeks later, the vigil was over. It was all so matter of fact, almost sterile in its simplicity. A form letter dated July 16, 1936 informed me that I had been too inconsistent and that because of my 'mediocre performances' I had not been selected to compete in the Olympic Games. For all my diligence during the past two years, a standing-room ticket for the week of the track and field events would be mine for asking. It concluded with *Heil Hitler*. Needless to say, I ignored this generous offer. Although the message in the letter came across loud and clear the first time, I read it again and again and again. And then, instead of tears, a stream of invectives came pouring out of my mouth. Although nobody seemed to be around to watch me, I felt that tears would show how deeply hurt I was – and, in my own mind, I did not want to give that satisfaction to my tormentors.

It was uncanny with what precision the Nazi master plan had worked out, undoubtedly already hatched at the time I was ordered back from England. To make absolutely sure that nothing would go wrong, that rejection letter to me was not mailed out until one day after the American team had left the United States by ship on July 15. The Nazis' speculation that the U.S. team would not turn back once on the high seas proved accurate. Instead of the customary three, only two

German women would compete in the high jump, one of them being Dora (Hermann!) Ratjen. The other was my friend, Elfriede Kaun. Many years later, after we had re-established contact, Elfriede told me that my absence had simply been explained by: 'Bergmann is hurt and cannot compete.'

It is difficult to put in the proper perspective my reaction to the swift and sadistic finale to two years of ups and downs, of high expectations and disappointment, of elation and dashed hopes. It was a cruel awakening from a beautiful dream that I may have been foolish to nurture. I had never before known such anger, such hatred, and such fury; yet, with all my raving and ranting, all of a sudden an immense feeling of relief came over me. No longer would I have to fear what would happen to me if I won, if I lost. No longer would I have to worry whether I was expected to raise my arm in the Hitler salute. No longer would these torturing questions wake me up in the middle of the night. All my anxieties had been eliminated – painfully, but oh so efficiently.

After sitting on the stoop for quite a while, I went into the house. Glad that nobody was home, I put the letter on the dining room table and went upstairs to my room, locked the door, and lay down on the bed. I felt I had to come to grips with the past, the present, and the future. But no matter how I tried I could not keep my mind off the significance of the notification. It was hard to accept that within less than 60 seconds, the time it took to read the fateful words, aspirations had been shattered. I was unable, then, and I am unable, now, to rationalize what was more hurtful, to be denied the thrill of participating on an Olympiad or to be denied the goal I had set myself. By competing in the Olympic Games – and I had no doubt that I would have done so successfully – I would have acted as a deputy for the Jewish people by destroying the picture Adolf Hitler had painted of us. Damn it, I was one of the four best high jumpers in the world and only through an accident of birth, by having been born Jewish, was I being cast aside like an old shoe. I could not just sit there and accept this without a whimper.

There was a phone in my parents' bedroom, and I decided to call the head of the RJF Schild in Berlin. For fear of a censor listening in, I simply read the letter to him without any comment. Unfortunately, my phone call had some very unpleasant consequences for this gentleman. Many years later, in the National Archives in Washington, I read a letter by the Stuttgart Consul General informing Ambassador Dodd that the head of the Schild, after lodging a vigorous protest with German Olympic Committee, had to report twice daily to the political police in order – and I quote – 'to prevent his leaving Germany to disseminate this intelligence.'

At the dinner table – the big meal was always eaten at midday – I could see the pity in my family's eyes. It was almost unbearable. I knew that I could not run away from myself and my frustration, but I also knew that nobody would be able to help me. I wanted no questions, no pity, no sanctimonious rationalizations: 'Well, maybe it is all for the best.' The healing process had to come from within. And for this, I needed desperately to be alone.[89]

Gretel left Germany for America in 1937 with $4 in her pocket and lived with her brother Rudolf who was already in Manhattan. She worked as a cleaner and a physiotherapist and was the American women's high jump champion in 1937 and 1938 and won the 'shot put' in 1937. In 1938 she married another German athlete, Bruno Lambert, a long jumper, and sponsored him to come to America, They had two sons and lived in Queens, New York.

Her parents and young Walter fled to Britain:

During the war they were interned and separated. When they were allowed to leave for the US they were taken to Liverpool under guard. The ship, though, was not ready and her parents were imprisoned for a couple of days – while her 12-year-old brother was sent to stay with a local Jewish family. 'I have never forgiven the English for that. There was no reason to put them in jail. They weren't criminals.' She said in a 1995 interview with the USC Shoah Foundation.[90]

Some recognition came late in her life. She only returned in 1999 when her hometown stadium in Laupheim was renamed in her honour. In 2009 Germany's athletic association restored her record as 'an act of justice and gesture of respect'.

For her 80th birthday, her sons bought her a computer and she wrote her autobiography, *By Leaps and Bounds*, published in 2004. The postscript to this sad tale made Gretel laugh. She recalled one of the athletes who did participate was Dora Ratjen, who was very shy and never undressed in front of the others. They had shared a room at a training camp and she noticed Dora shaved her legs each day.

In 1966, I was sitting in the dentist waiting room and reading a magazine on which they told Dora's story. I was flabbergasted and started laughing my head off. The other patients thought I was crazy, but I thought, 'This just adds to the absurdity of my own story'. Ratjen had been born to poor parents in Bremen, in northern Germany. Doctors said her sexual characteristics were ambiguous and advised her parents to bring her up as a girl. Only much later did medical experts deem Ratjen, who changed his name to Heinrich, to be a man. There is little evidence to suggest Ratgen was deliberately planted by the Nazis in an attempt to outdo the Jewish athlete. But sport historians, such as Volker Kluge, are in general agreement that they were aware of Ratjen's ambiguous sexuality.[91]

---

89 Margaret Bergmann-Lambert, *By Leaps and Bounds* (Washington: USHMM, 2005) pp.117–120

90 Obituary, *The Times*

91 *LA Times*

Bruno died in 2013.

Like so many Jews who fled the Nazis, Gretel had feelings of turmoil as she left her native land and her parents in 1937:

The pain of leaving my family and the agony I was causing them by going away started to hit home. The very real possibility that we might never see each again was almost unbearable. Although we avoided revealing these soul-searing feelings to each other, we knew only too well the other's innermost thoughts. I knew that I should and could not stay, yet I felt like a traitor for fleeing to freedom while they were trapped.

... At last, on May 9, 1937 the day came I had been looking forward to and dreading at the same time. My parents, my brother Walter, and I travelled by car to Ulm, where I was to take the train that would carry me to Hamburg. Walter, now almost 11 years old, was beside himself with grief. Crying his heart out and repeating over and over again: 'I can't stand it anymore. Why do I have to say good-bye to all the people I love so much.' His best friend Paul, and his brother Rudolph had left recently and now I, his big sister. He kept running away, not wanting to face the inevitable. It was hard for us grown-ups not to break down too; only the idea that some of the onlookers might thoroughly enjoy the spectacle of a Jewish family being torn apart made us determined not to lose our composure, at least outwardly. When I got on the train, the last look at my family, maybe forever, was blurred through eyes filled with tears. As I turned away from that train window, a feeling of immense rage came over me. Rage against a madman whose sick ideology, too readily accepted by too many people, forced me to flee a once-secure and wonderful life to enter an unknown world; rage against a system that spread fear, hate and suffering, ostracizing its victims purely for the crime of being born Jewish.[92]

Rita Levi-Montalcini

Rita Levi-Montalcini was another Jewish woman whose chosen career was disrupted by the Nazis. However, unlike Gretel Bergman-Lambert, she was ultimately able to achieve a successful career and recognition at the highest level.

Rita Levi-Montalcini was a neurobiologist who was awarded the 1986 Nobel Prize for Medicine with Stanley Cohen of the UK for their work on Nerve Growth Factor (NGF). This autobiographical piece was prepared for the Nobel committee in 1986:

My twin sister Paola and I were born in Turin on April 22, 1909, the youngest of four children. Our parents were Adamo Levi, an electrical engineer and gifted mathematician, and Adele Montalcini, a talented painter and an exquisite human being. Our older brother Gino, who

---

92 Bergman-Lambert pp.133–134

died twelve years ago of a heart attack, was one of the most well-known Italian architects and a professor at the University of Turin. Our sister Anna, five years older than Paola and myself, lives in Turin with her children and grandchildren. Ever since adolescence, she has been an enthusiastic admirer of the great Swedish writer, the Nobel Laureate, Selma Lagerlöf, and she infected me so much with her enthusiasm that I decided to become a writer and describe Italian saga "à la Lagerlöf". But things were to take a different turn.

The four of us enjoyed a most wonderful family atmosphere, filled with love and reciprocal devotion. Both parents were highly cultured and instilled in us their high appreciation of intellectual pursuit. It was, however, a typical Victorian style of life, all decisions being taken by the head of the family, the husband and father. He loved us dearly and had a great respect for women, but he believed that a professional career would interfere with the duties of a wife and mother. He therefore decided that the three of us – Anna, Paola and I – would not engage in studies which open the way to a professional career and that we would not enrol in the University.

Ever since childhood, Paola had shown an extraordinary artistic talent and father's decision did not prevent her full-time dedication to painting. She became one of the most outstanding women painters in Italy and is at present still in full activity. I had a more difficult time. At twenty, I realized that I could not possibly adjust to a feminine role as conceived by my father, and asked him permission to engage in a professional career. In eight months I filled my gaps in Latin, Greek and mathematics, graduated from high school, and entered medical school in Turin. Two of my university colleagues and close friends, Salvador Luria and Renato Dulbecco, were to receive the Nobel Prize in Physiology or Medicine, respectively, seventeen and eleven years before I would receive the same most prestigious award. All three of us were students of the famous Italian histologist, Giuseppe Levi. We are indebted to him for a superb training in biological science, and for having learned to approach scientific problems in a most rigorous way at a time when such an approach was still unusual.

In 1936 I graduated from medical school with a *summa cum laude* degree in Medicine and Surgery, and enrolled in the three year specialization in neurology and psychiatry, still uncertain whether I should devote myself fully to the medical profession or pursue at the same time basic research in neurology. My perplexity was not to last too long.

In 1936 Mussolini issued the "Manifesto per la Difesa della Razza", signed by ten Italian 'scientists'. The manifesto was soon followed by the promulgation of laws barring academic and professional careers to non-Aryan Italian citizens. After a short period spent in Brussels as a guest of a neurological institute, I returned to Turin on the verge of the invasion of Belgium by the German army, spring 1940, to join my family. The two alternatives left then to us were either to emigrate to the United States, or to pursue some activity that needed neither support nor connection with the outside Aryan world where we lived. My family chose this second alternative. I then decided to build a small research unit at home and installed it in my bedroom. My inspiration was a 1934 article by Viktor Hamburger reporting on the effects of limb extirpation in chick embryos. My project had barely started when Giuseppe Levi, who had escaped from Belgium invaded by Nazis, returned to Turin and joined me, thus becoming, to my great pride, my first and only assistant.

The heavy bombing of Turin by Anglo-American air forces in 1941 made it imperative to abandon Turin and move to a country cottage where I rebuilt my mini-laboratory and resumed my experiments. In the fall of 1943, the invasion of Italy by the German army forced us to abandon our now dangerous refuge in Piemonte and flee to Florence, where we lived underground until the end of the war.

In Florence I was in daily contact with many close, dear friends and courageous partisans of the "Partito di Azione". In August of 1944, the advancing Anglo-American armies forced the German invaders to leave Florence. At the Anglo-American Headquarters, I was hired as a medical doctor and assigned to a camp of war refugees who were brought to Florence by the hundreds from the North where the war was still raging. Epidemics of infectious diseases and of abdominal typhus spread death among the refugees, where I was in charge as nurse and medical doctor, sharing with them their suffering and the daily danger of death.

The war in Italy ended in May 1945. I returned with my family to Turin where I resumed my academic positions at the University. In the fall of 1947, an invitation from Professor Viktor Hamburger to join him [at the Washington University in St. Louis] and repeat the experiments which we had performed many years earlier in the chick embryo, was to change the course of my life.

Although I had planned to remain in St. Louis for only ten to twelve months, the excellent results of our research made it imperative for me to postpone my return to Italy. In 1956 I was offered the position of Associate Professor and in 1958 that of Full Professor, a position which I held until retirement in 1977. In 1962 I established a research unit in Rome, dividing my time between this city and St. Louis. From 1969 to 1978 I also held the position of Director of the Institute of Cell Biology of the Italian National Council of Research, in Rome. Upon retirement in 1979, I became Guest Professor of this same institute.

She was the first woman to be appointed to the Board of the *Enciclopedia Italiana*, serving from 1993 to 1998. In 1999 she was made an ambassador to the United Nations Food and Agriculture organization (FAO) and in 2001 the Italian Senate made her a Senator for life.[93]

Rita Levi-Montalcini died on 30 December 2012 at the age of 103. This means she was the longest-lived Nobel Laureate.

---

93 Rita Levi-Montalcini, 1986, later published in *Les Prix Nobel. The Nobel Prizes 1986*, Editor Wilhelm Odelberg, [Nobel Foundation], Stockholm, 1987, http://www.nobelprize.org/nobel_prizes/medicine/laureates/1986/levi-montalcini-bio.html accessed 26 August 2017.

Women Seeking Visas and Dealing with Other Documents

Kristallnacht was both a shock and watershed for the Jews of Europe. Many who had assumed that the Hitler Reich would not last long and that they should keep their heads down until it passed now realised that this was not the case. Documentation became a matter of life and death.

The women were forced to act when their men were taken to camps like Dachau and Buchenwald and only released on the condition that they left their native land in a relatively short period. This placed an extremely onerous task on the women of the family who had to organise paperwork and obtain visas through the labyrinthine process devised by the Nazis. It is hard to imagine how the Jewish women, who were mostly unused to dealing with bureaucracy, would have dealt with this when they also had to bear the anxiety of their husbands' situations and the family's future.

Historians tend to focus on the Jewish men who were arrested and taken away to camps. Marion Kaplan described the impact of *Kristallnacht* on women whose memoirs tend to focus on flying feathers when the mobs in their home tore pillows and feather bed-coverings:

This image of feathers flying, of a domestic scene gravely disturbed represents women's primary experience of the pogrom. The marauders beat and arrested Jewish men, sending more than thirty thousand to concentration camps. With brutal exceptions, which are worth noting because they may indicate more violence against women than historians have recognized to date, most women were forced to stand by and watch their homes torn apart and their men abused.

As women cleaned up the wreckage of the pogrom, their most crucial task was to rescue their men. Wives of prisoners were told that their husbands would be released only if they could present emigration papers. Although no statistics are available to indicate their success, these women displayed extraordinary nerve and tenacity in saving a large number of men and in facilitating a mass exodus of married couples in 1939. Women summoned the courage to overcome gender stereotypes of passivity in order to find any means to have husbands and fathers released from camps. They had to organize the papers, decide on the destination, sell property, and organize the departure. One example illuminates the ordeal facing many women. Mally Dienemann, whose sixty-three-year-old husband was deteriorating rapidly in Buchenwald, raced immediately to the Gestapo to prove that the couple were almost ready to emigrate. Next, she travelled to the passport office to obtain their passports, then to the Emigration Office in Frankfurt, the Gestapo, the police, and the Finance Office. She had to send requests to Buchenwald and the Gestapo in Darmstadt: 'Still it took until Tuesday of the third week, before my husband returned … Next came running around for the many papers that one needed for emigration. And while the Gestapo was in a rush, the Finance Office had so much and so many requests.'[94]

Mally Dienemann

Mally (1883–1963) married Rabbi Max Dienemann (1875–1939) in 1904 and they had three daughters. She was the daughter of a well-to-do merchant from Gollub in West Prussia. He was the head of the Liberal Rabbis' Association and served the city of Offenbach. He worked with Rabbi Leo Baeck. In December 1933, he was taken into 'protective custody' and sent to Osthofen for 'attitudes hostile to the state'. Apparently:

A history lecture he delivered to the Jewish community of Offenbach had been monitored by two policemen who later claimed that by drawing parallels between the era of King Herod and the present times, the rabbi had gravely insulted German authorities. Although Dienemann, his wife, and several other witnesses tried hard to rectify the authorities' twisting of words, the local police present had him deported to Osthofen.[95]

He ordained the first woman rabbi, Regina Jonas, in December 1935 but she was killed at Auschwitz in December 1944 without serving a congregation. It would be sixty years before another German woman rabbi would be ordained.

A year after *Kristallnacht*, Mally wrote a diary of their time in Germany under the Nazis:

… What do you do to get your husband released from prison? He [Max Dienemann] had been to the doctor in the days [leading up to his arrest]; he was suffering from severe foot pain and perhaps a certificate from his doctor, Dr. Hohmann, professor for orthopaedics at the Frankfurt University Clinic, could secure his release. I received a friendly answer when I phoned to inquire. Of course my husband was not fit for

---

94 Marion Kaplan, 'Jewish Women in Nazi Germany', in *Women in the Holocaust* pp.46–7

95 Kim Wünschmann, *Before Auschwitz: Jewish Prisoners in the Prewar Concentration Camps*, p.55

prison. A certificate was issued for me. At four o'clock [4.00pm on 10 November] I went to the police [the German Order Police as opposed to the Gestapo]. After a short wait I was brought before Superintendent [*Kommissar*] Richmann who was not impolite. I handed over the certificate and received a promise that it would be passed on. However, I needed to go back to the Gestapo. I asked for permission to speak briefly with my husband and to give him some food. This was permitted, and we were able to talk for a few minutes. He looked terribly ill, was resigned and brave, told me that he shared a room with 11 men, that they had just prayed together, that they were in good spirits. He did not mention any interrogation. I had to take my leave and again went to the Gestapo. Tress, their man in charge, had a bulldog face (he at one time had many connections to the Jewish community) but was not unfriendly and promised to help get the medical certificate accepted [so that Max Dienemann would be released]. I departed. In the street one could see shattered glass in front of Jewish firms and shops. Display windows were broken. Remnants of wares lay on the ground. Along the way I encountered women weeping; their husbands had been picked up during the day. I heard a whole string of frightful stories. Almost all Jewish men had been arrested; almost all Jewish apartments had been vandalized [*zerstört*]. Because the 'rage of the *Volk*' was not allowed to extend into the evening, they had not quite finished and thus some Jewish houses had not been touched. It was only that evening that we Offenbachers learned from the radio that this day had been a misfortune not only for our city, that not only the Offenbach synagogue had been set on fire but a whole wave of misfortunes had spread over all the Jewish communities of Germany. Not even the smallest village community had been spared. I lay down that night, beaten down [*zerschlagen*], dead tired. But sleep did not come. At five o'clock [5.00am on 11 November] friends phoned to say that the prisoners from Offenbach were supposed to be sent away. The car that would take them was leaving at six o'clock. Perhaps there was a chance that I could say goodbye at the police station beforehand and deliver some food [to her husband]. My girlfriend filled a basket with groceries, we went to the police, and when we arrived the driver was just starting the engine. We managed to get a brief glimpse inside a bus that was packed full with friends who were sitting and standing. We waved, and the bus drove away. We asked the policemen standing in front of the building, 'Where are the men being taken?' They answered gruffly, 'We don't know a thing.'

At eight o'clock I again went to Superintendent Richmann, who told me correctly that the men were being taken to Buchenwalde [*sic*] (concentration camp near Weimar). I mentioned my husband's illness, his age (63 years), his need for medical attention, and the certificate issued by the university professor stating that he was unfit for prison. 'Don't worry,' Kommissar Richmann told me, 'there will be medical services available. The prisoners are getting some Prussian treatment [*hart und preussisch angepackt*], but nothing will happen to them. At most they will lose a few pounds.'

I was so gullible that this provided some comfort on my way home. We had to wait and in the meantime pay visits to the police and Gestapo...

On Saturday, November 12, we heard that the Jewish prisoners were being released if they could prove they had a visa for some foreign country or a Palestine Certificate and that their departure was imminent. I sent a telegraph message on Saturday to my children in Palestine asking them to acquire a Palestine Certificate as quickly as possible ...

On November 17, I received a telegram from my married daughter in London, Frau Jakoby, saying that an entrance visa for both of us to go to England had been secured. I should go to the consulate immediately and pick it up. Owing to an error, I did not receive it right away, but the consulate sent it to me on Sunday [20 November]. And now I had the paper in my hands that I needed to free my husband.

I could prove to the Gestapo that nothing should interfere with our expedited departure. First I went to the passport office, to this [Mr] German in order to apply for passports. It appeared that I would be able to obtain it [*sic*] right away. There were still further issues to take care of and just when I believed I would be getting it on the spot, after being sent all morning from one office to the other, German said to me – this was a man who had known us for years –' Well, you need to show me evidence first that your husband has a doctoral degree. How do you intend to prove that to me?' I ran home and brought back his doctoral diploma, something about which he [Mr German] had no comprehension. He then said, 'Fine, in eight days you can pick up the passport.'

And now another series of offices awaited me. The official emigration office in Frankfurt, the Gestapo, the police, the finance office [*Finanzamt*], a petition to Buchenwald, a petition to the Gestapo in Darmstadt, and it still took until Tuesday of the third week [29 November] before my husband returned. On Tuesday at midday I was back at the official emigration advice bureau in Frankfurt. The director was very friendly, promised to do everything in his power, for he understood that every day presented a life-threatening situation for a 63-year-old man. When I returned home from making these rounds, I ran into some acquaintances who called to me, 'Frau Doktor, your husband is coming today. He is being released today. Make sure you have a great deal to drink on hand because he is terribly thirsty.' I dared not believe it, but at two o'clock a telegram arrived from Weimar giving his arrival time. I picked my husband up from the train station. This was not like picking him up when he was released from Osthofen[96] [concentration camp in late 1933]; this was not a man who had returned with his old familiar

---

96 Osthofen was a concentration camp for political prisoners. It opened 1 May 1933 and was the only camp where no one died. However, it was very primitive with appalling sanitary conditions, which resulted in many prisoners developing lifelong ailments. It was closed in July 1934. The Osthofen archive is http://www. ns-dokuzentrum-rlp.de/index.php?id=107&L=1 accessed 8 August 2017.

sense of humor intact. We greeted each other, and he said very gravely, 'If I go through this again, Mally, I will not survive.' We went home. But this deadly earnestness did not leave him. I was happy, but how could one remain happy for long? The husband of my daughter was still in a camp, and many a friend languished there as well …[97]

Mally, as the wife of an eminent rabbi, was better placed than many Jewish women to navigate her way through the Nazi bureaucracy. Just writing about her activities was exhausting. Mally also described their journey out of Germany a few weeks later, 30–31 December 1938. Not surprisingly that was not an easy undertaking:

… Our trip went smoothly until we got to Emmerich, the city before the Dutch border. In Emmerich two young SS men came into our compartment wearing their tight black uniforms, perhaps 20 or 22 years old. They inspected our passports and asked gruffly, 'Are you Jews?' We answered in the affirmative. 'Where is the *J* in your passport? What? I'm sure you'd like that, traveling through the world without having a *J* in your passport.[98] You need to get off the train and return to Offenbach, and above all, give us your passports. Come to the platform tomorrow morning and pick up your passports for the trip back.' We answered 'We were never again going to return to Germany' and that it must be all the same to him whether Jews who were emigrating and no longer living in Germany had the *J* or not. It was to no avail. We had to get off the train. We began to look for a hotel where we could spend the night. At two hotels we were told, 'We do not allow Jews to stay here.' We went to the Christian travelers' aid office at the station [*Bahnhofsmission*]. I could have spent the night there but not my husband. Naturally I would not be separated from my husband. In the fourth hotel no one enquired and we were finally able to put our things down. The weather was terrible, and we were dead tired after all this excitement. First we had to make a call to Holland, where we had been expected that evening. It took a long time before we got through to The Hague. We then lay down in bed – but we did not sleep that night. Early on a gloomy December morning, it was raining and snowing, we went to the train platform to face our tormentors. They appeared around eight o'clock and after drawn-out pleas gave us back our passports. After repeated requests they gave their consent for us to go to the police in Emmerich to have the *J* stamped into our passports. A long distance from the train station in Emmerich, through the city to the police station. There again we had to wait until it was out turn. Our hearts beating anxiously:

---

97 Mally Dienemann, diary entries pp.363–6 in *Jewish Responses to Persecution 1933–38*, eds. Matthäus & Roseman (Lanham: AltaMira Press, 2010)

98 It was mandatory for the letter *J* to be stamped in German Jews' passports after early October 1938 – usually in red.

would they provide it or not? The police official condescended to apply the *J* stamps. We were able to pick up our luggage and go to the train station and take the next express train heading for The Hague. A terrible hour still spent at the train station, for the train had been delayed by 40 minutes, and the two SS men constantly went up and down the platform and into the waiting room. Finally we could board, finally the train left. All of a sudden these young men clad in black, lads who felt all-powerful, examined our passports – but there were no questions about our luggage, no questions about what currency we were carrying. Perhaps they saw in our faces what this night in Emmerich had done to us. We arrived at the Dutch border, and our bitterness about everything that had been done to us was much greater than our feeling of happiness about being out of this land of anguish and ignominy. But then we changed over into the train to The Hague and saw the friendly, well-fed people, as we again heard a polite please and thank you (something one no longer hears in Germany), a true and intense feeling of gratitude and happiness arose with in us. We gave a prayer of thanks for our liberation and a prayer of supplication for all those who still remained in Germany.

After a two-month stay in England, we left for Palestine on March 15. We landed in Tel Aviv on March 21, 1939. Two weeks after we arrived, my husband became ill with a mild attack of pleurisy. The pain in his legs became very intense. The pain was attributed to all the standing he had to do and the exertion of being in a concentration camp. On April 10 he got up for the first time again. We were sitting in the sun in the garden that morning for an hour; in the afternoon a heart attack ended his life.

And now I'm sitting here in Palestine on Mount Canaan without my beloved life partner, without my circle of friends, without having saved even a fraction of our property. Because of the war we have lost any hope that the transfer payment [for moving funds from Germany to Palestine] can be made. I am truly 'Gone with the wind'.[99]

She wrote *Gone with the Wind* in English and of course the book was published in 1936 even though the film was not released until December 1939. Mally later went to America and died in Chicago in 1963.

The AJR's journal recorded the centenary of Max Dienemann's birth in October 1975. It stated that his 1933 imprisonment was due to one of his sermons being misinterpreted by the Nazis. It also stated that the visas for England were acquired as the result of Lily H. Montagu's efforts. [100] She was a leading figure in Liberal Judaism in England and a colleague of Leo Baeck's.[101]

---

99 Pp.374–6

100 *Max Dienemann Centenary,* in AJR Information October 1975 p.6

101 Umansky, Ellen M., "Lily Montagu." *Jewish Women: A Comprehensive Historical Encyclopedia.* 20 March 2009. Jewish Women's Archive. (Accessed 27 July 2017) <https://jwa.org/encyclopedia/article/montagu-lily>.

Andrew Sachs' Mother

I knew Andrew Sachs (1930–2016) was Jewish but it was only after he died that I read in his *Times* obituary that his family had fled Germany because his father was Jewish.[102] He wrote about his Catholic mother's efforts to get her husband Hans (1885–1944) safely out of Berlin and Germany. Their three children – Barbara, Tom and Andrew – were not regarded as Jewish. Hans 'had won the Iron Cross in the 1914 war. He had a solid-gold Prussian ancestry. He even had blue eyes and almost blond hair. None of that mattered.'[103]

Hans had studied law and had a doctorate, but in the 1930s he was an insurance broker in a virtual one-man business. The new anti-Jewish laws meant people were reluctant to deal with him as a Jew:

> Long-standing clients found it necessary, often reluctantly, to take their business elsewhere. 'Nothing personal you understand, Herr Doktor Sachs ... but our position ... family ... children, you understand ...' Ordinary people were scared and did not, behave decently, though they knew they were making life even harder for individual Jews they often liked and had been on good terms with.[104]

Andrew's father was arrested when he was found with a satirical article on him whilst out for dinner with his family. The arresting Nazis hauled him off to Nazi HQ saying, 'You will not see your husband again' to Katarina, Andrew's mother.[105] The restaurant owner, Gustav, whose own position was imperilled by allowing them to dine on his premises, instructed one of the waiters, Carlo, to escort her and the three children home.

> A few minutes later in the street, Mother collapsed with an awful cry ... Carlo took her gently by the arm and escorted us to our front door as she was recovering, her spirit by no means broken. She immediately got in touch with family members and friends, who hurried over to work out a plan of action. They hit on a potentially helpful contact: a high-ranking officer in the Berlin civil police. He had been a long-term client of my father's, but, like so many others, he had to stop his dealings with Jews. Our family nevertheless approached him in the faint hope of getting his support. They struck lucky. Ignoring the risk to his own career, he gave the necessary orders. It was a brave act and resulted in my father, grateful but distraught, coming back home just a few days later.
>
> But the danger had hardly gone away. Our top priority now was to ensure Father's safety. What was he, the one Jew in our family, to do? Our parents faced each other and nodded. 'Get out fast,' they said as one.

---

102 https://www.thetimes.co.uk/article/andrew-sachs–3j89ptn66 2 December 2016, accessed 4 December 2016.
103 Andrew Sachs, *I Know Nothing* (London: The Robson Press, 2015) p.5
104 Sachs p.17
105 Sachs p.23

Mother took charge. Father stayed out of the public eye as much as possible, while she marched along endless corridor of power to battle with an army of stony-faced officials. Nothing could daunt her. By turns bullying, cajoling, shouting, crying, bargaining or charming her way through, the bureaucrats finally agreed. 'Get your damned Jew out of the country! *Schnell! Schnell!*'

'*Heil Hitler*,' she said. It choked her, but she said it with a happy smile and left.

Father bought a one-way ticket to freedom. Actually, to Southampton. Armed with his UK entry visa and the address of his prospective employers in London, he packed his bags and saved his life. We still have his old passport stamped with 'J' for *Jude*, imprints of the German eagle and a spread of five swastikas.[106]

Five days after Hans arrived in London, his family witnessed the horrors of *Kristallnacht*. They followed soon afterwards sailing from Hamburg to Southampton. Andrew wrote that he was not keen to leave Germany but he was only young, born in 1930.

Only years later did I even begin to consider what my mother's feelings would have been that day. She was leaving behind brothers, sisters, nephews and nieces, aunts, uncles, both her parents, many close friends and a tragic number of her in-law relatives. She had lost her home and was now facing an unknown future in a foreign land. Yet her instinctive resilience, her refusal to despair and her gratitude for even the smallest blessings never deserted her. On that day she would certainly have appreciated the fact that – unlike millions of others in the coming years – she had escaped the Nazis with her husband alive and well, with three children she could surround with love, and with her own health and strength intact.[107]

Eva Reichmann

During my research, my eye was caught by a report of a woman being arrested on 10 November. Her name was Eva Reichmann, wife of Hans Reichmann. Hans, a lawyer, was taken to Sachsenhausen with 6,400 other Jews. At the end of December 1,064 were still there including Hans. He was released due to his wife's efforts, like so many other Jewish men. Between 1924 and 1939 they had both worked for the *Centralverein deutscher Staatsbürger jüdischen Glaubens* (Central Association of German Citizens of Jewish Faith – known as the Central Verein, or CV). Founded in 1893, its aim was to unite German citizens who were Jews and fight antisemitism. However, they were very patriotic, seeing themselves as German citizens with their own religion. They

---

106 Sachs p.25
107 Sachs p.29

therefore were not Zionists. From 1936 it was called the *Jüdischer Central Verein* (Jewish Central Association). It was banned after *Kristallnacht*.

Initially, I was unable to establish exactly what happened to Eva as some sources did not refer to her being arrested. A letter in German from Hans to Trudy and Paul (surname not known) written in late 1939 or early 1940 revealed the following:

> We went through the manuscript related to your request about Eva Reichmann. We found that she was not actually arrested as well. What happened is that, while her husband was imprisoned, she was asked by the Gestapo to appear at their headquarters on Alexanderplatz. She took this as a positive sign that her work of securing his release was working. But it was different than she expected. The Gestapo did not at the time say they would release her husband, but instead accused her of taking part in forbidden political activities and also of 'having numerous men visiting her at her home'. Eva explained to them who these visitors were, and was forced to pledge that she would no longer have more than three people at the same time in her apartment. She was then allowed to leave.[108]

Reichmann was only to be released from Sachsenhausen when they had papers to emigrate. So Eva had to organise the papers and visas. Then one day Hans was taken to Gestapo HQ and released. He asked Eva how she had managed it:

> I let Eva tell me the story of my liberation. Eva had looked tirelessly for every possibility to support my release, hours by hours in travel agencies, day by day at the emigration information centre and at the Gestapo, where uncounted women stood and waited, until they dropped from exhaustion...Eva managed to organize a visa for Paraguay; she had begged for it, booked a passage with great skill, sent calls and telegrams around the world. She didn't back down.[109]

Michael Simonson at the Leo Baeck Institute in New York added:

> The manuscript mentions she managed also to sell her trousseau, and was able to use part of that money to bribe an authority figure to take action in completing paperwork towards her husband's release and their emigration from Germany. The manuscript also mentions that nothing was done over the Christmas period, while he was still in Sachsenhausen, because all the offices needed were closed and the staff on vacation. Eva also had to rely on members of the Gestapo to file papers and pass on information which they wouldn't always do, either out of 'forgetfulness, anxiety or drunkenness', according to the manuscript of her husband.

---

108 Michael Simonson, Archivist at Leo Baeck Institute, New York email to author 7 August 2017. I am grateful to Michael Simonson for his painstaking assistance in providing this information. Accession No: ME1231
109 Michael Simonson email to author 8 August 2017.

As a result she would need to visit the Gestapo herself and resubmit papers. One British permit was organized for them by a woman named Ilse, but the manuscript says nothing more about this, nor identifies who Ilse is exactly. In the manuscript he praises the role of all the women who secured the release of their husbands and arranged safe passage out of Germany; 'These are the stations between fear and hope, the ordeal of a woman, all Jewish women experienced this.'

It appears that Hans was released in late December:

At the evening of December 27, Jacob Littauer was looking for me with great excitement: 'You will be released.' I go to Karl, who smiles at me: 'It is true, congratulations.' My companions give me tasks to do outside the camp ... I am sitting in the dark sitting room with Karl and Harzen and promise to take care of them, as good as I can outside the camp. From a bed someone whispers: 'Tomorrow you are at home, you lucky fellow. Think about us.'

At this night is no sleep ... I can't imagine the happiness to see Eva and the other good people outside the camp and the feeling of freedom ... I spread out the rest of my foods. We line up and I march to my last morning roll call (December 28, 1938) 'left-two-three-four'. An 'old' (in the camp for a longer time) Jew of my block falls: weakness, as so often, he is rubbed with snow, stood up by fellow prisoners, but sinks to the ground again immediately. 'Hats down-hats up. Work command complete!' I press Karl's hand: 'Thanks for everything, I will never forget you. – Fichtmann, Harzen, Littauer, Fritz Kauffman, see you all again in freedom.' The camp leader lets us line up for the 'final blessing'. I am standing 1 meter away from him and look in the glassy eyes of a stupid-brutal face. His speech in classic German I will never forget: 'All of you are Jews?' 'Yes.' 'You will be released today not because you behave well or you did work well. No! Your release today is so you will emigrate as fast as possible. If you leave the camp now, do your best to leave Germany immediately. I would like to say something: Any Jew that returns to Germany, will be sent back here again. Not for days, a few month or years, but until he dies.'[110]

They initially came to England on a collective visa and lived in Hampshire. Hans cooked for guests while Eva showed her expertise with wine. She worked at the BBC's Evesham monitoring service from 1942 to 1943. Finance from the US enabled her to acquire a second doctorate at the London School of Economics. Her thesis was published in 1950 as *Hostages of Civilization: The Social Sources of National Socialist Anti-Semitism*. She was heavily influenced by Rabbi Leo Baeck, whom she called 'the teacher of my youth'. Later she worked in the Wiener Library Research Department from 1945 to 1959, firstly as a fellow and then as its Director. She initiated interviews with Holocaust survivors.

---

110 Pp.279–280

Sometime after I had written this, I accidentally came across Elizabeth Jungmann, who became the second wife of Sir Max Beerbohm. She proved to be Eva's sister. She was a secretary and translator for Gerhart Hauptmann. In 1933 she fell in love with the ageing German poet and man of letters Rudolf G. Binding. Binding wanted to marry her but this was impossible under the Nuremberg Laws and:

> Binding's posture on the Jews was problematic. On one hand, Rütten & Loening Verlag of Frankfurt, a Jewish firm, had been his publisher for decades. Further, his last lover, Elisabeth Jungmann, was Jewish. Nevertheless, despite these connections, he was willing to go along with the regime's gradual removal of Jews from public life.[111]

She had met Sir Max Beerbohm in 1927 when working for Hauptmann, and when she fled Germany in 1939, Will Rothstein, who was an old Oxford chum of Beerbohm, had introduced them. Will Rothenstein, the son of a Jewish cloth merchant from Bradford, Yorkshire, was knighted in 1931. He provided her with a home when she came to England in 1939. When his first wife died in 1951, he contacted her and she became his secretary, confidante and carer. They married privately on 20 April 1956 when he was dying. In May 1956 she became his executor and when she died in 1958, Eva Reichmann became the executor of the Beerbohm literary estate.

Hans became a leader of the AJR and in a booklet published in 1951 by them he wrote a 'Tribute to Britain'. He wrote of the persecuted in Germany that 'the world will not put up with it', but the world did.[112]

Hilde Schwiening

Lothar Auerbach's reflections, in old age, on his home country featured in *Who Betrayed the Jews?*[113] He too had been arrested during *Kristallnacht* on 9 November 1938 and deported to Dachau concentration camp. His wife Hilde was left to struggle to sort out the paperwork. She had a son, Peter, born 1933 and twins Ruth and Michael born in 1935. In her case the situation was aggravated by her disability resulting from childhood polio, which affected her walking.

The Auerbachs ran a farm in *Schassbach*. Ruth's husband Jurgen told me:

> Schassbach was not really a village. It consisted of a few scattered farms. *Hoelzel*, the name of the farm, was very isolated. The nearest other farm was *Buchegger*, which belonged to the Moser family. The Auerbachs spoke *Hochdeutsch* with an admixture of Silesian dialect.

---

111 Jay W. Baird, *Hitler's War Poets* (New York: Cambridge UP, 2008) p.58
112 Hans Reichmann, *Tribute to Britain* in 'Britain's New Citizens' (London: AJR, 1951) p.7
113 Agnes Grunwald-Spier, *Who Betrayed the Jews?* (Stroud: Amberley Publishing, 2017) pp.500–502

Above and opposite: Postcards sent by Lothar Auerbach to his family: 9–12 Nov. 1938 Klagenfurt; 19 Nov. Dachau; 3 Dec. Dachau. The first card is transcribed as follows: "My dear Hilda and beloved children. Am very worried, since I am so far without news. I hope everything is alright, me too. Contact Moster or Fyn [people they knew from their time in Denmark] immediately to be able to stay there until you get the permit. Prepare everything for the sale even if price is low. Write to Gildemeester, Vienna I, Walbzeile 7 about transfer possibilities. Try urgently and as fast as possible by telegram confirmation to get English or Danish or other visa and tell me immediately. Gestapo Klagenfurt, best perhaps call in person with appropriate recommendations. Perhaps let Frieda [Lothar's sister; lived in Reichenbach, Silesia; perished in the Holocaust] and mother come, also money. You go (?) to Vienna Love, L." The text of the third postcard is as follows: "18.12.38. My dearest and beloved children. Hope you are well, I am well too. Up to now received 3 cards and telegram, including card from Ernst [must be Ernst Orbach from Berlin]. You are doing everything right. When you get my visa, inform Gestapo in Klagenfurt immediately. Yesterday I heard from the court in Wolfsberg that [a certain entry into the land register; unclear; perhaps a debt or mortgage on the land] has been cancelled. Get in touch with Vintler [the Nazi Ortsbauernführer who had been appointed administrator of the farm]. Perhaps he can request through Gestapo Klagenfurt my return, to enable me to settle things. I am very worried about you. Send 5 stamps. Love and kisses, Lothar." (Courtesy Auerbach family)

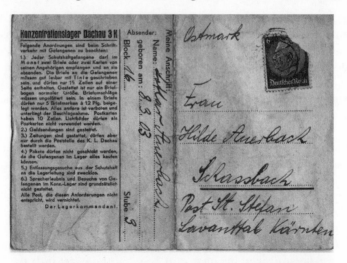

The local dialect in that part of Carinthia would have been almost unintelligible to the Auerbachs. Hilde had a library which marked her out as middle-class. We have a statement from someone who gave some evidence to the court that had to decide on the return of the property to the Auerbachs after the war. In this statement it said: '*a richtger Bua war er nicht*'. (A proper farmer he was not.) By language and lifestyle they were strangers. And then of course they were Jewish.[114]

Lothar sent an undated postcard from the Gestapo prison in Klagenfurt. He had been arrested with Gerhard Gadiel who was his farm worker.

> Dear Hilde and beloved children. I hope you are well. I am together with Gerhard. Through the Bauernfuehrer apply to the Gestapo Klagenfurt, also mention your handicap, best with a doctor's certificate or R.V. note, and ask for my release. I'll write to you from my new location as soon as I get permission. Send me photos of you and the sweet little ones. Chin up, don't worry about me, I can work, can't I. Your health is important for me. Love, Lothar. Drain water from the engine.

Lothar was sent to Dachau on 12 November and registered as No. 23,373. Whilst Lothar and Gerhard were in Dachau they had to wear the combination of yellow and red triangles, like most of the other Jews. That was designated 'Jewish Political' because the Nazis wanted to maintain that Jews were enemies of the state.

On 18 November 1938 Hilde received an expulsion order from her local police station in St. Andrä in Schassbach, which was where the family were living:

> By order of the State Police in Klagenfurt [Gestapo] we have to inform you that you and your family, so far as they are Jews, are instructed either to emigrate or to relocate to Vienna by 15 December 1939.
>
> If you relocate to Vienna you have to report to the appropriate police station after your arrival.
>
> Signed Der Postenkommandant, Nischelwitzer.[115]

The next day, 19 November, Lothar sent his first postcard from Dachau – an official Dachau postcard with very clear printed instructions from the *Lagerkommandant*. It shows he was born on 8 March 1903 and was in Block 16, *Stube* 3 (room). The message consists of 10 lines, which was the permitted maximum.

> Dear Hilde, beloved children. I hope you are all well which I can also say about myself. Please observe the instructions on the other

---

114 Jurgen Schwiening, email to author 23 July 2017 11.17.
115 Ruth and Jurgen Schwiening, *Ruth's Story*, unpublished memoir received 15 February 2014, Appendix I, p.6

side precisely. Here in the canteen you can buy everything, and per week I can shop for 15 Marks. Address it to me correctly using the sender on the reverse. Let someone take the double plough in and drain the engine water. Consult Herrn Vintler about the running of the farm. Greetings and kisses from your loving Lothar. Dachau, 19 Nov. 1938.

Answer cards only with cards and letters with letters.

The brief communication demonstrates his anxiety about Hilde managing to run the farm in his absence and that she should observe the Nazis' detailed instructions. The final sentence could have been written by someone else.

Two weeks later Hilde received a similar postcard, dated 3 December 1938, from Lothar from Dachau. In translation, he wrote:

My dear Hilde and beloved children. Am very worried, since I am so far without news. I hope everything is alright, me too. Contact Moster or Fyn immediately to be able to stay there until you get the permit. Prepare everything for the sale even if price is low. Write to Gildemeester, Vienna1, Walbzeile 7 about transfer possibilities. Try urgently and as fast as possible by telegram confirmation to get English or Danish or other visa and tell me immediately. Gestapo Klagenfurt, best perhaps call in person with appropriate recommendations. Perhaps let Frieda and mother come, also money. You then go to Vienna [?]. Love, L.[116]

The detailed instructions on the official Dachau postcard translate into English as:

1.) Every prisoner in protective custody may receive and send two letters or cards per month from or to his family. The letters to the prisoners must be written in ink and be easily legible and not have more than 15 lines per page. Only stationery of normal size is permitted. Envelopes must not be lined. No more than 5 stamps at 12 Pfennig are allowed in one letter. Everything else is prohibited and is liable to confiscation. Postcards have 10 lines. Photos must not be sent as postcards.
2.) It is not permitted to send money.
3.) Newspapers are permitted but may only be ordered through the post office of KL Dachau.
4.) Parcels must not be sent, since prisoners can buy everything at the camp.
5.) It is pointless to make requests for release to the camp authorities.
6.) Requests to speak to or visit prisoners in the camp are not permitted.

All mail that does not adhere to these regulations will be destroyed.
The Camp Commander

---

116 Jurgen Schwiening, email to author, 15 February 2017.

Hilde decided to go to Berlin, from where she would make her way to England:

> She was only allowed to sell some furniture in order to pay for the railfare to Berlin. She had an aunt and uncle in Berlin and also some friends, the Orbachs, where they stayed while Hilde made the arrangements for them to leave Germany and to go to England. The details of what must have been an enormous task for a handicapped woman with three small children and her husband in a concentration camp are unknown to us. We can only guess. What we do know is that Ruth's mother was extremely determined and energetic. We were told that she made representations to the Dachau Camp Commander to get her husband released. Whether this had any effect on his eventual release at the end of December 1938 we don't know. Between 27 and 31 December Ruth's father was released and joined the family in Berlin.[117]

The Schwienings don't know how Hilde managed. 'She was handicapped in walking, had to go to many offices, write letters, fill in forms and wait endless hours. How could she have looked after three young children at the same time?' I asked what happened between his release and his arrival in the UK. Jurgen replied:

> All we know is that Lothar first went back to Schassbach, found that his family had left, found out her new address in Berlin somehow and joined her. It may be that the neighbouring farmer, Moser, told him. We have a letter that Moser sent at the end of December to Hilda in Berlin. As far as we know Lothar did not know that his family had been expelled.
>
> It may be that Hilda had begun the process of getting a visa for her husband before he arrived. Unfortunately Ruth's parents never talked to the children about this time. They put that time behind them like a bad dream. How I wish I knew more![118]

Lothar's visa was dated 23 February 1939. However Ruth's parents did not speak about the period when Lothar returned from Dachau, so the details of how the precious visa was acquired are not known.[119] Ruth has written that her father's visa for entry to the UK was signed by C D Insall.

This turned out to be Cecil Dudley Insall (1898–1974). He was Frank Foley's deputy at the UK Passport Office in Berlin and worked there from 1933, shortly after the Reichstag fire, until he left with the rest of the embassy staff on a special diplomatic train in September 1939, just after war was declared. Apparently he once said he had issued as many visas as Frank Foley. He had to leave all his personal possessions in his flat when he and his wife left and they were destroyed by Allied bombing. His great nephew, Tony Insall,

---

117 *Ruth's Story* p.3
118 Jurgen Schwiening, email to author, 21 July 2017.
119 Jurgen Schwiening, email to author, 21 July 2017.

told me all his photographs of the period were destroyed.[120] Lothar was only released from Dachau on condition he left Germany or went to Vienna. His son-in-law Jurgen tracked down Insall's son and invited him and his wife to lunch at their home. Ruth, then thanked him in her father's name for rescuing him from certain death.[121]

The importance of women's roles in managing to get the visas to leave Germany and Austria is exemplified by the story of Gerhard Gadiel who was born in Breslau in 1914. He was one of the Auerbachs' farm workers (*praktikant*). After he was released from Dachau he went back to Schassbach. Amongst the family papers, Jurgen discovered an old faded letter dated 29 December 1938 addressed to '*Geehrte Familie Auerbach*' (Esteemed Family Auerbach).

> In this letter a Herr Moser wrote that he had 'heard from Gerhard' that Herr Auerbach had 'returned from the journey'. The 'journey' was, of course, Lothar's arrest by the Gestapo and imprisonment in Dachau. Gerhard, he wrote, was again working for the time being on the farm but didn't like it because he felt 'almost a stranger'. Herr Moser also mentioned that he was sending his neighbours some pork and two chickens. By this time, Frau Auerbach, having been expelled from their farm in Schassbach, had arrived in Berlin with her three young children and was trying desperately to obtain a visa to leave Germany. Herr Moser, we soon found out, was the owner of the neighbouring farm. Sending a Jewish family a friendly letter as well as food was clearly not without risk. It was an act of neighbourly kindness for which we are grateful even today. How lucky this letter has survived!

The International Tracing Service (ITS) at Bad Arolson put Jurgen in touch with Gerhard's sister who had emigrated to Palestine in 1936 and lost touch with her brother who had intended to follow her. It appears that he left the farm and returned home to Breslau, to his parents who were transported to Theresienstadt on 2 April 1943 and in October 1944 they were sent to Auschwitz.[122] It is not known whether Gerhardt was with them. Whatever his fate, he had no woman to obtain a visa for him to achieve his long-held dream of going to Palestine.

I was keen to pursue the impact of the visa requests on the British Passport Offices. I was fortunate that the Foreign and Commonwealth Office (FCO) has a Historians Group who have produced a set of papers entitled 'Frank Foley'. I do not have room for most of the information but I wanted to include the letter marked 'Top Secret' from Rear Admiral, Sir Hugh Sinclair, Chief of the Secret Intelligence Service to Sir Alexander Cadogan, Permanent

---

120 Tony Insall, emails to author 26 July 2017.
121 Ruth Schwiening, 'Not Only Nicholas Winton', letter in *AJR Journal* May 2016, p.8
122 Jurgen Schwiening, 'I am with Gerhard' – some family history rediscovered' in *AJR Journal* April 2012 p.10

Under Secretary of State for Foreign Affairs on 3 January 1938, enclosing a memorandum by the Director of Passport Control. He expressed concern at the amount of work being created by the 'aliens' wanting to come to the UK.

I am much disturbed at the increasing strain which is being placed on the personnel of the Passport Control Services in connection with the refugee question.

To meet requirements as they have arisen, I have increased the staff of the Passport Control offices, in Vienna from four to twenty-five employees, and in Berlin from eight to twenty-two, and still the officers in charge of these posts state that the work continues to be overwhelming and they ask that further assistance should be given them.

In Hungary, owing to the projected anti-Jewish measures, the Passport Control office in Budapest has daily had over 500 applications and I am again asked to despatch reinforcements.

In Czechoslovakia, it is reported that stringent anti-Jewish measures are to be adopted and pogroms are prophesied for the month of February, and it has been decided to reimpose visa requirements for Czechoslovak nationals from 1 April, 1939.

Up to date, over 35,000 visas have been granted to Refugees from Germany and Austria and now under the new scheme, the Home Office are delegating to the German Jewish Aid Committee in London powers by which they will be able to import refugees falling under the three following categories:-

a. Those refugees who desire to come to the United Kingdom to await permission to enter some other country overseas.
b. Any refugees who are coming here as trainees with a view to ultimate emigration overseas.
c. Refugees over the age of 60 who are to settle in the United Kingdom but with the obligation not to take employment.

This new scheme will place upon the Passport Control Officers abroad the responsibility of granting very many thousand further visas in addition to those which continue to be authorised in the ordinary way by the Home Office at the rate of some 200 a day.

It is increasingly difficult to recruit and train suitable extra staff for this work, more especially as I have no information as to the maximum number of refugee applications for visas for the United Kingdom with which Passport Control services may have to deal.

Signed by W.Jeffes 2/1/39[123]

---

123 I am grateful to Tony Insall and Dr Luke Gibbon for arranging for me to receive these documents from the FCO historians on 31 July 2017.

Resourceful Women

Alice Möller

Alice responded to my request for stories from women in the AJR Information newsletter. I visited her at home on 20 March 2017 and she told me her amazing story. At 105 she was incredibly vivacious and a real joy to meet. Her memory was very clear.

I was married in 1934 and was living in Vienna. I carried on working until February 1938 because they could not find a replacement. My daughter Susan was born on 5 March 1938 and I stayed at home with her. I had a Nanny for the first three weeks as well as a maid.

On 12 March Hitler marched into Austria under the Anschluss. We had all been fearful beforehand but I was so shocked that my milk dried up and Susan had to be bottle fed.

We didn't live in a Jewish area – we lived in the 8th district. We didn't see any persecution there but we heard about it. However Jews were not allowed to go in the public park with a pram. The non-Jews all wore Nazi supporting badges with a swastika so anyone not wearing one was identified as Jewish.

My husband Richard officially lost his job at the insurance company where they had both worked as soon as Hitler invaded. However fortunately he was able to continue his work unofficially from home and somebody brought the work to him. We were lucky he kept his salary and so we were OK. However this created a *fool's paradise* for us – without the continuation of his salary we would have left Austria earlier.

Accordingly in June 1938 we took another flat with a garden on the outskirts of Vienna. We told the landlord we were Jewish but he said he didn't care as long as we paid the rent. When we arrived by taxi with all our stuff and Susan there was a large banner in the shape of a shield declaring he was a top Nazi outside the property which had not been there before. It was a farmhouse and we had the ground floor.

He couldn't do enough for us and made a wonderful birthday party for Richard in July, but he never told his chums that he had Jews in his house. However in August he told us the Nazi Party had found out about us and unfortunately we had to go. He told us we should leave Austria as soon as possible – especially before the autumn when something dreadful was going to happen. So he knew about *Kristallnacht* in August in 1938. He told us he was very fond of us. Fortunately we had kept our old flat, so we just went back there.

Realising we would have to leave, we got a registration number from the US Embassy and then had to get a guarantor to get the required visa. I discovered that after the Anschluss, shops had set up in Vienna that sold addresses abroad. I bought the addresses of all the Möllers in the US – there were about 6 or 7 and I wrote to them all. I included a photo of all three of us in traditional Austrian dress holding Susan. A Mr Moller from Maryland and a Mr Holozapfel responded. I opted for Mr Möller because he lived closer to New York. He sent the affidavit and we waited for the Visa which came in November 1940. We had no alternative but to sit and wait. We were very comfortable and had no problems with getting food or other restrictions except that we could not keep our maid.

On 9 November someone telephoned us and told us not to go out because there would be trouble. Richard was being trained to be a hairdresser and had to go to the shop where they were training him. I tried to block the doorway with my body but he just pushed me aside and went out.

At 11.00am there was a knock on the door and from the kitchen I could see into the corridor and could see three or four suspicious-looking men with no uniforms. They shouted 'We know you are there you bloody Jew, so open the door before we smash it in.' They said they wanted all the Jews in one flat downstairs and told me to leave the flat. I phoned the hairdressers to ask Richard to come back but he didn't. I knew then he was in Dachau.

I refused to leave the flat and stayed there. Richard's mother had kept her husband's service revolver from WW1. He was called Emil and had been a doctor but he had died by then. There was edict that Jews could not hold weapons at this time. I had the gun because my father said he would throw it in the Danube and I was waiting for him to collect it. I had a slow combustion stove in the flat and put the weapon in it to hide it.

I went to the SR HQ which was opposite our flat and told them I wasn't leaving the flat. I said I was as good as them and had been born in Vienna, as was my mother. I said I had a child and wasn't leaving. I was so angry that I had no fear. Nothing happened and I went home to the flat.

I phoned an old boyfriend in London and told him what was going on and he promised to help us. He was called Lou Bloom and had a furniture factory. I had come to London in 1930 when I was 18 to improve my English. I thought I was going to a family but I was staying somewhere called The Priory near Clacton. I had travelled with two other girls and we had no opportunities to speak English because everyone there was foreign. I contacted the office in London and complained. They gave me a place in the Paragon Hotel in Blackheath, which still exists. I had a much older cousin living in London who came to see me and brought Lou Bloom who was 22. He fell in love with me and wanted to marry me but I went back to Vienna.

I gave notice on the flat and got rid of our furniture. My father had a business and the concierge there said he had a friend who would buy it. He came with an SS man and whilst I tried to negotiate a good price but didn't do well. I complained to the SS man that I would end up paying him.

The SS man wanted my piano but I wouldn't let him have it and said it was my mother-in law's. He came back an hour later and said he was sorry for me and asked where my husband was. He said he knew where he was and he would get him out and he would be back the next night. It was the longest night of my life but Richard did not come back. I think he did it as revenge for the piano.

I went home to my parents and gave the bedroom furniture to my former maid who was getting married. I left Susan with my mother-in-law who lived with her daughter who also had a child. I was determined to find Richard and now had no expenses.

I went to different coffee houses each day to gather information and listen to what people were saying. I needed a German passport now that Austria was occupied. I heard that visas from Ecuador were available, so I bought one for about 17 shillings. It covered all three of us and I then got three German passports.

I decided to visit Gestapo HQ in the Morzinplatz – it used to be a hotel. I rang up and made an appointment. My friends said I was crazy but I wasn't afraid. By then it was January 1939 and I went for the appointment. I gave my name and was saluted. I had a meeting with a man in his late 40s and we chatted for about 30 minutes. We talked about politics and he said he liked me and he would get my husband out in three weeks. However he said he wanted something in return. I said 'What can I do for you?' He asked me to visit him twice a week for the next three weeks as he wanted to talk to me. I agreed.

I went six times for 30 minutes each time. He was an educated man and I was a champion skier. We talked about art, music and politics – he never defended anti-Semitism. I thought he wanted sex but he didn't, but I would have done anything to get my husband back. Exactly to the date three weeks later Richard came home in a taxi. He looked terrible and he had to hold his trousers up as he had no belt. He never spoke about his experiences because they had to sign to say they wouldn't talk about it.

It was now mid-February 1939 and the English visa had arrived. We were allowed 10 marks each and couldn't take anything with us. We flew from Vienna to Croydon and I cried all the way because I knew I wouldn't see my parents again. We lived with Lou and his parents in their attic. We came for two months.

Beatrix Frank

I wrote about Steven's experiences in the chapter on 'Betrayal by Jews' in
Who Betrayed the Jews? Steven's father Leonard, an eminent Amsterdam
lawyer, had been arrested and was killed at Auschwitz in January 1943 aged
39. When Steven told me his story he hinted at his mother's courage and
resourcefulness in looking after her three sons after her husband had been
taken, so I asked him to tell me more.

My mother, Beatrix Frank (née Van Lier) 1910–2001 was born in
Eastbourne. Her parents were both born in Holland. They were popular
classical violinists who married in London at the Kensington Registry
Office around 1901. Ironically I married my first wife there in 1962
unaware of the connection. My grandfather, Simon van Lier, ran the
famous Palm Court Orchestra of the Grand Hotel in Eastbourne for many
years. Beatrix was born in 1910 and had two sisters. The elder Felicia
(Fifi) was born in 1902 and the younger Edura (Dori) was born in 1912.

When Beatrix finished her education in London, her parents sent her
to Amsterdam to go to a finishing school around 1928. One day she was
cycling in the park when she got a puncture. She was standing by her
bicycle feeling very forlorn when a gallant young man offered to repair it.
He was Leonard Frank (1903–1943) and as a result they started seeing
each other. They married in December 1931 in Holland as by then Beatrix's
parents had split up and her mother, Flora, was living in Scheveningen –
near The Hague. She was to die at Auschwitz in August 1942. My parents
started married life living in Amsterdam at 36 Merweerder Plein. Anne
Frank's family lived at No. 37 which was opposite, but later because they
only left Germany in 1933. It was also famous for having the very first
Dutch skyscraper, which was built in the 1920s.

They moved to a larger place when their first child Nicholas was born
in August 1932. I was born in 1935 and Carel in 1937.

It was a very happy marriage until my father was arrested in his
office in October 1942. He was taken to the Nazi HQ in Amsterdam
from there he was taken to Amersfoort prison where he was tortured.
My mother showed her initiative by disguising herself as a male cleaner
and smuggling herself into the prison where he was held. She was able
to speak to my father and he told her he had been tortured but had not
revealed anything. The family didn't know about this somewhat risky
venture, given she had three small boys at home waiting for her, until a
card she had written to her elder sister Felicia on 21–22 January 1943
came to light about two years ago. Postmarked Amsterdam, Beatrix
wrote 'Hello, much love. Leo was incredibly brave as always and that
also gives me great strength.' There is another card also sent to them but
its date is unknown. Beatrix wrote:

Dear Fee and Micky
I am writing to let you know that things have gone wrong with Leo and that
he left on Monday at 10.45, 'on orders from up high'. You'll understand

how I feel after all these terrible days of strain/tension – but I do not want to give up hope and remain confident that I will see him again. If Micky would like to come, rather not this week, because I do not want to see or speak with anyone until I have calmed down- else I would have taken care of everything for the boys and for the time being we are OK.

Steven thinks his mother was very wary of what she said, in case the Gestapo intercepted the mail. Without the postmark we are unable to know to which scenario she is referring. Leo was taken to Amersfoort Prison in December 1942. He was tortured there and then taken to Westerbork Transit Camp on 23 December 1942. He was taken to Auschwitz on 18 January 1943 and he was gassed on 21 January 1943. So when Beatrix posted the first card Leo was already dead.

Felicia was in hiding in Amsterdam with her husband Micky but they were arrested and died in Auschwitz in August 1943.

Without Dad's income she had no financial means to keep the family. We lived in quite a large house and she opened up part of the house as a school for Dutch Jewish children in early 1943. When the Nazis closed the Jewish *Joodse Lyceum* in Amsterdam, the teachers had asked her if they could use her house as a replacement school as the Nazis' restrictions meant Jewish children could not attend the ordinary schools anymore.

Dr Dienke Hondius who has written about the school confirmed 'that home schooling became a phenomenon in Amsterdam after the summer of 1941 when the schools were separated, and even more so once the deportations started, from 14 July 1942 onward.'[124]

Jews were also forbidden from going to the barbers so my mother cut people's hair as well. She had no qualifications or experience for these two activities but continued with them until we were sent to the Barneveld Castle in March 1943. I admire her initiative, but believe on one occasion whilst cutting a professor's hair, she nicked his ear.

After we were sent to Barneveld as a protected family, that special status was ignored and we were sent to Westerbork transit camp in September 1943. We lived in Barrack no. 85. It was split with men on the left and women and children on the right. There were trestle tables in front of each window and 12 people sat at each table for their 3 meals a day. This meant that the unit of 12 became very close. We were never hungry in Westerbork. My eldest brother Nicholas went to lessons but Carel and I just played. Our mother worked in the kitchens. I remember that she managed to get me a skipping rope for my 9th birthday which was 27 July 1944.

A year later we were sent to Theresienstadt in September 1944. You described our horrendous journey in your earlier book. A typhus epidemic was already in place when we arrived. To avoid catching the

---

124 Dr. Dienke Hondius, email to author, 20 July 2017. Dr. Hondius' book is *Absent: Herinneringen aan het Joods Lyceum in Amsterdam, 1941–1943* (Memories of the Jewish Lyceum in Amsterdam, 1941–43) Vassallucci, Amsterdam 2001.

disease you had to keep yourself and your clothing clean. My mother managed to get herself work in the camp laundry which was the only place in the camp with hot water. As well as her allocated tasks she surreptitiously washed our clothes to keep us clean and healthy. Somehow she also managed to wash clothes for other people and used this labour to barter extra food for us. She kept a laundry list of her 'customers' and my brother Carel has this. I remember that bandages and swabs were only washed in hot water. There was no sterilization and it is amazing that my mother never caught anything from that work.

In addition when trucks came into the camp with the food for the prisoners, she crawled underneath the truck to see if there was anything like a potato or any other scraps she could use. The laundry was outside the main camp and my mother had a long walk to it very early in the morning – around 4.00am. On the way she passed allotments where people were growing vegetables – she pinched vegetables for them to eat. Food was cooked in the cookhouse and was brought to us in the children's house but there was never enough. She bartered the private laundry work for a bitter bread she mixed with water to make a kind of bread porridge we called 'broodpap'. I have never forgotten the pain of the hunger we experienced in Theresienstadt.

In January 1945 the Germans and Red Cross agreed that most of the Barneveld group could be transferred to Switzerland. This was in exchange for Red Cross ambulances and medicines My mother was desperate to get transferred but she was denied because of her husband's underground activities. Her documents had *Gestraft* meaning 'punished' on them. She appealed unsuccessfully against this decision because she had been born in Eastbourne. About 15% of the Barneveldt Jews were left behind in the camp and she was very disappointed.

After the camp was liberated on 9th May 1945 by the Russian army, the camp was taken over by the Red Cross. She was able to write to her father in London on 19 May 1945. We were sent on the second Dutch transport for Holland and arrived in Falkenau (German name for Sokolov) on the Czech–German border. She asked the Red Cross to send her to the UK and it fell on good ears. She was told there was a Red Cross ambulance with space for her and the three of us going to Pilsen with French wounded soldiers who were being repatriated to France. Pilsen was occupied by the Americans at that time – June 1945. On arrival in Pilsen we were put in an awful DP camp. The next morning they went to the airfield where they were refused entry and told to go back to the camp. My mother refused and demanded to see the garrison commander. He eventually allowed them to be billeted in an unused barrack in the garrison. He enabled her to contact two RAF pilots who agreed to take us to Croydon airport quite illegally. On arrival they just dumped us on the runway and flew off. Another plane landed whilst they were on the runway and a lot of people got off. I think they were British who had been interned in Europe when war was declared. We were all taken by coach from Croydon to Cannons Park in Stanmore where they were all debriefed in the RAF Reception Centre Stanmore. My mother tried to telephone her father but she only had his office number and his secretary said he had gone home for the day. So it was only the next day she was able to talk to him and he was astounded to hear from her after all that time and to know she was safely in England with his three grandsons.

When she was 80 I spoke about her at the celebrations. I queried why was it that my father, a highly educated academic and well known lawyer, chose this non-academic but vivacious young girl, to be his wife and the mother of his children. He must have perceived something very special in her. This was borne out by her heroism and resourcefulness in keeping the four of us safe during the war. She was truly a most remarkable woman.

Gerda Abraham

Hildegard Abraham met her future mother-in-law in 1967 in New York, having previously met her future husband, Henry, when she was a student in Heidelberg. They moved to England in 1972 because Hildegard's post with the UN was moved to London. Hildegard had enormous respect and affection for Gerda and sent me this piece.

Gerda Abraham hailed from an upper-middle-class Jewish family in Berlin. Her father had been a much-respected doctor and her mother belonged to an old-established Berlin Jewish family. She was born on 26 February 1911. In 1935 Gerda, then just 24 years old, emigrated with her husband Siegfried and young son Hans (later Henry born 23 September 1933) from their comfortable home in Hamburg to Amsterdam. Having set up a successful stock brokerage business again, Siegfried was able to make a decent living for the family, but soon enough storm clouds gathered on the horizon. In the wake of the Sudeten crisis in October of 1938, the family, now with a baby daughter, spent a few weeks with friends in North London, but – ever optimistic – decided to return to Amsterdam.

A year later, in the autumn of 1939, Poland had been invaded and the war was in full swing. In November Siegfried was able to obtain a passage for the family on the SS *Simon Bolivar* with the aim to emigrate to Chile. The day before the ship was supposed to set sail Hans fell ill with a throat infection and high temperature. The family doctor was called and advised Gerda how to get the temperature down, unsure whether to encourage them to risk going on an extended sea voyage with a sick child. 'You do not know what conditions will be like on the ship and whether there will be a doctor on board. Why don't you take the next ship?' The next day the child was better but the ship had left from Rotterdam only to run on two mines on the way to Harwich with the loss of about 100 people. The other passengers were saved but the *Simon Bolivar* sank. After that, there was, however, no other ship to leave for South America from Dutch shores.

At first the Abrahams lived in the smart southern part of the city, but with the invasion by the Nazis in May 1940 things soon turned increasingly unpleasant and dangerous. From the spring of 1942 onwards all Jews over the age of 6 had to wear the yellow star and the Abrahams were forced to move to a poor working class district in the east of Amsterdam, a kind of ghetto. The flat that had been assigned to them was so small that they were unable to fit in the large pieces of furniture they had brought from Germany. Their son, now about 9 years old, attended a Talmud-Torah school after all the other schools had become out of bounds for him. Gerda, insisting on Hans obtaining as good an education as possible, sent him for English lessons to another part of Amsterdam; on the way he had to clutch his satchel to hide the yellow star for fear he might be arrested. Siegfried lost his brokerage business, but wisely took the initiative to re-train as an electrician. Gerda looked after the family as best she could under the circumstances. Jews were allowed to shop only between 4 and 5 pm, and decent food was extremely hard to come by. What she was able to find was often stored under the false bottom in her daughter's pram, even after the little girl would have been perfectly able to walk! Why? Bought on the black market, of course! How risky was that!

Jews constantly lived in hope of being liberated by the Allies but reliable news was scarce – listening to the BBC, for instance, would have been met with the severest punishment. In the unofficial ghetto there was a simple restaurant on the ground floor of the block of flats where the Abrahams lived. The owner was a German married to a Dutch woman, yet he was apparently not a Nazi. Occasionally he would slip Gerda some eggs, butter or cheese. One day, he asked Gerda a favour; a group of Wehrmacht officers had reserved tables for that evening and the restaurant owner found himself short-staffed. 'Frau Abraham, you have to help me. I need a waitress!' Gerda was horrified – she, a Jewish woman, was supposed to serve her bitterest enemies who could have her arrested and deported? However, she was tempted. The man had promised her a supply of food in return for her services; besides, she hoped she would be able to eavesdrop on the conversation of the officers and learn something about how the war was going. She agreed to the proposal and, kitted out in a smart black dress, a white apron and a lace bonnet to cover her dark hair, she discharged her duties as a waitress serving the German officers without ever being discovered.

In 1944 Gerda's husband was away from the family home doing manual work at Schiphol Airport while Gerda looked after the children. One day in May there was a knock at the flat door: a German soldier had come to round up the family. She stalled him, saying she would have to wait for her husband who was doing vital work at the airport. 'Your husband is waiting for you where I'm going to take you,' she was told. Actually Gerda had been expecting to be picked up and was ready, her luggage packed, only what she and the children could carry; in any case there was nothing she could have done. Her most precious material possession had been sown into her corset – just in case! In the event, the two beautiful diamonds never changed hands.

At the police station where the soldier took them, they were indeed united with Siegfried. The interrogating officer enquired about the family's nationality, and without hesitation Siegfried replied that they were Haitians. In fact, a friend who lived in Liechtenstein had sent the family Haitian passports in 1942 that had, by this time, expired. Asked where his mother was Siegfried said that she was in Haiti, when she was actually in Theresienstadt. After a few days at the Westerbork camp the family were taken by train to Bergen-Belsen near Hanover. Bergen-Belsen had been established as a holding camp for exchange prisoners in 1943, ie Jewish inmates in possession of mainly South American passports. At that point in the war, with the continuous bloodletting on the Russian front, Germany was trying to repatriate ethnic Germans from South America and British territories in exchange for Jews.

While her husband was a member of a work detail taking tree stumps from the ground, Gerda was assigned to the 'shoe commando', where she had to take shoes apart so that the leather could be used again. Being resourceful and foresighted, she had taken a length of washing line and some clothes pegs along and she now undertook washing for wealthy Jewish inmates from North Africa who were not used to performing such menial tasks for themselves. This way she was able to augment the starvation ration for her children with an extra piece of bread or a potato.

It was a bitter cold and dreary day when on 19 January 1945 Josef Kramer, the Kommandant of Bergen-Belsen concentration camp, entered one of the barracks. He was accompanied by two seemingly important personages from Berlin who had wanted to see for themselves what conditions in the so-called 'preferential' camp were like. That morning, Gerda had deliberately busied herself within earshot of the visitors tidying the bunk beds, because she liked to know what was going on. So when in the gloom of the hut she heard a member of the visiting party say to Kramer, 'Is it possible to switch on the light? We can't see a thing!' Addressing Gerda he added, 'Go and turn on the light!', only to be interrupted by Kramer, 'She won't understand German.' 'Oh yes, I understand German perfectly well; after all, I am from Berlin!' retorted Gerda. 'And I would love to switch on the light but it is not possible because there is no electricity in here.' She immediately regretted having spoken out of turn.

'What? Is it true you let these people live here in darkness?' the SS officer snapped at Kramer. Gerda's heart sank; she realized that having embarrassed the Kommandant could cost her life once the visitors had departed. She thought better of it and added quickly, 'Oh, but we have candles' and went to fetch a couple of stubs from her bunk and lit them.

During her stay in the camp she was a constant source of strength and hope not only for her own family but for countless others around her. She would time and again, when despair took hold, utter the words, 'Don't worry, we will get out of here one day and will again enjoy a happy life!' On 19 January 1945 the camp inmates had to assemble in the early morning in freezing conditions. The Kommandant had been told to call up 450 prisoners with South American papers. His aide-de-camp proceeded to read out individual names when Kramer yelled at him to just call up the different nationalities and their number in order to speed up the process. As there were apparently only four Haitians present, the Abraham family were included in the German-American exchange transport that left the camp on 21 January 1945. However, only 301 people were declared fit for transport by the camp doctors.

After a circuitous stop-and-start train journey through all of Germany the train arrived at the Swiss border four days later to be greeted by the Swiss border police with fixed bayonets. Despite the pitiful condition of the Bergen-Belsen survivors, the Swiss saw fit to put them up in barns and stables in the St Gallen area and to feed them a totally unsuitable diet. Six people died on Swiss soil, fifteen people were not fit for transport, and the rest were expelled from the country after only five days. Gerda was quite ill so that the Swiss army doctor examining the expellees decreed that she would not be allowed to travel with her husband and children. She told him words to the effect, 'You do not seriously think that I am going to let my family travel without me after all we have been through, do you? We have survived the war so far together and we will stay together wherever we may have to go.' And so, the next morning she hid herself away until the last moment to get on the train which was to take the 90 remaining former Bergen-Belsen inmates to Marseille and on to an UNRRA camp called Philipp Ville in Algeria. They arrived on 10 February 1945 and stayed there until October 1945 when they went to Algiers. The family stayed in a cheap hotel until January 1946. Finally they boarded their ship but even then there was a catastrophe when a fire broke out on the ship the night before they landed in Baltimore. Fortunately the crew managed to put it out. In February 1946 they finally reached the United States and the end of their odyssey. Gerda died in New York in 2000.

Gerda, Siegfried and their two children survived the Holocaust, in no small measure due to the extraordinary courage and fortitude of this wonderful woman. She is remembered by all who had the privilege to know her with great admiration and fondness, and with a great sense of loss.

Ruth Abraham: *Kristallnacht*

Ruth Abraham was a courageous young woman. Blessed with Aryan looks and being quite tall, she was able to move around more easily than most Jewish women. I came across her when I was researching women getting their men out of Dachau after Kristallnacht. *Ruth's memoir was published in English with additions from her daughter Reha Sokolow.*

On 9 November 1938 Ruth Abraham was warned by Fritz, her sister Edith's husband, not to venture out: 'Ruth, Berlin is burning. The synagogue on Fasanenstrasse is burning.' He added 'It is very dangerous. Whatever you do, don't leave the apartment.' However she did not heed his advice.[125]

> His warnings fell on deaf ears. Berlin was burning; this was shocking horrible news. I knew I had to go and see this for myself, with my own

---

125 Sokolow and Ruth Abraham, *Defying the Tide* (Jerusalem: Gefen, 2013) pp.46–50

eyes. I needed to be there and felt that I would be all right, that nothing would happen to me, as I could easily pass as a German.

So, I quickly put on my coat and left, carefully locking the apartment, and walked in the direction of Kurfürstendamm, to the synagogue on Fasanenstrasse. I didn't have to walk very far. In just a few minutes, I was in the middle of everything.

Even from the distance I could see the fires and smell the smoke. I could hear a terrible noise, the breaking and cracking of glass. Everywhere, the fires colored the night sky with bright flashes of orange. And there was a stench, a smell of burning that hung heavily in the air. When I got close, I thought I was in the middle of a horrible dream. This couldn't be real. The synagogue was burning. But even in my worst nightmares, I couldn't imagine what it was that fed the flames, what made them jump so high into the sky. It was everything that was holy to us; our prayer books, our prayer shawls, our sacred Torah scrolls, had been thrown from the synagogue, like rubbish, into big piles in the middle of the street and then lit with fire. All around the bonfires, dancing like at a merry carnival of madness, were the Stormtroopers, the SS, and big important Nazis, with puffed up chests, and youngsters of the Hitler Youth.

Their shirts, which were usually so clean and pressed, were filthy with soot and sweat from the shameful and dirty work they had undertaken. They had wild looks on their faces. They were happy, laughing and shouting, singing horrible songs against the Jews. They seemed drunk – if not from liquor, then from the wild power they got from burning the Torah scrolls. It was clear to me that this was what they had been waiting for. And, when the fires were not strong enough, they found more items with which to feed the flames. Then they took their axes and started to hack at the synagogue, destroying more and more so that the ferocious fires would continue to burn.

When they were through with the prayer shawls and the scrolls, they attacked the Jewish shops. These they could identify because they were already painted with yellow stars of David and the word 'JUDE' in big angry-looking letters. That we already had gotten used to, as well as seeing the Nazis standing in front of the shops with their arms folded across their chests, blocking the doors so that everyone would be afraid to shop there. But this was a million times worse. Now the Nazis took up their axes and shattered all the windows of these stores. They went inside and smashed the merchandise. They were all over, everywhere, running riot – breaking glass, smashing things, looting, throwing everything they could from windows onto the street.

I was standing near a dry goods store that sold blankets and pillows. These, the Nazis slashed open. That image remains frozen in my memory: goose feathers floating in the sky. The air billowed with smoke until the whole street smelled like a barnyard of fire. Ironically, there was a certain beauty to this, like the fall of an early winter snow, the goose feathers floating slowly, slowly down.

For an instant, I thought of Walter several miles away in another part of Berlin and wondered if the Nazis were also destroying his store, his sofas and fancy pillows, and if the goose feathers were floating there too.

Ruth and Walter were just dating but she cared for him and thought he would be her husband. It was not until the next morning she heard from him.

He was calling from his furniture store – his former store. It had been completely destroyed during the night. He had gotten there very early in the morning, and even as he spoke on the phone, he said, the Stormtroopers (SS) were still around, and he was terrified of leaving the store by himself. He was helpless and in shock. He saw no escape without running into the SS. His business was ruined. There was nothing to salvage. He was paralyzed with fear.

He asked if I would do him a favour. Was it possible for me to come and help him leave his store? He thought that perhaps I could get past the SS because I looked German, and maybe we could walk out together. At first, this took me by surprise. What nerve, I thought, for him to ask such a thing of me. We had met only a few times, and we weren't even engaged. But then, this was a person in great need, and I couldn't refuse him.

I agreed to come. It took me about 30 minutes by subway, across town to get to Alexanderplatz, and to find Walter's store. It was like walking through a war zone. All around, businesses had been destroyed. There was shattered glass everywhere. I could hardly walk for all the glass. I went to the address that Walter had given me, and I found the building that once housed *Fechner und Preidel*, one of the finest furniture stores in Berlin. There was nothing left. It was like a bomb had exploded there. The furniture was hacked to pieces – firewood. Each room, which had once been decorated with fine china and elegant furnishings, was smashed to bits.

Where in all this mess would I find Walter? I called, 'Walter! Walter!' Only silence. Only overturned sofas, shattered lamps, dining room tables hacked to pieces. I almost gave up on finding him. Then finally I spotted him – in the back, in a corner, where the ceiling was still intact. He was crouched on the floor, hiding behind something that was not broken.

But he was broken. He was not the same. I reached him and gently shook his hand, like you lead a lamb or a small child. He was in shock. He didn't know how to get out, only that he hoped the Stormtroopers would not see us. Together, we stumbled out of the store. And he was silent, completely silent. Finally, after thanking me for having come to help him, he started mumbling, 'My mother, my mother.' He was worried about his mother. The first thing he wanted was not food or water or fresh clothes or even to return home. He wanted to see if his mother in Mannheim was safe.

We made our way to a public phone. Miraculously, he somehow got though, but Walter could hardly understand her words for all her crying. I could even hear the sobs from where I stood, a few feet away. She was crying with relief at hearing Walter's voice, overjoyed that he was not harmed, and she cried when she told Walter what had happened on *Kristallnacht* to her, to his father and to the Jews of Mannheim.

The Nazis had thrown rocks and rotten eggs at Walter's mother, Elsa. And they had taken Walter's father, Julius, with all the other Jewish men, to a place called Dachau. 'Please, please come,' Elsa Abraham begged her son. She sounded completely lost.

Walter went to Mannheim to his mother and later Ruth joined them. His mother was wretched because her husband had been taken to Dachau. They talked and talked realizing it was hopeless.[126]

I remember saying to Walter, 'It makes no sense to talk about what we cannot change. Let me make a suggestion. I will go to Dachau to try to get your father, Julius Abraham, released.'

First they thought I was joking, then they thought I was crazy. Finally, Walter and his mother, Elsa, understood that I was totally serious and determined. I meant it.

They said, 'Absolutely not'. They would not permit me to put my life in danger again. They wouldn't hear of it.

But I was headstrong, and having recently put myself into dangerous situations, I couldn't stop and go back. I had a strong feeling, an intuition, that I would be successful. I would go.

Late that afternoon of November 16, 1938, Walter and his mother took me to the station to catch the next train to Munich, the city closest to Dachau. They gave me the train fare and two pictures – one of Walter and one of his father.

It was to be another long train ride for me, about eight hours through the night. There I was, alone, frightened and travelling further and further away from the security of my home and family. I had left Mannheim without a word to my parents and sisters. In addition to my parents saying I was out of my mind again, they would certainly have forbidden me to go, and I couldn't take that chance.

When I arrived in Munich, it was raining. I asked someone where Dachau was. I was pointed to a bus depot right around the corner. There were many buses, and I easily found one that was marked 'Dachau'. I got on the bus and found a seat. Nobody asked me for money. Pretty soon, the bus filled up with people, including many Nazis in uniform. Finally, the door closed, and we were on our way.

In about twenty minutes, we approached the camp and I became very tense. The first thing I noticed, right by the entrance was an electric wire fence to prevent people from leaving Dachau. This in itself was terrifying. What if I got into Dachau and they kept me there? I tried

---

126 *Defying the Tide* pp.54–59

to look for other exits – in case I would have to escape – but I also remembered that I had to appear calm, like a proper German lady.

When I got off the bus, I was asked why I had come. Most likely, I was taken for the wife or girlfriend of someone who worked there. 'I want to see the *Kommandant* (commander),' I stated.

'Do you have an appointment?' 'No.' 'It's very difficult to get an appointment with the *Kommandant*. Come with me. I will announce you.'

I was led into a small room where the only things were gray desks and metal chairs. While I waited, I could see from the window the *appel,* the roll call was taking place behind the barbed wire. This was where the prisoners were made to line up to be counted every day. After a short time passed, the *Kommandant* entered the room. He was very polite.

'What do you want?' he asked. 'There is an old man, a sick man, named Julius Abraham,' I said, 'He is here in your camp. He never did anything wrong. I want to bring him back to his family.'

Since Dachau is much further from Allenstein than from Berlin, I wanted to impress him with the sincerity of my request, so I lied and said, 'I have come all this way from Allenstein, East Prussia.'

The *Kommandant* promised to look into the matter. He scribbled his phone number down on a card and handed it to me. 'Call me in three days,' he said. Then he quickly turned and walked out of the room.

I was left standing there. The first thing I felt was great relief. At least the *Kommandant* hadn't laughed in my face or asked me why this old man was any of my business. I was still free! And, just as important, he hadn't automatically said no to my request.

But my relief lasted for only a moment, as there I was, by myself, in a dreadful place where I was a total stranger, without so much as a change of clothes. When I went outside, the rain was coming down even heavier than before. I walked right out of Dachau, through the front gate, but I didn't know where I would go and what I would do with myself, with three days to wait. My shoes and stockings were soaking wet.

Just then, a small car drove out of the gate. The driver was trying to get my attention. '*Fraulein* (young lady),' said the man in the car, 'hop in.'

At this point, I thought getting dry was more important than anything in the world, and I wanted human company. What would I do by myself hanging around Dachau for three days? I had no idea. But I was not the kind of young lady who could allow herself to just be picked up, right off the street. I knew the dangers of such things.

I said, 'If you're looking for a good time, then you've got the wrong person. Think again, I'm Jewish.'

'Don't worry,' the man said. 'I heard everything. I was in the room next to the *Kommandant's*. Please get in.'

I took a chance and got into the car. What else should I have done – stand there and get soaked for three days? I was surprised to see he wasn't wearing a uniform, and there was something about him that looked more compassionate than menacing.

He turned to me, suddenly very serious. 'What I do here can never be made good,' he said. 'But I want to help you.'

He said his name was Josef Müller. It was a name I would never forget. Josef Müller took me back to Munich. 'You're not permitted to go to a hotel here,' he said. 'You can, if you like, stay all night at my place of business. But you would have to leave early in the morning. Otherwise, I can take you to the Jewish-owned *Pension Spier* at St.Pauls-Platz.'

She chose the *Pension Spier*. Before he took her there he showed her the Munich beer cellar where Hitler started his 'maniacal speeches'. She had heard of it but never expected to go there. '...since I was always bold and somewhat curious, I did not turn down this invitation.' Afterwards he took her to the *pension*. A somewhat frosty reception melted when she mentioned Josef Müller.

Whoever this Josef Müller was, he must have been kind to the Jews. Or perhaps it was that whatever he did at Dachau was so awful that he tried to make up for it whenever he was outside the camp. Whatever it was, mentioning his name worked. They had a room for me.

For the next three days, except for going to the farmers' market and occasional walks around the area, I stayed in my room until it was time for me to call the *Kommandant*.

Finally, the day came. I called the *Kommandant*. He said 'Go to the Munich train station tonight and look for Julius Abraham.'

I went there and saw an old man in a striped prison uniform with his head shaved. He looked lost and confused. I knew from the photo that this was Walter's father. Julius Abraham had never met me, so to assure him that he was safe with me, I showed him the photographs that Walter's mother had given me. But he wouldn't even look at them. He had spent less than two weeks in Dachau, but already he was a broken man.

I knew he was in shock, but still I expected something – a small smile even for my rescuing him from that awful place. But nothing. No smile. No curiosity. No reaction at all.

I led him to the train platform, which was filled with soldiers. It must have appeared to them that I was a German woman helping an old Jewish prisoner, and this they did not like. They began spitting at me. 'Aren't you ashamed to keep company with such scum?' they hissed. What they would have done or said if they had known that I was Jewish too, I can only shudder to think.

During the long train ride back to Mannheim, Julius Abraham was totally silent. He didn't ask me a single question, not who I was or why I had rescued him. He was in a completely different world.

Our reunion back in Mannheim was bittersweet. One moment, they were happy to see a Jew rescued from Dachau; the next moment, they shed tears for those who remained there.

But Walter was overwhelmed. He and his mother could not believe it. I, myself, couldn't believe it. Our sages say that if you save one life, it is as though you have saved the entire world. I felt then as if I had done something quite miraculous. I had the feeling that Walter would propose marriage to me. I think his mother probably encouraged him to do so. And I was right.

On November 19, 1938, Walter proposed. With his father back home, Walter believed he could now leave Mannheim. We returned to Berlin together, an engaged couple. Now we would fight together.

Before we left Mannheim, I called Josef Müller to thank him for all he had done for me. He had shown me kindness, had given me support and hope by assuring me that if the *Kommandant* would not release Julius, then he would find a way to help me. He also told me that if I ever needed help again, he would be there for me.

I gave him my address in Berlin.

Marianne Wachstein: Ravensbrück

Ravensbrück, was the only predominantly women's camp. Marianne's story was important to me because she had written a surviving document outlining her grievances against the camp and was ultimately a victim of the Nazis' euthanasia programme.

Marianne Wachstein was born in Vienna as Marianne Kobler on 11 November 1895. She arrived in Ravensbrück on 27 July 1939 in a transport of 20 women. There were three Jewish women. Two were classified as *Rassenschande* (race contaminators). Wachstein was described as a 'political Jewess' and a *Simulantin-Jüdin* (malingerer –Jewess) and registered as number 2004/508. She was 44 years old and the mother of two sons. She had married Isak Ignatz Wachstein in 1917. He was born in 1883 near Lublin in Poland and was deported to Minsk where he was murdered around December 1941. Her story is unique because her uncensored report of what happened to her in Ravensbrück between May 1939 and February 1940 has survived to tell her terrible story, as she would have wished.

She arrived in Ravensbrück from a prison in Vienna. She was unconscious when she was put on the transport wearing only a nightdress and sandals. She claimed when she woke on the train, she thought it was a dream. She was pleased to learn she was going to a mental institution *(Nervenheilanstalt)* because of her mental and physical state. She soon realized the train was leaving Austria and going to Germany. Later she was beaten badly by one of the guards because she did not understand his order to stand up and this resulted in memory loss. She could neither walk nor stand when they arrived at Ravensbrück and was excused both work and *Appell* (roll-call). She was fortunate that a woman she knew from Vienna helped her get her memory back.

During the ten months she was there, Marianne was twice sentenced to solitary confinement in the prison. The first time she was sentenced to forty-two days in August 1939. She had refused to sign a document without reading it and was angry when the SS refused to allow it. She was put in a straitjacket by the head warden's deputy, Emma Zimmer and by a man who was a driver from the camp. She lay there for hours, had a screaming fit and lost consciousness. She woke to find herself lying in her excrement. She was sentenced to three weeks for her behaviour in the office and a further three weeks for soiling the cell and screaming.

After that period she was placed in a cell with an insane woman, who attacked her. She begged to leave the cell, which happened after two-an-a half days.

On 10 February a physician ordered her to attend the *Appelle*. The doctor refused to examine her when she asked him because she wanted to prove she could not stand at the *Appelle*. In desperation Marianne told the doctor and nurse she would tell the world the way people were being treated in the concentration camp. She was violently ejected from the room but repeated her threat in front of other prisoners. In her own barracks she told her co-prisoners what had happened and said it was the doctor's duty to examine her as a Jewish prisoner as he examined Aryans, because he had taken an oath as a doctor.

She was accused of slandering the state and its leaders and was again sentenced to twenty-eight days solitary. She was taken to the camp prison where she was left in a dark, frozen room for four days. On 23 February 1940 she was transferred to Vienna for interrogation. The journey took two weeks with various stops in Berlin and Plauen in Vogtland, where she was well treated. After a few months, when she wrote her report, she was returned to Ravensbrück. She was executed on 27 February 1942. It was only on 22 January 1943 that the Red Cross in Geneva was notified.

The report was dated 12 April 1940 and was addressed to The Honourable, Mr *Hofrat,* Dr Wilhelm. (A *Hofrat w*as a Court Counsellor.) Marianne Wachstein's Report is reproduced as written in translation.[127]

In the above-mentioned matter I allow myself respectfully to report about the following:

To begin with, I have to say the following in order to clarify the issue. The concentration camp Ravensbrück near Fürstenberg in Mecklenburg is a forced labour camp (*Zwangsarbeitslager*).

The labour that I saw women perform there, I myself have a nervous disease (*Nervenkrank*) and am therefore unable to work, is for example: there are two stone road rollers, a so-called small one and a big one. The road rollers have ropes attached to a handle. The women had to grab the handle and pull the road roller. Alternatively, they had to shovel

---

127 Irith Dublon-Knebel Ed., in *A Holocaust Crossroads: Jewish Women and Children in Ravensbrück* (London: Vallentine Mitchell, 2010)

sand, and other sand in wood boxes lying on a wooden base that had to be carried away etc. During the summer, the work hours were nine hours a day, on Saturday until noon.

Three times a day, the roll-call takes place, on Saturday and Sunday twice, that means that the whole camp has to stand. Each block (in one block there are about 140–150 people living in a wooden barrack) in front of its barrack, in groups of four women standing one behind the other erect and rigid like soldiers. They have to stand still with their hands pressed against their body, until the *Frau Oberin* [head guard] or one of the *Frau Aufseherinnen* [female guards] counts them. That means that the person responsible for the block announces the number of the women. Each *Appell* [roll-call] takes about twenty minutes.

The camp consists of seventeen barracks, each has room for about 150 persons. One barrack is a Jewish barrack. In addition, there is a prison-barrack built in 1940, which is still very humid. I, for example, stayed in solitary confinement in this building in cell 15. It was so damp that the wall with the window was covered with black mould stains.

In solitary confinement it is forbidden, with the exception of a few prisoners, to occupy oneself it any way, it is forbidden to read or write, nothing, just to sit the whole day on a small chair, there is not even a walk [for exercise].

Just before I was transferred (on February 23.2.40) from Ravensbrück over here to Vienna to the L.G. I was again sentenced to confinement for twenty-eight days, again totally unjustified. Detention in Ravensbrück consists of:

1. A hard bed
2. Food only every four days, the same ration as those who receive food every day which is approximately in quantity and quality similar to the food distributed here. On the three remaining days only the bread ration (about as much as we receive here) and twice a day black coffee (it is forbidden to drink the water there because it causes diarrhoea).
3. In a damp totally dark prison-cell worse than the above-mentioned from summer 1940. During the day the toilet and the sink can be seen.
4. Unheated (although the weather there is harsh and this winter is especially tough). I was confined there only four days out of the twenty-eight. At five o'clock God took me out of there by transporting me here. The first two days it was not heated at all, on the third and fourth day it was heated according to my estimation for one hour, hence insufficient.
5. Without any, even the smallest possibility of occupying oneself.
6. Without a walk.

This together, is defined by the small word 'Arrest'.

I got this detention as follows. When I was brought to the camp a physician examined each of the new arrivals, based on his examination he discharged me from standing at the *Appell*. I was allowed to sit during the *Appell* and I was discharged from work too. This physician was even so humane that he ordered me to wash in cold water three times a day (*Abwaschungen*). Because of my agitation I could hardly walk or stand. One day I was brought before a new doctor who deprived many others of the discharge cards. At that time the discharged people stayed in the barrack and did not take part in the roll-call outside. It was the depths of winter. When I entered the room, the physician told me harshly without even examining me: 'You have to attend the *Appell*.' This happened on Saturday, 10 February 1940. Because I have a nervous disease, it is impossible for me to stand for such a long period of time, because [standing] three times [a day at the *Appell*] means about an hour every day, I can't [stand] even 20 minutes. Therefore, I asked the doctor to examine me, because it was impossible for me to do it. He answered by shouting: 'You will attend your roll-call.' I answered that it was impossible for me and asked again to be examined. In spite of my requests to be examined he insisted that I had to stand and said something rude and disparaging about 'Jews', and the nurse sitting behind the desk followed with a jeering smile. In my distress, I answered: 'I will tell [people] abroad how one is treated in a concentration camp.' Upon that, the dark army physician grabbed my back and threw me violently out of the room without performing even the slightest examination. My ribs hurt but I said quietly; 'I will report that too.' Outside in the corridor, however, I screamed loudly in my pain because of the treatment and my ribs, that I would tell it everywhere. This happened in front of many prisoners, because usually every Saturday in Ravensbrück many prisoners stand (I was sitting) from 8 o'clock until noon [in order to receive medical treatment] and after that many are not treated, the nurse just comes out and says: 'Go home and come back next Saturday.'

A prisoner from hall B of the Jewish barrack called 'Rike' told me she had heard about the incident. I do not know who the many prisoners standing there were.

I was brought back to the barrack and talked about the incident in front of several prisoners in hall B of the Jewish barrack, and the *Stubeälteste* [hall-elder] Fräulein Hertl (or something like that) and the *Blockälteste* [block-elder] Fraulein Paula Keuselmeyer, both Aryans. I also said that: 'The physician has taken his oath and must examine me, the Jew, just as he examines an Aryan woman when he checks if she is fit or not.'

My excitement was only natural because when I was in solitary confinement and fainted, *Aufseberin* Frau Zimmer spilled water on me through the opening where the food is pushed in, and when this did not help she ordered the prisoner Frau Kaiser (everybody knows her, she counts the prisoners daily before they leave for work) who is no longer in the camp, to hit me through the same opening with a broom stick. When I woke up from the blows I received – I was wet all over and had to stay in the cold winter in a wet dress and wet slippers (in solitary confinement there are no shoes) for several days, the heating was not working and nothing dried. By the way, Frau Zimmer did not turn on the heating in my cell for days. I even did not know that it functioned and only when the guards changed and Frau Mandl came she asked me if I was warm and turned on the heating. Furthermore, I saw a young girl from the other barrack (a Gypsy) who had to stand in spite of what I thought was ongoing epileptic seizures. Frau Schenck from our Jewish-barrack *(Judenblock)* had seizures as well with terrible spasms and later stiffening of the limbs, and she too had to stand. Because all my life I have fainted when I stand for a long time, I was naturally very afraid if standing at the *Zählappell* (roll-call count) especially now because of everything I had been though since the coup, I find it even harder to stand because my knees do not hold me.

She then gives a long list of people who would be witnesses that on 10 February 1940 she only spoke about the doctor and his duty towards her. It is not clear if these people had agreed to be named.

Because of what I said I was accused of slandering the state and I think also the leaders, One of the 'colleagues' went to an *Aufseberin* who interrogated me, later I was interrogated by the *Frau Oberin* and on the same day I was put in solitary confinement.

In order to prove that I was not trying to dodge the freezing cold [during the *Appelle*], *I suggested to the Blockälteste* Fräulein Kemmelmayer that I should sit during the *Zahlappele* outside.

About a week later, I was brought from solitary confinement to the director. I could not walk in the slippers fast enough because of my nervous disease and my agitation. The *Aufseberin* (name unknown, she was the one who took me on 10.2.1940 to the solitary confinement) grabbed me from behind and pushed me the whole way. I stumbled, lost the slippers and was about to fall and asked: 'Please not so fast, slower please.' The Herr director screamed at me immediately: 'What did you shout?' although I spoke in a quiet tone, because over there I am always afraid. The way led through the hall. I answered quietly that I hadn't shouted. The Herr Director read to me from a piece of paper that on 10.2.1940 in the barrack I had slandered the state and I think the leadership too. I answered politely that I had only spoken, as I mentioned before, about the incident and what I had said about the doctor's oath. Upon that, the director took the file that was lying in front of him and hit me several times on the hands. I realized that I was not allowed to defend himself. Two days later I was brought to the *Frau Oberin* answered: 'You got that [the punishment] from the Herr director.' And immediately they took me to the arrest without considering that my feet were bleeding and frozen and that I was so emaciated that every single rib could be counted, in some places my skin was hanging like an empty sack, my feet are thin and get very swollen in the morning and when I stand up (I don't know if the flesh is already fluid or if the tissues have fluids in them). My flesh has come loose from the bones and on my face and throat too and the deterioration is evident. I served four days out of the 28 days I was sentenced to. On the fifth day, thanks to almighty God, I was transported to Vienna. The first two days there was no heating at all, the third and fourth day the heating was on for about an hour and of course that was not enough at all. Although I am a tough person, I was desperately freezing sitting the whole day with chattering teeth, starving, in complete darkness with bleeding feet. The light could very easily be turned on from the outside.

On the way, when I had to wait three and a half days in Berlin's prison on Alexanderplatz and 14 days in Plauen in Vogtland, because there was no room in the prison vehicle, I was lucky to meet noble physicians and *Aufseherinnen*. The doctor in Berlin gave me special dressings with ointment for the frostbite. The *Frau Aufseherin* in Plauen gave me ointment and dressings for both legs as ordered by the doctor and special daily baths for my feet. The wounds on my toes and feet healed and today only the skin is sensitive in some places and in other places there are small scabs. In Berlin and Plauen (I think it was court prison), I received a lot of very good food. In the morning two slices of real rye bread, butter or delicate sugar marmalade, so much that enough was left over for the coffee. In spite of that, I can't recover. I had already been, I think it was on 28 August 1939 (the date I remember because two days earlier I read in the barrack about the non-aggression agreement with Russia),[128] in solitary confinement for 42 days with an intermission of two-and-a-half days after being confined to the barrack for four days, because, as a colleague told me, two [prisoners] refused to work anymore. It is the custom in Ravensbrück to punish the whole block for the conduct of an individual.

She then describes an earlier incident in August 1939 when she received the first solitary confinement sentence of 42 days for the following incident:

I was brought into an office where they gave me some printed pages which I had to sign. I asked to read the pages prior to signing them and I was told it was only about leaving the country. Even then I did not want to sign without reading and because they were forcing me to sign, I said outright that I would not sign without reading and that I did not need any help. So help me God the communists would take revenge for what was happening to us. Upon that, I was put in dark-arrest (*Dunkel-Arrest*) which, during that time was still half-dark. Shortly after that, the windows were boarded up from outside and it became completely dark. This was the first time I was arrested and I did not know what it meant. Shortly after I was put inside, *Frau Aufseherin* Zimmer opened the door again, a man in uniform was beside her and he

---

128 The pact was signed on 23 August 1939.

shouted: 'You will rot away, starve, you will not get out alive.' (I later heard it must have been the driver of the men in the camp (soldiers)). Because I am a believer I answered quietly: 'If God wants me to die I will die here.' The man went away and the *Aufseherin* locked up. About an hour later the *Aufseherin Frau* Zimmer opened the door, asked me to step out, and in the corridor asked me to undress except for an undergarment, she then put me in a straightjacket (this is a favourite punishment in Ravensbrück). My hands were [fastened] so tight that about 14 days later my right hand was still swollen. My body was also tightly bound, near the neck too. Then I was put back in the cell and lay on the floor like a package. I did not struggle but lay submissive and quiet for an hour in my cell. That can be confirmed by the witnesses that I will name later. Because I was tied up so hard, I felt nauseous. I fainted and supposedly had a screaming fit. Somebody shook me and I woke up. Mr Chill [or Sill] stood in front of me (he is supposed to be a *Hauptsturmführer,* but I am not familiar with the different ranks)....

He hit me hard with his fist on the nose. For many weeks I felt the pain, he kicked me two or three times on my bare thigh and the *Aufseherin Frau* Zimmer grabbed me roughly from behind by the hair. My body, my hands were hurting because of being tied up so hard; all that [happened to me] a helpless tied-up package. Again I lost consciousness. Late in the evening, I woke up haunted by the pain, dirty from my own excrement.

I cannot reproduce her Report fully here but I was able to establish some background when the Jewish genealogy website *Geni* put me in touch with her grandson, Claude Thau. He is the son of her daughter Fritzi born 26 January 1920 who died on 28 February 1999 in Pacific Palisades, California. According to Claude she committed suicide aged 79, whilst she was in good health, but fearing what the future might bring.

His two uncles were Julius (1923–1950) – Claude said he met him briefly when he was two years old – and Ernest Vastene (1921–1998) whom Claude knew well. His wife, Hélène, who was Claude's father's daughter from his first marriage, is still alive in a nursing home in Paris. Ernest and his wife were stamp dealers on the Champs Elysée.

Claude says his grandfather, Marianne's husband, was called Isidor Isaac Wachstein (but he is Ignatz on the wedding certificate and also sometimes Izchak). He was born Korolovka in Poland on 5 December 1883 which was close to the border with Ukraine. Claude believes he was sent to the Minsk ghetto 28 November 1941. He says that everyone in the Minsk ghetto, which was the third largest, was killed at nearby Maly Trostinec on 30 July 1942. (I wrote about Maly Trostinec in connection with Otto Deutsch's family in *Who Betrayed the Jews?*)

I asked him about Marianne's background and illness but he was unable to help. 'I've been wondering about the illness since I read her report in Irith's book, which was the first I ever learned about her report or that she had been temporarily released from Ravensbrück.' He did not think his mother ever knew that either.

Claude explained that Marianne was released from Ravensbrück to testify in a trial in Vienna and was in hospital in Vienna at this time. She wrote her report that 'she expected that higher-level authorities would take action to end mistreatment at Ravensbrück if they knew what was happening'.[129]

Claude sent me a translation of the transcript dating 16 November 1939 about the trial. It states it is to the Ministry of Finance in Vienna and has a reference ReZ1. 17.854–6/39.[130]

> In criminal proceedings against Isaak Wachstein and affiliates on a suspicion of committing fraudulent actions and usury.
>
> In reply to your inquiry of November 10th 1939, following is stated: Isaak Wachstein is (remanded) in custody. For Isaak Wachstein and his wife Marianne Wachstein are currently standing accused of suspected fraud and usury.
>
> On May 6th 1938 Johann Wadura, a sawmill owner in Steinwandleiten 21, St. Veit an der Gölsen, filed a criminal complaint against the accused. Wadura asserted to have taken damage as a result of a fraudulent delivery of machines and was heard witness on August 5th 1938. His statements remained fundamentally unchanged and he decided to join in the criminal proceedings as a private party with a total amount of 15,000S. Due to considerable number of documents in the court record and the fact of them being currently under scrutiny by expert witness Hans Siegl, I would like to ask for permission to refrain from forwarding the court record.
>
> District Court Vienna.

Claude also sent me a transcript of a 'Verdict' from the Central Office of the Secret State Police Vienna dated 24 October 1938. It states:

> VERDICT
> In accordance with 2. Regulation on the Act of Reunification of Austria and the German Reich of 18.3.1938 RGBI. I.S. 262 read in conjunction with the Decree of the Reichsführer-SS and the Chief of the German Police and Ministry of the Interior as of 23.31938, C.D.S.B. Nr. 150/38; it is ruled for the entire assets of Isaak Isidor Wachstein, Jewish, and his wife Marianne Wachstein to be seized and his real property to be confiscated to the benefit of the Land of Austria.
>
> 1. Wien 13., Breitenseerstrasse Nr. 56, reference No 209 in the Land Register of Hietzing district.
> 2. Wien 6., Getreidemarkt Nr.1 and Papagenogasse Nr.1a, reference No 209, K.P.205 in the Land Register of Mariahilf district.

---

129 Claude Thau, email to author 7 September 2017.
130 Claude Thau, email to author 10 September 2017, various legal documents attached.

3. Wien 9., Grüne-Torgasse Nr.16 and Müllnergasse Nr.15, reference No 1307 and 1310 (repectively) in the Land Register of Alsergrund district.
4. Wien 10., Dampfgasse Nr. 4/6 and Laxenburgerstrasse Nr. 12, reference No 954, 2211, 2205, 2297 and 2298 in the Land Register of Favoriten district and
5. Municipality of Ueschendorf, reference No 410 in the Land Register of Neunkirchen.

All assets and rights of property will be passed on to the Land of Austria as of October 24th 1938.

Based on this verdict, which is enforceable at law, following is ruled:

The title of ownership in all Land Registers and cadastres (a comprehensive register of property) to be changed in favour of the Land of Austria.

Every right and claim of any third party to assets and properties is terminated.

No legal remedies against this verdict are permitted.

In attendance Dr. Pifrader. Attested by: Member(s) of legal staff.

Dr Pifrader was a veteran of World War I, who joined the Nazi party in 1931. He had studied law in Innsbruck in the early 1930s and that was how he came to be working for the State police as an administrative lawyer. After a period in Riga, he went to Berlin in 1943 where he received 'the German Cross' in silver for his services in arresting Claus von Stauffenberg (see page 201).

At the end of her *Report,* Marianne wrote: 'As for the matter 104c Vr 278/39 I feel that I am guilty, also regarding the matter of the machine'. Claude had written to me:

In her report, she was laser-focused on the treatment of detainees in Ravensbrück. It is amazing to me that she makes no mention of her family in her report. Her self-control was extremely strong.

My mother had told me when I was young, that she had visited her parents in a local Viennese jail once, which I had found surprising. That may be explained by the fact, which I had not known at that time, that there was going to be a trial. The property was seized in October 1938, but Marianne remained in the Viennese prison until July 1939. Perhaps Isidor continued to be held there while Marianne was sent to Ravensbrück. My mother had thought that her father was also sent to Ravensbrück and died, but Renee Steinig told me there was a report, written on Yad Vashem in 1957, that he died in Auschwitz. However, the attorney I hired to look into the trial told me that Isidor Wachstein was sent to Minsk on November 28, 1941, according to a letter he found that my mother's younger brother wrote on November 28, 1941. The attorney noted that the last surviving members of the Minsk ghetto were killed at Maly Trostinec on July 30, 1942 so he figured that Isidor was killed then, unless he died earlier.

I also asked Claude about Dr Wilhelm, to whom the *Report* was addressed. All he knew was that he was the head of the facility where Marianne was held during the trial. He put her *Report* in his desk, where it was found after the war.

The Librarian at the Wiener Library found a reference to Stolpersteine in Vienna at the property listed at No.2 on the 'Verdict' Wien 6, Getreidemarkt 1/12 which records her deportation and that she was killed at Bernburg, where the euthanasia programme was undertaken.

Marianne so wanted her story to be heard by the outside world. I hope that the soul of this unfortunate woman would be pleased to know it is published here. She was a particularly vulnerable victim of the Nazis' barbarity. The fact that she was killed as part of the *14f13* euthanasia scheme, makes our remembrance of her even more important. So many of the thousands of such victims were voiceless.

Community Leaders

Gisi (Gisela) Fleischmann (1892–1944)

I came across Gisi Fleischmann when I first started researching women leaders in the Holocaust. She was mentioned during the Eichmann Trial in 1961 and one of her colleagues Oscar Neumann (1894–1981), the head of the Zionists in Slovakia, wrote a brief biography for WIZO in 1970. She was described as 'one of the most outstanding Jewish personalities in Slovakia as well as throughout Europe ... she was widely known for her devotion, courage and rectitude'.[131]

Gisi Fleischmann's name appears in the Proceedings of the Eichmann Trial. According to the Court in Section XI:

> Mrs. Fleischmann's assignment who, at risk of her life, forwarded to addresses abroad the first authenticated eye-witness reports on the massacres and the use of gas. It was she who organized the rescue of Polish Jews to Slovakia. She was arrested twice and managed to be released; she did not heed repeated appeals to her to escape to Hungary and join her children in Palestine. She stayed on, unwavering. She was arrested while fulfilling her task, writing her last report, which was to be sent abroad. During the short time of her arrest, Gisi Fleischmann displayed the same courage, the same contempt of death, which had characterized her throughout her work. Gisi Fleischmann earned a special place of honour among the great women of Jewish history as a noble and wise women, warmhearted, courageous, truly a Woman of Valour!
>
> ... at her meeting with Brunner [Alois][132] at which he asked her for details about her contacts with Jewish organizations abroad and assured her that then nothing would happen to her. Her answer is: 'I would do

---

131 Leni Yahil, *The Holocaust* (Oxford: OUP, 1991) p.232
132 Alois Brunner (1912–2001 or 2010) was an Austrian SS officer who worked as Adolf Eichmann's assistant. Brunner is held responsible for sending over 100,000 European Jews to their deaths in ghettos and internment camps in eastern Europe.

that gladly, if I was sure that this would help my poor brethren; but just to save myself is not worth that much to me.' Brunner's reply was: 'You better watch out Fleischmann! Even if nobody else is taken away from here, I'll make sure that you are sent to Auschwitz by a special train!'

According to the Proceedings, Gisi Fleischmann attempted to escape but this was foiled by Brunner. She was deported to Auschwitz and taken to the gas chamber. On 8 January Eichmann sent a telegram to SS officer Kurt Becher saying:

> The Jewess Gisi Fleischmann was caught by the Slovak police in the act of composing an atrocity report about Slovak measures against Jews, addressed to a Swiss Jew of the Joint, despite the fact that she, that Jewess, had been assigned by Brunner to the task of trust of looking after the Jewish detainees. Moreover, the Jewess Fleischmann had also told the Swiss Consul in Pressburg [Bratislava] that the Germans were already so badly off as to require the economic assistance of the Jews.'[133]

Gisi was born in Pressburg (now Bratislava) the capital of Slovakia. She was the eldest of three children but the other two were boys, so her parents did not bother to educate her. They ran a kosher hotel and restaurant in the city. The Jews spoke both German and Hungarian and with the creation of the Czech Republic in 1918, 26-year-old Gisi became a citizen of a state whose language she couldn't speak.

Oscar Neumann, had a special role among the Zionists – he was in charge of the ÚŽ's (Jewish Centre) retraining department which enabled him to give help to the Zionist youth movements, which were now illegal.[134] He opened his brief biography:[135]

> She was then in her middle forties, the mother of two adolescent girls. Although she had been born in an orthodox family living in the Jewish quarter – with its ghetto atmosphere – of Bratislava, whose pride was the rabbinical authorities amongst its ancestors, she was an enlightened woman who knew how to make the most of her appearance, not out of vanity but in order to be accepted as a person of standing. She had great feminine charm, a profound knowledge of people, and much tolerance and compassion. Intelligent and well-informed, she was a first-class speaker able to hold an audience of thousands, and also knew when to keep silent and how to influence individuals privately. At the cost of her family life, and of her own survival, she devoted herself entirely to her work for the community.

---

133 The Eichmann Trial, *Record of the Proceedings* (Jerusalem: The Ministry of Justice, 1992) Section 50, p.910
134 Yehuda Bauer, *Jews For Sale?* (New Haven: Yale UP, 1994) p.70
135 Neumann p.7

Her most notable feature was her large, expressive eyes – inherited from her mother, Jetty Fischer, a Jewish matriarch of the type immortalised by Jewish writers. The family owned a popular kosher restaurant, on the premises of which the local Zionist organisation held its meetings; the two sons had joined it as students and became active in it. Through these meetings, and through the early Zionist literature, their sister Gisi also became familiar with Zionist ideology.

In 1915 she had married a wealthy man, Josef Fleischmann (1886–1942) and had two daughters – Alice born 1917 and Judith born 1920. At this time Gisi encountered Zionism and whilst the Orthodox community did not favour Zionism, her parents let their children use their kosher restaurant as the HQ for local Zionists. Neumann wrote some of the orthodox women objected to the Zionists raising funds to send abroad feeling the local poor were being deprived.

Gisi's public life began when she joined WIZO in the late 1920s and she quickly became Vice-Chair. In that capacity she started organising social work, educational activities and pioneer training in Slovakia. Wizo had a big impact on the Jewish women of Slovakia:

> ...it succeeded in recruiting Jewish women for Jewish social work and for Zionism. It achieved a certain revolution in their assimilated provincial lives, and brought them from the narrow environment of local charity work into the field of international Zionist and general activities.[136]

As early as 1933 the branch of WIZO that Gisi ran had to deal with Jews fleeing from Nazi Germany. Initially they had no idea that these problems would occur in Slovakia but gradually Gisi learnt to deal with these demands. She discovered her leadership skills, as she attended international conferences where she met other Jewish women leaders from other countries. She helped refugees fleeing Germany and after 1938 from Austria. Her efforts to help re-train them led to her becoming involved with the American Jewish Joint Distribution Committee (JDC or 'Joint') in Prague.

The JDC was created in 1914 to save Jews in Palestine, under the Ottoman Turkey, from starvation. Its initial purpose was to support Jews in eastern Europe and the near East during World War I. The work continued as the Russian revolution and the upheaval following the war impacted on Jews in eastern Europe. The rise of the Nazis led more funding to be sent to help German Jews and thousands were helped to leave Germany and Europe in the pre-war years.[137] The JDC still operates.

---

136 Neumann p.9
137 USHMM, *American Jewish Joint Distribution Committee and Refugee Aid*, accessed 12 October 2017, https://www.ushmm.org/wlc/en/article. php?ModuleId=10005367

Gisi then became the Joint's representative in Slovakia. Her visits to Paris and London in March 1939, to try to get visas proved fruitless as Jews were not given entry in these countries. However, in London Mrs. Rebecca Sieff, President of WIZO, held a large reception in her home to raise funds. Gisi spoke about the situation in Slovakia.

> While she was in London, even at this time, the WIZO Executive and friends advised Gisi to stay there instead of returning Slovakia. She refused to consider the possibility: she had come not to save herself but to look for ways and means of saving others. She wore herself out, going from the embassy of one overseas state to another in her search for countries to which people might be able to emigrate. All her efforts produced little result. The world had shut its doors against the victims of the Nazi persecution.[138]

A while later she was back in Paris for a JDC Conference and was therefore unable to attend WIZO's world conference in Geneva, held in August 1939. 'The 'Joint' was relying on her for their work in Slovakia, and she prioritised this. Despite great difficulties, she returned home from Paris, which involved a long detour following the start of the Second World War. She resumed her work.'

At that time Slovakia had many Jews from the neighbouring countries, including people without documents who were stranded in Bratislava. 300–400 people had been rescued from a camp at Sosnowitz, near Będzin, in Upper Silesia. They had to be looked after and required onward emigration before the authorities returned them across the border as 'undesirable aliens'.

Youngsters turned to Zionism and one of Gisi's colleagues wrote 'During the first one and a half years of the war we developed a huge network of training-farms for Eretz Israel, and also strong youth movements, much better and stronger than in normal times.'

In May 1940, the Slovak Zionist Organisation held its first conference and Gisi was elected to the Executive but on 29 September 1940, without any advance warning, the Slovak authorities ordered all Jewish organisations to be dissolved. In a letter she wrote two years later, Gisi summed up the situation:

> Our offices were sealed and what assets we had were confiscated. All our papers were seized by the authorities and work on behalf of the National Fund came to a full stop. This also applies to the strong Wizo organisation, and to the Maccabi sports organisation; its rooms and equipment were confiscated for other purposes. And so we were proscribed and had to stop all the various activities which we had been developing. It goes without saying that we nevertheless tried to maintain contact between the members of the organisation by means of emissaries, which was dangerous and not always easy.[139]

---

138 Neumann p.13
139 Neumann p.15

Soon after, the Nazis set about establishing a Central Jewish Office (*Judenrät*):

It was obvious that the Central Jewish Office was intended to reassure the Jews by leaving the execution of the measures to be taken against them apparently in their own hands. The Executive of the Slovak Zionist Organisation met to discuss whether they should cooperate with the new institution. Gisi Fleischmann was strongly in favour of cooperation, in order to attempt to save whatever was not yet lost.

In the letter quoted above Gisi wrote: 'Although we were faced with a difficult situation through the fact that the power was in the hands of the orthodox majority, which was to our disadvantage, we got two important people on to the Council of the Central Jewish Office ... and we also succeeded in getting a large number of our people employed in responsible positions and as clerks (again, some of them in responsible positions). The most important thing for us was the fact that one of our two people on the Council was able to secure the Retraining Department of the Central Jewish Office. This enabled us to legalise all the farm-training and educational activities of out three pioneer organisations and the youth movement within the framework of this Retraining Department. Systematic work enabled us to develop the training-farms to a greater extent than had been possible before...

Gisi was given a more subordinate position but still managed to achieve a great deal. The only remaining US Consul in Nazi Europe was in Budapest, so holders of affidavits had to go in person and that meant crossing the border. Accordingly, to make things easier Gisi's department sent whole bus-loads from Bratislava to Budapest.

Gisi's personal life became very hard. Her favourite brother, Dr Gustav Fischer (born 1896), a lawyer, was attacked in broad daylight on his way home in September 1939. He was butted through a gateway and thrown down some stairs and beaten up. He was so badly injured, that he died a few days later. His young wife became depressed and a few weeks later when she was staying with Gisi, she jumped from the third floor flat and died. Gisi's daughters had already been sent abroad to Eretz Israel before the war and her husband died of natural causes in 1942. This left Gisi with her mother, Jetty, who was born in 1871 and was seriously ill. Gisi and her other brother Desider (born 1894) placed their mother in the local Christian hospital. Desider and his wife and family went into hiding and survived to collect Jetty after the war, although she died in December 1945.

In the spring of 1941, the head of the *Judenrät*, Heinrich Schwarz, was dismissed because he was not as compliant as required by the Nazis and if he disagreed with an order, he resisted. His replacement was an outsider – more of a quisling. They had no chance of influencing the new man and consequently a small resistance group started in Gisi's office, which was now at No. 6 Edelgasse, away from the main *Judenrät* office. It became a natural meeting place and later one of the centres of illegal activities.[140]

In September 1941, a new Jewish code with 270 paragraphs was published by the Minister of the Interior. It specified baptised Slovak Jews (10–15,000) were to be treated as full Jews. Deportations started slowly in October 1941. The leaders appealed to the Head of State, the Catholic priest, Dr Josef Tiso in vain. A minority fled either to the woods, Hungary and some churches. By the end of the year about 7,000 Jews, nearly a tenth of Slovak Jews, had found refuge in Hungary.

In a letter dated 1943,[141] Gisi wrote:

The tragedy began in March with the deportation of the best people we had, our boys and girls above the age of 16. Their behaviour was devastatingly heroic, especially that of our young Zionists who went singing with their heads held high towards their fate which no one at that time suspected, though people were afraid.

These first transports of young people were the prelude to even greater tragedy, which continued with the separation of families, the deportation of the very old, the seriously ill, large families, throughout the whole of last summer until October, and so carried nearly 60,000 of the 80,000 Jews here to their doom. The whole tragedy was carried out at a speed which it probably did not achieve anywhere else, so that sixty thousand people were sent away in less than four months. It is hard to describe the terrible scenes which took place before and during the journey amongst the young, the old, the sick, the dying, the mentally ill, all together in cattle trucks which were closed and sealed. People were deprived of all their belongings and ill-treated already in the collection centres while they were waiting to be deported, and in these camps there were also terrible scenes...

As soon as the deportations had started, we tried to organise help from abroad for those who had been deported, in the form of parcels and medicines to be sent to them collectively, and we also sent money from here, as soon as the addresses of those who had been transported became known, but this applied unfortunately only to a disproportionately small number, as the large majority sent not a sign of life from the day of their deportation. When we became convinced that it would not be possible for us to provide them with the necessary help in this way, we began to establish direct contact with the people abroad with the help of suitable emissaries. In this way we managed to carry out relief measures on a large scale. The emissaries went to the resettlement area/Lublin district in which the majority of the people were those from the family transports. Into all the various villages we put people whom we knew and trusted, to whom we sent money and other things. Contemporary reports provide convincing evidence that

---

140 Neumann p.17
141 Neumann pp.18–23

this was the only way in which to offer substantial help. The recipients confirmed the gifts of money and things with their signatures. We were glad to have found the way to help...

Last year we received the terrible news that there had been an action against the Jews in the region of the General Government,[142] in the course of which all those who had been resettled were again deported. In spite of our desperate attempts, it was months before we traced those who had been transported, although our emissaries were continually on the move. About the beginning of February, we succeeded in finding out that several hundred thousand of our people had been deported to the region between Rawaruska and Przemysl as part of the Final Solution. Until now, we have had no reports from there, or rather, we have received such news from the villages in which people have remained that it is rather unlikely that those exposed to the repeated transports are still alive...

So far, the following has been confirmed without doubt:

The men and women capable of working are in the three main centres, Auschwitz, Birkenau and Lublin. Their life in these camps is that of prisoners. As long as the individual continues to be capable of working he justifies his right to exist. Should he become weak, or prevented by illness from carrying out his work, he simply ceases to exist. It is extremely difficult for the emissaries to get right into the labour camps, nevertheless we have already managed to establish contact there. Certainly, it will not be possible to provide anything except relatively limited relief measures here, because the work is incomparably more difficult here than in any of the other reception districts.

At the height of the deportations, Gisi wrote in the same letter:

...we were told that according to further orders, the remaining roughly twenty thousand people would be deported at the latest by the middle of September and the country be made *Judenrein*. At this time, there came together a small group of unselfish people, some of them members of our movement, but also some orthodox and newly-acquired colleagues, who have now become a close, unified community and who have made it their task to fight in all respects against further deportations. Through successful interventions and other systemic work, the group has succeeded in acquiring friends and collaborators in Government circles, in order to carry out the rescue work. To carry it out, it was first necessary to provide the friends in the Government who were willing to help with an appropriate argument to oppose the absolute necessity of the deportation. This argument was the plan was the plan for establishing labour camps, in which the Jews were to be completely

---

142 The rump Polish state left under the German Governor, Hans Frank, based in Krakow.

isolated from the rest of the population, while their work potential was being exploited for the benefit of the State. Jews were gradually being excluded from the economy, instead of being deported, were to become liable for the labour camps…On the other hand, the camps were not to become a charge on the State and we had to give an undertaking that we would obtain subsidies in foreign exchange from the Jews abroad to cover the entire cost of their maintenance. Moreover, we had to commit ourselves to certain personal obligations in order to ensure the cooperation of the relevant authorities at all times.

We have three such camps, containing altogether 3,000 Jews. These camps represent huge communities, which in an unbelievably short time have established a series of workshops which have already become models of their kind, performing important services to the State, as during the prevailing labour shortage it would not otherwise be possible to do the work which is being done there. There are large carpentry, textile, clothing and other workshops in the camps, which obtain their orders for the most part from the State itself, but also partly from private enterprises. The income from the work supports the entire community, including those who are unable to work, children and old people. Payments are comparatively low and the maintenance of the camps (provision of their most essential hygienic and social requirements: infant welfare, care of the sick and the aged, schools etc.) presents a great problem; the income of inmates is not sufficient and outside assistance is essential to cover the cost…Of course, life in the labour camps is hard for those concerned, but when it is considered that this measure has saved people from deportation, i.e. certain death, it means nevertheless that we have been very successful…We would like to point out, that the Jews in the highest positions in the labour camps are some of our Zionists, which guarantees to a certain extent that from a Jewish and humane point of view the work is done as well as it possibly can be.

…There are in these camps also many boys and girls belonging to the various movements; in all three camps are *hechalutz* groups engaged in cultural activities and in learning Hebrew besides doing physical work, who are receiving help from is regularly. The fact that one of our leading people is also responsible for the labour camps makes it possible to visit there frequently and to maintain a real and continually growing contact with the people there. Our people have also succeeded in establishing general cultural activities in these camps, and some very impressive events have already been arranged there – the only place in the whole country where such things are even possible.

Besides the camps of Sered, Novaky and Vynne, there were eight satellite labour camps for hard labour. All these camps were in fact destined to serve as assembly points for deportation, but it is not clear when and how this changed.

In this long letter (Neumann does not reveal its exact date, nor to whom it was sent) Gisi noted that agreement on the labour camps was made in October and was to last until the end of March 1943. She wrote:

In fact, no deportations took place during these five months. We are aware that we took an insane risk in coming to such an agreement, as we had nothing more definite than the expectations of promises from friends...In order to be able to fulfil our huge obligations, therefore we borrowed considerable sums locally and from friends abroad ...and so far have been unable to repay this debt of honour.

Hauptsturmführer Dieter Wisleceny was a close friend of Eichmann and was advisor on the Jewish question in Bratislava. This 'rosy, corpulent and self-indulgent' man was prepared to stop deportations, not because he was kind, but for payment by the Slovak Jewish Community. In March 1942 he was offered 55,000 dollars and after payment he flew to Berlin to speak to Eichmann. He returned to Bratislava in early September and the deportations stopped.

According to Neumann, in the summer of 1942 the Slovak government had two warnings that the deported Jews were being murdered. In December 1942 Wisleceny said they would stop the deportations everywhere except Poland for two million dollars. This led to the 'Europe Plan' where the WJC set the money aside within three months but nothing seemed to happen for a year. At the same time Father Tiso told Himmler's envoy the deportations would start again in April.

Gisi Fleischmann wrote on 7 May 1943 to her contacts abroad, saying she had spoken to 'Willy' – her code-name for Wisleceny, about 'the big plan'.[143]

...he was very interested but did not himself have the authority to decide about it. He had already spoken on the telephone to Berlin and was planning to go there to make the proposal in person. She recorded that she and a colleague had made him a preliminary offer of one thousand dollars to stop all the deportations for a time, during which it ought to be possible to reach a definite agreement. 'Willy' could not commit himself until he had spoken to his Superior, but she asked her contacts to see that the money would be available.

At the same time, she recorded, she was negotiating to have the exterminations stopped, although according to the information that was reaching them, this would come too late for most of those who had been deported.

On 11 May 1943 she added a postscript to her letter:

I have just come from Willy...He has spoken to the boss of his department and been empowered to negotiate concerning the big plan. On principle, they are prepared to stop the deportation entirely, but

---

143 Neumann pp.24

they are asking out friends to make a definite proposal. I told him that in view of the difficulties of communicating we would need some time, and asked him to tell me the amount we would have to expect. To this he answered that it would have to be fairly large and that we ought to allow two or three million dollars...

I suggested the following to him:

I shall pass the information on at once. Roughly between 1st and 10th June I will call him and let him know whether our friends are in a position to enter into such large commitments. I would then make one thousand dollars available as a preliminary payment and in return be granted several weeks further extension during which the deportations will be halted. Within this period an agreement would have to be reached and the planned instalments be determined.

On the whole, Willy has agreed to my suggestion, only, he is asking for a preliminary payment of two thousand dollars, because below this sum he would not be able to negotiate for the moratorium. In any case, I have an assurance that there will be no deportations before 10 June 1943...

Gisi did not get the answer she was hoping for from abroad. They offered to pay in such a manner that funds would not be available until after the war – Gisi was not willing to pass this offer on. She was not convinced the 'plan' would be able to go ahead. She felt those abroad were being impractical as they wanted Jewish observers to supervise the cessation of the deportations. Gisi felt 'Willy' would not want many people involved in the 'plan'. However she would discuss it with him, if she had assurance that commitments would be met.

But to present myself with this negative reaction and to make strict conditions would be impossible if times were normal and our partners kind. Therefore if nothing should come of the plan through our fault I refuse to be held responsible ...It is incredible that we were given such a chance and will not be able to make use of it for reasons which are incomprehensible to us.

However her friends said there had been deportations recently and she queried when. She had begun her negotiations on 10 May and since then large-scale deportations had ceased even though all the preparations were in place. She tried to pacify them by saying 'Willy' had the authority to negotiate and she had always found him a man of his word.

On 20 July 1943 she wrote:

You must realise that it is impossible to carry on important negotiations and to make fundamental conditions and demands without showing a single sign of trying to take our commitments seriously. I cannot even plead lack of time, as after all there has been plenty of time since 10 May to receive an answer from our friends. I shall absolutely have to know definitely what their attitude is, by the end of the month – the final date, and whether the sums for the future instalments are assured. Surely when I wrote I pointed out clearly enough that we will have to expect the possibility of having to pay a further large instalment after the first payment and the break which was to follow it, in other words that it is essential to get these sums ready. I have nothing further to add to my letter now. I don't think that I have to emphasise that until now I have done the utmost I could in this matter and it goes without saying that I shall continue to regard this my task as my most holy mission. Everything else depends on the extent to which our friends abroad will contribute to the realisation of the plan...

Meanwhile they were still trying to help those already deported. In spring 1943, Gisi wrote:

We have found isolated groups of people, including some in places which had been thought to have been abandoned; our people are living in hiding in the woods, in ruined huts etc. Their physical condition is so bad that it is only a question of time before they will no longer be able to hold out. We are sending them money and other valuables[144] so they will be able to help themselves.

The only real help is escape and this has succeeded so far in 40 cases. But it is out of the question to save certain people...the possibility to help them depends on the physical condition of the individuals. We have charged our emissaries with organising this work and we have reason to hope that it will be possible to develop this branch of our activity. We already have about 50 people here with us, who will first of all have to be fed and clothed before they will look like human beings again. On no account will they be able to remain here for long and therefore the organisation will have to be further developed so that we will be able to send them on...The organisation is not yet making enough provisions and we are trying to improve matters. As we have come to the conclusion that all those who are in...will sooner or later be exterminated, this is the only constructive kind of help, unless our bold plan will succeed in this respect as well. But it goes without saying that this help requires a large sum.

We have had the opportunity of talking with some of the refugees... Undoubtedly the news is entirely true, as the refugees come from different places and reported the same or similar things. Indiscriminate extermination of men, women and children in large numbers is an everyday occurrence, and this extermination is carried out systematically by a few people. Mountains of corpses are lying in the graves which they themselves have dug and the hill covering them sometimes continues to move, which indicates that those still alive are buries as well. Thousands

---

144 'Other valuables' meant forged papers.

of children have been collected from the camps and ghettos and wiped out with machine guns. People, regardless of sex, have to undress completely before the shooting, and are often chased and hunted for days in a kind of *battue,* before they receive the death-blow.

Gisi also wrote about Poland: 'Unfortunately we are receiving less and less news from there. It is as if people buried under debris one after another cease to show signs of life.' When funds were low Gisi decided to try the Jews in Hungary, who had hardly been touched so far. She went to Budapest, was well received by influential Jews there coming back with lavish promises. A second visit was less successful as she received no promises. However she made contact with Christian Church leaders and told them the situation in Poland and Slovakia, ensuring the Jews abroad would be told.

When the *Judenrät* in Bratislava first heard about the death camps, Gisi wanted Dr Isidor Koso, the Slovak President of the Council to receive the information and contacted his wife. In the winter of 1943 Gisi contacted her again over the planned rescue of a thousand Jewish children to be sent to Eretz Israel. Mrs Koso asked Gisi for a letter of introduction so she could collect funds herself in Switzerland. A woman sewed the letter into her coat, but she told the Gestapo who let Mrs Koso travel to the Swiss border where they arrested her on arrival. She secretly brought back to Bratislava but the Office heard just before the Gestapo came to arrest Gisi. She was taken into solitary confinement with normal concessions to prisoners denied. It was a few days before she could make contact with her friends. However it appeared that the Gestapo were more interested in Mrs Kaso's contacts. Gisi was treated reasonably well and released after a few days providing she kept quiet about it.

Sometime later they went back to the Office to arrest her, but she was warned and wasn't there. The Gestapo went to her home and finding nothing arrested her elderly mother, who did not give anything away and was released but Gisi's brother David was taken as a hostage instead.

Gisi spent the next four months in various prisons, most of the time in solitary confinement. When she was eventually released, friends urged her to leave the country, since from now on, as a suspected person, she would no longer be able to do her work. They had already made the necessary arrangements for her escape to Hungary, and from there she could have joined her two daughters in Eretz Israel. Gisi refused, and three days later she was back at her desk.

She was in touch with her daughters and before her arrest wrote to one of them:

It was to be our fate to be separated for a few years...You must put up with this, because we must put the Jewish community before personal suffering. Apart from this, all my thoughts and desires concern you, and you have all my love. My greatest wish is to ne together with you in Eretz Israel. I believe that it will soon be time for this dream to come true. Until then, we will have to be strong, even if we are homesick for each other.

During the past few years, I have seen such terrible suffering and have had to witness the terrible persecutions and torture to which our people have been exposed, have had to see our marvellous young people, amongst them also all the girls of your own age, sent away to the horrors in Poland. When I see all this like a spectre before me, I daily thank God to know my children are in Eretz Israel; in Eretz, the fulfilment of the ideal for which I live and work…This life is neither pleasant nor easy. But we, who continue to believe in humanity, have to do everything possible both as individuals and as people to be strong and resilient.

After she was released she wrote to a friend:

I want to thank you and all the other people for the trouble you are taking over my Aliyah. Please believe me that I am confronted with an unbearable conflict.' She had just received word that one of her daughters was seriously ill. She knew, she said, that the truth had been kept from her until then 'because you knew that I would find this terrible anxiety about the wellbeing of the beloved child so hard to bear that it is extremely difficult for me to devote myself to other important concerns.' Her mother was also seriously ill. 'And so I am thrown to and fro as a plaything by fate, between my duties as a child to my mother and as a mother to my child. In addition…there is also my feeling of responsibility to the community, for after all, no harm must befall the Jews of our community, because of personal worries. There are so few of us who have in this so difficult time the opportunity and the strength to do anything…' She would be glad to have a certificate and a visa in her possession, she concluded '…and thus prepared, I shall continue to serve the community for as long as I can…'

In March 1944, Himmler brought the Final Solution to Hungary. Thousands of Slovak Jews tried to get back home. Many parents in hiding had sent their children to Hungary for safety. These children passed through their homeland on the way to Auschwitz.

In the summer of 1944, Dr. Kazstner came to ask the Bratislava Jewish Resistance group to help with supplying goods Eichmann had agreed to accept in exchange for Jews. Gisi's group agreed to help but it was too late. There was a rebellion against the German-dominated Slovak government and Hitler's troops marched into Bratislava. The Jews were all concentrated in Sered – the former labour camp.

From the High Tatra mountains, the eastern part of Slovakia ruled by the partisans, a former member of the group sent a messenger to take Gisi to safety. She refused to leave, yet again saying: 'I shall stay at my post with my comrades.'

A final effort to avoid the imminent deportations was made by contacting Wisleceny who was in Budapest with Eichmann. This time using Kurt Becher, a horse dealer, who had previously negotiated for the SS with Joel Brand during the summer. Himmler had visited Bratislava on 21 September and ordered the total deportation of the Jews. Becher flew to Berlin to talk to him but had no success. By the time he returned on 25 September the Jews had been handed over to *Sturmbannführer* Alois Brunner, who had been transferred from France.

He ordered all remaining Jews to the Sered concentration camp within two weeks. But a few days later on 28 September there was a round-up of Jews by the SS who collected 1,890 Jews including most of Gisi's group, who were sent to Sered. On 30 September the first transport of the second wave of deportations left Slovakia for Auschwitz. That was the end of the two-year period of grace for the Slovakian Jews.

The building at Edelgasse 6, which housed Gisi's office, was now a Gestapo prison and Gisi and one of her colleagues were employed to look after the prisoners providing for them out of their illegal funds. Although they were both at liberty and could sleep at home, they were under constant surveillance. Gisi had managed to hide her mother as an Aryan in a hospital. They heard from those in Sered of the resumption of the deportations.

In the middle of October, news spread that Gisi had been brought there and was being interrogated by Brunner.

> That same night, the writer (Neumann), visited her in her hut and heard from her what happened: She had received a letter asking for news from one of her colleagues who was then in hiding. Sitting in her office in Edelgasse 6, with a Gestapo man in the next room, she began to write him her answer: 'Unfortunately, I too am in the lion's mouth.' At that moment the Gestapo man entered. Gisi tore the letter into small pieces but the man retrieved them from the waste paper basket and painstakingly put them together again. Then he informed Brunner.

Someone who was at Sered at that time, recorded later:

> On the way to the hut I saw Gisi escorted by an SS man, going towards the main building; I recognised the SS man as a former fellow soldier Cerno, but though his eyes met mine we did not speak. After the interrogation which lasted for several hours, Gisi was brought to the hut in which I was being kept. She was as courageous as ever. She told me she had tried to influence Brunner but failed and that he had sworn at her: '*Verlogene Saujüdin* (lying Jewish sow) you have cheated us.'

Most of the transports leaving Sered in September and October 1944 which took about fifteen thousand Jews went to Sachsenhausen, Stutthof, Theresienstadt, Bergen-Belsen and other German camps. These were not specifically extermination camps and so people had a chance of survival.

The transport assembled there on 16 October was the last one for Auschwitz. Gisi apparently tried to appeal to Brunner but he turned his back on her.

We were labelled R.U (*Rückkehrun erwünscht* – return undesirable)' the same survivor recorded. 'Possible escape plans were discussed, but Gisi would not consider them because she did not want to endanger her friends and colleagues who were still in the camp, though she encouraged me. The transport left on 17th October 1944, making straight for Auschwitz; some survivors told me that as soon as the train arrived three names were called and they saw Gisi being led away…

I was curious about what happened to Gisi's daughters. Apparently Aliza (Alice) Fleischmann Hartoch died in 1996 and Judith Fleischmann Roder died in 1997. Both are buried in Israel.[145]

What are we to make of this woman? Yehuda Bauer, an eminent Israeli Holocaust historian born in Prague in 1926 has written:

…from the aspect of social history of the Jews, the story of a woman and a leader who climbed the ladder of traditional female involvement in Jewish welfare and migration matters and became the only political leader of a Jewish underground – the only underground anywhere in Europe that united all the political factions of a country (with the exception of the communists), and the only group anywhere in Europe that tried to rescue not just its own Jews but Jews of other countries as well – is significant. The case of Gisi Fleischmann can and should be addressed as an important manifestation of the development of Jewish society and of the female role in it. She was a courageous woman, a brave leader, a person who wanted to enjoy life, who had a happy family around her, but who chose to stand at the head of a group that tried to save a community. I don't know of any other woman who did something similar during the Holocaust, or indeed even before that. All I can say is that I think she did her best, and that she should be recognized as a role model, despite all her mistakes. She was the stuff heroines are made of.[146]

Telšiai, Lithuania

Professor Dan Michman told me about this town where all the men were killed first and then some months later the women were all killed. So for a while the community was run by women.

Jews started settling in Telšiai (Jews called it Telz) in the fifteenth century. By the end of the nineteenth century there were 3,000 Jews in the town

---

145 Maya Shaham, Yad Vashem, email to author 31 October 2017.
146 Yehuda Bauer, 'Gisi Fleischmann', in *Women in the Holocaust* pp.262–3.

representing 51% of the population. By 1940 there were 2,800 Jews, roughly 48%. Most of them worked in crafts, commerce and as pedlars. It was famed for its educational institutions which included a girls school founded in 1865 by the Jewish poet Yehuda Leib Gordon and the Great yeshiva opened in 1880 with 400 students.

Lithuania was annexed by the Soviets on 31 July 1940 and the shops were nationalized and the Jewish educational institutions were closed. The Yeshiva was moved out of its building but functioned elsewhere until Passover 1941. The students were dispersed in the surrounding towns and part of the valued Library as saved in the Samogitian 'Alka' Museum. Telšiai was occupied by the German army on 26/27 June 1941. The Jews were driven to the Rainiai estate several kilometres away from the town. On 14–15 July the Jewish men were murdered in Rainiai forest and the women and children were sent to a camp in Geruliai village on 22 July. Jewish women from other towns in the area were also brought there. At the end of August 1941, some of them were murdered, while 500 young females were driven to Telšiai. They were put in a ghetto created in the poor part of town between the Market Square and Lake Mastis. During the 1941 Jewish New Year and Yom Kippur (the High holidays) the women prayed in the Tailors' Synagogue which was within the area of the ghetto. Until 24–25 December Telz was a town of women, but then the ghetto was liquidated and the entire Jewish population was murdered in the Rainai Forest.[147]

The Yeshiva of Telz became a significant institution when Eli'ezer Gordon became the Rabbi of Telz in 1883. He introduced modern educational innovations such as yearly examinations, progress relied on grades and an academic year with clearly defined terms. During the inter-war years it became one of the most important yeshivas in Lithuania with students coming not only from Eastern Europe but also America, Germany and Palestine. Most of the staff and students were murdered in the Holocaust. In 1940, two Telz rabbis had gone to America to try to rescue the yeshiva. Although unsuccessful, in 1945 they re-established it using the same name of Telz in Cleveland, Ohio where it became one of the leading yeshivas in the US. [148]

The narrative according to Yad Vashem's *The Untold Stories of the Murder Sites of the Jews in the Occupied Territories of the Former USSR*:

The German army entered Telšiai on June 26, 1941. The following day, the town's Jewish inhabitants were driven out of their homes and their property was plundered. They were then imprisoned in cowsheds and barns on the Rainiai estate.

The commander of the Lithuanians appointed a council to represent the Jews, which strove to improve their difficult living conditions. On

147 *Synagogues in Lithuania Catalogue* (Vilnius Academy of Arts Press, 2012), p.172.
148 Stampfer, Shaul. *Telz, Yeshiva of*. YIVO Encyclopedia of Jews in Eastern Europe 10 February 2014. Accessed 13 August 2017, http://www.yivoencyclopedia.org/article.aspx/Telz_Yeshiva_of

July 14, 1941, a number of Germans and Lithuanians appeared at the estate and began to abuse the Jews as a crowd of Telšiai residents looked on. That day and the next, all the Jewish men at the estate were murdered, as were Jews from Alsedziai and from a number of nearby towns and villages.

On July 22, 1941, the women and children were taken from the Rainiai estate to the Geruliai camp, which was severely overcrowded. They were held together with the women and children of nearby towns, almost 2,000 people in total. On Saturday, August 30, 1941, the women and children were driven out of their huts. Five hundred women and young girls were then marched to Telšiai, while the others were murdered by Lithuanians.

In Telšiai, the 500 women and children were imprisoned in a ghetto near the lake under very harsh conditions. Encircled by a high wooden fence topped by barbed wire, the ghetto's gate was guarded by Lithuanians. A number of the women toiled for Lithuanian farmers, who fully exploited their workers, while others worked in Lithuanian homes as servants.

Female inhabitants of the ghetto, Dr. Blat, Dr. Shapira, and Dr. Srolovits, established a makeshift clinic to treat women that were ill or in labor. Despite their efforts, all of the babies born in the ghetto died shortly after their birth. A typhus epidemic also raged in the ghetto.

On Rosh Hashanah and Yom Kippur of 5702 (September 1941), the women of the ghetto gathered to pray – with several leading the prayers – in the Beit Midrash inside the ghetto. Other women, having undergone brutal hardships and suffering, turned to the local priest seeking to convert to Christianity.

From December 22, 1941, the women who worked in the villages were returned to the ghetto. The development was construed as a sign of the ghetto's impending liquidation, prompting many women to flee the ghetto via the lake or under the fence. Dozens of the women who escaped reached the Siauliai ghetto.

On December 24–25, 1941, all the women remaining in the ghetto were taken to the Rainiai estate, where they were murdered. Of those who escaped, sixty-four survived until liberation.

Telšiai was liberated by the Red Army in the summer of 1944 but by then there were hardly any Jews left in the town where they had lived for more than 500 years

Two women have given testimony recorded by Yad Vashem.[149] Chana Pelc (Khana Peltz) said:

After three hours, it stopped raining, the skies cleared, and the murderers reappeared. They rounded up the remaining men, brought

---

149 *Telšiai – Written Testimonies in Untold Stories,* Yad Vashem. Accessed 9 August 2017, http://www.yadvashem.org/untoldstories/database/index.asp?cid=555

them to the pits and shot them all dead. Shmuel Pelc and a number of other men who returned from the pit told us what they had witnessed. One interesting event happened there. During the rain, a lightning bolt badly damaged their shack and the roof collapsed and yet nobody was injured. All this happened on Shabbat (Saturday) July 15, 1941. They shot all the men from Telšiai, varniai, Seda, Zarenai, Luike and other towns in the region...All those remaining in the ghetto were brought across the Mastis Lake, to the Rainiai camp where pits had already been dug. That year, the winter was especially harsh. The women were forced to undress completely. They stood there at the edge of the pit, frozen with cold. They stood, and waited to die...

Galina Masyulis and Susanna Kogan testified:

One of these camps, Rainiai, was located near the estate of a popular Lithuanian opera singer named Petrauskas. The woods near the estate became a mass murder site...The ones doomed to death dug the pits themselves. Vodka was brought to the forest and the executioners got drunk while the ones condemned to death did the digging...People were forced to strip naked and lie down in the pits they had dug; the grenades were thrown into the pits. Children were flung into the pits with bayonets, or they were knocked in with a rifle butt or kicked in...

Leah Tayts (also Lea Taic née Poplak) wrote in Yiddish to her brother, I Poplak, who lived in Cape Town in South Africa on 30 December 1941. The letter is held in the Vilna Gaon Jewish Museum in Vilnius.

I and my two babies are the only people still alive of all our family. Today, the 30th of December 1941, my children and I are to be killed. They have murdered all the Lithuanian Jews here and nobody can stay alive. I managed to escape several times – a Lithuanian Jucius P. from the village of Stulpenai [?] helped me. So if the world survives, please give him some of my things. Because that Lithuanian tried to hide me, but he did not succeed. When you are to say *Kaddish* for us I do not know either. My husband [Yitshak?] was shot on the fifteenth of Tammuz [10 July 1941]. From my heart I wish you all the best. It is from the depths of despair that your doomed sister and her two babies are writing to you. My regards to all my dear people abroad. Make sure that our innocent blood is avenged.[150]

In fact although a Yitshak Tayts was listed as killed, her husband was named as Shneiur (Schnauer) Taic on a testimony form at Yad Vashem submitted

---

150 Gershon Greenberg, *The Vanished World of Lithuanian Jews,*(Amsterdam: Rodopi, 2004) Footnote 35 pp.252–3

by a relative Knana Zak. She was born in Kupiskis and was a teacher Her children were named as Vana aged 4 and Bentsion aged 2.[151]

With the help of the South African Board of Deputies, I was able to establish that her brother was Judel Poplak who was born in 1908 and arrived in Cape Town in 1929. I was able to identify him because he came from the same town although it is listed as Kibisk.[152]

Kazys Idzelevicius, was described as a perpetrator and his testimony was taken from KGB files. He testified that:

> The killing of women and children took place in Geruliai in August 1941. A pit of 150 meters in length, 3 meters in width and 3 meters wide, was dug. We herded the women and children there and started shooting them. We shot them in groups of 30–40 people throughout the day. We killed ultimately about 2,000. During the killings some women could not stand the horror and collapsed into the pit alive... There were women with small children or babies in their arms. All the Jewish women and children were shot in one day. The killing started at six o'clock in the morning and ended between eleven and twelve o'clock in the afternoon...All Jewish belongings were brought for storage in Telšiai.

The Lithuanians and Germans treated the Jews with terrible cruelty and tortured them before murdering them. What was known as the 'Devil's Dance' was imposed on the male Jews before death and the women would have been aware of this if not actual witnesses. In the devil's dance the men had to move about on their knees with their hands in the air or run in circles, fall down and get up as commanded.[153]

> The mass murders began at Rainiai on 15 July after a 'devil's dance' where the men were beaten with planks. They went back to the stables, where they had been kept, 'with heads split, teeth knocked out and eyes swollen. Then they were removed in groups of twenty-five into the forest, forced to dig pits, undress to their underwear and shot. In his 23 January 1945 testimony in Telšiai against Lithuanian guard Kazys Sulcas, Adam Desyatnik of Telšiai described how Sulcas beat those who couldn't run, get up and down quickly enough during the devil's dance: how the Germans gave Sulcas gold and silver valuables taken from the prisoners.

Desyatnik was 'allowed to stay behind because of his youth'. He was described as single and a gymnasium graduate'. Hannah Peltz is quoted as

---

151 Form no 93266, Leah Taic Nee Poplak, in Central DB of Shoah Victims' Names accessed 10 August 2017, https://yvng.yadvashem.org/index.html?language=en&s_lastName=Taic&s_firstName=Lea&s_place=Telšiai I am grateful to Nigel Salomon for translating the entries made by her relative Khana Zak.
152 Shirley and Jordan Beagle of South Africa, email to author 14 August 2017.
153 P.233

saying men's beards were torn off with pieces of flesh, when they reached the pits. However because of the storm they were told to dress again and return to the stables. She continued:

> They no longer looked human; their faces were grey and half-wild. The pious Jews thought heaven had intervened [by having it rain]. They sat like pieces of clay, stones, frozen statues. The rain, thunder and lightning continued for another three hours. They moaned and tore out their hair. The guards stood outside, preventing them from running. They were exhausted and their bones were broken. The sky cleared. The killers took the Jews back to the pits and shot them. Some escaped and reported what happened.[154]

A conference was held in the Zemaite Theatre in Telšiai on 12 October 2011, entitled 'Names Emerge from the Past' to remember the residents of the Telšiai ghetto who were killed in 1941. It was attended by 300 local students and 30 teachers and was organised by the local Gymnasium, the theatre and the IHRA. Some of those present gave recollections from their families. Jadvyga Stulpinaite-Blaziene spoke of her father Boleslovas Stulpinas who hid 26 Jews in an underground bunker he dug in his courtyard for three-and-a-half years. The name has a similarity with the man poor Lea Paic mentioned as having helped her. The local priest Andriejus Sabatiauskas, a participant at the conference, said: 'We must analyse the events which happened in 1941 in Lithuania, discuss about them and talk about them continually. Our talking is not sufficient enough.'[155]

---

154 Cited in GG p.234
155 *'Names Emerge From the Past' Conference Remembers Jewish Community of Telšiai/ IHRA Press Release,* 19 October 2011, https://www. holocaustremembrance.com/media-room/news-archive/%E2%80%9Cnames-emerge-past%E2%80%9D-conference-remembers-jewish-community-telsiai Accessed 9 August 2017.

Slave Labourers

Bernard Ferencz and Judge Bejsky

The Nazis' use of slave labour is a vast topic. I have dealt with it elsewhere[156] but to put the Markkleeberg camp into context, I looked at the writing of Bernard Ferencz (born 1920) who was a young lawyer at the Nuremberg trials and was involved in collecting evidence from the camps. He wrote 'I had peered into Hell.'

> Camp inmates seldom knew or cared which particular company or agency was the beneficiary of their toll, sweat and tears. Every concentration camp inmate was a slave laborer. Jews in particular were less than slaves since they were all marked for extermination; for those unable to work, the next stop was the gas chamber or the crematorium.[157]

His book *Less Than Slaves* describes the painstaking efforts that were made to persuade German industrial firms such as I. G. Farben, Krupp, AEG, Rheinmetall, and Daimler-Benz to compensate camp inmates who were exploited as forced laborers. The meagre outcome of these efforts emerges from searing pages that detail the difficulties confronted by Ferencz and his dedicated colleagues.

He wrote about Siemens of Germany which he described as 'the second largest electrical concern in the world' Whilst some acknowledgement of their use of slave labour was made by Hermann von Siemens, the Chairman 1941- 46, in January 1946.

> He acknowledged that prisoners of the concentration camps at Oranienberg and Buchenwald did work in shops put at the company's disposal by the camp administration, but he could not recall how many persons were involved. He expressed the view that the prisoners

---

156 Agnes Grunwald-Spier, *Who Betrayed the Jews?*
157 Website of Benjamin Ferencz, http://www.benferencz.org/assets/prefaceslaves. pdf, 2015, accessed 26 October 2017.

welcomed the opportunity to work and he was not aware of any undernourishment or ill treatment.

This version was also repeated in their official *History of the House of Siemens,* published by the company after the war. Ferencz commented:

Not a word appeared in the official company history about Auschwitz, Flossenberg, Sachsenhausen, Buchenwald, Gross Rosen, Ravensbrück or Mauthausen. It was as if Siemens had nothing whatsoever to do with those dreaded camps. The evidence later uncovered as a result of the intensive searches by the Claims Conference and the reports of the survivors painted quite a different picture.

Auschwitz commandant Höss swore he provided 1,200 females to Siemens in 1943 and about 1,500 in 1944. They bore tattoo numbers between 150000 and 200000 and worked in the fertilizer factory, which had been altered for the manufacture of electrical switches for aircraft... When Göring complained to Himmler that not enough concentration camp inmates were being used for aircraft production, Himmler referred to Siemen's work in Auschwitz.

Five hundred and fifty Jewish women, bearing tattoo numbers 55740 to 56290, were sent to Flossenberg concentration camp and from there were shipped to the Siemens factory in Nuremberg. The original invoices were found, showing that Siemens was charged RM4 per day and received a credit of 65 pfenning per prisoner for having provided the food.

Twelve hundred female prisoners had been taken from Sachsenhausen to work at the Werner Works in Siemenstadt Berlin, and when the Werner Works was bombed out, Siemens transferred the operation to Buchenwald. Transport lists found in the archives of the International Tracing Service showed the identity of other inmates from Buchenwald who worked for Siemens at Neustadt bei Coburg in Bavaria. Another list showed the Gross Rosen inmates who had worked for Siemens at Christianstadt in Brandenburg. A letter was found which Lieutenant General Pohl has sent to Himmler on October 20, 1942 in which Pohl assured Himmler that the Siemens company was building new barracks at Ravensbrück to house 2,500 female inmates who would work on telecommunications equipment for the army.[158]

In this section, there are two personal descriptions of experiences in labour camps by very young girls 13, 14 and 15. In this extract from the Eichmann Trial Proceedings, Judge Bejsky, one of Schindler's Jews, spoke about the Plaszów camp near Cracow:

I don't know what the significance of a labour camp is. A labour camp is a different concept. For us, it was an extermination camp...There was

---

158 Benjamin B. Ferencz, *Less than Slaves* (Cambridge: Harvard UP,1979) pp.117–8

work within the camp which was done solely by women, and this was the task of dragging stones from the quarry which was below that new area being prepared for building a road. They used to load stones on to eight to ten waggons on the short railway tracks. At the end of the train, there were long ropes and along the ropes on both sides, women of the camp were harnessed. And in this way they would walk up a fairly steep road from the quarry below, for a distance of two and a half kilometres, up the hill, under all weather conditions for twelve hours. The most horrible thing was that the women were dressed like us, with wooden shoes which used to slip in the snow and the mud. And in this way one could visualize the picture which I am unable to describe – and I do not know whether others would be able to describe – how women walked for a whole night, stumbling and pulling these waggons.[159]

Judge Moshe Bejsky (1920–2007) was Schindler's document forger. He made rubber stamps with the Nazis' symbol and later become a Supreme Court Judge in Israel (1979–1991). He was also the President of Yad Vashem's Commission of the Righteous (1970–75).[160]

Another witness at the Eichmann trial, Zivia Lubetkin, who was a survivor of the Warsaw Ghetto (see pages 226–32) also spoke about slave labour as an aspect of the Nazis' anarchy:

...beyond the scope of any law, was the kidnapping for forced labour. A person would leave his house in the morning, and would never know when he would return, and if he would return. Various formations of Germans were able to come in during the day, in the morning, or towards evening, to close a street, and with screams of such a nature as it would be difficult to describe them as actually being human voices, they would first of all collect people by shooting, and without regard of age or sex, seize people and take them off to work. Some of them on their return, related that they had never engaged in any work...Again it was clear that this was a method of torture, of terror, of making our lives worthless.[161]

Whilst reading these young girls' harrowing experiences, we must remember that the Nazis were paid by the industrialists for the provision of these slave labourers and these companies thrived on this cheap labour. This must lead to the question of how much of Germany's great post-war economic success was based on not having the normal costs of employing labour in their accounts, under the Nazis.

---

159 Judge Beisky, *The Eichmann Trial Proceedings 1962*, pp.2152–3
160 Agnes Grunwald-Spier, *The Other Schindlers*, pp.126–132. Judge Bejsky spelt his name with a 'j' but the Trial Proceedings spell it with an 'i'.
161 Zivia Lubetkin, *The Eichmann Trial Proceedings 1962*, pp.2153–4

Junkers-Markkleeberg Labour Camp

In writing about women I needed to cover how they were treated as slave labourers. I found this story in the Wiener Library – the girls' youth and Hungarian origins influenced my choice of subject.

Zahava Szasz Stessel (Katalin Szász) spoke at a dedication at the Markkleeberg Labour Camp on 13 June 1998.

I am number 50226, and my sister, who is here in the audience, is number 50225 on the list of Hungarian Jewish women, slave laborers arriving from Bergen-Belsen to the camp at Junkers-Markkleeberg on December 8, 1944. Being here today after years of striving to distance myself is an overwhelming experience.

My return was not easy. Similar to many survivors, I hesitated to come, to renew memories and deal with issues that I worked so hard to suppress. Yet I am here with you, respected audience, and I am pleased. I can see the world outside my former prison. Here are the small houses, close to the camp, that always reminded of my home back in Abaújszántó, Hungary. I can now observe the daytime view of the homes that I once saw only by night from the lights of distant windows, as we marched from Markkleeberg to Theresienstadt in April 1945.

By being here, I pay tribute to my fellow inmates in Markkleeberg with whom I dreamed of freedom and a better world. Many perished, leaving no grave site for remembrance. I returned also because I yearned to reinforce my belief that it was wrong to take my parents, grandparents, my sister, and me so far from my home, from our town, to Auschwitz. How unjust it was to make my sister and me orphans and slave-laborers at the ages thirteen and fourteen.

As we stood there on that clear day in May 1944 in Auschwitz, asking what had happened to our parents, we were told, 'Look at the sparks of fire from the smoking chimney. There is your old world, your family, your loved ones, who are now being burned.' More terrible than the words was the fact that it was true; our nightmare was our reality. We continued in that dreadful world in Markkleeberg, standing barefoot in wooden shoes on the frozen snow and ice, motionless for hours, while our tormentors celebrated the holiday in December 1944. Our nightmarish reality extended throughout the forced Death March in April 1945.

Amidst all the evil, there were also acts of kindness, minutes of good feelings, creating a kind of a flower in the frost of icy existence. Such a bouquet of flowers was the love my sister Erzsike –or Hava – and I shared. We each wanted, for instance, that the other one should have the small ration of bread we received. We saved it until someone stole both our portions. The memory of our sisterly devotion today outlives the remembrance of the crudest treatment we received.

Another flower in the frost was the kindness of a worker in the factory of Markkleeberg who gave my sister a jam sandwich. We never saw that good man again, but I hope my words of thanks may yet reach him.

The facts that we were young during the Holocaust and we had a warm family upbringing helped us to continue our lives. My sister chose to be a nurse and was in charge of the emergency room in a large hospital of Israel. I myself became a librarian and served at the information desk of the New York Public Library, at Fifth Avenue, as well as a freelance writer.

The loss of my family and home has never been forgotten. I feel echoes of the camps each time I say good-bye, and the Holocaust enters every important decision of my life. My twelve-year-old granddaughter writes poems evoking the flames of Auschwitz for a school assignment. I know that even her daughter will carry the scars. Yet I am not as bitter as I could be. I feel, somehow, that the Holocaust experience exists to prevent the world from ever going so far again in mistreating a human being.

I thank you for your kind attention. I offer my gratitude to those who organized the memorial and made this event possible.[162]

A munitions factory was created at Markkleeberg, near Leipzig, in October 1943 by the Junkers Aircraft and Engine Company (*Junkers Flugzeug und Motorenwerke*) Originally created to house foreign forced labourers and workers from Germany, it was mostly destroyed by Allied bombing. It then became a women's labour camp in February 1944 and transports of Hungarian Jewish women arrived between August and December 1944 to perform heavy and demanding physical labour. At its peak there were 1,539 Hungarian Jews and some French political prisoners. The camp was evacuated on 13 April 1945 when the women were sent on a death march to Theresienstadt. Roughly 700 women arrived between 30 April and 4 May 1945. The others had either escaped en route or died through the harsh conditions or were killed by the SS.[163]

Katalin and Erzsébet (Erzsike) Szàsz were fourteen and thirteen when they were sent from Auschwitz-Birkenau via Bergen-Belsen to work in Markkleeberg where the factory was

> ... producing aircraft engines for the Germany war industry. The factory belonged to Junkers, and the majority of the laborers who stood twelve hours per shift, day or night, by the machines or who cut heavy logs of iron bars were fragile Jewish girls from Hungary...even though we could hardly reach the machines.[164]

---

162 *Snow Flowers: Hungarian Jewish Women in an Airplane Factory, Markkleeberg, Germany* (Lanham: Rowman & Littlefield Publishing, 2013) pp.323–4
163 The Azrieli Foundation Glossary of Holocaust Terms, *The Holocaust Survivor Memoirs Program 2015*, Accessed 1 August 2017, http://memoirs. azrielifoundation.org/glossary?q=Markkleeberg
164 *Snow Flowers* p.15

Katalin stressed the fact that as initially there were only Hungarian Jews, the labourers had a bond. 'Although born in different parts of Hungary, the culture we shared was common to us all. The new rules were cruelly incomprehensible, as were the commands in German that we hardly understood.'

The Nazi racial ideology and practice of persecution was aimed not only at the individual, but also at the specific culture and civilization embodied in each person. My research strengthened the idea that what we had learned at home and the impact of our city or small town of origin governed our mental lives and behaviour. As our possessions, clothing, and all vestiges of human identity were gradually taken from us, we retained only what remained in our minds and souls...

The Nazi universe destroyed the families and community, but not the interpersonal relationship of its victims. Self-help and close friendship were important means to survive and existed in a number of different frameworks. A girl who was separated or lost her family attached herself to a group or to another girl and formed a new relationship that became a source of mutual assistance and strength. Some became 'camp-sisters' and supported each other. If they remained alone or isolated and had no one to encourage them, to give them help and company, they perished faster than the others.[165]

Originally, employees in the aircraft industry had elite status with considerable benefits, but when the war drained men away that foreign labourers or concentration camp prisoners were considered suitable. The surviving documentation gives limited information on the use of Jewish slave labour by the major German firms.

Among the hundreds of corporations to which nearly one-half million camp or ghetto inmates were sent by the end of 1944, the greatest offenders were the munitions and arms makers in the narrowest sense: Dynamit Nobel, Rheinmetall-Borsing, Krupp, Messerschmitt, Heinkel and Junkers.

Between 1932–1939 the JU 52 was the most widely used transport airplane in the world and was seen regularly during the war at Nazi airports. The Nazis changed the company into a government-controlled one. Its main business was the production of aircraft and their engines. On 1 May 1939 the factory at Dessau and in Halberstad were decorated as 'Nazi Model Factories'.

In 1944, plants were appealing for workers wherever they could be found, mostly for construction projects at first, and then for assembly-line service. In the use of prisoners, Junkers and Messerschmitt were granted first choice.

---

165 *Snow Flowers* pp.16–7

The representatives of the German armaments industry were sent to select the workers. Standing next to the SS officers, Junkers representatives were given the opportunity to pick prisoners with both intelligence and physical endurance. The Junkers' delegation of civilian engineers and managers came to Auschwitz and Bergen-Belsen. Wearing their gray civilian business suits they inspected the rows of prospective slave laborers and picked out the women they considered most suitable for factory work. During this process, we all had to disrobe and walk naked, one by one, holding our clothing in our left hands and raising our right hands. Whenever a girl raised suspicions of trying to hide a sore or a pimple with her clothing or her hand, she was asked to uncover herself and they examined her even more carefully. The civilians in business suits laughed and talked as we passed. The process was both degrading and humiliating, but the terror and fear for our lives surmounted our natural instinct for modesty and eliminated the full impact of the sense of shame. In my eyes, the SS were not men, not human beings, but a kind of life-menacing, pain-inducing monstrous machine. They were part of that reprehensible other world that crushed all that was human and civilized.

Parading naked in front of German SS guards engendered strong emotions: but, in an absurd and ironic way, men in business suits represented civilized society with all its rules, morals, and obligations. Being nude, shaved all over, and observed by these men in civilian outfits with their watchful eyes was especially disturbing for us teenage girls from sheltered, small-town environments. Personal modesty had been ingrained into Jewish women from childhood. To undress in front of strange men was unthinkable and caused a dreadful, disorienting shock and threat to our personal integrity.[166]

There were four transports to Markkleeberg: the sisters were on the fourth with 300 women, on 8 December 1944. They marched from the station to the camp – a short distance. On arrival girls called out to them in Hungarian, wanting news of their families. The camp was very pleasant – 'The barracks were built of cement with glass windows, and they had electricity!' The others said:

'You've arrived at a good place! Here we are treated as workers.' It was encouraging that we were no longer in an annihilation camp. The women in the barracks next to ours came from various cities and towns all over Hungary. They asked us, as new arrivals, many questions about the world of concentration camps and about Auschwitz and Bergen-Belsen, where they had been before.

We had ten three-tiered bunk beds in our room. On every bed was a mattress made of jute cotton filled with straw and an army blanket. We were all Hungarian except two girls, Hanka and her friend, who were from Poland. We could hardly sleep that night, despite the fact that it was the first time in our camp life that we each had a separate bed.

---

166 *SF* pp.36–7

We were so excited to be in a new place, which was, of all the camps, the most bearable. Later, as we became adjusted, we found that, for prisoners, life even in Markkleeberg, was not easy.[167]

New prisoners could not work with the German civilians and foreign workers in the factory until they had been quarantined to show a lack of communicable diseases. At this time Katalin and her sister were only 14 and 13.

We were assigned instead to work crews outside of the camps. Some of the girls were added to existing commandos. Twenty girls were assigned to woodcutting; twenty to the carpentry shop; others to tailoring; some to the shoemaker's shop; twelve to collect garbage; twenty for gardening; twenty for road repair; and eight for coal shoveling. The rest of us, a large group of sixty girls, Erzsike and I among them, were assigned to work in the quarry as our initiation to Markkleeberg.

Shortly, as we were standing and waiting to leave, an SS soldier of the lowest rank appeared. He led us out of the camp. At the gate, they counted us, and from the storage area we picked up shovels, pickaxes, and spades to carry to the quarry.

The work in these squads of prisoners was among the hardest physical torment we had to endure. The rock quarry was a notorious place, designed for special uninterrupted ill-treatment by the SS. The women toiled in the bitter cold without protective clothing. Some axed out the stone, others crushed it to load onto carts or wheelbarrows and move it, using primitive methods, to other parts of the camp where they had to pile it up. The work was not only physically gruelling, but also dangerous. It was the kind of December weather with dry cold and heavy winds. With each breath, our lungs filled with bitter cold air. Our hands froze as we walked, carrying the heavy shovels on our shoulders to the quarry. Some of the girls wrapped their feet in pieces of cloth they had taken from the lining of their coats. We were afraid to do it, so our bare feet became icy in the wooden shoes.[168]

The quarry was just over the road and was a cavity two metre deep in the ground. An elderly SS man, whom they called *Lófogú* (horse-teeth) because of his large extruding teeth, was in charge. 'He was the most vicious of the SS guards.' They had to produce gravel for the road to beautify the camp. 'We all knew that it was not necessary, and the only purpose of it was to keep us working to torture us.' *Lófogú* instructed them:

First, those with pickaxes, such as Erzsike, had to cut into the soil as the first step in producing the gravel. He showed how to push pickax [sic] into the hard wall of sand and gravel. Even he had difficulties doing it

167 *SF* pp.59–60
168 *SF* p.65

because the soil was all frozen. Then those with the spades had to dig deep into the loosened soil. The resulting gravel had to be shovelled and lifted up over the top of the two-meter-deep pit.

The soil was so frozen that only with tremendous effort with the pickax and spade could the girls produce a small amount of gravel. *Lófogú* was angry. He expected us to work like strong men. I watched Erzsike as she tried with all her strength to cut into the frozen wall of earth and stone. Then those of us with shovels also had trouble scooping and throwing the stones to the surface of the pit. The earth and stones on the shovel were very heavy and they tumbled right back. I could hardly move the shovel once the stones were on it, and *Lófogú* complained that we did not raise the shovels high enough...

Lófogú screamed at the girls on top of the pit to fill the carriage higher. Finally satisfied, he assigned the thirty girls to be horses. Seven stood at each side of the carriage, the rest standing at the front and the back. In addition to his whip, *Lófogú* picked up a big tree branch to hit the girls. The group tried to pull the heavy load with the crushed rock and gravel, but they could move it. In desperation, the girls accused one another of not pulling hard enough. As they were maneuvering [*sic*], the unstable carriage laden with its heavy cargo derailed, striking those who failed to get out of the way in time.

Replacing the stones and gravel on the collapsed cart, the girls started anew to pull. Down in the pit we could rest a bit as *Lófogú* tortured the others above. We watched, petrified, how the veins bulged on the necks of those who pulled the carriage in front, their heads bent and one foot forward. We were afraid that they might tear themselves in half as they unsuccessfully pulled and pushed the heavy cargo. *Lófogú* started to scream and curse, raising his whip high to come down in force and bludgeon his victims; then as if by a miracle, the carriage started to roll.[169]

Junkers paid the SS *Haftlingsentgelte* a fixed amount for each labourer per day. This was transferred to the SS WVHA which ran all concentration camps. The companies took 40% for the prisoners' upkeep. 'Considering our poor nutrition, unheated and overcrowded barracks, and the surrounding fences in which the workers were caged, the charge of 40 per cent was outlandish.' For unskilled female labourers the factories paid four RM per day ($1.60 today). Of course the prisoners received nothing. 'No taxes or social insurance would be paid for them. Thus, private industry could not find cheaper labor than prisoners.'

The SS WVHA collected large sums. In December 1944 Junkers paid 96,356 RM for 31,669 days work at Markkleeberg. In February 1945 the payments increased to 34,116 days work. Whilst the SS reaped this benefit, Junkers also benefitted from using the slave labour. Kaitlin reflected:

The Holocaust was not just calculated genocide; it also included a plan for profiteering from the victims. No laws, of course, protected the

---

169 *SF* pp.65–67

Jewish prisoners. The SS placed almost no restrictions on employers concerning the safety or welfare of the workers. The result was that companies did whatever they pleased. Their physical capital was greatly valued. The machinery was operated with care, oiled, greased, and allowed to rest. We prisoners, on the other hand, were like a bit of sandpaper that, rubbed a few times, becomes useless and is thrown away. When concentration camp prisoners died, the statements from Markkleeberg and Buchenwald listed the names but not the causes of death. The diminished number of inmates was reported only so that a new shipment of slave laborers would be sent.

In the SS policy of extermination through work (*Vernichtung durch Arbeit*), the concentration camp played a central role. The Jews were worked until they were no longer useful, and then they were pushed aside to die. The potentially useful would be cared for minimally. Those who were judged by the staff doctors (prisoner doctors were never involved in these decisions) to be incapable of working were returned by sub-camps back to the main camps of Auschwitz or Bergen-Belsen, to their deaths. [170]

Eventually the girls were sent to work in the aircraft factory. Katalin and her sister were sent to the main factory – a twenty-minute walk at around 6.00am. They shivered walking with armed guards on both sides and *Aufseherinnen* with whips at the front and back. They went through 'The Jews Gate' which only opened for them. Still in columns of five, they were ordered to keep the lines straight. The factory was not heated, although some of the machinery generated heat. There was a heated office. The factory was very noisy with hammering, sawing and polishing assaulting their ears.

The girls discovered their dates of birth had been altered on the transport list by the Jewish inmates who registered them. It was dangerous to be too young and so they made her sister seven years older and Katalin four years older.[171]

Apparently the first transport had received two weeks proper training. But Katalin and Erzsike only had an hour, but even though it was explained in Hungarian, there were a lot of German technical words which were difficult to remember as they were 'hungry, tired and scared'.

Katalin detailed the terrible conditions in the camp. I cannot cover all the aspects here, but one incident involving the Commandant Alois Knittel cannot be excluded.

The first Saturday night after the New Year, the inmates from the whole camp were taken for a shower and disinfection. We had to tie our garments in a bundle, which was numbered. After the shower we were chased out naked and wet to wait outside in the snow until all the others joined us and our clothing was disinfected. It was unreal; the wintry cold was freezing our wet bodies. The water quickly turned to icicles in our hair and everywhere else. There was no means of protection from

---

170 *SF* pp.126–127
171 *SF* pp.128–9

the burn of the relentless winter wind. Our teeth chattering, Erzsike pulled me closer for warmth...The snow melted under our bare feet. The flaked flurries of crystal snow were drifting in the air; those few that reached the ground turned to black slush around this. Still we continued to stand in the relentless, unbearable cold. Many girls sobbed aloud. Others whimpered, with teeth clenched, and some recited phrases they remembered from the Psalms. As we were on the edge of falling into the tranquillity of death, our clothing arrived and we were allowed to go to the barracks. The next day, the *Revier* was crowded with women suffering from pneumonia, pleurisy, and infections of the urinary tract that troubled them for years to come.

The night of the shower was documented by survivors at the Center of Federal Justice Bureau for the Clarification of Nazi Crimes in Germany. The following was reported: 'In the winter of 1944–45 (the exact date was not remembered), the women were not scheduled to work that night and were taken for a shower. Knittel then ordered the women to go out to the *Appelplatz* naked and wait there for all the others. He left them standing in the freezing cold from 8 until 11 at night. Three young women died as a result.[172]

At the end of her remarkable book Zahava described their return to the family home in Abújzántó, in northern Hungary in the Tokay wine region, in July 1945. Their beloved parents did not return but there was a poignant reminder of their mother:

> Like Erzsike and I, many other returnees, after all their difficulties, arrived in their town or city only to find that strangers occupied their homes and their personal belongings were held by townspeople. Each of us has painful memories of seeing our precious things used by others. Some were able to reclaim part of their property with the aid of the police, but the majority had no strength or spirit to fight for things. When I saw my mother's suit being worn on the street, I collected my strength and dared to ask for it back. Mother's elegant black costume had much sentimental value for us, and I remembered the times she had prayed in the synagogue wearing her favourite [religious] holiday outfit. The woman in my mother's suit, a local resident, angrily rebuked me for stopping her in the street and said I was an audacious, impudent teenager with no manners and shame. 'I bought the suit legitimately at an auction conducted by the government, and you have no right to it!' she said, using the law as an excuse as she walked provocatively away. I was lucky she did not ask her son, who was with her to beat me up. I stood there helpless and dumbfounded; the only thing I could do was to cry, which I did.[173]

Before we leave this section we should note that Hugo Junkers (1859–1935) who had inherited the family business was an engineer of remarkable foresight

---

172 *SF* p.192. Alois Knittel was the Commandant of the camp.
173 Stessel pp.291–2

who developed the company to produce aircraft. He also had an interest in the arts. He was a main sponsor of the Bauhaus movement and assisted with the 1925 move from Weimar to Dessau, where his factory was based.

When the Nazis came to power, Hermann Göring, who was the *Reichscommissar* of Aviation, asked Junkers to help with German re-armament. Junkers refused. The Nazis subsequently threatened him that unless he handed over all his companies' patents and market shares he would be imprisoned for High Treason. At that time he was in his seventies and fearing for the safety of his wife and twelve children, agreed, but he was still confined to house arrest. The 3rd of February 1935 was his 76th birthday. The Nazis came again to pester him for the rights to his companies. The circumstances are unclear, but he died at home that day and shortly afterwards, his wife sold all the rights and patents for a fraction of their true worth. It is alleged that Göring was taking revenge for being rejected as a test pilot in the early 1920s.[174]

Hugo Junkers was a decent family man – a scholar and an engineer who would have been horrified had he known what the Nazis did in his company's name.

Browarna St. Labour Camp[175]

I found this piece in the writings of Rabbi Huberband published in 1982. I have searched for corroborating evidence about the camp but found very little. However, the story is so detailed and he was such a man of integrity that I have accepted it as valid.

Rabbi Shimon Huberband (1909–1942) had lived in Piotrków but within days of the start of the war a German bomb killed his wife, children and father-in-law. Only his faith sustained him. In 1940 he moved to Warsaw. He had known Emmanuel Ringelblum (1900–1944) before the war through YIVO. He joined Ringelblum's Oyneg Shabbat group. He was made head of the Department of Religious Affairs in Aleynhilf, the main welfare organization of the ghetto. He also remarried.

When the Great Deportation began, the Rabbi was found work in Emil Weitz's brush shop. It was raided by the SS in August 1942 and he was sent straight to the Umschlagplatz. There was no time to bribe the guards to release him.[176] He and his second wife were both killed at Treblinka.

He was regarded as deeply religious but very tolerant. He was described as 'A great scholar, highly erudite in the Torah, Mishna, and Talmud, a man of noble virtue, a fervent Hassid with a flaming heart, he nevertheless always tried to use common sense.'[177]

174 Carly Courtney, *Disciples of Flight: Hugo Junkers*, 9 January 2017
175 Shimon Huberband, *The Labor Camp for Women*, in 'Kiddush Hashem' pp.421–442
176 Simon D. Kassow, *Who Will Write Our History* pp.165–9
177 Menakhem Mendel Kon, cited in Kassow p.166

His writings and notes were handwritten in Yiddish. After his death they were incorporated in the Oneg Shabbat archive and buried. One part of the archive was discovered in September 1946 and another, on the same site, in December 1950. The third part has not so far been uncovered. His writings were assembled into a Hebrew edition in 1969 and in 1982 the first English version was published. Huberband's writing was described as 'part diary, part autobiography, part eyewitness account and part historical monograph'.[178]

He did not believe the Nazis' behaviour excused Jewish failings and was particularly hard on women in his essay 'Moral Lapses of Jewish Women During the War'. The other work of interest describes a labour camp in Lublin. Little background is provided but it is written in the first person by a fifteen-year-old girl from Warsaw.

In early 1942 the Germans asked the Lublin community to provide 300 women to work at plucking feathers under the supervision of the SS. Although 'a fine salary plus meals' was offered the word went round that the conditions would be terrible and so very few women volunteered. Accordingly the *Judenrät* sent out many Jewish policemen and 'prisoners' from the labour camp to seize Jewish girls and women and over fifty women were taken away. These included wives, mothers and even twelve-year-old girls. This was organised by the head of the *Judenrät* 's labour bureau, Mr Bradt.

They were taken to the Browarna Street labour camp where Jewish craftsmen such as tailors, shoemakers and hatters worked. The women were locked in the barracks with no food. Permission was given for food to be brought to them from home. However, since Browarna Street was outside the ghetto, everyone taking food to these captured women had to have permission to leave the ghetto. The fifty women were inadequate to the task and so in the middle of the night Jewish homes were raided and sixty women and girls taken from their beds to Browarna street. Some rich women bought their freedom and others had been warned and had hidden themselves away.

The 15-year-old girl explained she had left Warsaw at the beginning of summer in 1941 because of the hunger and poverty in the ghetto and come to a relative in Lublin. Her mother died in Warsaw and with the house full of small children someone had to care for them. It had taken weeks to get a travel pass back to Warsaw from Mr Bradt. On 14 January at 10.00 she went to the door to buy potatoes when it burst open. Five men were there including Bradt, who said they were taking her to the women's camp. Bradt said he had been beaten because there weren't enough women and they would only take her for one day.

She waited in the courtyard and eventually Bradt and the others came back with 10 prisoners including two 12-year-old girls. They were taken to a garage for German trucks and eventually there were about 250 women, from elderly to the very young girls, as many had been brought from Browarna Street. She described the conditions:

It was freezing cold that day, and the garage wasn't heated. During the several hours we were there, we nearly froze to death. We were all

---

178 Jeffrey S. Gurock, 'Introduction to the English Language Edition', in *Kiddush Hashem* 1987 pp.xvii-xix

terribly hungry; they gave us absolutely no food. We simply collapsed due to the freezing cold, hunger and exhaustion.

There were many officers in the garage, and they were headed by the Chief of the SS, who held a long thick whip in his hand. At the door to the garage, there stood many mothers, fathers, and brothers of captured girls, who had brought clothing and food for them. The girls went over to the door to take the things which had been brought for them. At that point the chief of the SS began to beat the girls brutally with his whip, hitting their heads. We immediately realized what kind of situation we had fallen into.

At about 4.00am we were led out of the garage to the square in the market, where we were lined up in rows of four and counted. The SS announced, 'If one girl runs away, the other three girls from her row will be shot.' They began to take us to the steambath on Trzeciego Maja Street.

In the freezing cold of 20 degrees Fahrenheit, and on terribly slippery roads of ice, the Germans led us to the steambath. We were followed by a taxi filled with German officers.

Then suddenly, they began to beat us and force us to run. The taxi literally ran over the last few rows of girls and pushed everyone forward. The rows turned into a crowded, panicking mob. The slipperiness made everyone fall, and we all fell on top of each other. That was apparently what they wanted. They began to trample on the bodies of the women who fell; they beat everyone brutally. Many girls became bloodied and wounded.

We finally arrived at the bathhouse. When we were left stark-naked, they moved about in our midst and sent in the Jewish policemen, group leaders and 'prisoners' to do the same. We noted that the Jews dropped their eyes. One girl covered her body with something; when a German officer passed alongside her, he beat her for doing so.

The order was given for all of us to get dressed within two minutes. We were overjoyed when we were finally out of the bathhouse.

From there, they took us to the building of the former Home for Polish Soldiers. We were led across a large yard, up a stairwell to the second storey, and across various rooms and halls, both large and small. We were finally taken into a large hall, all of whose exits were guarded by SS men.

In the hall, there were a number of rows of tables, and between tables there was a large wooden crate. One of the walls was lined with huge sacks of unplucked feathers. When we entered the hall part of it was already occupied by approximately 150 female convicts, both Jewish and Christian, who were plucking[179] and pulling feathers.

---

179 The translator used the word plucking. In fact plucking is removing the feathers from the animal. This had already been done as the feathers were delivered in bags. What the women were doing was 'quilling' removing the hard quill from the down feathers. I am grateful to Rachel Parker of Gressingham Foods for her advice.

Two military guards stayed behind, as did the chief of the worksite. He went over to a sack, took out a handful of feathers and put them down on a table. He then proceeded to pull a feather, showing us how it is plucked – the down should be pulled off and thrown in the crate; the hard feathers should be kept separately. When a pile of hard feathers had accumulated it should be taken away. The work must be performed efficiently. If a hard feather is found in a crate, the responsible workers will be punished with lashes.

Our contingent was called the 'ghetto'; the contingent of convicts was called the 'prison'. Four girls were placed at each table to take feathers out of the sack and put them on the table. Each girl took feathers from the table and plucked their down into the crate. There were four girls to a crate. Each one of the 'prison' girls had a chair to sit on, but not every 'ghetto' girl had a chair. There were only a few chairs, which were rotated and passed on from one girl to the next.

The SS chief with the whip issued the order: 'Get to work!' We sat down at once to pluck feathers. The chief also announced that if any of us dozed off for an instant whilst at work, that girl would be whipped. He roamed across the hall like a wild animal. back and forth, looking to find some sort of transgression. But everyone was watching out for their skin. Even those girls who had chairs stood up so they wouldn't fall asleep.

It was close to twelve midnight. Our fingers were swollen due to the continuous work, our arms and legs were about to break, our eyes were growing heavy. We were weak and famished. The chief suddenly jumped up and announced that a commission had arrived to examine our work. The commission consisted of four people – three military men and one civilian. They went from crate to crate, looking for feather among the plucked down. When they found a feather in a crate, the chief addressed the four female workers at the responsible table: 'Come this way, come!' And he ordered them to step to the side.

Thirty Jewish forced laborers, in all, assembled at the side of the room, including young girls and elderly women. The chief then placed a table in the middle of the room, selected one of the women, placed her on the table and rolled up her dress. He removed her underwear and beat her naked body with a rod twenty-five times at 'a certain place'.

Blood began to run after the first few blows, but this did not calm the evil one's anger. On the contrary, like the bull in a bullfight, the sight of blood provoked him even more, and he completed the beating with even more fury.

As soon as the punishments began to be executed, all the girls began to cry out loud and shriek. At that point the chief announced that any girl who shouted and anyone being beaten who screamed would be given twice as many blows.

The girl who was the first to be beaten became hysterical, but this did not matter to him in the least. After beating her, he took her into the washroom to let her calm down, and told her to clean off her blood.

He conducted the same procedure for all the subjects, including a number of elderly women. The terror and fear of this cruel man was so great that all the beaten women, upon returning from the washroom, calmed themselves of their hysteria. They all washed off their blood and bandaged their wounds. They returned at once to work.

The four commission members who witnessed the punishments laughed loudly during them and repeated constantly, 'Very good, very good.'

The chief ran from one table to the next, shouting endlessly the two Polish words he knew: *Predko robicz* – 'work quickly'. We were afraid to look him straight in the face. The commission members spent over two hours with us, until all the punishments had been meted out.

At 2.00am the chief ordered the 'prison' to go to sleep and the 'ghetto' to continue working. The 'bedroom' was a large hall with four windows. The floor was covered with straw, but there wasn't a single pillow of straw or hay, and not a single blanket. The 'prison girls' lay down alongside each other in their clothes and slept.

We continued working. Those girls who had been standing for hours because of the shortage of chairs in the 'ghetto' were filled with pleasure when they sat on the chairs vacated from the 'prison'.

At about 5.00am the chief awakened the 'prison' to return to work. They were given food to eat. Each female convict received a quarter-kilogram of black bread and a cup of black coffee. All we were given was a little tin can of jam; nothing to eat or drink with it. In our state of hunger, the food given to the 'prison' workers sharpened and heightened our appetites. The chief announced that the *Judenrät* was supposed to provide our food, but was in no rush to do so.

The 'prison' sat down to work. We had to return the chairs to them and continue our work while standing. At about 11.00am a few 'prisoners' from the Lublin labor camp arrived with a cauldron of food which had been sent by the *Kehilah*. It was a soup made of water. The whole cauldron had just a few potatoes – unpeeled.

The chief ordered us to stop work for half an hour and then ordered us to 'continue working'. Our fingers hurt terribly; it was simply impossible to move them. Our eyes were gradually growing heavier.

The chief, holding his whip in his hand, was hiding in the next room. From there he watched through a glass pane to see which girl was falling asleep. As soon as he noticed such a girl, he went over to her and beat her with his whip over the head. He punished a number of 'sleepers' by placing them under a freezing-cold shower for some time. When the girl returned from the shower he shouted at her, 'Now you won't sleep any more!'

One girl fainted due to exhaustion, and we all ran over to resuscitate her. The chief began to beat people, and shouted that no one was allowed to go over to save anyone. He would resuscitate everyone himself. Whoever went over to save someone else would be given twenty-five blows.

The girl lay stretched out on the floor unconscious. No one dared to go over to her, and the chief was in no hurry. Eventually, he and a soldier carried away the unconscious girl to the washroom, put her under the shower, and poured water on her for as long as it took until she regained consciousness. After resting for a few minutes, she was ordered to return to work at once.

The same thing happened several times. At noon food was brought in for the 'convicts' with only the leftovers given to the 'ghetto' women. Later the same day the prison director came with others to inspect the camp. The convicts complained about the SS chief beating them and allowing them little sleep. As result the chief was told to improve their conditions and the convicts were removed from the chief's supervision. The same day, two female guards arrived in the workroom – one was Polish and the other Ukrainian. The chief and two soldiers were replaced by them.

As if the previous hardships weren't enough, we now faced a new problem – both women were terrible anti-Semites. They beat us, cursed at us, harrassed us every other minute. The camp chief no longer had the authority to beat the convicts, but the female guards *did* have the authority to beat us. After all, we were Jews! Especially the Ukrainian woman made our lives miserable. 'I've been waiting twenty years,' she said, 'for the day when I could get back at the Jews.'

At 6.00pm they were given the convicts' leftovers of watery soup and raisin bread. Finally the 'ghetto' were told they could sleep.

We went into the 'bedroom' and lay down on the same straw which the 'prison' girls had slept on the night before. After one and a half hours of sleep, preceded by forty-eight hours of work, the chief came in, shouted 'Everybody up!' and started beating people with his rod. At 9.00pm we sat down once again to begin work.

The description of her terrible experiences continues for several more pages. She eventually became seriously ill with five other girls. Even the Ukrainians sent to beat them back to work realised how ill they were. They were released and told they were going to hospital. However the Nazis' mendacity continued as they were sent home. However getting back to Warsaw was not easy.

I began to work at obtaining a travel permit to Warsaw, and learned that all the train passes were forged. So I had no choice but to buy a pass from a forger for two hundred zlotys.

I also learned that extensive searches were conducted at the railroad station in Deblin; military policemen were said to search all the cars for Jews. When I boarded the train in Lublin. I bargained with the conductor, gave him forty zlotys, and he hid me underneath a pile of luggage in the last car. And that is how I reached Warsaw safely.

In Warsaw, I went to the transfer bureau and received permission to enter the ghetto on the basis of my travel permit. When I reached the gate at the corner of Leszno and Zelazna Streets, I showed the guard my entry permit from the transfer bureau. The Polish policeman nonetheless threatened to arrest me unless I gave him money. We, a group of five people, decided not to give him a single groschen because we had valid transfer permits. The policeman proceeded to arrest us and began to take us to the station house at 40 Leszno Street.

When we saw that he wasn't joking, we started to bargain with him. He released us in front of the station house for the price of fifteen zlotys.

Now I'm in the Warsaw ghetto. The work continues at that hell on earth called the Lublin Labor Camp for Women.

Most of the residents of the Warsaw Ghetto were deported to Treblinka in 1942. I suspect that the young girl whose story Rabbi Huberband recorded did not survive the Holocaust. Had she done so, I feel that she would have made herself known.

I tried to find more information about the camp but it was not easy. The Museum at Majdanek told me they did not have much information but knew that it was a small penal camp for Jews taken there as a result of roundups. It was established in 1940 in a tenement building and was subordinate to the German Employment Bureau. They confirmed Jewish women worked there.[180]

The young girl does not give the SS Chief's name – probably she did not know it. I discovered that an Austrian, Odilo Globočnik, supervised SS activities in Lublin including the forced labour camps. Odilo was an early member of the Nazi party, joining in Carinthia in 1930. He rose through the ranks but was imprisoned for over a year for political offences and may have murdered a Jewish jeweller, Futterweiss. Although he was made *Gauleiter* of Vienna in May 1938, Göring had him suspended. Later Himmler pardoned him and in September 1939 he was appointed as SS and Police Leader for the Lublin district in Poland where he was known as brutal. He was a central figure in Operation *Reinhard*.[181] He was arrested by the British Army on 31 May 1945 but committed suicide with a cyanide capsule before trial. A photo of him dying was taken by a German sergeant who wanted a record of 'the worst man in the world'. The local priest refused to bury him in consecrated ground. The historian Michael Allen described him as 'the vilest individual in the vilest organization ever known'.

---

180 Jakub Chmielewski, Majdanek State Museum, email to author 7 September 2017.
181 HEART, *Odilo Globocnik 'The Worst Man in the World'* http://www. holocaustresearchproject.org/ar/globocknik.html 2007, accessed 10 September 2017

Resistance

The next section covers Jewish women's involvement in Resistance of various forms. To explain the many different aspects of Resistance, I have reproduced a text I found in Israel in 1997. It was in the Beit Lohamei Haghetaot Museum, which is part of the Ghetto Fighters' Kibbutz. I have always found it very important and poignant in describing the grades and levels of resistance and rescue.

To smuggle a loaf of bread – was to resist
To teach in secret – was to resist
To cry out warning and shatter illusions – was to resist
To forge documents – was to resist
To smuggle people across borders – was to resist
To chronicle events and conceal the records – was to resist
To hold out a helping hand to the needy – was to resist
To contact those under siege and smuggle weapons – was to resist
To fight with weapons in streets, mountains and forests – was to resist
To rebel in death camps – was to resist
To rise up in ghettos, among the crumbling walls, in the most desperate revolt – was to resist.[182]

The eminent Israeli Holocaust historian, Yehuda Bauer, was interviewed at Yad Vashem in 1998. The question of resistance was discussed at length. Much of what he says resonates with Avrahmi's piece. For example, speaking about diarists 'Writing diaries was a way of expressing opposition and resistance.'[183]

From that he turned to physical resistance such as that undertaken by the *Sonderkommando* in Auschwitz. There were several revenge acts and on one occasion an SS man was thrown alive into the ovens. Bauer commented

---

182 Monia Avrahmi, *Flames in the Ashes* – written in 1985 for the film. Monia worked at the museum.
183 Yad Vashem, *An Interview with Professor Yehuda Bauer,* 18 January 1998, Jerusalem. Interviewer Amos Goldberg. P.23, http://www.yadvashem.org/odot_pdf/Microsoft%20Word%20-%203856.pdf, accessed 29 October 2017.

'From a psychological point of view, this is an extreme example of what people can be forced to do when absolute terror is exercised against them.'

Bauer refers to Filip Müller, who described the actions of the dancer Franceska Mann (see pages 266–71) in his memoirs of his time as a member of the *Sonderkommando*. At one time he planned to commit suicide but a woman friend pushed him out of the gas chamber saying he must survive to tell the story. This of course was a continual message in the Holocaust 'people were told by their relatives, friends, or inner voices that they must survive in order to tell the story. It was a major element in the desire for survival.'

When asked about a general pattern of Jewish response during the Holocaust, Bauer said the reaction runs the whole gamut of possible responses:

...from utter disorientation, helplessness and desperate obedience to anything the murderers said, to a full realization of what was happening. Knowing there was no way out, some proudly went to their death in the pits and gas chambers, whereas others chose various forms of resistance. In some instances, Jews did collaborate with the Nazis; an example is a number of cases of Jewish agents or Jewish policemen...[184]

Examples of these were Stella (the Black Panther) described in *Who Betrayed the Jews*? And another is Stella Goldschlag in Berlin who betrayed fellow Jews thinking she was protecting her parents and herself. However, in most cases when the Nazis had what they wanted, they sent the betrayers to be killed like everyone else.

In other cases people went to the other extreme. Mostly the young, who thought there was no other way, resorted to arms, limited though they might be with what was available. There was fighting physically against the Germans but there were also in-between reactions – from running schools and prayer groups to organising literary and artistic activities as a protest against the Germans desire to reduce the morale of the Jews. An enormous flowering of cultural activities were seen in the ghettos of Warsaw and Theresienstadt.

Bauer regarded the smuggling food of food into the ghettos as unarmed resistance. Likewise we shall see later that women in prison were encouraged to maintain their self-respect by washing themselves, doing their hair and keeping the cell tidy. This was regarded as 'spiritual resistance'.

Bauer refers to those who had lost all hope, being willing to go wherever they were led. This happens in other genocides. However I think this partly ignores the fact that many people were law-abiding, believed the Nazis' lies about a new life in the East and also thought if they did as they were told and kept their heads down, all would be well and Hitler and his Nazis would soon be gone.

Different Jews had different reactions. People who don't have arms cannot fight and many groups of Jews consisted of women and children, with the able-bodied men all taken away. You cannot flee to the forests if you live

---

184 P.24

in the suburbs. Partisans need some local support and classes do not occur without teachers.

There were also different attitudes from those of different traditions. The very orthodox expressed the view that it was the will of God and did not react, such as was demonstrated at Telšiai (see pages 155–60).

Bauer then refers to a hidden ideology, a tradition:

A woman protects her children. Now that is true for any woman anywhere, but she becomes an active person, she pushes her children to rescue themselves, even when she knows she can't rescue herself. She pushes others, she fights for them. Now again, this is not specific to Jews. But in this extreme circumstance it changes a Jewish tradition, while it continues other traditions. She's responsible now; the husband has disappeared. He's been killed and she is alone, fighting for her children's lives, in order to protect them. She draws strength from certain types of Jewish traditions, and opposes others in order to fight. I think this is the classic reaction for a whole series of situations.

The question of the reaction of Jewish women in the Holocaust is part of the Holocaust. Women were targeted just as were men. Jewish women (for the first time for thousands of years in Jewish communities) assumed leadership positions. Politically, Jewish women had always been disenfranchised, but in the Holocaust, there was no room for this disenfranchisement. They became leaders of political and social groups in France, Holland, Bohemia and Slovakia, as well as the underground groups in Eastern Europe.[185]

The question of armed Jewish resistance has to be seen in proportion as it was on the margins of the Holocaust. The numbers of fighters is very small compared with the millions of dead. Before the Holocaust the Jews had no access to arms and no tradition of an independent military force even though an unexpectedly large proportion fought in the First World War. There was no united leadership either. Nothing much changed during the Holocaust when there was opposition or indifference from the non-Jews around them or an insistence that Jews should join the general resistance. This all impacted on Jewish resistance. People question how many Germans the armed Jews killed. Not many, but the intention was to make a statement against the German murders. Resistance was a moral imperative:

This was, of course, particularly true for youth, and the overall picture of Jewish resistance in Europe is much larger, despite it being marginal, than we originally thought. We estimate today that approximately 30,000 Jews participated in partisan fighting in the forests of Eastern Europe against the Germans. This is a rather large number. Most of them died. It didn't prove to be a major way of rescue but it made a statement.

In the ghettos of Poland and Lithuania, we know of some 17 ghettos where Jews organized some sort of resistance. Only in a few places did

---

185 Bauer pp.26–7

it result in actual resistance. But in a large number of ghettos, especially in what is now Belarus (which was partly Eastern Poland and, therefore, the former Soviet Union after World War II) we estimate that there were some 65 ghettos where there were armed groups, who then escaped into the forests and joined the tens of thousands of Jewish people who tried to resist. They didn't always manage to get arms (and therefore fight) but they tried.

It should be remembered there were even Jewish rebellions in the extermination camps – in Sobibor, Treblinka and Auschwitz. It was only Jews who rebelled in the Nazi concentrations camps. There were other resistance groups such as the 'International Resistance in Buchenwald'. They took over the camp after the Nazis left, they did not fight them, but occupied the camp until the Americans arrived. The only armed resistance in the camps was Jewish resistance according to Bauer.

> There was Jewish armed resistance in France (quite massively, considering the small number of young men who remained) and in Italy and in Bulgaria. Over 7,000 Jewish men and women joined the Tito partisans in Yugoslavia; this is a large number considering the number of Jews there. There were 1,600 Jews fighting in the hills of Slovakia in 1944 and there was a Jewish underground resistance group in Germany. In other words, it occurred almost everywhere, and it is significant as a symbol.
>
> It is less important whether German lines of communication were vitally disrupted by mines that the Jews had laid – that is not the issue at all. The important issue is that they laid the mines. Jewish armed resistance was massive, nevertheless marginal, but very important because it became a symbol of Jewish reaction. However, Jewish unarmed active resistance was much more widespread than Jewish armed resistance.[186]

Women Parachutists

Haviva was one of a group of Jewish men and women from Palestine (now Israel) who volunteered to join the British Army and be parachuted into occupied Europe. They were to organize resistance to the Germans as well as helping to rescue Allied personnel. There were originally 250 volunteers of whom 110 were chosen to be trained. Of these, 32 were eventually parachuted into Europe and five arrived by other methods. Most of them were emigrants from Europe and were sent to their original country because of their personal knowledge both of the terrain and the language. Of the 32, only three of them were women.[187]

---

186 Bauer p.28
187 USHMM, *Jewish Parachutists from Palestine*, accessed 22 January 2017.

The idea of this group came from Reuven Shiloah (1909–1959) who was born in Jerusalem. He was a political advisor in the Jewish Agency and later to the Ministry of Foreign Affairs. From 1936 to 1948, he was liaison officer between the Jewish Agency and the British Army authorities in Palestine and it was in this role that the parachute project was developed. In 1945, he was a Jewish Agency observer at the United Nations founding conference in San Francisco and later he was responsible for the creation of Mossad.[188]

The project with the British used the courage and eagerness of young Jews who had emigrated to Israel before the war. These youngsters responded to the dire conditions for their fellow Jews in Nazi-occupied Europe.

Voices – the voices of brothers crying from the death wagons, gas chambers and mass graves – filled the hearts of the parachutists and gave them no peace.

'I could not resist the voice which called me,' said Enzo Sereni.

'I went because the voice called,' said Hannah Senesh.

'Duty called – I could not live in peace if I did not answer the call,' wrote Zvi Ben Ya'acov.

'I must go to Hungarian Jewry; to arouse them; prepare them; arm them,' said Joel Nusbacher.

This was the feeling of every parachutist toward the Jewry in the land of his birth where he was designated to jump. Each knew the danger attached to such a mission; they were parachutists in fascist territory; and Jewish parachutists, even though wearing the uniform of British officers. In the case of the women, death was certain if caught, for they could not pretend to be lost pilots – they stood revealed as spies beyond the shadow of doubt. Still they wrote, 'It is necessary to do even the impossible...It is necessary to try even at the cost of life.'[189]

Many of the youngsters wanted to volunteer as parachutists but very few were chosen. They mostly came from the country from agricultural settlements – 'straight from the plough and the barn'. But there were also fishermen. They had all arrived by different means in Eretz Israel by different means. They had all helped to found new settlements, creating fertile land out of swamps and preparing the land for the others who would come. 'They regard us as heroes,' said one of the parachutists after meeting the Jews in the Diaspora. 'I couldn't seem to explain to them that every kibbutznik would be glad to do our work, if only he were permitted.'

---

188 JTA, *Reuven Shiloah, Leading Israeli Diplomat, Dead.* 11 May 1959, accessed 13 August 2017.
    http://www.jta.org/1959/05/11/archive/reuven-shiloah-leading-israeli-diplomat-dead-served-in-washington

189 Dorothy and Pessach Bar-Adon, *Seven Who Fell*, Zionist Organization Youth Department (1947), p.10

The first two were dropped in Roumania and were caught by the fascists. They were followed by others in Yugoslavia, Slovakia, Hungary, Roumania and Bulgaria. Everywhere they left a good impression. The following note from Colonel William Jones who served with the partisans, is typical of others. Colonel Jones wrote from London regarding Hannah Senesh:

By the way, I had the pleasure of meeting a young lady who parachuted in Slovenia to my headquarters and then proceeded overland to another part of Europe. She was a grand girl and was plucky as anyone could be. She was accompanied by two other young men from Palestine. They were all excellent and will be regarded as great heroes as time goes on. Should you ever meet them, please give them all my love...[190]

Hannah's British commanding officer wrote:

The 1943 volunteers were urgently required to work in the Balkans in connection with the rescue of Allied Military Personnel stranded or in prison in enemy-occupied territory. Miss Hannah Senesh was one of the earliest volunteers. The conditions and qualifications required were comprehensive and strict. Hannah possessed sense; the remainder she achieved by hard work and devotion to duty. Her comment when asked if she was frightened on her first parachute jump was typical:
    'Not more than anyone else in the plane.'
    Her cheerfulness and enthusiasm were infectious and she set a hard pace for her male associates to maintain. When the time came for her to go to Jugoslavia as the first step on her errand of mercy she did not flinch nor display any last minute temperament. To Hannah it was her duty and as such it was done. She died at the hands of the Nazi butchers whilst trying to rescue allied prisoners of war in Hungary. Just a girl of 23 but one possessing a flame of patriotism and devotion to duty that is worth remembering these days. Let us profit by the memory of gallantry and courage displayed by thus young girl and ensure that Hannah Senesh and others did not die in vain.[191]

Their job was to relay information back to the British on 'enemy strength, factories, bridges and troop movements'. They used three Hebrew phrases to contact the Allied military bases from behind the enemy lines – Am Israel Hai (The people of Israel live) Aliyah Hofshit (Free Immigration) and Medina Ivrit (Jewish State). 'Their additional mission to the despairing Jews trapped in those countries was to bring the glad tidings of Eretz Israel Rebuilt; to save lives; to organise the Jews for defence; to expand the Jewish underground; to distribute funds.'[192]

---

190 *Seven Who Fell* p.13
191 P.14
192 P.9

The three women were Sarah (Surika) Braverman, born in Romania in 1919, Haviva Reik, born in Slovakia in 1914 and Hannah Szenes, born in Budapest in 1921. Only Surika survived – she said: 'Of course we thought we'd return. We weren't adventurers, nor were we setting out to commit suicide. We were all convinced that we would see our loved ones, our friends, our families again.'

Haim Hermesh, the only Slovakian to return alive added: 'Haviva was afraid she wouldn't return. More than once she told me that even if she were to survive – and she had serious doubts about that – it was already too late for her to become a mother.'[193]

During training at Ramat David, when it came to the first parachute jumps, most had no problems.

Haviva Reik, one of the oldest members of the group, had injured her hand during the Palmach drills the previous summer, and there was concern that it was not yet strong enough to handle a parachute. The first jump proved this fear to be groundless. Haim Hermesh recalled how, flying over the fields of Ramat David, Reik first peered down at the green fields and then resolutely walked over to the doorway of the aircraft. Darting a quick glance at the instructor, a sergeant and teacher from a small English village, she vanished through the doorway, a smile on her lips. Hermesh remembers how calm she was during the jump: 'She jumped quietly and boldly, with the parachute canopy covering her. We felt that something extraordinary and fateful had just occurred: the second Jewish woman had parachuted from the skies of Palestine and had embarked on a tale of daring and affliction.'

In contrast to the relative psychological ease with which Reik accomplished her first jump...the vivacious Braverman – referred to by her British commanders as the 'blond bombshell' – could not overcome her fear of jumping from an airplane. Braverman recalled the seconds of fear that pursued her long after. 'It was already my turn to jump from the plane, but when the English sergeant shouted "Go!" I automatically moved back and stayed on the floor of the plane, while those in line behind me jumped, one after another. Showing tremendous solidarity with her plight, her comrades offered to jump with her in tandem – one on either side of her – until she could overcame her fear. She repeatedly refused their generous offer until the British officer suggested a compromise by assigning her a part in the operation that did not involve a parachute drop.[194]

The work was secret and the parachutists' families did not know what was happening.

Surika Braverman remembers how she left twenty postcards with her operators in Bari with descriptions of her supposed doings in Italy.

193 Judith Tydor Baumel-Schwartz, *Perfect Heroes* (Madison: U of Wisconsin, 2010) p.3
194 P.17

Throughout her active duty the postcards were sent to her sister once a week to hide the true nature of her mission in Europe.[195]

Reflecting on the impact of the project:

> Apart from their successful or unsuccessful military activities, the parachutists contributed considerably to encouraging, emboldening, inspiring, and raising the morale of the local Jews if only by means of the rumors about their presence that circulated. Enzo Sereni, who was captured immediately after landing and subsequently perished in Dachau, is a case in point. The rumor about the presence of a Jewish parachutist in the camp spread like wildfire. According to Ruth Bondy, 'in the eyes of the Jews, many of them Zionists, a Jew from the land of Israel and a British officer appeared like an angel who descended from another world that had long sunk into oblivion.'[196]

Haviva Reik

Haviva Reik who was born in Slovakia in 1914 came from a large family and was a keen member of a Zionist youth group. Her plans to emigrate to Palestine had to be put on hold when her family needed her to bring some money home. She got a sales job for a factory making agricultural machinery, making her rounds on a motorcycle. 'Being the first woman in the country to dare to manipulate such a speed demon, she was a spectacle on the roads.'[197] In 1938 she managed to start her emigration training in Bratislava. She married another Zionist and in 1939 they left for Palestine settling on Kibbutz Ma'anit. Haviva trained with the underground military in the *Palmah*. Hearing about the parachute unit, she joined it hoping to be sent to Slovakia to help rescue Jews there.

In the late summer of 1944, Reik was sent to Bari in Italy to await posting. However she was thwarted by British military rules which prohibited women doing 'blind drops'. Therefore she was prevented from joining her male colleagues on the Slovakian mission. 'How can I stay here in Bari when there will be no representative of Hashomer Hatsair among the parachutists?' she asked her friend who was trying to persuade her that she was fated not to go with the men. However Reik was not giving up. She found an American military transport bound for Banska Bustrica in Slovakia, held by anti-German forces. The parachutists were headed there and she actually got there before the men.

On 21 September 1944 Reik parachuted into Slovakia just in the middle of the national Slovak rising. She was meant to reach the capital and connect with the leaders of an underground Jewish rescue unit called the 'Working

---

195 P.34
196 P.41
197 *Seven Who Fell* p.143

Group'. Three other parachutists had arrived in the previous week and another one, Abba Berdiczew, arrived at the end of September with the radio transmitters for everyone. They made contact with the local Hashomer Hatsair and the leader Egon Rot. For six weeks they were performing two tasks – getting Allied pilots back home and dealing with the thousands of Slovakian Jewish refugees seeking safety in the area. Haviva ran a large public kitchen feeding the thousands of hungry refugee Jews.[198]

Haviva, who was past thirty when she undertook her mission to the Jews of Slovakia, was known as 'the mother' of the younger parachutists. Efficient, level-headed, straight as a die, in the end, Haviva became a legend among the entrapped Slovakian Jews whom she helped to organise as fighting partisans.[199]

Her life started and ended in the Carpathian mountains, spanning the two world wars. Having no outstanding gifts, being in no way a 'career' woman, Haviva's dream expressed in many letters was simply 'to settle down after it's all over and have babies.'[200]

Her letters reveal her feelings as she waited in Egypt for the mission to begin:

On the one hand, she is filled with the zest of living and tries to devour the pleasures of Egypt. There are the accounts of the park, the zoo on Sundays, cruises on the Nile, climbing the Pyramids and 'descending like gazelles,' an evening of 'Bambi'. On the other hand, there is the ledger-balancing of a mature woman who knows very well what faces her.

On April 16, 1944 she wrote: 'In a few days I will be thirty. It is difficult for me to say that I feel that age. The years go by quickly and there is still so much to accomplish. I have no feeling of not having exploited the years, but who knows, perhaps I didn't think enough of myself. But this has been a war within me ever since I joined the movement. Private happiness versus the filling of duty. More than once the two have collided and the stronger won out.'

May 3, 1944, 'I too wanted a quiet life, a family life. To give up having a child was not easy. But my optimism says that it is never too late. Perhaps I will also fulfil that duty – surely the greatest for a woman.'

Toward the end of May, she is studying for her secret service activities and writes, 'Most of my time I fill with study. I am busy until eight in the evening with only short recesses. I progress well and often and I am surprised that I have the power to concentrate and grasp things under these nerve-racking conditions.'

July 6, 1944. 'I pass through different moods. Sometimes there are days of tension without measure and afterwards days of quiet and contentment. I try to control myself and to meet the future quietly.

---

198 Judith Tydor Baumel, *Havivah Reik 1914–1944*, Jewish Women's Archive (JWA) 1 March 2009, accessed 22 January 2017. https://jwa.org/encyclopedia/article/reik-havivah

199 *Seven Who Fell* p.141

200 *Seven Who Fell* p.142

I know that the last moment will be difficult because we are only people of flesh and blood. But I am sure that I will reach my goal. I am sure that I will do everything demanded of me and I am sure that I will return. Then I will remember I am a woman. For is man made for war? Is the Jew made to kill? Is a woman made to wage battles? But I will return to my settlement – I will have a family, children...'

On July 30, 1944, after her last leave in Eretz Israel, Haviva wrote of her leave-taking from her nephew, Michael, aged eighteen months. 'Michael stood up in his crib and asked me, 'When will you come back?' It was the first time he had ever said those words. Did he feel that I had no answer for him? And at that moment, I felt a prick in my heart.'

The next letter is written to her comrades in Ma'anit, an hour before her plane takes off for Slovakia. 'I think of you and that strengthens me. I am quiet and look with clear eyes to the future. We will meet soon.'

Haviva arrives in Banka Bystrica and writes her first letter to Ma'anit. 'If I were to write all that I lived through in these two weeks, I would have to write a novel and we will leave that until I return home. Yes? The first days were very difficult. I worried about R. Z. and Ch. Who came only after nine or ten days. In addition to that, everything had changed here and the addresses I had were old. Luckily, I knew the surroundings and the people and after four days I made the necessary contacts and started to work. My position was – and is today – complicated and difficult because they know me here, both the gentiles and our people.

'Up to now, I was able to take care that nobody recognised me except the people whom I had to get in touch with for our work. In spite of everything, people try to identify me.

'A few days ago, they swooped down on my apartment, but luckily, I wasn't there that night. So I remained, as you see, alive. We hope that all will end well. We work at a quick tempo; there are many worries, arrangements, much work. But I live with only one thought; to save what is possible...'[201]

In November 1944 they had to evacuate the settlement at Banksa Bystrica because of the oncoming German forces. They had two options – to go to the hills with the younger, fitter and healthier leaving most of the Jews to their fate or trying to take the whole group to safety. Reik's preference was the latter course and she persuaded the others to agree, however when they reached Bukovice they were attacked by *Hiwis* (Hil*fs*williger, meaning 'voluntary assistant', or, more literally, 'willing helper', in this case Ukrainian Nazi collaborators in the SS). Reik and Reiss were taken to prison. Early on 20 November 1944, together with a group of captured Jews, they were murdered in the Kremnica Forest. All the bodies were dumped in a ditch.

After the war the bodies were exhumed and identified by their uniforms. They were reburied in the British military cemetery in Prague with crosses over the graves. After many Zionist protests, in 1949 the crosses were replaced by

201 *Seven Who Fell* pp.147–9

Stars of David. The British normally buried soldiers near the place of death, but uniquely in September 1952 the British War Office allowed the Israeli government to take the bodies to Mount Herzl in Jerusalem and bury them in the 'Parachutists' section'.

Haviva Reik is regarded as a Zionist hero. She is remembered in Kibbutz Lahavot Haviva, the ship *Haviva Reik*, which brought Jewish immigrants to Palestine after the war, and the Israeli educational centre Givat Haviva.[202]

Surika Braverman

Surika was a friend of Haviva Reik – both were enthusiastic members of Hashomer Hatzair. Both of them were kibbutzniks – Reik lived on Kibbutz Ma'anit and Surika on Kibbutz Shamir very close to the Golan heights. Before the mission Haviva had problems on her kibbutz as she had become involved with the son of wealthy landowners in Zichon Yaacov. The very socialist-minded kibbutzniks regarded the family as 'capitalist', which made the son unsuitable to partner her. She was given an ultimatum – either him or us. Haviva went to stay with Surika to think it over. Surika admitted she had been afraid to jump and she was the last person to see Reik before she parachuted into Slovakia. Surika did get to Europe to work for the Resistance, 'but landed on the ground in a small plane'.

At a ceremony to commemorate the seven who did not return, in the presence of President Peres in Spring 2010, Surika spoke of her parachuting comrades as being 'simple people who believed in what they were doing for their people and the Zionist, socialist and political movements they belonged to'. The event was organised by Moreshet, created in the 1960s to collect testimony from camp survivors and resistance fighters. They also focus on women fighters. 'Among the many related topics we deal with is the contribution of women in actual active fighting in the ghettoes and the forests, and their role in the underground units,' explained Yonat Rotbein Director of Moreshet Educational Programs, herself the daughter of a resistance fighter.[203]

Surika was born in Romania in 1919 in Botosani in the far north of the country. Her family were Zionists and she joined Hashomer Hatsair as a child. She arrived in Palestine in 1938. The outbreak of war in 1939 and the Romanians' alliance with the Nazis meant contact with Jews left behind was lost.

In an obituary written on 28 February 2013 following Surika's death in January 2013, Seth Frantzman referred to when they last met in December 2009. Braverman spoke excitedly about her experiences in World War II as though they had happened yesterday. Although almost everyone in Israel and many Jewish communities abroad, learns the story of Hanna Szenes,

202 Reik, Haviva, Shoah Resource Centre, The International School for Holocaust Studies at Yad Vashem.
203 Lydia Aisenberg, 'Journey of a Lifetime', *Esra Magazine* Issue No: 154, April/May 2010

the most famous of the Jewish parachutists, who was executed by the Nazis in Hungary in November of 1944, few people knew that one of Szenes's colleagues was still alive in the country.

He also recalled:

Braverman remembered that she and the others selected for the mission were very realistic about its ability to change events. 'You have to understand, we didn't go to Europe to overthrow the Third Reich…We didn't think they would make us heroes, we wanted to go to the Jews of Europe and say we had come to help.'

Braverman was flown into Yugoslavia in July 1944. Like all the parachutists her cover was as an English officer and journalist in the army. The partisans called her Sarah. Because of the events in Romania, she was unable to be sent there, so she spent most of her war in partisans' camps in the mountains in Yugoslavia. She spoke of seeing German POWs milking cows and nursing the wounded.

When we were in the partisan camp, they didn't know who we were. They knew we were English soldiers and we were not the only foreigners there – there were also Americans. Every morning there would be a partisan girl who came with a cow and she would give each of us some milk. We were all in English uniforms with officers' insignia. When she saw that I knew about livestock, she was surprised to see an Englishwoman who knew such things. But of course, for me it wasn't surprising, I had taken a course in farming in Ness Ziona.

Eventually she was evacuated to Italy and returned home via Cairo. She went back to her kibbutz where she lived until she passed away at the age of 95.

When the Israeli War of Independence broke out in 1948, she was summoned to Tel Aviv by the Chief of Staff Yaakov Dori. There was another woman there, Shoshana Gershowitz, and Dori said they needed a women's corps in the Israeli army as they would be drafting all the women who had fought in WWII. Braverman recalled saying 'How do we do that?' Dori said come back with answers. 'In the end, we went out and found 32 women who had been in the Hagana. We took them down to the Borochov quarter, in today's Givatayim, and we trained them with firearms. They signed up to the army, and I signed last, so I received military number 33.'

The IDF is one of the few armies that conscripts both men and women and women now reach the highest levels. Surika died on 10 February 2013. Minister Limor Livnat said of her:

Sarah (Surika) Braverman, of blessed memory, was a woman larger than life, a trailblazer who inspired thousands of women in the pre-state Jewish community and later in Israel. In many ways Sarah's life story is the story of Zionism itself, as an illegal immigrant, a pioneer, a parachutist and a fearless fighter for the war for the Jewish people and the establishment of the land of Israel. Surika…was also a courageous fighter for women's rights in Israel, and this paved the way for the service of women in the IDF when she brought about the establishment of the Women's Corps.[204]

Interviewed about heroes on her kibbutz on 6 September 1993, she said: 'This country is inundated with heroism; there's a new hero every second. That's not what the nation lacks today. What it lacks are people with a mission.'[205]

Hannah Szenes

Hannah was born on 17 July 1921 into an assimilated Hungarian Jewish family in Budapest. Her father, Bela Szenes (1894–1927), was a well-known author and playwright. He died aged 33 when his children were 7 and 6. Perhaps Hannah inherited her writing skills from her father. Perhaps she also inherited her fatalistic approach to life from him too. After he died, her mother recalled a conversation they had a few weeks earlier. He was up unusually early to complete an unfinished play. He was looking well as they had recently returned from a holiday at Lake Balaton. Suddenly he said:

> You know, I was just thinking – I could end my life now. I've attained everything a Jewish writer possibly can in Hungary. I'm a respected columnist on the foremost newspaper [*Pesti Hirlap*], my plays are performed with casts of my own choosing...the ink barely has time to dry before my work is in print. What more can there be? The gates of the National Theatre will never be open to a Jewish writer; but even if I had a choice, I think my plays are better suited to the Comedy Theatre. So what more can happen? Success abroad? Films? Money? I've had it all. Really, I could calmly go now.[206]

Hannah received a modern Hungarian education and it was only when she was exposed to anti-Semitism at her high school that she decided to learn more about Judaism. This led her towards Zionism and she joined a Youth movement and learnt Hebrew. In 1939 she went to Palestine to study at the Nahalal agricultural school for two years. She wrote about this time in the diary she had started when she was 13. On 11 July 1939, she wrote in her diary that in future she would write it in Hebrew.[207]

---

204 'Sarah Braverman, IDF's First Lady Passes Away' in *Jewish Voice* 13 February 2013, accessed 12 August 2017, http://jewishvoiceny.com/index.php?option=com_content&view=article&id=3201:sarah-braverman-idfs-first-lady-passes-away&catid=127&Itemid=783

205 *Perfect Heroes* p.182

206 Catherine Senesh, 'Memories of Hannah's childhood', in *Hannah Senesh: Her Life and Diary* (New York: Schocken, 1973) p.6

207 Life & Diary p.74

The Austrian Anschluss increased anti-Semitism in Hungary and Hannah writes about the Jewish Bill being discussed in the Hungarian Parliament on 24 April 1938:

The debate on the Jewish Bill is now in progress. There has been, and continues to be, terrible tension about it, and conjecture as to whether there will be a law concerning this Bill. People are talking about it everywhere. Commerce, industry, the theatre, cafes – everything is at a standstill while this matter is under discussion in Parliament. I wonder how all this will end?[208]

The Jewish Bill became the first 'Jewish Law' and reduced the ratio of Jewish representation in the economic fields to twenty per cent. It was also stated that 'the expansion of the Jews is as detrimental to the nation as it is dangerous; we must take steps to defend ourselves against their propagation. Their regulation to the background is a national duty.'

Later Hannah wrote about the second Jewish Law announced in 1939. The number of Jews in intellectual life was to be reduced to six per cent, in commerce and in industry to twelve per cent. A Jew could no longer be a member of Parliament, or a judge, teacher, lawyer. In addition on 3 February 1939, a bomb was thrown into the largest synagogue in Budapest during the Friday evening service. This was the Dohany Utca synagogue, in fact the largest in Europe. I remember my mother telling me she nearly went there that evening, but at the last minute decided against it.

On 10 March 1939 she included a copy of her application to Nahalal in the diary – she said with pride she had written it in Hebrew. She includes the following: 'Even before the tragic turn of events concerning our people in my native land, I longed to live in Palestine, and for the way of life there.'[209]

Her parachute drop was doomed. Reufen Dafne, who was on the same mission, described what happened.[210] Hannah was 22 when they arrived in Yugoslavia. On 9 June 1944 she was due to cross into Hungary. At the border there were concerns about her going that day but she refused to listen and insisted. She asked him for a cyanide capsule, which he refused, to remove all doubts about her success. As she left she said 'Till we meet again – soon, I hope, in enemy territory.'

She was captured almost as soon as she touched Hungarian soil and taken to prison in Budapest. She was severely tortured to get her Allied wireless codes, but she did not reveal anything. To try to break her, they arrested her mother and took her to the prison. Her poor mother had told the police her daughter was in Haifa, as she had no idea of Hannah's plans and had not seen her for five years. Both women stayed strong and Hannah still refused to divulge anything. Hannah was tried as a spy and sentenced to death. Hannah's eloquence about the war ending and the judges soon being judged

208 P.50–51
209 P.72
210 Pp.170–9

affronted the officer-in-charge, Colonel Simon, who offered her the choice of being shot or begging for mercy. She refused to beg and was shot without a blindfold. In 1950 her body was moved to Israel to the 'Parachutists' section' on Mount Herzl. Her mother was able to join her son in Israel, having written of her own experiences.[211]

One epitaph for Hannah is provided by her nephew, whom she never knew. Dr. David Senesh is the son of Hannah's brother Giora (György) who was one year older. He is a famous clinical psychologist based in Israel who specialises in 'post-traumatic stress disorder, moral resilience, and restorative processes'.

He speculated on why Hannah had become so inspirational: 'It's not a simple story, there are many ways to look at it. Her diaries weren't meant to be published, but they were a way for Hannah to let her passions and desires come to life through poetry and prose.' They were published and so the next generation can feel what she went through both before and during the Holocaust. Hannah wrote when she was seventeen:

> I don't know whether I've mentioned that I've become a Zionist. This word stands for a tremendous number of things. To me it means, in short, that I now consciously and strongly feel a Jew, and am proud of it…One needs something to believe in, something for which one has a whole-hearted enthusiasm, One needs to feel that one's life has meaning. That one is needed in this world. Zionism fulfils this for me.

David spoke about what psychologists call the 'complicated bereavement' of his own father and grandmother, Hannah's mother, Catherine. She experienced the trauma of a 'reverse-order death' but also lived to a very old age both in the shadow and light of her daughter. She never overcame the tragedy and Davis's father too was deeply affected by his sister's early and tragic death. The following poem was found in Hannah's death cell after her execution:

> One – two – three … eight feet long
> Two strides across, the rest is dark…
> Life is a fleeting question mark
> One – two – three … maybe another week.
> Or the next month may still find me here,
> But death, I feel is very near.
> I could have been 23 next July
> I gambled on what mattered most, the dice were cast. I lost.

Dr. Senesh revealed a story his father had told him and his brother Eitan:

> Giora mentioned that, after years of separation from his beloved sister, he finally made it to the Land of Israel and was reunited with Hannah

---

211 Pp.202–242

on the eve of what was to be her fatal mission. They only spent one day together and then parted forever. He told his sons that if Hannah would have told him the exact nature of her proposed mission he would have talked her out of it. But she never told him the details of her mission (maybe figuring that he would talk her out of it) and the rest is history.

As her nephew said, 'the world lost an incredibly bright and talented woman who would have gone on to make a huge impact and contribution.' She chose the codename *Hagar* for the mission according to David. It was as if she knew that she would be cast out into the wilderness, never to return and in her honour his daughter's middle name is Hagar. Seventy years after her ill-fated mission Hannah's legacy lives on in her poetry and her writing. Her eulogy could be her own words:

> There are stars whose radiance is visible on earth
> Though they have long been extinct
> There are people whose brilliance continues to light the world
> Though they are no longer among the living
> These lights are particularly bright when the night is dark
> They light the way for mankind.[212]

Rafi Benshalom (born Richard Friedl in 1926) wrote of the parachutists' effort, that in spite of its failure and the loss of life: 'During those tragic times, when we stood abandoned and isolated, [their mission], nevertheless, had great symbolic import that will not be overlooked in the history of Jewish defense and rescue.'[213]

Melitta Stauffenberg

My interest in Melitta was aroused by meeting Clare Mulley at a book launch in early 2017. I told her about this book and she told me about her shortly to-be-published title about two rival female German aviators. She told me Melitta was half-Jewish and I recognised the name from the plot to kill Hitler.

Melitta was born on 8 January 1903. 'As a child, flying held an irresistible fascination for me, and as I had a very scientific interest in intellectual things, I opted to focus my studies on aeronautics. From there, it seemed inevitable that I would give everything I could to complete my full pilot's training.'

At a lecture in Stockholm in December 1943 Melitta said 'The decision to devote my life to flying and thus to a job which…right from the start,

---

212 Tuvia Book, *'Being David Senesh: Hannah Senesh's nephew reflects on his aunt's legacy'*, in *The Times of Israel* 16 December 2013, accessed 18 March 2017. http://blogs.timesofisrael.com/being-david-senesh-chana-seneshs-nephew-reflects-on-his-aunts-legacy/
213 Rafi Benshalom, cited by Yahil p.646

appeared to be a specifically masculine one was, admittedly, unusual for a young girl.'[214]

Melitta was eleven when World War I broke out in 1914. 'The days of my youth, where one can look for the origins and secret roots shaping a life, were a time when there was nothing but deep tribulation for Germany.' Her father was too old to fight at 53, but with his Russian he was made a reserve officer and acted as a censor and interpreter at a POW camp. This eventually earned him an Iron Cross, Second Class.

In the 1920s she enrolled to study mathematics, physics and engineering – she was an unusual student at the Munich Technical University – the only female. By the end of the decade she was regarded as an expert in aerodynamics, leaving her mark on aviation research and the defence industry. In the 1920s, because of the lack of funding due to the problems of the German economy, there was a shortage of engineers and so she was able to find a role testing propeller and engine assemblies on the Junkers G31. During WW2 she was working almost exclusively in the top-secret restricted areas of Rechlin and Berlin-Gatow. The role of women was ambivalent:

> Exactly where did they fit in a sport that celebrated 'the whole man' and prized 'fellowship' above all? A number of critics doubted the ability of women to master the physical tasks that aviation required. Women generally lacked decisiveness, a sense of comradeship, and technical expertise, claimed Hans-Georg Schulze, press spokesman for the German Airsport League. These debilities kept them from being good glider pilots, although he conceded that a number of women had gone onto become airplane pilots whose enthusiasm and contributions deserved recognition. And indeed some of Nazi Germany's best known pilots – Hanna Reitsch, in particular – were women. All in all, Schulze concluded that women had undeniable, but not equal rights to the airstream. It is significant, however, that these assumptions did not go unchallenged. Nazi sport officials, for example, reminded local authorities not to exclude women from gliding courses, the demands of training the ranks of the Luftwaffe notwithstanding. Although women could not be full members of the paramilitary German Airsport League, they were encouraged to join auxiliary gliding clubs. It was particularly important to keep women flying, argued one official in the Reich Education Ministry, because, later, in life, as airminded mothers, they would not stand in the way of their sons taking up flying or serving the nation in the Luftwaffe.[215]

The Germans never provided a space for women pilots in the German war machine, unlike the British. Although they had contacts in the Nazi high command, which they cultivated carefully, they were ultimately driven along by the sheer force of will. Melitta declared 'We women pilots are not

---

214 Clare Mulley pp.2–3
215 Peter Fritzsche, *A Nation of Fliers* (Cambridge Mass: Harvard UP, 1992)

suffragettes' and neither she nor Hannah Reitsch, her rival, played the gender card. They simply outperformed the men.

Her father was Michael Schiller, born in 1861. He was a civil engineer, architect and civil servant. His family came from Odessa and had been involved in the fur trade. His family was Jewish but when he was about to go to the university he was baptised as a Protestant. He had been brought up in that faith and would bring up his own children in it. His own father, Moses, was a non-religious Jew. He admired German culture and Michael's baptism seemed like the end of their Jewish connections. They were German patriots and never discussed their Jewish roots. No one was aware of Michael's real background.

It is not clear when Melitta found out but certainly the introduction of the Nuremberg Laws in 1935 would have made her situation clear. She was already known for being critical of the Nazis from her university days in Munich and perhaps she was aware of his speeches calling Jews 'vermin' and stated 'the Jew can never become German however often he may affirm that he can.' After the Nuremberg Laws were introduced Hitler was rather vague, which was out of character. When interviewed he claimed 'the legislation was not anti-Jewish, but pro-German. The rights of Germans are hereby protected against destructive Jewish influence.'

Michael Schiller was 74 in 1935. Therefore it must have been around 1880 when he went to university. This was a time when many Jews were converting to ensure a better career in the academic and professional spheres. At that time being a Jew was still a handicap and career conversions were common. Antisemitism revived in the new German Empire in the last quarter of the nineteenth century. Jews were blocked from occupational and social mobility leading to the increase in conversions. In Prussia in the mid-1870s about 50 Jews became Christians each year; by the late 1880s this had increased to 300; in 1902 the figure was 400. For Germany as a whole figures are only available after 1880. In the early 1880s it was at least 200 conversions a year and twenty years later it was more than 500. Felix A. Theilhaber calculated that around 1900, German Jewry was losing at least 1000 people a year. In 1914 The German Jewish population was 620,000 but there may have been as many as 100,000 converts and their descendants. [216]

In Vienna the figures were even higher – 1868–79 there was one convert for every 1,200 Jews; in the 1880s, one for every 420 Jews and 1900–10 one for every 230 Jews. The situation was probably aggravated by the ban on Jews and Christians marrying. If one chose to marry one had to convert. This law did not exist in Germany. The situation in Hungary was not so serious until after the collapse of the Hungarian Empire.

At the end of 1935 Michael Schiller submitted a three-page article to the magazine *Nature and Spirit* making a case for raising children to be 'fully human' by developing logical thinking and the exclusion of belief in supernatural powers. He wasn't defending Jews or human rights but merely

---

216 Todd M. Endelman, 'Conversion as a Response to Antisemitism', in *Living with Antisemitism*, ed. Reinharz (London: Brandeis U.P, 1987) pp 62–64.

his own family. Initially the Schiller family were not affected by the racial laws because to be defined as a Jew you had to have three or four 'racially' Jewish grandparents or two if they were practising Jews. This excluded Michael's five children. Additionally, at first decorated veterans, people over 65 and those married to Aryans were exempt, so again Michael and his family were OK. However, they were no longer the equal German citizens they had felt.

From late 1935 'Aryan certificates' were required for college, work and marriage. Melitta's family exploited the fact that their father was now a Polish citizen since the frontier changes and they pretended they had to get their papers from Odessa. Later they claimed nothing was found. Melitta was a patriot and affirmed her loyalty to Germany but

> ...she now saw a clear distinction between her adored country with its rich cultural heritage and the so-called Third Reich, from whom she suddenly had to hide her family history. Knowing that her aviation development work at DVL was of national importance, she focused on making sure she was regarded as an invaluable member of the team before her Jewish heritage could be revealed and her job called into question. She now spent long days on the airfield and in her office, talked a little less about politics, and very rarely mentioned her family.[217]

(The DVL was the *Deutsche Versuchsanstalt für Luftfahrt* which meant German Research Institute for Aeronautics.)

In 1931 she met her future husband Alexander von Stauffenberg. He was the twin brother of Berthold and the older brother of Claus von Stauffenberg who would attempt to assassinate Hitler. Although he was a historian, he viewed himself as a poet. Melitta spent most of her time in Berlin but Alexander drifted around in the early 1930s as an unpaid lecturer from university to university before he finally became a professor at Würzburg in 1936.[218] Meanwhile the German consulate in Odessa was searching for Michael Schiller's birth certificate. The state policy was to encourage single staff at universities to 'marry someone desirable for the Third Reich'. Alexander may have volunteered with a cavalry regiment when he was 18 and been a reservist since 1936, but he was not a member of the Nazi party and his nephew, Count Berthold, described in 2012 how Alexander was 'against the Nazis from the very beginning and said so, many times – thoughtlessly as was his way'.

Melitta and Alexander loved each other, respected each other and shared views about the current state of their country. There were also practical advantages:

> Melitta would become a member of one of Germany's oldest and most distinguished families, affirming both her national identity and her patriotism. Alexander could silence his critics, and would become eligible for academic advancement open only to married men. But

---

217 Mulley pp.48–51
218 Medicus p.5

Alexander also knew that he was marrying a woman whose father had been born Jewish: a bold step in Nazi Germany. 'Of course it was brave for Alex to marry Litta.' Claus's eldest son later commented. Under the Nuremberg race laws, it was also illegal.[219]

They were married quietly on 11 August 1937 in a Berlin registry office. The claim that the family papers were lost in Odessa was accepted by the registrar but perhaps they were very lucky or perhaps the Stauffenberg name carried weight. In Breslau a man with a Jewish mother and an Aryan father was not so fortunate. The day before his wedding booked for 9 October 1935, the Prussian Registry Office cancelled his wedding because of his ancestry. It was not until June 1956 that the marriage was recognised from the original date and their two daughters became legitimate.[220]

Melitta had known about her Jewish ancestry for some time but a letter in 1940 from the German Genealogical Research Board officially classified her as 'half Jewish' This had severe implications for her career and safety. She determined to become indispensable to the Luftwaffe – and was successful, as she was never sent to a camp.

Beginning in 1933, Jews were written out of the annals of German aviation and systematically excluded from air sports. Walter Zuerl's compilation of the accomplishments of *Pour le Mérite* aces during World War I, does not include the several Jewish recipients. At the same time, Robert Kronfeld, an Austrian Jew and perhaps the most accomplished glider pilot in the early 1930s, left Germany, where he no longer felt welcome, for England. Less well-known fliers found themselves excluded from the German Airsport League as well. Adolf Brieger, a Münsterberg gliding instructor whose references included Freiherr von Gablentz, a director at Luft Hansa, Ernst Udet, and a half-dozen local club officials and notables, all of whom testified to his enthusiasm, patriotism, and good character, could not find a place in the new national community because he was Jewish. His students, 'young fliers and athletes from Munsterberg,' signed a petition on Brieger's behalf. 'Like us in thinking and nature,' Brieger was a 'a pioneer of the national idea' and 'German to the last drop of blood.' 'He cannot belong to the Juda' they insisted, because 'we, who belong to the national front and in the great majority stand behind the swastika,' have followed him. 'We are proof' that 'he is to be seen as German,' the thirty-eight young fliers concluded. As it was, Brieger had to quit all gliding clubs and cease teaching in 1935, a fate he undoubtedly shared with many aviators.[221]

Robert Kronfeld (1904–1948) joined the RAF in the UK and became a Squadron Leader during World War II. He was awarded the Air Force Cross

---

219 Mulley p.73
220 Agnes Grunwald-Spier, *Who Betrayed the Jews* (Stroud: Amberley, 2017) pp.435–8
221 Fritzsche pp.198–9

(AFC) for his work on tailless gliders. He was a test pilot after the war and was killed in an air crash in 1948.[222]

Meanwhile Melitta's proud and patriotic parents, like so many thousands of German Jews, were facing the prospect of transportation to a concentration camp. Whilst the first deportations of German Jews began in January 1941, they were initially protected because Margarete was not Jewish. They also has a close friend with the right connections but this was a perilous situation.

By this time Melitta's amazing work with dive-bombers had both proved her worth but also caused her to be regarded as irreplaceable. Dr. Georg Pasewaldt testified: 'This woman's achievements could scarcely have been performed by anyone else.' However although her racial background was not discussed either at Rechlin or the Aviation Ministry, Göring himself personally intervened to see that Melitta's work was defined as 'war-essential' to make her situation secure. Consequently, on 25 June 1941, Melitta received a *Reichssippenamt* – a certificate from the 'Reich Kinship Bureau' which confirmed both her 'German blood' and her official status as 'equal to Aryan'.[223]

This special position saved her life. However she decided to seek the same status for her father and siblings. She was not alone. In the period 1935–1941 around 10,000 Germans descended from Jewish families applied for 'equal to Aryan' status. Only 300 had success and lived with the fact it could be revoked at any time. In 1942 Martin Bormann decided only new applications would be considered.

> Melitta's timely application may well not only have saved her family from deportation but, although she did not yet know it, ultimately prevented their murders. From this point on, Melitta knew that her Rechlin work was of vital importance not just for her fellow pilots, or even her country, but directly for the safety of her own family. She could not afford to take any unnecessary risks, but neither could she afford to be anything less than exceptional.[224]

Dr. George Pasewaldt was visiting Rechlin in early 1942. It was the most important flight test centre in the *Luftwaffe* and he was a colonel in the General staff and Chief of Development at the Technical Office of the Aviation Ministry. Rechlin was 150 kilometres northwest of Berlin and was where various aircraft and their weapons were tested together with aircraft instruments and bombs. When the Nazis took power various villages were cleared and an almost circular flight field, about a mile in diameter, had been created.

---

222 South-East History Boards, http://sussexhistoryforum.co.uk/index.php?action=p rintpage;topic=9772.0 accessed 15 October 2017
223 Mulley pp.134–5
224 Mulley p.135

In this restricted area, one could fly planes day and night, shooting at or blowing up targets and making measurements – all in the service of a German 'final victory'. When Pasewaldt looked out at the sky above Rechlin in early 1942 he could hardly believe his eyes. Was that Ju 88 twin-engine bomber with a full-view cabin, designed by the Junkers Factory in Dessau, about to be crash-landed? The colonel demanded to know the reason for such a daring nose dive that must have produced huge vibrations. Could the dive still be interrupted and the aircraft maneuvered back to normal? And who was that pilot flying at the 'limits of the permissible.' Apparently able to withstand enormous acceleration forces?

As he learned from onlookers, it was just 'Melitta making a crash-test'. After World War II, Pasewaldt – an educated jurist and battle-tested fighter pilot – recalled that taking a plane into a moderate nose dive like that would have been considered a 'heroic act by many a male pilot'. Yet for Melitta von Stauffenberg, taking the most extreme risks had been an everyday occurrence for several years.[225]

On 26 October 1942, Melitta's father, then aged 81, took it upon himself to send a handwritten letter to Hermann Göring without discussing it with his daughter. He argued that while Melitta's mathematical modelling and engineering work 'must definitely continue to be used in the interests of the Fatherland' he felt she should be relieved from undertaking the nosedive test flights. He added 'According to medical opinion these could prevent the possibility of issue'. He concluded by suggesting with some audacity that a 'well-earned further honour for her services' might help overcome any resistance from her to the idea. Mulley comments 'Michael Schiller did not know that the enforced sterilization of "half-Jews" had been discussed in Berlin earlier that year, so his chosen line of argument was unlikely to carry much weight.'[226]

It was Georg Pasewaldt who suggested to Erhard Milch, Göring's number two at the Reich Aviation Ministry, that Melitta should receive an honour. He had been thinking about pushing for this for a year. 'Countess Stauffenberg, with hundreds, more than a thousand experimental flights, beyond anything so far achieved in our special field, is most deserving,' he told Milch. He added that she should receive an Iron Cross, Second Class. Milch had never heard of Melitta with her married name but he knew a modest aeronautical engineer called Melitta Schiller and he asked Pasewaldt to tell him more.

This woman has sacrificed herself beyond description with her tireless practical trials for research in the service of the Luftwaffe. She has made technical and scientific evaluations and produced a complete report on

---

225 Thomas Medicus, *Melitta von Stauffenberg: A German Life* (Berlin: Rowohlt, 2012) Trans. David Brenner, pp.7–8.
226 Mulley p.157

each of her flights which include innumerable dives and night flights. This data is unobtainable by other means and of unique value.

Milch was very impressed. Accordingly on 22 January 1943, Melitta received a telegram from Göring. 'The Führer awarded you today with the Iron Cross 2.' Six days later, another delayed telegram arrived. 'I will present you with the Iron Cross, awarded by the Führer to you, personally, on January 29.' Melitta had to go to his villa on Berlin's, Leipziger Strasse close to the Aviation Ministry. When she arrived she was shown into a massive room with tapestries and old masters that Göring had acquired. His wife Emmy was there with her sister and her niece and when Göring arrived they went into his private office. They talked about her work and she later told her family, 'He cannot believe that I fly heavy bombers, like the Ju 88, and even do nose dives with them. He is also surprised by the number of my dives' which he checked in his file. When he was satisfied, he pinned the medal on her and expressed his 'deep, sincere admiration' for her and her work. He joked that it would be easier to list the planes she could not fly, rather than the ones she could. Melitta wrote, 'The thing was clearly fun for him.'

Göring later asked Melitta why she worked for a company rather than directly for the Reich.

After some thought, I answered that would be convenient in a way, because the other companies wouldn't see me as competition any more, as they sometimes do, even though I've been seconded from Askania since the beginning of the war. Göring was obviously annoyed that commercial interests were still influential, even in wartime, and he said he would arrange for her release and transfer.

His wife was also kind giving her a package of coffee and tea and inviting her and Alexander to use their box at the theatre and stay at their guesthouse whenever they chose.

All in all, 'it was really cosy,' Melitta told her family with some astonishment. 'The tone was pleasant and good-humoured, and you got the impression of an honest and touching heartiness.' Göring even noted the event in his diary that evening: 'Gräfin Schenk (von Stauffenberg) awarded Iron Cross II'. It was an extraordinary moment for a woman who the previous year had been under investigation as a 'Jewish *Mischling*'.

The media covered the honour extensively and her name was on everyone's lips. 'Brave Woman Receives the Iron Cross' ran the headlines and the comment that it was 'rare for a woman'. Professor Herrmann, head of the Technical Academy at Gatow wrote, 'She liked to wear the decoration' because it was reassuring to know she was valued since she was proud of her work and it was good to have it recognized. Herrmann however wrote she wore it, 'in spite of her reservations which were becoming increasingly clear to those who were initiated into her personal thoughts'.[227]

Her parents did not give up. Her mother wrote a follow up asking Göring to ignore her husband's letter. However, Michael wrote again the following year on 4 September 1943, still expressing 'concern for her life'. 'There is no record of any reply from Göring, but if neither Melitta's gender nor her 'Jewish blood' was enough to prevent her work for the Luftwaffe, then her father's letters stood no chance. Michael was only lucky that there were not 'greater repercussions'.[228]

Her brother-in-law was Claus von Stauffenberg, the one eyed colonel who placed a briefcase bomb under Hitler's map table in 1944. In a conversation on a dinghy on Wannsee lake so they could not be overheard, Melitta agreed to fly him there by faking an emergency landing. In the event Claus used other means but when the plot failed, her name implicated her and she was arrested with the rest of the family. She had to plead with Göring himself.

Two of her brothers-in-law were executed, the other adults were put in camps and the children were taken away. Melitta herself was released on 2 September and was referred to as Gräfin Schenk, as the Stauffenberg name was unacceptable. Medicus speculates on her involvement in the plot:

> After World War II, there were claims that she had been involved in the logistical planning for [the] assassination attempt of 20 July 1944. Others maintain that she had been personally briefed by Claus von Stauffenberg on the military resistance. In addition, the countess is alleged to have flown her brother-in-law back to Berlin in a Fieseler Storch after his attempt on the *Führer's* life, so that he could then implement the Valkyrie Plan. Did Melitta von Stauffenberg thus participate in some way in the preparations for the 20th of July? If so, she would have been the only woman who played an active role in the armed resistance, something thought to have been carried out exclusively by men. Is it possible that the extensive, decades-long research on the Hitler assassination has omitted this up to now?[229]

Sara Ginaite (1924–)

Sara Ginaite was a Jewish Lithuanian partisan who fought against Nazi occupation during the Second World War.

Ginaite was born in 1924 in Kovno (Kaunas since 1940), Lithuania. She was educated in a Lithuanian-speaking school and she was about to graduate

---

227 Mulley p.163–167
228 Mulley p.158
229 Medicus p.6

Sarah Ginaite, 11 July 1944.

when Nazi Germany invaded the country in 1941. Three of Ginaite's uncles were killed in the Kaunas Pogrom on 26 June 1941, a massacre of Jewish people that the Nazis encouraged the Lithuanian population to perform. The pogrom resulted in the deaths of 9,200 people, almost half of them children. The surviving members of Ginaite's family were incarcerated in the Kovno Ghetto, along with 40,000 others.

While living in the ghetto Ginaite joined the Anti-Fascist Fighting Organization (AFO) to take part in the resistance against the Nazis. She began a relationship with their charismatic youth leader, Misha Rubinsonas who was secretary of the Young Communist League. He and his sister Sonya had managed to secure a cache of arms for the underground from a shed near a German field hospital. Sonya managed to copy the key that had been left in the door, so the ghetto underground were able to raid the shed and took the arms to the nearby cemetery. From there they took them by truck to a safe-house in the city.

The two were married in a civil ceremony in the Ghetto on 7 November 1943. The pair were among the first group of 17 members of the underground who on 14–15 December 1943 left the Kovno Ghetto to escape to the Rudninkai Forest where they joined a partisan military unit named 'Death to the Occupiers'. Sonya then re-entered the ghetto on 7 January 1944 with four others to bring more partisans to the forest. She claimed to be a nurse and said she needed to escort four sick workers to the ghetto hospital. It was such a success that they did it again on 8 February 1944. They operated in the area of Vilnius.

In her book *Resistance and Survival* Sara wrote a chapter called 'Women of our Detachment'.[230]

---

230 Ginaite-Rubinson, S., *Resistance and Survival: The Jewish Community in Kaunas, Lithuania, 1941–1944* (Mosaic Press, 2006), pp.174–9

All the partisans of Rudninkai Forest lived according to the well-established rules and traditions of the Soviet Union. We observed Soviet holidays with great fanfare. At the beginning of March 1944, we began preparations for the celebration of International Women's Day. We invited Jurgis (Zimanas) and the women from his unit and also the women from other detachments. I was asked to deliver the official address.

I sat at a desk in the headquarters' dugout with a blank sheet of paper before me. I didn't know what to write or what I should say. I knew very little about the International Women's Movement or about how it was run in Lithuania or in the Soviet Union. I had no knowledge of war heroines or their achievements. Noticing my confusion, the commissar offered his help. I accepted without hesitation and he proceeded to prepare an appropriate introduction for me to read. First, I was to thank the Communist Party of the Soviet Union and its leaders for having freed women from their 'double yoke'. Although it was not very clear to me exactly what this equality and freedom from the 'double yoke' consisted of, I did not bother to argue. I simply did what was asked of me and then proceeded to write about the women of our detachment, about their responsibilities and their bravery.

Sitting at my desk, I did not think of the inequality of women partisans. At that time, I, personally, did not feel any gender discrimination. I also did not feel any dependence on my husband, or any male, because I was a female. But, looking back today, I ask myself if there were any problems for a woman in that man's world. Certainly the life of the women in our, and in other, detachments in Rudninkai Forest was somewhat different from the lives of their counterparts, the men.

The main issue for the girls who wanted to join the partisans was to find a way to be enrolled in the ranks of the escapees from the Kaunas Ghetto. The most important requirement was to be an active member of the AFO. Women who were members were the first to join the partisans. Those women who were less active or did not belong to the underground organization had to acquire a gun or pay the equivalent black market price of a weapon. Only then would they be included in a group escaping from the ghetto to the forest.

Most of the men – ghetto resisters – had girlfriends or were already married. At the beginning of 1944, many of these men were already in the forest or were soon to leave with an upcoming group. Their wives and girlfriends would later be enrolled on the list of escapees and many of them came with guns. I would say that seventy and eighty per cent of all Jewish women in the detachment were themselves members of AFO and (or) married to ghetto resisters. It is important to note, however, that all the marriages in the ghetto were about true love, not a means to escape. We all married at a very young age. We felt there was no point in waiting any longer for a better time to come. Young couples wanted to be together, to fight together, and to survive or die together.

All the women who came to the forest did not come to save their own lives or avoid death. As soon as a new group from the ghetto was admitted to our detachment, the Jewish women were treated as equals to the Jewish men. Upon entry to the detachments, the same basic rules applied to men and women. All the Jewish partisan men were equally motivated to fight the enemy by any and all possible means.

Of course, there were the centuries-old male–female divisions in responsibilities and duties, The women were regarded as weak, frail, and unfit to play a part in difficult and dangerous missions. Their participation in combat was often not appreciated. Even the Jewish partisans were not eager to take women along on dangerous missions far from our base. They felt that girls would only make a difficult situation worse, that they might require shielding during a retreat or a battle, that they might be a burden. Since the Soviet government rejected such distinctions, our women were not discouraged from carrying arms and they did participate in military endeavors.

Most of our girls were perfectly suited to the demands of forest life. They were young, physically strong, fearless and courageous. But, I must emphasize, they were not super-women. None of us was unique. We were ordinary women with all the shortcomings of any average person. Altogether, then, the lives of the women in our detachment were not that different form the lives of the men aside from the fact that duties and responsibilities were divided along gender lines.

There were only four women in the 'Death To The Occupiers' Detachment when the eleven of us joined the partisans. They were Jekaterina Radionova, Lisa Orlova, our nurse, Ania Borisova, and lastly, Taibele Vinishki, who fled the Vilnius Ghetto. Later on, women would make up about fifteen per cent of our detachment. Our daily life was complicated and unusual. We trekked the winding, snow-blown paths alongside the men, usually with only brief periods of rest. Nobody taught us how to fight or to perform our duties. We learned by ourselves, not only how to clean and use a gun, but how to conduct ourselves in combat and battle, how to blow up a bridge or a train, how to cut communication lines, and how to stand on guard. And all of us, young but fully self-reliant adults, managed to do all that was required of us.

For a long time, we had neither a bathhouse nor an outhouse. We had to go far into the woods through deep snow in order to simply to wash. The female partisans were often plagued by lice. They sucked our blood mercilessly and our attempts to eradicate them always proved fruitless. Our menstrual periods were as tortuous as the assault of the parasites, particularly when we were on missions or on guard duty. Because we had no female hygiene products, we resorted to shredding sheets or buying rags from the local peasants which we washed in cold water in the woods. Very often they would not dry thoroughly and we had no choice but to use them anyway.

In addition, the women had to bear the brunt of the daily chores around the camp. When we were not on sorties or on guard duty, we were peeling potatoes or doing kitchen chores. We washed 'our' men's clothes and also the clothes of the men who were not 'ours'. The diminutive Beile Ganelina, with hands raw and swollen from the cold, voluntarily washed, rinsed, and dried almost all the men's clothing. Our record-setting potato peeler, Leja Sher, was first at everything. Following a successful mission, she helped her husband, Liova Sher, clean and polish his gun. Other women, such as Ania Borisova and Zoja Tintate-Sherman, attended to the ill and wounded around the clock. An experienced head nurse, Riva Epshteinaite-Kaganiene, performed operations that should have been done by a surgeon.

Sara Gordon arrived from the Kaunas Ghetto the day after her husband, Peisach Gordon-Stein, was killed in action. She had the fortitude to continue on after his loss and avenged herself as best she could for his needless death. At sixteen, Sulamita Lermanaite-Gelperniene was the youngest girl in our unit, but she worked and fought the enemy alongside the rest. Alte Boruchovich-Teper was not only a fighting partisan but, just as she had been in the ghetto, she was second mother to the girls. In our unit, she served as our confidante and supporter and we continued to call her our *Mamele* (little mother). One could safely say she was both a fearless warrior and an affectionate, devoted friend.

During my time with partisans, I became close friends with Tiva Bloch. We looked somewhat alike and shared similar tastes. We were both tall and blonde and preferred similar trousers and knee-high boots. We were both poor singers and shared a dislike for women's work. For a time we were assigned to work in reconnaissance and would go together to Senoji Macele where the local people thought we were sisters. Janchevski, our liaison in Inklerishkes, often mistook Riva Bloch for me. Once, when we went to Inklerishkes together, Janchevski asked which one I was, Tiva or Zose. Laughingly, I simply told him that I was Riva when I wanted to be, and Zose when I needed to be.

In the spring, our daily life and food supply improved. We saw the construction of the bathhouse, baking oven, field hospital and a workshop at our base. We also had a number of cows that needed grazing, feeding and milking. These chores, once again, became the responsibility of the women. There were no meadows in the forest so we tried to find relatively flat and less densely wooded area for the cows to graze on. I was never able to manage this task easily. The cows would never listen to me. They would trip over themselves or get caught on large branches and tree trunks that had fallen on the ground. I would no sooner finish helping one get itself out of a mess when another would find itself in a similar situation. After consistent failures, my eyes swollen from crying, our commanders agreed to free me from the burden of taking the cows to graze.

Our partisan women experienced all the severity of partisan life, fought bravely against the enemy and never complained. At the same time, we were able to maintain our feminine sensitivity and softness, which was a comfort to our companions, our male friends and our husbands, both in combat and in the daily life at our base. We did everything in our power to temper the difficulties we all experienced as warriors, friends, wives and partisans in Rudninkai Forest.

So, on March 8, to celebrate International Women's Day, all the women in the unit were given a day of rest. We were not required to do work or be in guard duty, and even the most 'womanly' work was done by the men. Early in the morning, the men, wanting to be particularly attentive and respectful to the women, lit the stove in the recently built bathhouse. All the women took showers with what was, under the circumstances, the greatest level of luxury. We put up our hair and helped each other to dress attractively as we could. Some of us wished to appear especially feminine and we wore skirts and blouses and put on lipstick. Others wished to dress so as to underline their equality with men and wore trousers, jackets and belts.

I put on a new pair of pants that had been made for me by Tevje Friedman, one of our partisans, and a warm brown shirt. I wore two belts, one for my pants and the second belt for my pistol...I was becoming extremely nervous at the thought of standing on the podium to deliver an address. As I stood in front of almost 300 people, my voice wavered and all I wanted to do was disappear into the dugout. It was only when I came to speak about the women of our unit that I managed to calm down.

On that special celebration on March 8, I spoke not only of the women of our detachment but also of the women in the Kaunas Ghetto and the city's underground movement. I told the Janina Czizinauskaite who was a member of the underground resistance movement in Kaunas and was shot at the Ninth Fort. She shared a death row cell with AFO member Polia (Pesha) Karnauskaite-Musel. Later on, Polia, after being miraculously released from the Ninth Fort, continued to be an active member of the AFO. Among other assignments, Polia risked her life when she smuggled a Jewish child to safety. I also mentioned our ghetto resisters, Ida Shater, who participated in smuggling Jewish children from the ghetto, but did not manage to join the partisans...I also spoke of our courageous women: Malke Sinjor, Sheina Levi, Esya Shtrom, Ida Pilovnik-Vilenchiuk and others. All of them were fearless fighters; dutiful and conscientious workers.

On the occasion of International Women's Day, many women of our detachment were honoured by our commanders and officially thanked for their bravery and valour in combat. My happiest surprise was the receipt of a rifle from Kostas, our commander. It was so unexpected and I was so joyful that I forgot to thank him and just kissed my prize. I was one of the first women of the detachment to receive her own personal rifle.

In 1944 Ginaite and Rubinsonas took part in the liberation of the Vilna and Kovno ghettos, although by this time 90% of the Jewish populations inside had been killed. Ginaite's own family were all dead, save for her sister and a young niece.

Both Sara and Misha survived and settled in Vilnius. Sara's father had died of natural causes in the ghetto. Her mother and sister Alice were sent to Stutthof concentration camp, where her mother became sick and died. Alice survived to be liberated from Stutthof and her husband came back from Dachau.

Ginaite fought against rampant anti-semitism to become a professor of Political Economics at Vilnius University, where she published award-winning books on the Holocaust in Lithuania. Following her husband's death in 1983, she moved to Canada to live with her two daughters and continue her academic career. She wrote five books on economics.

Miriem Golda (Gola) Mire (1911–1943)

I knew
that machine guns are better than the strongest words
and ranks of soldiers better than the trustworthiest lines of poetry.
I knew
that a rhyme written even in the most burning pain
cannot compare to the thunderous drum of fighters
going into battle.
And this too I shall know:
The red flag flying in the stormy wind
is more precious than anything sung.
But how can I help it if I allowed the words, gathered in pain,
to burst out in song before my heart broke?
O poems, you are like arms that yearn in vain.
So let my tortured cry be: To battle! To battle!
(Translated from the Hebrew)

Gola wrote this poem in prison in March 1943. Some of her poems were dedicated to her husband and dead child but others like this one, *Instead of Progress,* were more revolutionary.

She was born in Rzeszow in 1911, in the Lvov district of Galicia, Poland, which is now in the Ukraine. She lived in a comfortable Jewish home with religious but tolerant parents. She attended the Polish schools, doing well and showing leadership qualities from an early age. She joined the local Hashomer Hatsair group when quite young. Aged only seventeen she was elected to the leadership and after persuading her parents moved to Lvov. However when the family moved to Belgium in 1932, Gola refused to go and ran away the day her parents left.

At this time she was expelled from Hashomer because of her radical views. She became involved with the Communists and in 1936 helped to organise a strike at the factory where she worked. She was arrested with twelve other strike leaders and spent six months in prison. On her release, her parents tried to persuade her to give up her protests, but she continued. She was in Przemysl and was founding Communist cells in the surrounding villages.

She was arrested again with other young women and a show trial was held by the right-wing Polish government. They were refused a lawyer and all were silenced when they tried to defend themselves except for Gola who spoke for 90 minutes uninterrupted. She made such an impact that the Chief Prosecutor visited her in her cell and gave her three roses, but she was still sentenced to twelve years in prison.

Even in prison she fought for an improvement in the conditions and the relationship between the warders and prisoners. In 1938 they were moved to Fordon Prison near the German border. The guards fled when war broke out on 1 September 1939. They left the prisoners locked inside but the women, led by Gola managed to escape just before the Germans arrived.

She heard her boyfriend Alexander (Olek) Hausman was in Warsaw, but by the time she got there he had moved to Bialystok, so she followed him. Both Bialystok and Lvov were under Soviet control but they went to Lvov together and got married. She was appointed a member of the city council and commissar. However, after the German conquest of June 1941 Olek fled east to join the Red Army. Nothing more was ever heard of him. Gola was heavily pregnant and stayed behind but she knew the Germans were looking for her. She hid in a dilapidated basement where she gave birth on her own, cutting the umbilical cord herself. She struggled alone for several weeks before she contacted relatives in the Cracow Ghetto. A Pole was sent to bring her to them but by the time she arrived at the Ghetto in early 1942, the baby had died.

It took her time to recover from the ordeal and she sat writing poems to her son and husband. Then the tone changed and she seemed renewed. She thought her husband was still alive and wrote him a long letter telling him what had happened to her and how she had felt betrayed by their colleagues in Lvov.

She and her cousin Vuschka Spiner went to work in a German factory, where they sabotaged the cans of food intended for the German army by making holes in them. Gola decided this was not worth the risk and they stopped. Vuschka's husband, Dolek Liebeskind (1912–1942), was head of the Akiva movement and they discussed tactics for acting against the Nazis. Gola always said the deportations would mean annihilation and they should defend themselves. In the end she decided to leave the ghetto and go back to her Communist friends who, following an order from Stalin, were active with the PPR (*Polska Partia Robotnicza* – Polish Workers' Party) in January 1942.

On 20 November 1942 she wrote to her parents who were in Switzerland: 'I am now with old friends of mine and my husband's. Through them, I found work in my old profession [the publication of a newspaper and pamphlets]. My work has given me back the independence and inner peace I lacked after my child died.'

Gola wanted to recruit her family and friends from the ghetto for the struggle against the Nazis. However her party comrades did not feel that the time was right and also they were ill-equipped. She was concerned because she felt as a Jew they were in a race against time to avoid annihilation. Her efforts enabled Dolek and his colleagues to get some help from the PPR – such as guides to the forest, hiding places outside the ghetto. This was mainly through another organization, *Iskra* (Russian for 'Spark'), led by Heshek Bauminger (1919–1943) which merged with the PPR.

Tova Draenger said they all saw Gola as

… a superb example of a woman of refined spirit, experienced [in the underground] and a courageous fighter. They believed that her personality and unique spirit reflected the values of the party. It was not long before it became clear that not only were the risks unequal, but the amount of dedication was unequal too …They provided no help, either in the form of weapons, trainers or guides, nor did they give financial assistance.

Gola was very hurt by this, but Liebeskind and Shimshon Draenger (1917–1943) felt they couldn't work with or submit themselves to a party whose ideology was alien to them.

On 22 December 1942, two groups, *Iskra,* which Gola belonged to, and a group under Liebeskind, undertook a major bombing attack on the Germans in Cracow. It was named *Cyganeria* after the café the German officers used. Several casualties occurred amongst the officers. But informants betrayed many of the members of the other group, whilst *Iskra* managed to continue bombing targets outside the city under Gola's influence.

In February 1943, Heshek Bauminger was ill and was captured in his room. He managed to shoot his attackers, saving the last bullet for himself. Early in March 1943, Gola herself was captured at the PPR printing office in Cracow and taken to the Montelupich prison – known as one of the harshest. Other members caught after the café bombing were also there. After 14 days of solitary confinement and terrible torture, during which she did not reveal anything, she was transferred to Cell 15 in the women's wing where her colleagues were being held. Genia Meltzer-Scheinberg, the only one of the group to survive the war, testified that the women in the cell were horrified by Gola's appearance. Her hair and fingernails had been torn out and she looked grey and exhausted. However even here Gola earned her tormentors' respect, which she had done previously in other prisons.

The women from the groups became very close and Gola became especially close to Tova Draenger. When they were put in the basement, they sensed the end was near. Draenger and Gola planned escaping and Genia said she did too. They would escape when they were taken to the truck to take them to the 'Hill of Death' in Plaszów. The men came up with the same idea quite independently. Genia said they did not expect to succeed but they wanted 'to prevent the Germans from leading them to their death, and to let the world know that the Jewish women organized this escape'.

They planned that when they were taken to the truck across the street, at a given signal they would all run and surprise the guards. On 19 April 1943, at dawn, most of the women were taken and did as agreed. Unfortunately, as it was so early there were no other people around for them to hide amongst. The women ran but the guards chased them and shot at them. Most of them were killed as they ran. Genia hid herself between a gate and a wall and Gola, who was wounded in the arm, saw there was no room for her and ran into the street. She was shot and fell.

In 1946 the Polish government awarded Gola Mire it's highest decoration for military valour – the *Order Virtuti Militari.*

Jamila Kolonomos (1922–2013)

Jamila was a Jewish partisan in Macedonia. She was born in 1922 in Monastir (Bitola). Mark Lowen interviewed her for the BBC in November 2011. She sat looking at an old photograph album and with her finger traced the outline of members of her family:

'My mother Estef, my father Isaac,' she begins, moving through them slowly. 'Then my brothers and sisters.' She goes on naming all 18 of her relatives killed in the Holocaust. 'I was the only one not taken. I didn't even say goodbye to them, 'she muses, grappling with the memories. Jamila Kolonomos is one of the few Jews still remaining in Macedonia – a country that lost 98% of its Jewish population, the highest proportion anywhere in the world ...

At 89 years old, she is one of the few who remembers the deportation of the Macedonian Jews, sent by the occupying Bulgarian forces to the Nazi German death camp at Treblinka in Poland. Jamila only survived by hiding in Macedonia and then joining Tito's partisan resistance. As she casts her mind back, her kindly eyes suddenly narrow and a look of sheer anger fills her elderly face.

'I cannot forget the screams as the soldiers arrived,' she says, almost shouting. 'I still dream about them. And now when I laugh, something aches in my heart.'[231]

Shlomo Alboher's family also came from Monastir and he has written about his visit in June 1998 and outlined the fate of the Jewish community:

On March 11, 1943 all the Jews of Macedonia, all 7,215 of them were taken from their homes by Bulgarian soldiers, policeman, and clerks to the Monopol tobacco factory in the city of Skopje, capital of the Republic of Macedonia. They spent the following days on the wooden benches of the factory, ten on a bench, starving, thirsty, and fearful as to their fate. For the five days until their deportation, they were without food, locked in the halls of the factory and guarded by the Bulgarian soldiers. There were three shipments from the Monopol, 80 Jews in each cattle car of the train, each car sealed and locked on March 22, 25 and 29, all of them with one destination, the Treblinka extermination camp in Poland....

---

231 Mark Lowen, 'Last survivors of the Holocaust keep memories alive' in *BBC News Magazine*, 27 November 2011, accessed 14 March 2017, http://www.bbc. co.uk/news/magazine–15877299

Fighters in the Macedonian 'Goce Delchev' Brigade, among them the Jewish fighters Estreja Ovadja, Estreja (Stella) Levi, Jamila Kolonomos and Adela Faradji. (Courtesy Yad Vashem)

Monastir is shown in southern Macedonia. (Thanks to Robert Bedford of the Foundation for the Advancement of Sephardic Studies and culture, FASSC. From *Monastir Without Jews*)

In June 1998, I accompanied several family members in a visit to Macedonia, the land of our heritage. The sights were difficult, even horrifying. The two big synagogues of Monastir, Portugal and Aragon had disappeared. The Jewish cemetery in Monastir '*Beit Haim*' (the Home of the Living), founded in 1497, five years after the expulsion from Spain, was abandoned and in miserable condition. The Bulgarian soldiers had used the gravestones to pave their military camp, the parade grounds, the floors of the barracks, the swimming pool, the walls of the washrooms, sidewalks, etc. The Macedonian peasant farmers also took part in the destruction. They used the gravestones to pave their yards or to build dining-room tables.

All that was left were smashed pieces of gravestones strewn all over the cemetery. Swastikas and Nazi slogans were drawn on the tent that the Jews of Monastir had put up over the grave of the great Abraham Aroesti, one of the head rabbis of the city. The iron fence round the cemetery and the *Magen David* (Jewish Star) adornments that were built in the 1920s were broken apart, and Macedonian shepherds were herding their sheep among the graves.[232]

The situation in Macedonia was confusing. Yugoslavia had reluctantly joined the Axis alliance, but its government fell after an anti-Germany military coup on 27 March 1941. Accordingly the Nazis invaded Yugoslavia and Greece in early April. Yugoslavia was partitioned amongst the Axis powers and Bulgaria annexed Macedonia, which included Skopje and Monastir (also known as Bitola). At the time there were 78,000 Jews living in Yugoslavia including 4,000 Jewish refugees who had come in the 1930s.

Bizarrely, on 4 October 1941 the Bulgarians began persecuting the Macedonian Jews by prohibiting them from engaging in any industry or commerce. All current businesses had only three months to be transferred to non-Jews or close down. A law was imposed that only permitted Jews to live in certain areas of Monastir. The Jews in the more prosperous area east of the Dragor River had to move to the poorer area near the old Jewish quarter and this became the ghetto. With them all gathered together it was relatively easy to steal their property and on 2 July 1942 the Bulgarian government forced the Jews to hand over 20% of their assets. There were committees to assess the value held by the Jews and those who couldn't pay the tax had their possessions auctioned to meet the demand.

Normal Jewish life was completely disrupted. Jamila Kolonomos wrote 'Thus life was so greatly changed and there were no get-togethers, no festivals, no weddings, no celebrations.'

It is important to remember that Bulgaria is always held as an example; although he was a German ally, King Boris refused to hand over the Bulgarian Jews. However, the Macedonian Jews living in Yugoslavia and Greece, who lacked Bulgarian nationality, were deported beginning on 11 March 1943.

---

232 Shlomo Alboher, *The Jews of Monastir, Macedonia* (Macedonia: The Holocaust Fund of the Jews from Macedonia, 2010) p.5

The Jews were told they were going to other parts of Bulgaria and they would return after the war but they were still terrified and confused. Kolonomos had advance notice of this action and accordingly decided to hide. She described what happened:

> At dawn we heard the uproar of groups of police. In a moment there was the sound of horses' footsteps and the noise of carts. Then all was calm. Then came a noise like thunder...We asked each other what it could be. Then we were able to discern the sound of voices, shouts, the crying of many people, of babies, of women! We were able to distinguish the words of the Bulgarians who shouted : 'Quickly! Quickly!' The prayers, moans, curses, the crying was clear...They were taking all the Jews, old and young, not just the youths who could work...A river of people passed alongside us.

At 7.00am the Jews were forced to walk to the railway station, where a train was waiting to take them to Skopje where a detention centre had been created in the state tobacco monopoly warehouse called Monopol. It had the advantage of being alongside the railway and could hold thousands of people. Albert Sarfati, one of only five people from Monastir who managed to escape from the camp, fled on 26 March and survived the war. He recorded:

> They loaded us into cattle wagons, fifty to sixty people per wagon, including luggage. There wasn't enough space and many had to stand. There was no water. The children were crying...A woman in one wagon was giving birth...but there was no doctor. We reached Skopje at midnight. Night. Darkness. They opened the wagons and in the darkness pushed us into two large building. Cars carrying the Jews from Shtip had been added to our train. Stumbling over one another in the darkness, dragging our luggage and continuously being beaten by the Bulgarian soldiers, the children, the aged and infirm tried to squeeze into the building. When the sun rose, we realized we were in Skopje in the building of the Monopoly, and that all the Jews of Monastir had been rounded up that same day.

The prisoners were kept under strict conditions at the camp – speaking to or meeting anyone outside the camp was forbidden. Those that were ill were looked after by Jewish doctors also imprisoned. They were not allowed to smoke, play games, read newspapers, drink alcohol, receive food from outside the camp, look through the windows, write to each other or move from room to room. They were only allowed to visit the toilets in groups with a guard and only 15 were provided for 7,300 people. There was a lot of disease and at least one person died each day. One of the doctors, Helena Leon Ishach wrote:

> In one room there were over 500 of us. We arrived in Skopje around midnight and were locked up in the building of the Monopoly. The entire following day we and the Jews from Stip were kept under lock, because the search and plunder of the Jews from Skopje was still going on.

Having been locked up in the wagons the day before, and now the whole day in the building without latrines, people were compelled to relieve themselves in the corners and thus the air soon became unbearable.

Whenever one of us would peek through the window, a police officer would fire his pistol into the air. On 13 March they finally let us use the latrines. They let out the 500 of us who were in the room for half an hour then locked us up again, so that more than half the people were unable to relieve themselves or get water.

They let us out only once a day, section by section and then for such a short time that many of the weak, ill and invalids could not get down the stairs. Hunger pervaded, only on the fifth day did the camp authorities set up a kitchen, but for over 7,000 of us there were too many stoves.

Food was doled out starting at eleven in the morning, and the last ones were fed around five in the evening. Food was distributed once daily and consisted of 250 grams of bread and plain, watery beans or rice. They also gave us smoked meat, but it was so bad that despite our hunger we couldn't eat it. Not even one-fifth of us had dishes, so that several people had to use the same dish.

Under the pretext of searching us to find hidden money, gold or foreign currency, they sadistically forced us to undress entirely... in some cases they even took away baby diapers. If anything was found on somebody, he was beaten.[233]

Jamila Kolonomos' memoirs, written in Ladino, her first language, were published in 2006. The extract below describes her time as a Partisan during the period when the Jews of Monastir were being rounded up and deported. Jamila was the second of five children – two boys and three girls. One sister (Bela) married in 1941 and had a son. They were all killed at Treblinka – only Jamila survived. She was modest about her achievements. As early as June 1941 Jamila created three youth groups and one women's group. When they joined the Yugoslav Resistance, *Damyan Gruev,* in April 1943 she learnt how to use weapons and replaced the Commissar. In August on the Karaorman mountain the first Macedonian Partisan battalion was created from three former detachments and comprised 130 people in three groups. She was one of the three Commissars – the others were men. In September the group was expanded with a battalion of Kosovo Serbs and a group of Slovenes from a prisoner camp in Greece that they liberated. In addition a group of Italians who surrendered also joined the Resistance against the Germans. Jamila was made Commissar of the Macedonian battalion with a great many responsibilities.[234]

She was continually promoted and in August 1944 her brigade tried to liberate Debar in the west, but had to retreat. She was wounded in the

233 The Fate of The Bulgarian Jews, HEART 2008, http://www.holocaustresearch project.org/nazioccupation/bulgarianjews.html accessed 25 July 2017.
234 Jamila p.90

back by an exploding shell but was pulled to safety by a fellow soldier. On 30 October 1944 she was involved in the liberation of Ohrid and later, with great difficulty, Struga.

After the war Jamila received considerable recognition for her bravery and effectiveness in the war. She was a leading official in many organisations including the Alliance of Yugoslav Resistance, the Union for the Protection of childhood of Macedonia and the Alliance of Anti-Fascist Women of Macedonia. She also served as a Deputy in the Macedonian Assembly. In 1962, she was named Professor Emeritus in the Faculty of Philosophy at Sts Cyril and Methodus University in Skopje. She also wrote extensively on Ladino and the Yugoslav-Macedonian Resistance.

She had married Avram Sadikario in June 1947 and they had one son, Samuel, who is a Professor at Skopje University. Her brief marriage to Chede brought her a daughter Mira born in 1945, a month after her father's death. Tragically Mira was killed in the 1963 Skopje earthquake when the family home collapsed. Jamila and Avram were rescued in time, but Mira was suffocated in the rubble.[235]

Jamila died in Skopje on 16 June 2013.[236] The following is an extract from her book translated into English.

How Did I Survive The Holocaust? By Fighting![237]

On April 18, 1941 Macedonia was occupied by the Fascist armies – German, Bulgarian and Italian. Monastir was quickly occupied the Germans and Bulgarians. The anti-Semitic laws were put into effect from the very first day. All these laws were approved by the Bulgarian King Boris III. Today, in spite of out protests to *Karen Kayemeth* and the Israeli government, there exists in the Holy Land a plaque of thanks to King Boris, which offends both the dead and the living!

My father, the Director of the Banque Franco-Serbe in Monastir, was denounced to the German authorities because he was Jewish. Two German soldiers took him from the house, forced him to open the bank vault and confiscated the money and other valuables. We rejoiced when he returned home.

My mother had died one month prior to the start of the war. My sister Bela was engaged to Mois Kasoria. Escaping from Belgrade ahead of the advancing Germans, they settled in Skopje and were married. The police refused to give us a permit so we did not attend the wedding. There was a law prohibiting Jews to travel or leave the city. My brothers Kalef and Menahem were forbidden to continue with their schooling, and began to learn office work like most of the Jewish youth. My younger sister Rachela and I stayed at home, learning to sew shirts and take care of my grandmother Djamila who was bedridden with gout.

235 Jamila p.120
236 Nancy Hartman at USHMM, email to author 16 March 2017.
237 Jamila Kolonomos, *Monastir Without Jews: Recollections of a Jewish Partisan in Macedonia* (FASSAC: New York, 2008) Chapter 8 pp.57–63

The Communist Party alone had organized the Resistance against Fascism. The Jews had no choice, and they supported the party that led the Resistance. The majority of the Jewish youth belonged to *Hashomer Hatsair*, which completely associated itself with the Resistance. More than 600 Jews were secretly organized. Thus, from 1941, we helped in any way we could.

From day to day. The situation was becoming unbearable. Forced to wear the Star of David on our coats, we could not leave the ghetto. The Bulgarians forbade all work, or running an office, and closed all the Jewish shops. We became impoverished. Solidarity amongst us grew as much as possible. We all lived with the hope that the war would not last long.

In Macedonia, in the winter of 1943, there existed only a few armed units of the Resistance. Because of the awful terror, these fighters were located in villages far from the cities. Contact with these units were very tenuous, and the organized youth were not able to join them. In the cities, the largest part of the underground organizations were betrayed, and many members were imprisoned and killed by the Bulgarians.

On March 9, 1943, a leader of the Resistance, Borche Milyovski, advised me not to sleep at home for a few days, as he did not know what plans the police had for me. He gave me an address where I could hide and spend the night.

I spoke with my father. I told him, 'It looks as though we must leave the house and go into hiding.' He replied, 'We cannot, I don't believe it is necessary. I cannot leave my mother who is bedridden. The Bulgarians say they will only take the young men who can work. Kalef and Menahem are not yet eighteen. Rachel is young, she is thirteen. You should hide.' He knew that I worked for the Resistance and did not give me any difficulties on that subject.

The address I was given was that of a kiosk which sold cigarettes. It was located very near a police station. The owner was an invalid, with one leg. His name was Bogoya Silyanovski, later declared as *Tsaduke H'aolam* (Righteous Among the Nations) by Yad Vashem. He took me in and quickly closed the kiosk. The night passed calmly, and in the morning, I returned home. All the Jews were anxious, not knowing what might happen to them. They lay in bed, fully dressed, with the lights on. My father advised me to prepare a change of clothes for all of us, for who knows? ...

I straightened the house, cooked *fijonis* (beans) for dinner, and bathed and fed grandmother. I prepared for all of us a small parcel of underwear, socks and a few *biskochos* (biscuits). Thinking again that I would return the following morning, I did not say goodbye to anyone and took nothing with me.

When it became dark, I took Estela Levi with me, and we went to the kiosk. The owner locked the door and left. We sat, one next to the other shaking from the cold, in the black darkness, for there was no window and nothing could be seen. We couldn't sleep, wondering what the next day would bring. It was after midnight, when we heard muffled voices from the nearby police station. The hoof beats of horses and the creaking of rolling carts broke the night silence. Bulgarian soldiers and police had seemingly surrounded the city. The hours stretched and we did not know what was happening. At dawn, we heard voices coming nearer. The shouts, cries and prayers of the women and rending of their garments (a sign of mourning among Jews) were becoming so loud we became deathly afraid and pained. We began to cry, and we wanted to come out and join our loved ones. But we were locked in. Nothing could be seen through a small hole in the door, only that snow was falling.

No one came during the entire day. Like a dead city, it was silent beyond our kiosk, as no one walked the streets. In the evening, the owner came back with three Jewish women: Roza Ruso (nee Kamhi), Estreya Ovadya, and Adela Faradji. They told us that the Bulgarians took everybody, locked the houses, and the police took the keys. The Jews were taken to the rail station and searched, the Bulgarians looking for money, valuables and anything that struck their fancy. The Jews were then taken to Skopje in cattle cars. Much later we would learn of the horrors and indignities to which they were subjected at the Tobacco Monopol in Skopje.

Thus, five Jewish women were enclosed in a kiosk of three square meters (32 square feet). Only a curtain separated us from the side where the cigarettes were sold. We were without food, without water, with no means for hygienic purposes, not even a blanket for cover. Seated on the planks, we couldn't move during day or night. Every day the policemen came to the kiosk to buy cigarettes and would stay to talk to the owner. Being so near, we could hear everything, but we couldn't talk, cough, or breathe.

We remained in these unbearable conditions for a month. Seeing the days pass, and exposed to many risky situations, we felt obliged to insist that we be taken to the mountains as soon as possible. On April 7, our request was met. The Partisans received us cordially. The Jews who had joined the Partisans since 1942 approached us and, with great interest, inquired after our loved ones. We knew, of course, nothing.

From these first days in the mountain we were given *noms de guerre,* or aliases. I was called *Tsveta* (Flower). Because the Bulgarian propaganda portrayed the Partisans as Serbs, Jews and Communists, we pretended to be *Vlachs*.[238] There was a perception among the general public that Jews were weak, feeble and not good fighters. Because of that, we, the Jewish Partisans, jointly swore to fight Fascism, which had caused us so much harm, with all our strength – we were going to be an example for all. And that is the way it went...

A new life began for us, different than anything we had experienced before. We lost the fear that, at any moment, we would fall into the hands of the Fascists who would torture us and in the end kill us. I don't know from where we got the strength and courage to be at the front line of combat. It was as if we wanted to avenge our loved ones without knowing what befell them.

---

238 In this case, the complex term *Vlachs* refers to an ethnic minority of Romanians.

Allied against us was the Bulgarian Army, joined by the Germans and the *Ballistas*[239] of the Albanian Fascists. They burned the villages that supported us, and many villagers were imprisoned or killed.

The winter of 1943–1944 was harsh, with a lot of snow and hardship. February was the toughest month. For fifteen days joint enemy forces surrounded us. Led by our brigade commander, we were able to fight our way out and find a route from one mountain to another one. As there were many soldiers in the villages, we could not find food. Hungry and tired from lack of rest, the Partisans began to weaken and freeze. We had to be constantly walking, otherwise one succumbed to the cold's *muerte blanka* or 'white death'. We didn't lack for hallucinations – in some, one thought of falling into a fire with outstretched arms and a smiling face; in others, one imagined slicing their backpack as if it were bread. And there were some about lying on the snow, falling immediately asleep and never awakening. I caught the same 'disease' – I saw villages in front of me, heard disagreeable voices and was eating a very tasty roast of young lamb. Even now I can feel the taste in my mouth.

A friend, whom I have dubbed '*Salvador*' – 'Saviour'[240] – saved my life from certain death five times. Seeing me fall behind, he would take my hand and drag me along the path by force. There were a few Englishmen with our unit serving as liaison with the Allies. They gave us a couple of pieces of sugar, which restored us…

On February 13, 1944 we arrived at a great obstacle. In front of us was the river Tsrna Reka (Black River), greatly swollen. It carried rocks, tree trunks, trees. From one direction, the Bulgarians were constantly firing at us. We had to cross the river. We found a villager who showed us a place where the river was less deep. So with great difficulty, we tried to ford the river, holding each other's hands. The river swallowed some fighters, carrying them downstream too quickly – they were not saved.

In my group we were concerned about being shot in the back by the enemy. My comrades crossed the river and I remained the last one alone. I decided to cross. The water came up to my mouth and began to drag me to the bottom. I turned back…Here will be my end! I thought of detonating the grenade I had with me and killing myself – better to die that fall in enemy hands! At that moment, from the other river bank, my 'Savior' appeared, signalling me to wait. He undressed, crossed the river, grabbed my back and saved me. I had a great fright, and it took some time before I calmed down.

The snow did not abate. Wherever we march we left tracks in the snow and the Fascists found us quickly. The cold air froze our garments, which became stiff like a drum skin. We received help from other brigades, though, and we positioned ourselves in more secure places,

---

239 *Ballistas* were Kosovar Albanian Fascist militias (mainly Moslem) who murdered and deported Serbs 1941–1943.

240 'Salvador' was Chede Filipovski, whom Jamila married in early 1945. He was tragically killed in a motorcycle accident very soon afterwards.

got a little rest and comforted ourselves. From my brigade, 80 fighters remained in the mountains and snow – we lost them forever.

It was not easy to move each night from place to place to fool the enemy. During the day, we hid in the depth of the forest. Many were hungry. Many gave their lives in this war.

And our young men and women fell in combat. We always remember them and we will never forget them. I will mention only a few: Estreya Ovadia – later proclaimed Yugoslav Heroine; Rafael Batino: Mordehai Nahamias; Aron Aruesti; Marsel Demayo; Samuel and Salamon Sadikario; Mois Bahar; Josif Shurna; David Navaro and many others. All the Jews who took in the Resistance rose to high levels of command in brigades and divisions. I ended up as *Komesaryo* – Commissar of the 42nd Yugoslav Division. We were all decorated with high medals and awards.

At the end of 1944, Macedonia was liberated. All the population, happy that the war had ended, were embracing members of their families. Only the Jews were bitter in their thoughts – we found no one, the houses were empty, and we had no reason, and no one with whom to rejoice. We cannot forget what we went through and what our loved ones went though.

Today, there is war in all places in the world and in our own neighborhood. Everything is being repeated in ever worse ways. Now we must fight to have peace. All we desire is for the coming generations to live without the pains we suffered, and not to go through what we endured.

A postscript to the tragedy of Monastir without its Jews is represented by the census that was undertaken between 31 January and 2 January 1942. The Bulgarian authorities ordered the head of every Jewish household to present himself at the registry office with a photograph of himself, his wife and any grown-up children. Three volumes of the census of the Monastir Jews survived and are held in Yad Vashem's archives.

These volumes provide a unique historical record of a Jewish community shortly prior to its annihilation. Each page recorded from left to right: order number of registration, date of registration, full name, occupation, date and place of birth, nationality, religion, family status, physical traits, address, registration, photograph and signature.

The photos give a visual picture of these Jews of Monastir – young, middle-aged and elderly – 'the face of an entire community now extinct'. However not all the photos are still there – some were removed by their relatives in Israel.

In 1959 three men originally from Monastir deciphered the registers and the details were all printed out using a simple press on 800 pages. They collated all the details and created 3,013 biographies of the Jews of Monastir. However each one had the same ending: 'Sent by the German-Bulgarian fascists, on 11 March 1943, to the camp of mass murder of innocents'; 3013 times over.[241]

---

241 Yad Vashem, *Population census of the Jews of Monastir, accessed,* 11 August 2017, http://www.yadvashem.org/yv/en/exhibitions/communities/monastir/names.asp

Women of the Warsaw Ghetto

The women in the Warsaw Ghetto suffered the whole gamut of the horrors of the Nazis' Final Solution. Thanks to the efforts of the chronicler Emmanuel Ringelblum, we know much more than could have been anticipated. The women included below are just a tiny sample of the thousands who suffered in that awful place.

Rachel Auerbach/Rokhl Auerbakh (1903–1976)

Rachel was born in Lanowce in Poland (now Lanovtsy in Ukraine) on 18 December 1903. Her brother died in 1935 and her parents died before the Holocaust. She attended the gymnasium and university in Lemberg where she studied psychology, philosophy and history.[242]

Her life can be divided into three periods. Up to 1933 she laid the foundations of her academic, literary and journalistic career. During the Holocaust (either in the Warsaw Ghetto or hiding on the Aryan side) she used her skills to document her personal encounters and the events occurring around her. After the Holocaust she wrote about her inter-war experiences in Lemberg and Warsaw, which were major Jewish cultural centres and her work as running a soup kitchen for three years in the Warsaw Ghetto. She also wrote a great deal about the friends, colleagues, acquaintances and family who died in the Holocaust.

Rachel started writing in Yiddish and Polish and had her first articles published in 1925 in the local Lemberg Polish daily paper called *Chwila*. Later she had various roles with a Yiddish daily paper called *Morgn* until 1930.

Jan and Antonina Zabinski ran the Warsaw Zoo during the Holocaust and hid many Jews in underground pathways at the zoo.[243] Jan, who was the zoo's Director, was a member of the Polish Resistance and Rachel knew him.

---

242 Carrie Friedman-Cohen, *Rokhl Auerbakh 1903–1976*, in Jewish Women's Archive, 1 March 2009, accessed 23 March 2017, This biographical section is based on the JWA article unless otherwise indicated.

243 Agnes Grunwald-Spier, *Who Betrayed the Jews?* (Stroud: Amberley, 2017) See pp.333–4

Rachel Auerbach, who took part in the attempts to create a clandestine ghetto archive and who played an important role in documenting the story of the Warsaw ghetto, was in contact with Zabinski all through that period. After the ghetto was liquidated, she went into hiding and continued to work on her diary, recording events for posterity. As the front came closer to Warsaw, she gave one of her notebooks to Zabinski. He put it in a glass jar and buried it in the zoo grounds. In April 1945 Rachel Auerbach was able to retrieve her manuscript and publish it.[244]

Rachel never married but lived with a Polish Jewish poet, Itzik Manger (1901–1969), in pre-war Warsaw. She was apparently the inspiration for some of his poems. She rescued his archive and after the war returned it to him in London.

After the German occupation Dr Emmanuel Ringelblum, a teacher who organized the Ghetto's archive called *Oneg Shabbat,* asked Auerbach to organize a soup kitchen. Premises were found at 40 Leszno Street and she ran it for three years. Ringelblum encouraged her to record what happened in the Ghetto and her memoir *Soup Kitchen, Leszno 40* is one of the few of her works that has been translated into English. She also wrote about the hunger the Jews suffered in the first two-and-a-half years of the occupation *Gets a teller ésn: monografie fun a folks kikh* ('Give me a plate of food: Monograph of a Folk-Kitchen') which is one of her most vivid portrayals of the ghetto period. These writings were all buried with the rest of the archive in three milk churns and after the war two were recovered. The third milk churn has never been found – so far.

Auerbach left the ghetto for the 'Aryan' part of Warsaw on 9 March 1943 and survived due to her command of German and her 'non-Jewish' looks. She was able to work as a Polish secretary during the day and at night she carried on with her documentation of ghetto life She wrote two reports during late 1943 and early 1944: 'They Called it Deportation' which described the 'Great Deportation' from the Warsaw Ghetto during the summer of 1942 and 'Together with the People', which described the cultural life of the ghetto. Whilst these were distributed in the ghetto, they later became the basis of her post-war works.

Even before the end of the war, she became involved in the documentation of the events in Poland and collecting testimony and materials. She moved to Israel in 1950 and spent the rest of her life working on Holocaust testimonies and continuing to write about the Holocaust. She was the founder and Director of Yad Vashem's Department for the Collection of Witness Testimony. She reviewed publications about the Holocaust and was critical of Holocaust fiction claiming to be based on historical facts.

She was keen to record the cultural creativity of the Jews both before and during the Holocaust and the significant role of the Jewish women.

---

244 *Jan and Antonina Zabinski, in 'The Righteous Among The Nations'* from Yad Vashem, http://www.yadvashem.org/righteous/stories/zabinski accessed 15 July 2017

Emmanuel Ringelblum:

Rachel Auerbach, told me that there's a pot in use there that is now serving the third generation of one family – the first two generations have died out. This happens often in families who get all their food from the public kitchens. The lunches served at the public kitchens have deteriorated badly. The oats that used to be milled on the Other Side are now milled in the Ghetto. They're more expensive here than on the Other Side, and poorer in quality. Why was the milling transferred to the Ghetto? There are two answers. The official answer. The mills on the Other Side have to work for the Others; they can't work for the Ghetto. And then, some people say, the real answer is that it's a typical swindle perpetrated by the food-supply office of the Jewish Council.[245]

Seymour Levitan translated Auerbach's memoir of her soup kitchen into English and it is reproduced below. In his introduction Levitan wrote 'During the war she felt despair about the real usefulness of the soup kitchen; she saw their great communal and moral value as part of the immense Jewish effort of resistance.' In Samuel Kassow's *Who Will Write Our History?* he wrote; 'Auerbach was a superb observer of the Jewish everyday' and her writings are 'an indispensable source for any cultural or social history of the Warsaw Ghetto'.[246]

Soup Kitchen, Leszno, 40 by Rachel Auerbach, translated from Yiddish by Samuel Levitan

Our heads were full of ash and soot from the fires that engulfed the city only a little while before. The heels of our shoes were split from trudging through the stone and bricks of buildings destroyed by bombs and our nostrils filled with smoke and the smell of corpses. The noise of planes and exploding bombs still echoed in our ears.

It looked as if an earthquake had hit the city. The government was dead but the body wasn't yet buried, and we were the mourners for the burial. These were the last days of September 1939. After the capitulation of Warsaw and just before the German army officially marched in.

Near the end of September, on the first or second of a 'Series of Black Days' of the first German placards on the walls, the poet Rajzel Zychlinsky came to me with the news that Emanuel Ringelblum was looking for me. He'd asked her to let me know I was wanted at the 'Joint' office.

After the destruction of its building on Jasna 11, the 'Joint' had moved to Wielka Street. We had heard that Ringelblum carried on

---

245 Emmanuel Ringelblum, *The Journal*, edited by Jacob Sloan (New York: McGraw-Hill, 1958) pp.201–2
246 Seymour Levitan p.97

with his work during the entire siege, in the most intense days of bombardment, even on that frightening Monday, 25 September, when the bombardment lasted without let-up from eight in the morning till six at night. The day that marked the beginning of the fall of Warsaw.

I was broken, despairing, desperate. And penniless. When I came to Wielka Street, Ringelblum told me that a decision had been made to busy as many intellectuals as possible in the Jewish institutions – to save 'the cadre'. Moreover, he made clear to me that not everyone could escape – and not everyone should.

The Germans were uprooting Jews living in the West. There were already tens of thousands of refugees in Warsaw, along with the Jews driven out of the countryside. We couldn't just let these people fend for themselves. He sent me to Leszno 40, the local of the Small Businessman's Association. The building hadn't been destroyed, and we ought to establish a kitchen there. Ringelblum introduced me to Tsalel, the secretary of the Association.

I was given a sum of money, and set off scrambling over the ruins with Tsalel, over the broken barricades and unfilled anti-tank trenches. We wandered through the living quarters of former businessmen, looking for cooking utensils, plates, spoons and food. In a 'Joint' stockroom there was a bit of food that hadn't been burnt or soaked through. And so, on the first of October, the day of Hitler's arrival in Warsaw, at the very hour of his victory parade at Saxony Square, Pyotr Sulin, the Polish caretaker of the Small Businessman's Association, and I were clambering over the ruins of the side-streets which we were permitted to use, avoiding the German military divisions that were converging on the parade. I carried a pack of accounting books to help manage the administration of the new kitchen and a carton of dried plums. Pyotr hauled a half sack of rice on his shoulders. And I had obtained several of dried fish a day earlier.

That's how it began...

On out first day we handed out fifty portions. We served our last two thousand bowls of soup at the time of the liquidations at the end of July 1942, just before our kitchen was transformed into a 'shop kitchen' under the authority of the German firm W.C.Többens. I apparently have endurance. I held out at our workplace until that very moment. In the course of nearly three years I stood at the very center of Jewish suffering, on the front lines of the struggle against hunger. I experienced the fate of the Jewish masses so close up it would be impossible to be any closer to it.

Adolf as in Hitler, Bund as in Völkerbund

Adolf as in Hitler, Bund as in Völkerbund (League of Nations). That was how he – jokingly- introduced himself. I don't remember the way he'd come to Warsaw. He was originally from Vienna. He had escaped or been deported and may have made his way here though Zbonshin.

He seemed to be about 30. Not tall; a slim elegant figure, a little Viennese gentleman, with a neatly combed wave in his hair and a courteous smile on his lips, still clean, still well-groomed. He came to us when he had run through the last of his ten zlotys, the money he'd gotten by selling the heavy gold pocket watch he had inherited and managed to hold on to till he reached Poland. He obtained an identity card allowing him to eat at our kitchen. He'd buy his meal ticket and eat his soup at a table where he spoke with people from Germany.

When his last single zloty was just about gone, he moved from the front hall to the row near the kitchen and began to take his soup in a tin can hanging from his arm on a bit of string. At the same time – in a sort of joking way – he made an effort to draw my attention. He had probably convinced himself, like others, that if I chose to, I could do something for him. He wouldn't leave the corridor after eating; he would stand behind the wall reading a bit of an old German newspaper and wait patiently for the mad rush to be over, so that he could initiate a conversation with me as I went by.

His good sense told him that it would be pointless to cry about his condition. So he made an effort to maintain the manner of an easy-going conversation you might have in a coffee house or on the train. One time he worked up his courage, knocked on the office door and said he'd like to ask me something. In as much as had heard that I used to write for the newspapers before the war, he's like to know my opinion regarding the situation in Germany. One had to define it, *nicht war*? (isn't that so?) What was happening there? He ventured to say that he'd read Ernst Haeckel's *Welt Rätsel* (World Riddle) and wanted to get to a scholarly explanation of the problem. 'How could it happen that Hitler with his paranoid obsessions could rise to power in a country of the greatest scientists and scholars and with their help become the ruler of all Europe? How on earth could this happen in the 20th century!' – Every second or third Jewish refugee from Germany was forever preoccupied with the 20th century.

He grew agitated and his voice rose, he sermonized with emotion, and I felt that there was a subtext beneath his words. 'Herr Bund,' I said to him, 'excuse me. I'm expecting someone soon. Can you tell me something about your personal life?'

As if that was exactly what he'd been waiting for, and with the same intense manner, he began to convince me that it would make sense to save him, that *unberufen* (touch wood), he had something to live for. There was a living waiting for him in Vienna the minute Hitler leaves. His *gotselige* (blessed) parents had fled the war zone in Galicia in 1914 and thereafter stayed in Vienna. His father, a clock maker, had worked his way up, established a successful jewelry business in the 2nd Bezirk. After Hitler marched in, his father grew seriously sick and left the world. *Die gotselige Muter* (his blessed mother) had died earlier. There was a Catholic partner who was still running the jewelry shop, a respectable Christian doing well at the business. When the time comes, 'if only it were now' he would have no difficulty getting his living back, even if only in part. He was already engaged. When he was deported, his fiancée remained in Vienna, and he's received no more letters from her. But that problem – he added in a humourous [sic] tone – could wait till after the war.

Bund parted from me elegantly, requesting that I should not be annoyed with him – he'd only wanted me to take into account that if he were rescued, he had something to live for…

The weeks went by. By now, Bund was living in a refugee shelter. He received his soup from us, with or without purchasing a ticket, and also received a soup a day there. After a while I learned that thanks to a private initiative of some kind, a group of 'declassed intellectuals' was to be given an additional breakfast that consisted of a glass of ersatz tea with yellow sugar and fifty grams of bread. With the help of Dr. Weisberg, the director of the refugee shelter, I added bund to the list of these declassed people. A few weeks later, I had the opportunity to obtain for Bund a small packet of dry products. But that was all that I could do for him. After a while he took to waiting for me in the corridor again. Once, with a gesture from the distance, I indicated that nothing more could be done. From that time on he stopped lying in ambush for me. Apparently he still had enough will and shame not to make me feel that I had to avoid him.

Some time later I was told that Bund was standing in the gate of the bazaar at Leszno 42 dealing in our soup tickets. Tickets? His identity card allowed him to purchase just one ticket – I was taken aback. But actually I knew full well that all sorts of deals were done with our meal tickets. The price of 20 groshen for a soup that was worth more than a zloty impelled the poor to try earning something this way. Depending on what we cooked on a particular day, the soups went at a higher or lower rate of exchange. If they heard there was bean soup, consumers bought up meal tickets for the next day, without great difficulty changed the date and sold them at a higher rate of exchange. As a result, there were occasions when we ran out of soup for the late arrivals. And because of this there were some difficult situations. We caught on to the trick and stopped selling meal tickets for the following day. Of course, the other kitchens had the same problems, and Kitchen Headquarters gave us strict orders not to tolerate these violations. We were asked to confiscate the identity cards of the dealers in meal tickets.

I sent for Bund, and around three or four in the afternoon he showed up. I asked him to have a bowl of soup from the pot of food that stood reserved for people who finished work late. He thanked me nicely but refused to eat.

'*Spiren Sie zich beleidigt, Herr Bund*? (Do you feel insulted, Herr Bund?)' I asked, and began telling him what he was doing made no sense, that nothing he bought with the money he made could have greater food value than our soup. I kept speaking until I realized he was silent, and the words faded on my lips.

'*Gnedige Frau, aber schauen Sie mir an!* (Gracious lady, look at me!)' he finally stammered.

I looked at him. With the thumbs of both hands he pinched his cheeks under his eyes, and when he took his hands away from his face, there were two holes that were very slow to disappear. A spark of irony and angry satisfaction showed in his eyes. As if to say, 'You see, that's what your help amounts to...'

Both his fingers and the little mounds under his eyes clearly said; swollen! A swollen person daren't eat any liquid. He could now do without my soups and my friendly rebuke. He shook his head: '*Sie haben Recht, Sie haben Recht, küss di Hand, gnedige Frau* (You're absolutely right. I kiss your hand, *gnedige Frau*).'

It was sometime before I saw Bund again. It was nearly spring, and there were occasional warm days.

Walking once on Leszno, I suddenly saw him in the distance. Apparently he saw me too, but he didn't greet me, didn't hurry over. He turned into the passing crowd and headed for the nearest building. This was a large double house 52/54. Bund was barefoot. His small, almost childlike feet were dead white, as if made of dough, and spotted with dirt from the melting snow.

It pierced my heart. It drove me to run over to him, feverishly trying to think of what effort I could still make on his behalf. By the time I reached the gateway of the double house, he had disappeared. Possibly he was no longer able to get his shoes on his feet because of the swelling. But it could also be that he'd let himself be misled again by the vain hope of doing some kind of deal with the money he'd make from his pair of old shoes, and when he had the few zlotys in hand, couldn't resist the temptation and gave them away for a loaf of bread – wanting to fill his stomach with solid food.

A new springtime approached...

He had probably run from me because he was ashamed to show himself barefoot, muddy, unshaven. And maybe he didn't want to speak to me at all and hear me go through the same pointless reprimand again.

Adolf as in Hitler, Bund as in Völkerbund...

Zivia Lubetkin, Warsaw Ghetto Fighter (1914–1978)

'She had blazing eyes and a penetrating glance. She was simple and direct, demanding the maximum of others and of herself. For her, thought and action were one.' That was how Zivia (Celina) Lubetkin was remembered by those who knew her.

She was born in 1914 in Byten in eastern Poland. Her family was comfortable She was one of six girls and one son born to her parents. Of the nine members of the family only three survived the Holocaust; the son and one daughter emigrated to Palestine (now Israel) before the war and Zivia afterwards.[247]

Zivia attended the normal Polish school but had private Hebrew lessons. From an early age she was a member of *Freiheit* (Freedom), a Zionist-Socialist youth movement. In the group she learnt to work in the bakery, the laundry, the fields and latrines. This was preparation for emigrating to Israel. She also joined *Hehalutz Hatzair* movement and was keen that the two should combine which they did in 1938. This led to an increase in the number of members of the joint group known as *Freiheit-Hehalutz Hatzair.*

During the winter of 1938–9 she was involved in re-organising the training centres and this gave her leadership status in the movement, The young people admired her, as did her colleagues in education and administration. In 1939 she went to Geneva for the 21st Zionist Congress and returned just before the outbreak of war. It was decided that emissaries from Palestine were to go home. A new board was created and Zivia was included.

A footnote in her book, presumably written by one of the editors states:

An alternate Central Committee composed entirely of women was elected in case the men were drafted. Zivia was a member of this committee.

On September 7, a government order required all the [Jewish] men to move towards the east. Zivia and Edek Golowner were made responsible for closing down the Movement's rest house at Józefów outside Warsaw, evacuating the young people who had fled from Germany, from the training farm of Grochow, and sending them to the eastern provinces of Poland. On finding the people at Grochow had already vacated the premises, Zivia and Edek travelled alone and on foot to Kowel in eastern Poland, where they arranged to absorb the members of the Central Committee and the training farms who were making their way eastward through bombarded Poland. After the Red Army invasion of eastern Poland on September 17, Zivia and others were sent to the Rumanian border to open up an escape route to Eretz Israel. It was Zivia's task to travel from town to town through eastern Poland and direct the Movement members southwards to the Rumanian border or northwards to Vilna. After four months of operating in Soviet territory, and while still maintaining contact with the Movement in the German occupied zone, the Dror leadership in the Soviet occupied zone held an underground meeting in Lvov. They reviewed the operations of the preceding months and agreed on their future course. In reply to an urgent request from Frumka Plotnitzka for Zivia's help in the German zone, the Central Committee of the Movement decided to send Zivia

---

247 Biographical details are mainly from the Jewish Women's Archive. Fatal-Kna'ani, Tikva. "Zivia Lubetkin." Jewish Women: A Comprehensive Historical Encyclopedia. 1 March 2009. Jewish Women's Archive. Accessed on 13 December 2016, https://jwa.org/encyclopedia/article/lubetkin-zivia.

there. The occasion of this underground meeting also marked Zivia's departure. Zivia begins her story with this underground meeting.[248]

Edek Golowner, was from Vienna but lived in Lvov. He was a gifted educator and lecturer. He was a founder of the *Hehalutz* underground. His fate is not known, but his age is given as 27.[249]

Later in January 1940 she went to Warsaw and continued her underground activity. In the ghetto she was responsible for organizing and communications with the outside. She negotiated with the Joint Distribution Committee (JDC) and the *Judenrät* for funds to help members and their families. She made decisions at critical times such as when the situation in Lodz deteriorated, she insisted that the women members should be evacuated so they were not endangered. She also was active in discussions to create farms which would give members work, an income and a social life. They also created a distance from the miseries of ghetto life.

In autumn 1941, Zivia began to understand the intended overall extermination and decided to resist. As she testified at the trial of Adolf Eichmann: 'After we heard about Vilna on the one hand and about Chelmno on the other, we realized this was indeed systematic ... We stopped our cultural activities ... and all our work was now dedicated to active defense.'

Zivia was one of the initiators of the armed combat against the Germans. On 28 July 1942 when mass deportations were underway she was one of the founders of the Jewish Fighting Organization (*Zydowska Organizacja Bojowa*) known as ZOB. She was a member of its command and one of its organizers. She took part in ZOB's first resistance operation in January 1943 and the Warsaw Ghetto Uprising in April 1943.

Once the Ghetto Uprising had started the fighters trapped in the ghetto were doomed. Zivia serves as a liaison between fighters dug into bunkers as she visited different bunkers and maintained their contact with the leadership. The day before the ZOB command at 18 Mila Street was discovered by the Germans, Zivia was sent to find a way out, through the sewers, to the 'Aryan' side. On 10 May 1943 she went through the sewers with the last of the fighters but she was always haunted by the thought that she had abandoned her friends to certain death. She stayed in Polish Warsaw until the end of the war working in the underground and the rebellion from August to October 1944. She was part of the ZOB that fought with *Gwardia Ludowa* (the People's Guard, a Polish underground army organization). She was rescued with the last of the fighters, from a hideout in November 1944 (see Basia Temkin-Berman's story, pages 240–7).

Zivia died in her kibbutz home aged 64 on 11 July 1978. Perhaps one of the finest postscripts to Zivia's courage and foresight came after her death. In 2001, her granddaughter Roni Zuckerman became the first Israeli woman fighter pilot in the Israeli Air Force flying F-16s. However, Zivia would not have been so impressed as the *Telegraph* report on this achievement only

---

248 P.11–12
249 Pp.303–4

referred to her grandfather 'Antek' Zuckerman's role in the Warsaw Ghetto Uprising and not that of Zivia Lubetkin.[250] They had married in 1947.

Her book was written in 1946 when she arrived in Israel 'in the Days of Destruction and Revolt':

I am saddened by this meeting.

I have dreamt of it for twelve years. Many of you must remember your first encounter with Israel, with your comrades, with the Kibbutz collective settlement movement. Nevertheless, you are not capable of imagining what this meeting means to me, after living through these past six years. For we never imagined that any of us would still be alive to meet with you.

A gathering such as this is certainly encouraging, radiating a sense of power and strength. Yet I cannot say that my heart is filled with joy. The images of people, some of whom you knew and others you did not, appear before me – the hundreds, the thousands, the millions of Jews who are no longer. This burning memory follows my every step in this land.

It is sad. I never thought that we would meet this way: a lone survivor of the millions. Nor did we expect that the few who did survive would not be here with us. Nor did we imagine that when we emerged from our isolation into freedom we should find the world that we did.

It is difficult for me to speak. There must be some ultimate limit to the level of emotional experience and shock that a person can absorb. I don't believe that I would be able to bear it all and continue to live. In that reality, when we were surrounded only by destruction and death without any ray of hope, without any sign that the image of Man had still not been totally obliterated from the earth, and we had already lost our ability to feel and be shocked – you were the only force that supported us, that kept us going: the Land of Israel, the labor movement, the Kibbutz, this distant home.

I am incapable of describing what the Kibbutz meant for us. I would not be exaggerating if I said that the very few, the lone survivors, survived only because of you. During those six years there were moments and hours when it seemed that there was no reason to remain alive, that taking your own life was the only way out, the right way. And only that feeling, that there were comrades in that far-off Land, that there was a home where they thought about us and were concerned for our welfare, only this kept us alive.

I cannot find the words to express my feelings. Words are unfit, they no longer have any value. They are the same words that were uttered before the war, and at its outset, and all through it. And now, after it is all over, we are forced to rely on those very same words.

---

250 Tom Gross, 'Female Fighter Pilot Joins Israel's Top Guns', The *Telegraph*, 8 July 2001, accessed 22 September 2017, http://www.telegraph.co.uk/news/worldnews/middleeast/israel/1333264/Female-fighter-pilot-joins-Israels-top-guns.html

It is my desire to transmit, describe, recount – so that you may hear and judge.

The Secret of the Movement's Strength

...I believe that no man is capable of adequately expressing the tragedy of what happened. Perhaps the best way is to sit down together and weep, or cry out in a single voice as the tale is told. I have tried to recount those events in a way that we are able to understand and assess what we heard, together and as individuals. I do not know if this is the suitable way to express what we are feeling, nor what I feel as one who has lived through the entire experience. Fate determined that I should survive, and I am left with no other way.

I do not want to sum up. There are a few things, however, that I would like to add.

There are certain questions which have consistently troubled us all, whether there in Poland, or here in Eretz Israel. The first is: How did it happen than an entire nation was led off bare-necked to slaughter? I have tried my best to explain. I don't know what conclusion may be drawn from my words. I do want to say, however, although it may not help, nor does it make it easier, that I doubt whether any other nation would have reacted differently against the well-oiled highly perfected German machine under those same conditions of dreadful isolation. We know very well how the Poles and Russian prisoners went off to slaughter, and how entire European nations surrendered to the Nazis.

The second question is, from where did the pioneer movement derive its strength? The Zionist pioneer-youth movements took on the responsibility of all Jewish public life, a bit too late perhaps, during the most difficult days. I believe that one does not have to probe too far to find the answer. It would be wrong, painfully wrong, to assume that the resistance displayed by the youth during the stormy days of destruction was the response of a few individuals, of Yitzhak, or Zivia, or Mordechai, or Frumka. We have lived and still live with the conviction that our fate would have been very different had we not been members of the Movement, if we had not absorbed the values that it gave us from childhood.

This is the real secret of the Movement's strength. The Movement always knew how to demand everything from its members. The Movement's goal has always been to educate a new kind of man, capable of enduring the most adverse conditions and difficult times while standing up for the emancipation of our people, of the Jew, of mankind. It was our Movement education which gave us the strength to endure.

I don't know if I succeeded in describing how much we were almost obsessed at times with preserving the unblemished personal morality of each of our members as individuals, and of the Movement as a whole.

During the intense starvation in the ghetto, we received various things which could have improved our living conditions immeasurably.

They did not involve our having to live at the expense of others. For example during the initial period of the war, the bakeries were doing a very profitable business. We were offered the management of one of the bakeries, because it was known that members of Hehalutz would not cheat the people by using inferior or inaccurate scales. Since none of us were bakers, however and we would have had to hire workers and reap the profits of their labor, we refused. It was against our Socialist principles. This example crystallizes the moral values we tried to maintain during the entire period of the war.

What gave us this moral strength? We were able to endure the life in the ghetto because we knew that we were a *collective,* a movement. Each of us knew he wasn't alone. Every other Jew faced his fate alone, one man before the overpowering, invincible enemy. From the very first moment until the bitter end, we stood together, as a collective, as a movement. The feeling that there was a movement, a community of people who cared about each other, who shared ideas and values in common, made it possible for each of us to do what we did. The greatest tragedy was that the Jews did not know what to do. From the very first days of demoralization in the ghetto until the final days of destruction and death, they did not know what to do. We knew. Our movement values showed us our goals and how to achieve them. This was the source of our strength to live. It is the very same source which keeps the survivors alive even today.

I spoke mostly of the pioneer underground and the Warsaw Ghetto Uprising, although I know what occurred in other places from stories that I have heard from people whom I have met. It is difficult, however, to speak about places where I did not witness the events. I did not speak at length about those who fell before the mass destruction. Nor did I discuss those ghettos, which for various reasons never reached the stage of armed resistance and revolt. Nor did I speak of the Bialystock Ghetto Uprising whose value was probably equal to our own. Our comrades in Bialystock were totally isolated, but they fulfilled their duty nevertheless.

Other places, such as Czenstochowa and Bendzin, are equally worthy of mention. They began their uprising but failed. We haven't the right to judge events merely by their success. Take Czenstochowa, for example. Rivka Glanz visited us after the Warsaw Ghetto Uprising and I said to her: 'I believe that since the uprising ended as it did, it would be better for you to join the partisans. You will be able to kill more Germans and save more Jews.' She replied: 'We too want to stay with our own people until the very last.'

And they did. They remained. They remained behind to die. They didn't succeed in carrying out a full-scale uprising, but their bravery was equal to our own. They were with us until the end of the uprising, they witnessed its final, tragic moments. Nevertheless, they wanted to resist. They planned an uprising of their own, as did our comrades in Bendzin and in many other places. These courageous deeds and those who fell must always be remembered. We must never forget ... and so many others. All of these names are dear to us. They are the real heroes.

I have been told that I have mentioned people's names without always discussing their movement affiliation. The truth is that I no longer attach any importance to movement affiliation. I, myself, can no longer recall many of the movement affiliations of the real heroes whose names I have mentioned here. There were periods when we all, Hashomer Hatzair and Dror in the beginning, and then later all the pioneer- youth movements, looked upon ourselves as a single movement with a single leadership and a shared concern for the welfare of all of us together. I mentioned the first German *Aktion* in Warsaw and the problems that ensued after we sent some of our people to fight with the partisans and then tried to use the few remaining weapons in the ghetto. We sent almost all the members of the Dzielna kibbutz to Czerniakow and to the partisans near Mesritsch and Hrubieszow. Only a few individuals remained in the kibbutz. There was absolutely no one left from the Hashomer Hatzair leadership. Josef Kaplan was in prison, Shmuel Braslaw was murdered and Mordechai Anilewicz had left Warsaw. Tosia Altman and Aryeh Vilner were on the Aryan side. Only a few of our own people from Dror were left. We knew that under these circumstances there was very little we could do. We decided, however, not to leave the ghetto because the members of Hashomer Hatzair had remained behind without any of their leaders. We moved in with them without taking into consideration who belonged to Hashomer Hatzair and who to Dror. Later the same was true for Gordonia, Hanoar Hatzioni, and the political parties of the ghetto. For this reason I have not always pointed out the movement affiliation of the people I have mentioned.

Many of our comrades fell before they were privileged to take part in the first battle. I am referring to those who operated in the Soviet-occupied zone ...

We also had a cadre of young men and women that grew up and developed within the ghetto. We shall never forget them. I cannot even begin to tell you about Shaul Dobuchna, a young boy from Warsaw who was physically weak but displayed a moral strength beyond description. What can be said about those comrades who did not live to participate in the uprising, but whose courage and bravery were equal to our own. I would like to add a few words about the broader picture. I mentioned the Poles and their attitude towards us on various occasions. It is clear to all that if our Polish, Lithuanian and Ukrainian neighbours had behaved differently, many more Jews would have survived. I must add, however, that we did receive moral support (although it was not always sufficient) from the Communists (PPR) and Polish democratic circles.

Certain individuals, Righteous Gentiles, supported us and helped us. I've already mentioned the contacts and aid we received from the Polish

Government-in-exile in London, even if it was late in coming and very limited in scope.

Our bond with Eretz Israel: The importance of this bond cannot be measured in intangible or practical benefits, but rather by the encouragement we received, even if it was a bit late. You cannot imagine what a letter or a word from Eretz Israel meant to us. There were times that we believed that the entire world, including the Jewish world, had forgotten us, Many Jews died cursing their Jewish brothers in the neutral countries and across the Atlantic. Why were they so silent? We wanted to believe that the Jews of Eretz Israel were doing everything in their power to help us. Was this true?

I have heard that when Josef Kornianski and other comrades arrived in 1944, there were many in Eretz Israel who didn't want to believe what these comrades told. We, who knew the truth, constantly looked for ways of contacting you. We wanted to tell the world. We didn't want the world to remain silent, especially not the Jews, not you. We tried to get through to you in many different ways, but we never succeeded.

At the end of 1943 we realized that death and destruction were awaiting us. We wanted you to know of our life, our struggle, and our death. We decided to do everything in our power to keep two comrades alive: Hancia Plotnitzka from Dror and Mira Fuchrer from Hashomer Hatzair. Even though they refused to abandon us and make their way across the border, we ordered them to do so. As you know, it never came to be. We wanted you to know not only for the sake of history, but for the future as well. Let our people know. Let the survivors know. You, too, should know. Remember the past and learn for the future.

I didn't speak about the attempts made by the Jews in small towns throughout occupied Poland to preserve their dignity and honor. There were many successes and many failures. Many Jews rose with guns in their hands and later escaped to the forests.

I didn't tell the stories of the Jewish partisans, of the Vilna Ghetto, and of the various other towns, for it is difficult for me to speak of places where I have not been. But the people did resist.

The Jewish People Stood The Test.

Cecylia Slapakowa/Cecila Slepak (1900–1942/3)

Cecylia was a Polish-Jewish translator and journalist who came from Vilnius. Her family were Russian-speaking Jews. Her major work was the translation from Russian to Polish of Simon Dubnov's twelve-volume History of the Jews. *This was published posthumously in 1948. I came across her as a colleague of Emmanuel Ringelblum. He asked her to undertake a survey of women's lives.*

Cecylia was part of the intellectual elite involved in both secular Jewish culture and Polish culture in Warsaw. Her husband was an engineer and there was a daughter it is believed. When the Germans had invaded but before the Ghetto was created Rachel Auerbach was present at a meeting at Cecylia's home for one of her Sunday afternoon 'coffee hours', which brought together Jewish intellectuals, actors and writers. Apparently this was a dangerous activity as German patrols were marauding around Warsaw breaking into private homes looking for both valuables and forced labourers. Cecylia was determined to fight the gloomy mood and her 'five o'clocks' were reminiscent of pre-war salons where good conversation and modest food enabled the guests to forget the war briefly. Sometimes chamber music was played.

However in spring 1940 the Slapakowas had to leave their spacious flat and the salons ended. Rachel Auerbach recalled Slapakowa asking her about her work in the soup kitchen (see page 220).The manner of her questions led Rachel to assume she was researching a project for the *Oyneg Shabes* (Oneg Shabbat). After the war the papers for Cecylia's project were found in the boxes which contained Part 1 of the project.

It is believed Cecylia and her husband had a daughter of school age. It is assumed that mother and daughter were killed in Treblinka in 1942 or perhaps 1943.[251]

Cecylia thought the project would be useful in the reawakening of Jewish society after the war and she felt the women's role was crucial: 'Women are playing an important role in the positive trends of our life.'[252] She regarded women as a buttress against the increasing pressures of moral collapse, preserving basic communal values. Whilst Sara Horowitz saw the change in women's role as a 'measure of atrocity' Slapakowa saw it is as a good sign for the future. She thought women were adapting to continually changing circumstances remarkably:

> Women's individuality, so long hemmed in by ethical-cultural norms, has now become [a source of dynamic strength]. The particular circumstances of our socioeconomic life have impelled the Jewish woman to positions in the fight for life that are far more prominent than those occupied by women of other nationalities. The Jewish woman has penetrated into almost every aspect of life. In many areas she has a acquired a dominant position and has become the positive factor in the formation of our new economic and moral reality. In her individual and communal activity she brings forward many models of behaviour from the past; however, with a subtle and amazing sense of intuition she adapts this experience to new conditions, thus achieving very positive results. It is important to remember that the Jewish woman wants more than to simply 'endure' [*przetrwać*]. She also wants to construct the foundations for the future socioeconomic rebirth [of our people]. Therefore we see the drive to acquire skills and professions ... But the

---

251 Kassow p.178
252 Kassow p.243

influence of the Jewish woman is also strong in the moral sphere. She is imparting a ray of hope and courage into our dull and dark life, a touch of humanity and...even heroism.

Women were motivated by their sense of obligation both to their families and their own sense of self to do many things as at once – in modern parlance 'multi-tasking'. They might be caring for their children, learning new skills or risking leaving the ghetto to do some smuggling.

Cecylia followed the guidelines given and questioned seventeen women about their pre-war life, the outbreak of war, the siege, whether their husbands had fled or stayed, how they coped with the beginning of the occupation and how they had been affected by the creation of the ghetto. It is known she was conducting interviews as late as May 1942 and perhaps even later. It is presumed she handed over her notebooks after the beginning of the Great Deportation on 22 July 1942 and before 2–3 August 1942 when the first cache was buried. Kassow says Cecylia and 'her children' died in Treblinka in 1942 but the evidence of her offspring is sparse.

The women interviewed were identified only by an initial. They were a very diverse group – some were highly educated with several languages, others were housewives with little education. 'They ran the gamut from Basia Temkin Berman, a librarian and an important figure in the Jewish underground, to Ms. P. who survived by becoming a high-class prostitute in a ghetto nightclub.'[253]

Ms. C. and Ms. F. were the first two interviewees – both were from 'lower middle-class backgrounds' – Ms. C. had made corsets and Ms. F. sold shoes. Since the start of the war neither husband had provided economic help:

Mr. C cowered in the house, constantly sick and afraid to go outside, and Mr. F had been beaten so badly during a stint of forced labour that he was unable to work for a long time. Both women relied on their pre-war contacts with friendly Poles in order to trade and support their family. After the ghetto was established, both would slip out to the Aryan side to smuggle. In November 1941 the Germans announced the death penalty for Jews caught outside the ghetto. Ms. C had a number of close calls. After being caught by a police agent who freed her in exchange for a bribe of fifteen hundred zlotys, she finally decided to give up smuggling, even though she had been earning up to seven thousand zlotys a month. She told Slapakowa that she was now surviving by petty trade and by selling personal effects. But the risk of getting shot was not worth it ...

Her associate, Ms. F, was not so lucky. She had three children to support, and the oldest was thirteen. In 1941 she had another child – and redoubled her frantic journeys that took her under the ghetto walls to the Aryan side. ('She was haunted by the fact that now she had to feed one more soul. She tried to store reserve supplies of food.') Making

---

253 Kassow p.244

matters worse, her husband came down with typhus in September 1941. Ms. F took enormous risks to crawl out of the ghetto, through holes and cracks she found in the ghetto walls. Even the announcement of the death penalty did not deter her. Caught in November, Ms. F did not have the money to pay the high bribe that the agent demanded. She was among the first group of Jews executed in November 1941 for exiting the ghetto illegally.[254]

Cecylia was not coy about describing strategies that would upset pre-war conventions. She interviewed one woman who grew up in a home marred by alcoholism and 'sexual brutality'. Although she married before the war, her husband fled to the East on 6 September 1939. Her parents ran a restaurant so they were not short of food in the siege. After the German occupation her husband contacted her from Vilna (now Vilnius) where he was hiding and asked her to join him but her attempt failed. When she returned to Warsaw she found the Germans had taken all the food the family had stored at the restaurant. Unfazed by this, Ms. C became the lover of a Polish lodger her parents had let a room to. He was free to travel all over occupied Poland and the Reich and returned with goods that Ms. C sold for a handsome profit. This stopped when the ghetto was created but she then set up a restaurant with food supplies brought in by her Aryan lover. When he lost interest in her, the restaurant failed. She began smuggling on the Aryan side using a house on the border of the ghetto to get out of the ghetto. On another occasion she was nearly shot escaping the Germans. The borders of the ghetto were changed in October 1941 and that option was lost. Instead she became a waitress in a ghetto restaurant. This time she continued her petty trade as well as holding erotic conversations with customers over lots of vodka. By the time she was interviewed by Slapakowa she was the 'top girl'. 'For the price of having to sell herself … she can ensure her own and her family's economic survival.'[255]

Another woman Ms. G, also had Aryan lovers, which divided her parents. Her father condemned the affairs but her mother thought they were necessary for their survival and helped him come to terms with them. The first relationship went on for a long time, which was risky for the man because of the racial laws. When the relationship ended she found another, this time a Polish tailor who helped her smuggle goods, then another Pole, a police inspector called Bolek. They were very ostentatious about the relationship, running up huge bills in the most expensive ghetto cafes. Ms. G also earned money by trading on Bolek's ability to free Jewish prisoners. He managed to free Ms. G's brother the first time he was sent to a labour camp in April 1942 but couldn't do it the next month.

This overt relationship upset even the unflappable Slapakowa:

The open pleasure Ms. G took in Bolek, the expensive wines they consumed together, and the fact that Ms. G felt no embarrassment in

---

254 Kassow p.245
255 P.246

front of her friends all puzzled Slapakowa. She wondered whether Ms. G's behaviour might be explained by a tendency she noticed on the part of many Jewish women to 'eat, drink and be merry'. Perhaps she thought her brazen behaviour would reassure Bolek and tie him more closely to her. Slapakowa admitted that there was something 'repellent' in what her subject was doing. But she also quoted Ms. G's mother: 'If it hadn't been for Guta,' she said 'our whole family would have been in the Gesia cemetery long ago.'[256]

It is felt that the best interviews came from women of her own class. Ms. F was a refugee from Lodz with a doctorate in philology. She spoke four languages and had a good job as an executive secretary in an artificial silk factory. When the factory changed hands, she left because her responsibilities were reduced. She then had a job where she could use her fluent French. Like most interviewees, she relied on help from pre-war Polish acquaintances. When the Germans occupied Lodz, as elsewhere, they imposed restrictions on Jews' access to the shops, but her Polish friends brought her food and other basic supplies. However, after the Nazis' plans for a ghetto were announced in April 1940, she decided to go to Warsaw. With her sister, she risked a terrible journey across the border from the Reich and the General Government. The border guards made her strip naked and then beat her. She was thrown off the bus and not allowed to cross the border because she was a Jew. She managed to cross on foot even though she was grazed by a border guard's bullet. Eventually she reached Warsaw, where she failed as a street trader and so learnt how to give manicures.

By 1942 had tried various means of survival; she had worked in both an ink and a box factory where she earned six zlotys and a bowl of soup each day. She decided not to get a better job because she didn't want to help the German war effort. In a factory where both Poles and Jews worked, she suffered petty anti-Semitism. When she tried to sell manicures to raise more money, or even reading fortune cards, she was betrayed by Poles and had to stop.

When the interviews ended, Ms. F, who had been a business secretary, was selling sweets in the street. She told Cecylia that educated women like her had to think about what they would do after the war as she was unlikely to regain her former standing. She might emigrate and so needed a marketable skill.[257] Ms. F said 'The woman of tomorrow will be a skilled craftswoman.'

Slapakowa noted Ms. F had 'a biological drive to survive' while maintaining her own moral standards and personal dignity. She did not mind what job she did as long as it did not compromise her integrity. She also refused to seek help and supported herself no matter what.

As in normal times, some women derive energy from feeling useful to others. Ms. B was forty-eight when the war started and performed heroic service as an anti-aircraft warden. She helped put out fires, cared for refugees

---

256 Pp.246–7
257 P.247

and nursed the wounded. During the terrible air raids on 26 and 27 September 1939, she stayed in post even though she knew her house was being bombed and she did not try to save her possessions. After the occupation, she worked in an orphanage and later as a hygienist in a ghetto refugee shelter. Even her husband's death in November 1941 did not stop her. During the typhus epidemic she helped the sick, risking her own life. Slapakowa saw her as the kind of woman who needed these volunteer activities to fight for her own survival.

Basia is believed to be the only interviewee who survived the war and to have a child. She too survived by serving others and set up a children's library in the ghetto. Before the war, she was one of the few Jewish librarians in Warsaw Public Library. The working conditions were excellent and she had several good Polish colleagues who helped her during the war. However, she told Slapakowa that she found the work in the ghetto more satisfying as it meant immediate achievement and also she was preparing Jewish children for life after the war. She encouraged the children to read Yiddish books, as she told Cecylia 'enjoying their own literature and reconnecting with their language would make them happier and better-adjusted human beings.'

Apparently she also helped a Polish Catholic engineer who hid over 26 Jews in Warsaw. Feliks Cywinski (1902–1985) rented apartments for Jews and brought them food several times a day in his briefcase so as not to arouse suspicion. Those who survived went to Israel after the war and invited him in 1965. He was greeted like a hero and in 1966 was recognized as Righteous Amongst the Nations by Yad Vashem.

She and her husband relocated to the 'Aryan' side of Warsaw on 5 September 1942, and the difficulties of their first period there were recorded in a six-page memoir, handwritten in Polish held at the Ghetto Fighters' House. She particularly noted the characteristics of those who dared during that time to go over to the 'Aryan' side (people of means and from among the intelligentsia, who had personal connections 'outside') and described the harsh reality facing those who went into hiding. In her memoirs she reviews the difficulties of making initial underground connections.[258] (Read her own story on pages 240–7.)

It appears that some educated women found the war presented new opportunities that had not been available before. Ms R who was a married woman of thirty-seven, was a trained agronomist. She worked for CEKABE (an interest-free Credit Union) but was bored with the work. A female colleague who was equally bored declared she wished the war would start so they would have challenges and important tasks like running soup kitchens and war relief. She said 'We'll do things. We'll live!'[259]

All the women in the survey struggled to hang on with various levels of success. Ms. D cleaned and did laundry, rummaged through rubbish looking for food. Before the war she and her husband had a modest 'lower-middle-class' lifestyle. They soon lost their home and lived in an awful *punkten*

---

258 Ghetto Fighters' House records.
259 P.248

(refugee centres). Ms. D tried to keep a sense of dignity and autonomy by putting a blanket around their space. She wanted to get a job as a maid so she could leave to live 'in a real room'. Her husband got blood poisoning after doing forced labour for the Germans and she gave blood to help him – but he died. She told Cecylia, as she continued scavenging for food, 'You know, I so much want to survive!'

The fragility of economic life in the ghetto was demonstrated by Mrs K, who was a very religious woman. Before the war her husband had a successful shop that sold women's coats and she looked after their children – a girl of ten and a boy of seven. During the siege a German bomb destroyed their home and all they had. Her husband was then afraid to leave the house so with her two sisters, she started a vegetable and fish stall. She was exhausted but pleased she could feed the children. Her marriage failed but her strong family ties helped her cope with the creation of the ghetto. They had to leave the old stall but the three women started selling bread instead. The women took a loan in the morning to buy the bread and they made about 25 zlotys each day. It was barely enough to feed three families, but they managed until August 1941.[260] Mrs K caught typhus but recovered although her two sisters both died. She then became responsible for four orphaned children plus her own two. She sank deeper into poverty and started selling her possessions. In the winter of 1941–42 she couldn't afford to light the stove and the children had to stay in bed fully clothed. If she worked she earned five zlotys but a loaf of bread cost twelve. In desperation she sold all the family's ration cards for bread, sugar and soap. She used the proceeds to buy porridge, which she supplemented with potato peelings from her neighbours. On the days she had no work, they didn't eat.

Mrs K knew her appearance had deteriorated and she told Slapakowa that when she had wanted to buy some sweets for the children the stall owner thought she was a beggar and chased her away. She had always been scrupulous about the Jewish dietary laws, but now she ate what she could get:

> But the war has not distorted her soul or spoiled her sense of right and wrong, her ideas of honor and morality. Even in the worst times, even when she faced the death of her loved ones, she never went into the street to beg or steal. She never sent her children out to beg. (A neighbor has confirmed this.)

The survey ends with Mrs K. It is not known whether the *Oyneg Shabes* were given all her notebooks before she was killed. However, the project was not completed. From what remains it can be seen that Slapakowa was looking at the social and cultural pressures in Jewish society that limited women's aspirations and ambitions. Following YIVO's traditions she tried to study the present to change the future. Before the war, Jewish women struggled to get political and communal leaders to take notice of them. Perhaps she thought her study would help change attitudes after the war.

---

260 P.249

Ringelblum realised in late 1942 or early 1943 that the study was incomplete and he would have liked more material. A few months before he was captured by the Gestapo, Ringelblum made a further comment about Jewish women in the war. This time he was referring to young women – the members of the Zionist combat groups that he had personally witnessed during the Warsaw ghetto battle. 'Their courage, ingenuity and combat skills left the men far behind.'

Basia Temkin-Berman (1907–1953)

I became interested in Basia because she was the only one of Cecylia Slapakowa's interviewees to survive the Holocaust. This was probably due to her leaving the Warsaw Ghetto to live on the Aryan side with her husband. She had a son born in 1946 who lives in Israel. She was a librarian and had achieved great career success in the Warsaw public library system before the war.

Basia Temkin-Berman war diary was published first in 1956 in Hebrew. It was only published in English in 2012 as *City Within a City*. It covers the period 5 May 1944 to 14 January 1945. Israel Gutman in his introduction writes that the diary displays two distinguishing characteristics:

> ...first in addition to factual information, it makes room for the personal impressions and raw feelings surrounding the author's daily struggle with the unbearable challenge of rescuing thousands of Jews before and after the final destruction of the Warsaw ghetto. Second, unlike other works in this genre, written by people hiding on the Polish side of Warsaw, which focused on describing the course of events and the weight of the tragedy that struck the families and ghetto Jews as a whole, Basia Berman's diary reflects the dynamics of the activity and unfolding events in the Polish area, as well as the contacts between Poles and Jews. Furthermore, it includes information on the vicissitudes of Jews in various hiding places in Warsaw in the months August-September 1944, i.e. during the valiant Polish uprising against the German occupation forces, an uprising which ended in destruction, displacement and catastrophe.[261]

Gutman also points out the difficult situation for Holocaust survivors in the new state of Israel when the Bermans arrived in 1950. The War of Independence (May 1948–March 1949) had taken a heavy toll and was an existential fight for Israel's survival. Whilst many diaries and memoirs were being published:

> Most of these works dealt with manifestations of the Jewish armed resistance and chapters in the lives of the heroes of the ghetto uprising.

---

261 Gutman pp.1–2

The Israeli leadership at that time admired the ghetto fighters and the partisans in the forests, as bearing witness to the valiant Zionist ethos of the Land of Israel. Conversely, the suffering of the concentration camp survivors, as well as the daily struggle of those who survived thanks to the efforts of non-Jews who risked their lives in saving Jews, did not attract as much attention and acceptance. It is therefore not surprising that Basia's diary did not meet with the response it deserved at the time.[262]

Basia was a librarian and was active in this area.

Even in the darkest days of the ghetto, books were always in great demand and changed hands quite often, including books banned by the Germans, such as works of Y.L.Peretz, Leo Tolstoy, Franz Werfel and Stefan Zweig. Homeless children sold books for a few pennies out in the street making them accessible to readers. Books served as a window to another world and helped to alleviate the horror of daily life.

Basia Berman made books her responsibility, and made sure they were available, especially children's books. For the children books served not just as reading material, but as a means of learning about the outside world, about the distant, imaginary life on the other side of the wall, the world with trees, trains, animals and vast spaces.

Basia personified the connection with books and its significance in the ghetto. Even those who didn't know her or never met her knew about her as the woman of the books in the ghetto.[263]

Dr Emanuel Berman wrote what he called 'The Paper Bridge' as an introduction to his mother's memoir. She was born on 21 August 1907 and died on 30 April 1953 when he was almost seven. The paper documents he had, and those also found after his father's death in 1978, are 'the paper bridge' connecting him to his mother 'in order to allow at least a glimpse into the broader picture of her life both before and after the war'.[264]

He found a notebook written in Yiddish entitled 'Your family' and dedicated 'To my son Emmanuel'. He assumed it was written in the late 1940s before they went to Israel in 1950 – he was born in Warsaw in 1946. It begins:

Almost none of them survived. I start forgetting their faces, even their names. When you grow up, when you can understand this, it will all fade from my memory. But I want you to know where you come from. Not because your family had some distinguished pedigree. They were

---

262 P.3
263 P.8–9
264 P.34

simple Jews: a ramified, variegated, colourful family There were many like it. But for me it was the dearest and the best.

Everyone needs to know his origins, and not settle for stock phrases like *'petite bourgeois'* or *'hassidic'*. This says nothing. One needs to know the unique colour of one's family, to take the good from it and erase the bad. It amazes me that the Jews, an ancient people with such a long history, gave little attention to family history. Other nations have pedigrees extending for hundreds of years. And we, with thousands of years behind us, rarely know where we come from personally. It's so important – historically, psychologically, sociologically – especially now after the destruction. We must hold on to any crumb that survived.[265]

These two paragraphs really resonated with me for two reasons. Firstly, as someone who is interested in my own family's history, I am continually amazed by British Jews who have no idea in which country their grandparents originated. Secondly, in the late 1990s when I first began to explore the Holocaust so my teenage sons could understand their past, I found the following quotation. Even now I cannot read it aloud without a lump in my throat:

There is no way of knowing what my children will make of ancestors from the age of dusty roads and long afternoons on the shaded veranda deep in the Russian countryside. But I want to leave the road marked and lighted, so that they can travel into the darkness ahead, as I do, sure of the road behind.[266]

Basia abandoned her project after about 30 pages before she had got to describe her own parents, siblings and childhood. She wrote of her grandfather as an old man and that she inherited her father's eyes – grey and sharp.

The only document Emanuel found from the pre-war period was his mother's proof of studies at the Polish Open University where she studied Political and Social Sciences between 1926 and 1930. Later she studied at Warsaw University to become a librarian and became a director of a branch of the Warsaw Public Library. She published a research study on Warsaw Jewish libraries. She joined the left-wing Poalei-Zion party where she met Adolf Berman, whom she married in 1936.

She kept a diary from her youth and continued in the ghetto but around ten notebooks were lost when they escaped the ghetto in September 1942. Emanuel explains that the book is the last part of her diary covering the last part of the war with flashbacks to the three difficult years in the Warsaw Ghetto where they maintained double identities. Openly they were head of a childcare organization and a librarian but secretly they were organizers

---

265 P.35
266 Michael Ignatieff, *The Russian Album* (London: Penguin, 1988) p.2.

of the Jewish underground. When they lived on the Aryan side they were a Christian Polish brother and sister, Barbara and Michal Biernacki.[267]

On 27 August 1944 she describes her disguise for the streets of Warsaw. As Emanuel wrote, it was intended to 'confuse the Germans and their collaborators who prey on Jews in hiding':

> In the first period I pretended I was a poor woman, part of an impoverished *intelligentsia*, refugee from eastern Poland, where I had never set my foot, but I had to adjust myself to the birth certificate made for me, which stated I was born in Krynki. I was walking around dressed very shabbily, with patched up shoes and a terrible, worn out, dark-red coat (it was the old coat of Dora [Akerman] which she used to cover herself in the winter for several years). It was so ragged, especially the sleeves, that I had to patch it up; since I didn't have matching fabric, I used a strip cut off from the bottom of a dark underskirt, a gift from Irena [Krenicka-Berman], which earlier belonged to Mrs. Kramsztyk (who had passed away). I made symmetrical patches which reached almost to the elbows, and the whole looked tip-top. And then the black collar, a 'fox' made of goat's fur or a similar domestic animal, lent to me by [Maria] Ossowska, appropriately threadbare and turned russet – something that a self-respecting servant wouldn't wear and then the crown of it all: a beret with the notorious widow's veil (the first was from Zosia R[odziewicz] and the second from Janka N.): it was worn-out from the beginning during the constant tram travels, and finally, torn from all directions, worn during worst rains without an umbrella, it was shredded into strips…To this one should add the briefcase, torn up one side, stitched together with grey thread and bound by a cord instead of the missing strap.
>
> I believed in this briefcase and in the veil as I would believe in a talisman. Until today I am convinced that thanks to this uniform I avoided many blackmail attempts, which I definitely stood in danger of, especially in the beginning when I conducted myself not as surely as I did afterward. Fortunately, no self-respecting blackmailer would risk getting involved with a wretch like me.[268]

The following entry imparts two pieces of information: 'Today May 5, 1944, for the first time in four months, A[dolf] went to the meeting of the Council [for Aid to the Jews], something he avoided after our adventure.'[269]

The Council was known in Polish as *Rada Pomocy Żydom (RPŻ)* and was generally known as Żegota. It was established in October 1942 with the help of the main Polish political parties and representatives of the Jewish National Committee, an umbrella organisation. The Council gave help to Jews on the 'Aryan' side and in the concentration camps. It was funded by

---

267 P.41
268 Pp.142–4
269 P.63

money donated by Jewish bodies in the West and transferred through the Polish government-in-exile in London. Basia's husband, Dr Adolf Berman, was the Council's secretary.

Żegota was the body that Irena Sendlerova worked with, in a special section, to save about 2,500 children who were smuggled out of the Warsaw Ghetto after homes were found for them. These children required false documents and stories to match them. If the children were old enough they had to learn their new identities.[270]

The adventure mentioned was Dr Berman's arrest by two agents of the German Criminal Police called Lubarski and Szwed. The matter was resolved by a blackmail payment but the two agents were executed by the Polish underground. According to Gutman the organizations in Żegota were also policing the blackmailers and Jew-hunters and eliminating the gangs of hunters who fearlessly prowled the streets.[271]

On 6 November 1944 she wrote at length:

I would like to describe this state within a state, or rather city within a city, this most underground of all underground communities, whose members met with each other, worked and talked in the midst of a population which didn't suspect anything; where every street, every coffee shop, every tram stop called to mind dozens of unique adventures. Every name was false, every word that was uttered carried a double meaning, and every telephone conversation was more encrypted than the secret diplomatic documents of embassies.[272]

I wanted to describe the history of those contemporary *marranos*, hunted down and persecuted with cruelty unknown in history, where a handful of *desperados* set for itself a task of protecting the remnants of the people from annihilation, of saving its honor, and preserving documents bearing witness to the truth. This handful, which could not be distinguished from those among whom it hid, pretended to live a normal life, while in reality the life it led could not be dreamed up by any author of detective stories, nor could it be imagined by the most secretive revolutionary operators in tsarist Russia. [They constituted a kind of secret fraternity which used a special lingo to communicate about its matters, had its own identifying signs, hundreds of meeting points and a special way of dressing. Every detail was significant and calculated] ...

Previously, every nook and cranny called to mind the events that took place there; now, when all these places disappeared from the surface of the earth, and not only 'the city within a city' but the city itself ceased to exist – I cannot write.

---

270 Hans Stanislav Kopec-Gdansk, Żegota, for HEART. Accessed 14 October 2017, http://www.holocaustresearchproject.org/revolt/zegota.html

271 P.19

272 Pp.263–4

On 10 November 1944, she wrote:

> The woman who sells us bread every day (one kilogram of white bread costs 40 zlotys) tells us that Warsawians are being deported all the time from the nearby locality of Babice. Today, one of our neighbors travelled to Warsaw together with the Germans he works for. He told us that despite everything, many streets and buildings in the city center are still standing. They are partially burned but not completely destroyed. Valuable items have been looted. Streets are strewn with rotting bedding. It is possible to find untouched crystal and porcelain vessels.
>
> Yesterday we made purchases from our neighbor, Dr. D, who makes a living by selling items belonging to his deceased wife, and also some of his own stuff. After surveying what he calls his 'store' we chose the following: a bed sheet with some holes in it; several pairs of regular and thermal underwear, women's underwear and two handkerchiefs – all for 595 zlotys. He was very pleased with the transaction, because so much merchandise is being brought from Warsaw that it's difficult to sell anything. We were very sad; he is such a nice person.[273]

On 14 November 1944 she discussed various medical issues and the doctors concerned. One aspect was rather a surprise to me – she called it 'cosmetic surgery' – disguising circumcision.[274]

> At first we thought it was extremely stupid believing that this would help anyone who was caught. Furthermore, they were very expensive – as far as I remember the cost was anywhere from 3,000 to 10,000 zlotys. However, if someone requested a special allowance for such surgery I didn't refuse, taking into consideration the possible positive psychological effect, namely strengthening the patient's self-confidence.
>
> At the same time, however, I know of two cases in which surgery of this kind saved lives. In one case, Stasio [Rogalski], a young man with 'bad' looks [Jewish looking], was accidentally arrested in the street as a J[ew], but he recited the Christian prayer fluently, and after the physical examination also turned out to be positive he was released. In another case a bribe was needed, but the alleged reason for release was a whole [i.e, uncircumcised] mem[ber]. In case of children, not only surgeries were involved, but also sophisticated massages and tying on weights. I was told about it by Franka Kuszyńska, but I didn't quite understand the technique. I heard that there were some results and it was difficult to say whether the child was circumcised or not.
>
> In any event, I know of one authentic case, where during a random search on Szczygła Street, the specialist 'visual inspector' examined the genitals of two suspicious looking men, and when the *gendarme* asked him '*Was ist den los?*' 'What's the matter?', replied decisively '*Alles in*

---

273 P.278
274 Pp.292–4

Ordung!' 'Everything's all right'. This happened to the Bankier brothers and I was told about it by the wife of one of them, Ewa W.

Later on 29 November 1944, Basia wrote about recent activity when on 28 September the AL unit was told to move to Wilson Square. There was fighting and many soldiers fell but no one from their little group was hurt. They had hoped to cross the Vistula River but left it too late so hid in basements the next day, 30 September.

> Celina [Lubetkin] got lost somewhere and she could not be found anywhere even though they kept looking for her all day. Later it emerged that someone gave her an order to guard some dugout or shelter and somehow they forgot to relieve her during the retreat. She was left all alone, a rifle on her shoulder, grenades hanging from her belt, and it was a miracle that the G[ermans] didn't kill her right then and there. It was only in the evening [on Sunday, October 1] that Marek [Edelman] ran into her by accident, took her with him, and after a long search they found the others.[275]

She ends on 14 January 1945: 'I cannot write any more; the candle is going out. Once again sounds of the front come from the direction of the Vistula.'[276]

Three days later the Russians liberated Warsaw from the Germans. The Bermans lived busy lives in the post-war period and their son Emanuel was born in 1946. They decided to leave for Israel and went in March 1950. Life was tough in Israel and when they arrived in Tel Aviv it was hot and humid. First they lived in a cheap hotel and then in a cockroach-infested temporary flat before they got their own place. Meanwhile Basia was diligently learning Hebrew.

Emanuel writes that he learned from his father's notes that his mother's health problems started in July 1950 and she went to stay in Safed in the mountains where the climate was better. She wrote to Emanuel and her husband in Polish. When she returned home she wrote a letter in Hebrew – Emanuel said the language was clear but sometimes awkward.

To the Municipal Library, Tel Aviv

I ask to give me work at the municipal library. I have a diploma as a librarian from the University of Warsaw. The topic of my thesis was 'Jewish libraries in Warsaw'. I have worked in this profession for 20 years. First in the Popular Library of Poland, in the bibliography department of Hebrew and Yiddish periodicals. Later I worked at the Warsaw Municipal Library, where I was the director of one of the departments for seven years, till the war. In the Ghetto I was the director of the central children's library of Centos (association for helping children and orphans) till deportation. After the war I collected

---

275 P.322
276 P.427

books in Hebrew and Yiddish which survived, and organized a central library with the help of the Committee of Polish Jews. I collected 120,000 books, 80,000 of which we donated to the Hebrew University in Jerusalem. The last year before immigrating I returned to the Popular Library of Poland. Organizing their Hebrew and Yiddish books which survived the war. Half a year ago I came to Israel, and now I learn Hebrew. I want very much to start working in a library. I want to give all the knowledge I accumulated for 20 years to the city of Tel Aviv, which I love. Respectfully, Batya Berman.

This letter received no reply, according to Tom Segev.[277] It was two years before Basia found work at an elementary school librarian. Her son speculates that 'Her marginal and passive position after reaching her "promised land" standing in such contrast with her intense social involvement in Poland in the preceding years, must have hurt her tremendously.' His father was elected to the Knesset (Israeli Parliament) which meant he spent half the week in Jerusalem. He later gave evidence at the Eichmann trial and served on the board of Yad Vashem.

Basia and Adolf's relationship became more strained and they seemed less close.[278] Basia's health declined and 1951 was a bad year with a diary entry for August reading: 'I am again awfully sad. I don't feel like living. I cannot find one thought that would cheer me up. At the end of 1951 she spent 24 days in hospital and then more time in sanatoria. In April 1952 she wrote: 'The day after tomorrow will mark two years since our arrival. Writing is harder and harder; as I feared, the illness [Parkinson's disease] moves to the right arm. I believe this may still be reversed. But I am sad.'

Her last diary entry was on 12 April 1953 in shakier writing: 'I haven't written in almost a year. I have been working for some time. I felt much better mentally. Now I am somewhat indisposed. I must love my boys, and not let my spirit fall down.'

Dr Emanuel Berman wrote he was touched by my interest in his mother.[279] She was a remarkable woman, as are all the women in this book, and deserves to be remembered. It is sad that her life after the war was such a disappointment after all the years of suffering, which took such a toll on her health.

277 Tom Segev, *Between Warsaw and Tel Aviv, in Haaretz* – 3 April 2008, accessed 14 October 2017, https://www.haaretz.com/between-warsaw-and-tel-aviv-1.243311
278 Pp.52–3
279 Dr. E. Berman, email to author 21 August 2017.

The *Kashariyot*

I had not heard of the kashariyot *until I started this research. When I found out about them I was overwhelmed by their courage and resourcefulness, especially as they were such young women. I have written about them at some length because I think it is so important their story is better known, particularly as the majority died.*

The *kashariyot* were young Jewish women who were couriers between Jews in ghettos and other places. The name comes from the Hebrew word *kesher* meaning 'connection'. The singular is *kasharit* for the female. The English words courier/couriers can be used but they 'do not capture the heroic connotation of the Hebrew words' according to Lenore Weitzman.[280] The *kashariyot* travelled on illegal missions for the Jewish resistance in German-occupied Eastern Europe during the Holocaust. Weitzman describes their role:

> Using false papers to conceal their Jewish identities, they smuggled secret documents, weapons, underground newspapers, money, medical supplies, news of German activities, forged identity cards, ammunition – and other Jews – in and out of the ghettos of Poland, Lithuania and parts of Russia...The *kashariyot* were a lifeline – a 'human radio' for news and information, a trusted contact for supplies and resources and a personal one for hope and resilience.

During the Holocaust these women were seen as fearless and were a source of pride. The great Polish chronicler of the Holocaust, Emmanuel Ringelblum, wrote of them in his diary on 19 May 1942:

> These heroic girls, Chajke and Frumka, are a theme that calls for the pen of a great writer. Boldly they travel back and forth through the cities and towns of Poland...They are in mortal danger every day...They rely entirely on their 'Aryan' faces and on the peasant kerchiefs that cover

---

280 Lenore J. Weitzman, *Kashariyot (Couriers) in the Jewish Resistance during the Holocaust*, JWA, https://jwa.org/encyclopedia/article/kashariyot-couriers-in-jewish-resistance-during-holocaust accessed 6 Nov. 2017

Chavka Folman Raban. (Courtesy Ghetto Fighters' House)

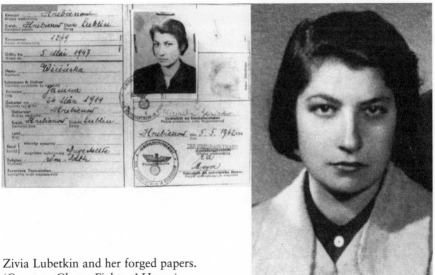

Zivia Lubetkin and her forged papers. (Courtesy Ghetto Fighters' House)

Bronka Klibanski's forged papers. (Courtesy Ghetto Fighters' House)

Rachel Auerbach at Eichmann's trial. (Courtesy Ghetto Fighters' House)

their heads. Without a murmur, without a moment of hesitation, they accept and carry out the most dangerous missions. Is someone needed for Vilna, Bialystok, Lemberg, Kowel, Lublin, Czestochowa or Radom to smuggle in contraband such as illegal publications, goods, money? The girls volunteer as though it were the most natural thing in the world... They undertake the mission. Nothing stands in their way. Nothing deters them...How many times have they been arrested and searched?... The story of the Jewish woman will be a glorious page in the history of Jewry during the present war. And the Chajkes and Frumkes will be the leading figures in this story. For these girls are indefatigable.[281]

However the *kashariyot* did not receive the attention and adulation the Ringelblum predicted. They were only young girls – some as young as fifteen – with the others in their late teens and early twenties. After looking at what they did we will consider why their courageous work has been so ignored.

The Nazis not only segregated the Jews from their Christian neighbours when they enclosed them in ghettos, they also cut them off from other Jews. Jews could not travel, their mail was censored and radios were forbidden. The Jews sealed in the ghettos had no way of knowing what was going on beyond the ghetto walls and all the Jewish organizations and youth movements could no longer communicate with their members:

> The ghetto walls were designed to isolate the Jews from news, information, supplies and assistance that might help them survive. To overcome that paralyzing isolation, the Jewish resistance developed a 'secret weapon' the *kashariyot*, who could break through the walls of

---

281 Ringelblum pp.273–4

the ghettos throughout the vast territory of prewar Poland and who could deliver news, help and hope.[282]

In the early stages of the occupation, such work was done by men and women who had been the leaders of Jewish organizations. However it became more dangerous for men to travel as circumcision made them easy to identify as Jews. Moreover, men wandering in the streets aroused suspicion – why were they not at work or away fighting? It was far easier for women to stroll around in a casual manner – going shopping or meeting a friend.

There were also issues of language. Polish girls had attended local Polish schools, whilst the men tended to have attended religious schools where Hebrew and Yiddish were spoken. Therefore when they spoke Polish they gave themselves away because they were not fluent, might use a Jewish inflection or have an accent. The women were able to speak more naturally on a Polish street. Another factor was female intuition. Bronka Klibanski (1923–2011) who was born in Grodno was a member of the Dror Youth Movement and joined the Bialystock ghetto underground. She worked connecting the ghettos in the area of Bialystok and Grodno in Poland: 'In comparison to men, it seemed to me that we women were more loyal to the cause, more sensitive to our surroundings, wiser – or perhaps more generously endowed with intuition.'[283] That intuition helped them sense when someone was staring a tad too long, who could be trusted and who was a collaborator and when it was time to run.

Lenore Weitzman wrote at length about why the *kashariyot* have been in effect ignored in the post Holocaust period when they were so appreciated when they were at work. Zivia Lubetkin who was part of the central command of the Warsaw Ghetto Uprising (see pages 226–32) wrote: 'one cannot possibly describe this work of organising the Jewish resistance, or the uprising itself, without mentioning the role of these valiant women'[284] In addition Mordechai Tenenbaum, who commanded the Jewish uprising in the Bialystok ghetto, wrote of the missions of Tema Sznajderman as the real 'centre' of resistance activities. Likewise Yitzhak Zuckerman, a leader of the Jewish fighters in Warsaw described Lonka Korzybrodska as having the intelligence, wisdom and charm of 'a high priest with her long blond braids arranged like a halo around her head'.[285]

Lonka was born in 1917 near Warsaw. Her father was a teacher and Lonka went to Polish schools and mixed with Poles in the Socialist youth movement. When the war started she made herself available as one of the

---

282 Weitzman p.1
283 Bronka Klibanski p.186
284 Zivia Lubetkin p.75
285 Cited by Weitzman p.9

first female liaisons – helped by her blond hair and Aryan features. She spoke eight languages. Zuckerman said of her:

> Lonka was truly born to serve as a liaison. She had all the natural attributes for it...She knew how to hide her true identity and a lot of her work was conducted via Germans. She developed contacts with soldiers, officers, railway workers, who never knew what they were transporting and what they were doing when they delivered her suitcases or performed other services for her.

She was captured in June 1942 and interrogated as a Polish woman in the Pawiak prison in Warsaw. She was sent to Auschwitz with 53 other women from the prison in November 1942. She caught typhus and died on 18 March 1943 aged only 26.[286]

Such women were shown great respect by the leaders of the Jewish resistance. At a historic meeting in Vilna on 31 December 1941 to unite Zionist youth organizations, Abba Kovner, a poet and leader in Vilna, first made his speech in Yiddish calling for armed resistance. He warned:

> ...those who waver put aside all illusion. Your children, your wives and husbands are no more. Ponar is no concentration camp. All were shot dead there. Hitler conspires to kill all the Jews of Europe and the Jews of Lithuania have been picked as the first line. Let us not be led like sheep to the slaughter![287]

He then turned to Tosia Altman, the *kasharit* who had just arrived in Vilna from Moscow and she repeated the powerful speech in Hebrew:

> The symbolic recognition and status accorded to Tosia Altman was not only a reflection of her personal stature as a *kasharit* from Warsaw. It was also an indication of the legendary importance of the *kashariyot* as those who would carry the call for resistance. If fact, as we have seen, the *kashariyot* literally carried the text of Kovner's speech and delivered its powerful message in other ghettos.

Why then were the *kashariyot*, who were so well respected by their contemporaries, neglected ever since in subsequent historical accounts? Weitzman suggests that whilst ignorance, poor scholarship or sexism could be responsible, it is also possible that modern historians have their own perceptions about what constitutes a hero. They use the term for those who physically fought the Germans in the ghettos. Some *kashariyot*, like Frumka Plotniczki, whom Ringelblum praised, led the ghetto fighters in the Bedzin ghetto and did engage in combat. Most did not.

---

286 Sara Bender, *Lonka Korzybrodska 1917–1943*, Jewish Women's Archive, accessed 6 November 2017, *https://jwa.org/encyclopedia/article/korzybrodska-lonka*
287 Cited in Kassow p.456, note 7.

The *kashariyot* also risked their lives and were in constant danger. They too assumed they would be killed. Fighters were only active for a few months – in Warsaw January to May 1943 and in Bialystok for about three weeks in August 1943. Certainly the couriers faced the risk of death for over six months and many of them faced it for several years. Like the fighters, they were killed. However because they worked alone and carried nothing that gave their true identity, the circumstances of their deaths is not always known. Most of them are known to have died. For instance, of twenty-three who started as couriers in the Grodno-Bialystok area, eighteen lost their lives, so only five of them survived.

With the ghetto fighters there were a few survivors, recognised as 'heroes'. It appears that not all those described as 'fighters' were actually involved in the fighting in the ghetto. For example, Yitzhak Zuckerman, one of the commanders of the Warsaw Ghetto Uprising, was actually on the 'Aryan' side when the uprising occurred because he was trying to buy more arms in April 1943. According to Weitzman he was 'engaged in the same type of strategic missions as the *kashariyot*'. So it would appear that the term 'hero' is applied more readily to those who fought with guns.

With the shortage of guns and arms, many of those fighting in the uprising used homemade weapons like Molotov cocktails or physical means such as their fists. The evaluation of who was deemed most valuable at the time was demonstrated towards the end of the fight at Warsaw and Bialystok:

> When the final liquidations and uprisings began, the leaders had to decide whether the *kashariyot* should remain in the ghetto to fight in the uprising, or if they should leave the ghetto to continue their work on the Aryan side. In both cities the leaders made the same decision: They 'ordered' the *kashariyot* to leave the ghetto (or to remain outside the ghetto) because they considered the *kashariyot's* missions on the Aryan side – i.e. securing weapons and rescuing others – as more important and more valuable to the resistance than having them fight in the ghetto.
>
> This analysis underscores the fact that it is inappropriate to superimpose today's views of who and what is heroic if we are trying to understand Jewish resistance during the Holocaust. The *kashariyot* were not conventional fighters: they did not use conventional weapons and they did not fight conventional battles. Their times called for daring innovations and different modes of fighting the Germans. But the *kashariyot* were clearly engaged in fighting the Germans and we deny them the heroic recognition they deserve if we impose inappropriate post hoc standards that disregard or diminish their heroism.[288]

From this Weitzman concludes that the role of the *kashariyot* was essential to the Jewish resistance whether it is defined as 'informing, persuading and organizing others to resist, evade or thwart the Germans. or as the armed

---

288 Weitzman p.10

struggle against the Germans. She states: 'If they had done nothing else, their efforts to spread the news of the mass murders, and their effectiveness in mobilizing others, place the *kashariyot* at the very heart of the Jewish resistance.'

It is self-evident that without the resourcefulness of the women who sourced arms for the fighters, as exposed to death whilst doing their duty as the fighters, the latter would not have had their arms.

> Their exposure to risk and death, the amount of time at risk of death and the loss of life in the line of duty – the *kashariyot* were more that equal to other participants in the ghetto resistance. It is, in fact, difficult to imagine a Jewish resistance during the Holocaust without them. It is therefore appropriate to correct the historical record to include what Dr. Ringelblum referred to as the *kashariyot's* 'glorious page' in the history of the Jewish resistance during the Holocaust.[289]

When the ghettos were first established the *kashariyot* helped reconnect Jewish communities, political parties and youth groups. So many of the first couriers were from the youth groups because they had such passion and loyalty. They were keen to do anything and they took information, news and written bulletins between ghettos. Many came from Dror – a socialist-Zionist youth movement.

Chavka Folman Raban (1924–2014) was a courier for Dror and was captured and sent to Auschwitz. She survived and in 1997 wrote a memoir:

> It should be remembered that one of the Germans' goals was to isolate the Jews, cut them off from each other. The purpose of the trips by couriers like myself, was to meet with our [Dror] people, maintain contact, hand over bulletins and other movement publications and to tell them what was happening in the center and the various branches. Sixteen-and-a-half, seventeen-year-old me was expected to transmit information about an active center, about ideas on resistance, report that there was still a movement, that not everyone was depressed...[290]

The *kashariyot* were regarded as beacons of hope during the dark days. They provided advice, encouraged the Jews not to give up, they gave people inspiration by bringing news of their families and communities. The members of the movements rejoiced when the young girls arrived. Chavka added:

> One of the most difficult concerns that filled the hearts of Jews was the feeling that the entire world had forgotten about us, that we had

---

289 P.11
290 Chavka Folman Raban, 'They Are Still With Me', p.67, cited by Sheryl Ochayon *The Female Couriers During the Holocaust*, Yad Vashem 2017, accessed 4 February 2017.

no hope and certainly no future; this was loneliness and all its horror. With meagre abilities, we young women worked to ease this feeling of loneliness, so that it would be less suffocation. We let them know they could depend on contact and activity.[291]

Chavka was born in Kielce, but grew up in Warsaw where she attended a Jewish High School. She joined ZOB and became a *kasharit*. In the obituary in the *Jerusalem Post* when she died in 2014, it described the *kashariyot* as

chosen for their non-Jewish looks and for their perfect command of Polish, enunciated without any trace of a Yiddish accent. Travelling across Poland by train, they picked up information by listening to conversations around them. It was often frightening work, because there was no dearth of anti-Semites among the Poles, and the couriers never knew when someone might catch them out.[292]

Chavka's codename outside the ghetto was Ewa Marczinek and although she was interrogated several times both by the Polish and German authorities, she was always successful in persuading them she was a Polish Catholic. However on 22 December 1942, the Cyganeria Café was attacked by the Jews (see page 209). This resulted in 11 dead Germans and 13 wounded. Chavka was amongst those arrested and this time she failed to talk her way out. She was, however, sent to Auschwitz as a political prisoner, not as a Jew. She was tattooed on her arm and her long blond hair was cut off. She was sent to Ravensbrück for the last six months of the war and was liberated in April 1945.

She already knew her father Abraham-Benjamin Folman had been murdered at Treblinka, but after the war she found her two older brothers Wolf and Mordechai had died fighting the Germans in Warsaw. Her mother Rosalie was still alive and together they went to Mandate Palestine in November 1947. She was one of the founders of Kibbutz Beit Lochamei Hagetaot, known as the Ghetto Fighters House and had three children with her husband Yehezkiel Raban. She was a teacher at the kibbutz and took youth groups to Poland showing the house where she grew up and the path she walked along to school. She wanted them to know about Jewish life in Poland before the Holocaust.

On hearing of her death President Shimon Peres said she was 'an outstanding example of Jewish courage'. She was buried in the cemetery at the Kibbutz she helped to create.

291 Folman Raban p.85

292 Greer Fay Cashman, 'Death of a Warsaw Ghetto Heroine', *The Jerusalem Post*, 13 January 2014, accessed 7 November 2017, http://www.jpost.com/Jewish-World/Jewish-Features/Death-of-a-heroine-337818

Frumka Plotnicka was a leader of the Hehalutz youth movement and was one of the most travelled couriers. She was called 'Die Mameh', Yiddish for 'the Mama'. When she arrived at a community:

Jews would flock around her from all sides. One would ask her if he should return home or continue his way eastward to the Soviet-dominated provinces. Another would come in search of a hot meal or a loaf of bread for wife and children. They called her 'Die Mameh' and indeed she was a devoted mother to them all.

Sheryl Ochayon states that the role of the *kashariyot* changed once the Nazis starting exterminating the Jews. It started with the *Einsatzgruppen* who were mobile killing units that followed the Wehrmacht into Russia in late 1941. The Jews were not yet aware that the Germans 'Final Solution' was to kill all the Jews.

A key role was played by the *kashariyot* who spread the word about the killing units and the shooting operations. It was the information spread by the *kashariyot* that enabled the Jewish leaders in far-flung places and in different communities to put the pieces of the puzzle together and to realize that the German plan was not merely to massacre Jews in certain locations, but to kill all the Jews of Europe.

Now the *kashariyot* took on yet another role – once they had seen what was in store, they had to warn communities where slaughter had not yet occurred, so that they could take some action. These young girls found themselves having to detail the mass murders. They were witnesses. Frumka Plotnicka saw the destruction of many Jewish communities. She witnessed Jews being loaded into cattle cars and deported to death camps. She reported the annihilation of so many Jewish towns and ghettos that she began to refer to herself as 'the gravedigger of the Jewish people'.[293]

Frumka 'followed the traces of annihilation' and was described by Yitzhak Zuckerman (1915–1981), known as Antek, who was married to Zivia Lubetkin and was regarded as the leader of the Warsaw Ghetto Uprising. He explained how they heard about the mass murders. They heard about the small Jewish community of Troki being annihilated and tens of thousands in Vilna. It was clear that 'the annihilation is beginning both in the east and in the west' and this was what 'we tried to explain to our veteran party members, to the Jewish community, to the activists'.[294]

---

293 Ochayon p.4
294 Yitzhak Zuckerman, *A Surplus of Memory* (Berkeley: University of California Press, 1993) p.156

He writes of Frumka, Lonka and Tema travelling around from city to city at this time. Lonka told him how she and Frumka tried to save Yitzhak's sister's son, but had not managed it. He wrote:

Then it was clear to me that my family was no longer alive. My family – my father and my mother, my sister, her husband, and the child Ben-Zion whom the girls had decided to rescue, only him, because they couldn't save any more and ultimately, they couldn't save him either... Uncles, aunts, a big tribe of the Kleinstein and Zuckerman families, a big widespread clan, in Vilna.

The horror of what was happening was emphasized by the story of 'the gravedigger of Chelmno' who was a young man called Yakov Groyanowski from Izbicza near Lublin:

The 'Gravedigger' was a young man who was taken by the Germans from one of the towns in the Baltics where there were still Jews. With the members of his community, he was taken to an abandoned castle near the city of Chelmno. Men, women and children were brought there in one of the transports and gathered together. At that stage they weren't beaten. That was apparently in December 1941. Then a tall, stocky German appeared; his face was kind, he was smoking a cigar, and he delivered a speech. He said he knew how much the Jews in the ghettoes in the occupied areas were suffering, and now their torments had come to an end. After the advance of the German army and the occupation of the Soviet areas, they were to be settled in villages and other places where their labor was demanded, and schools for their children would be established. He calmed them down, apparently he looked trustworthy. He caressed the children's heads. The people believed him.

Because the Jews in the ghetto were dirty and typhus was raging, he told them to undress and shower, and he promised them new clothes. He took them to another room (I don't exactly know the plan of the abandoned castle), and then German gendarmes appeared with whips and herded the Jews into an hermetically sealed truck parked outside. The doors were shut, the German driver started the motor, and exhaust gas streamed inside. As I recall, after a trip of about sixteen kilometres, they came to a wood near Kolmdorf, where Germans appeared along with young Jews from previous transports, the gravediggers, who dug the pits, put the bodies in and covered them. When they finished their work, they were taken back to the jail near the castle or that woods. At night, they were led away in chains.

The 'Gravedigger' was one of them. Most of the people they dealt with had suffocated to death in the truck. But there were a few exceptions, including babies who were still alive; this was because their mothers held the children in blankets and covered them with their hands so the gas wouldn't get to them. In these cases, the Germans would split the heads of the infants on trees, killing them on the spot.

After a few weeks, the young man managed to escape: 'He went through Jewish communities, places where Jews were still left. He would go to the rabbis of the city and the notables, and tell his story; but they didn't believe him.'[295]

He gave the testimony to Ringelblum's Oneg Shabbat, who recorded it in both Polish and German. The Polish version was sent to the *Delegatura*, the underground representatives of the Polish government-in-exile.[296]

Frumka was sent to Będzin by the Warsaw Jewish resistance in the autumn 1942 to encourage similar resistance groups. The members of the Jewish youth groups had been preparing for a revolt for several months. Then the ghetto was brutally cleared with about 6000 Jews being sent to Auschwitz in August 1943. Frumka died in the bunker of a resistance group in Kamonica on 3 August 1943, aged 29. She had been asked to go to Eretz Israel to take living testimony of the annihilation of the Jewish people. She refused fearing such a journey would be seen as an attempt to save herself. Her sister, Hancia, had already been killed on 20 April 1943, aged 25. There was also a brother Hershel who died aged 22 but details are unknown.[297]

It is recorded that some of the youngsters continued fighting until the bitter end – even on the trains to Auschwitz. Jochanan Ranz recalled:

> ... from one train the Nazis didn't let the people out, but opened the doors and shot in with machine guns killing them all. They did this because the train was mutinous on the way, many jumping off and one SS guard was killed. The troopers were afraid of a possible desperate resistance before the gas chambers.[298]

'When you receive this letter, none of us will be alive.' The letter in question was sent by the leaders of ZOB stationed in Będzin on 17 July 1943.[299] They open with 'For years we have dreamed of an opportunity to tell you about our life and our fight,' so there were obviously problems in communicating with the leaders in Palestine. Their uprising started in Kamionka and Środula in August 1943 but ended for the authors in their bunker underneath the house on 24 Podsiadły Street. It was addressed to the leaders of the parent organization who were in Palestine already – Wania, Mendel and Zev – and was signed by Cwi Brandes, Frumka Płotnicka, Herszel Szpringiet, and Baruch Gaftek who were repelling the Germans attacks.

The letter was given to the JHI by the grandson of a Warsaw doctor who found it amongst his personal papers. There was also a statement from a witness about help that the doctor gave a Jewish couple in occupied Warsaw.

The letter outlines the situation as the signatories understood it:

295 Zuckerman pp.157–8
296 Shoah Resource Center, *Grojanowski Report*, Yad Vashem
297 Zivia's book, pp.322–3
298 Mary Fulbrook, *A Small Town Near Auschwitz*, p.294
299 Aleksandra Sajdak, *The Last Letter From Będzin*, Jewish Historical Institute, 21 June 2013, accessed 23 Sept. 2017, http://www.jhi.pl/en/blog/2013-06-21-the-last-letter-from-bedzin

Following the organization of the ghettoes, a systematic plan of extermination began. It began in Warthegau, in the districts of Łódź and Poznań. About 80,000 Jews were poisoned by gas (officially it was known as evacuation).

In Lodz, there was a small, closed and sealed community that numbered some 40,000 who were undoubtedly dying from hunger and tuberculosis. At the moment, we don't have any information from there. This place of destruction is called Chelmno (Kulmhof). After this, came the extermination of Lithuanian Jews who were shot to death in Ponar. Altogether, about 20,000 Jews remained in Vilna, Kovno and Shavl. For several months now, we have had no word from their either, and it appears that they have been made *Judenrein*. We prepared our defenses, but unfortunately they've been unsuccessful. In the area known as 'Government' Warsaw, Lublin, Czestochowa, Krakow and the surroundings, there are no Jews at all. The extermination was carried out by gas in Treblinka near Malkinia. This is an infamous place of destruction, not only for the Jews of Poland, but also for the Jews of Holland, Belgium, and so forth.

Our finest chapter was in Warsaw...Terrible battles took place in the ghetto. Sadly, only several hundred of the enemy were killed – some 800. The result was that all the Jews were killed; the ghetto was destroyed and not a trace of it remained. In the 'Government' region there is no longer a Jewish settlement, apart from three labor camps, Trevnik, Poniatov and Prokochim, numbering up to 30,000 people. In a few weeks' time there will be nobody left.

In Warsaw a few thousand people survived among the gentiles in an illicit manner, on the Aryan side...The Ukraine and Polesia are *Judenrein*. In Bialystock about 20,000 Jews survived in slightly better conditions. Those from the Lublin district were completely exterminated in Belzec and Sobibor.

The last Jewish settlement, which had existed under relatively better conditions, was Upper Eastern Silesia. Some three weeks ago 7,000 Jews were exiled. They are being killed in Auschwitz. They are being shot and incinerated. In the coming weeks, our district will be without Jews. When you receive this letter, none of us will be alive.

Sadly, their prediction was correct.

Vladka Meed wrote about the next stage which was organising armed resistance to the Germans once the youth movements in the ghetto agreed to the policy. So the couriers took the risk of delivering guns and ammunition into the ghettos. Vladka was a courier working on the Aryan side of Warsaw for the Bund and she wrote:

The major problem on both sides of the wall was getting weapons, weapons with which to resist the Germans...Deep in every heart, bringing us ever closer together, lay the yearning for vengeance, vengeance for our families taken to the death camps, for the wrongs and sufferings we ourselves had borne…It was a great event for me when I managed to procure my first revolver.[300]

She also described having to quickly repack a carton of dynamite into smaller packages so they would go through the grating of a factory window into the ghetto. She and the gentile watchman who had been bribed, worked frantically in the dark with the watchman trembling like a leaf. When it was finally done, the watchman stood there flushed, drenched in perspiration and unnerved … 'I'll never risk it again, I was scared to death.'

Vladka Meed, who was born Feigele Peltel on 29 December 1921, was unusual because she was one of the few who lived to tell the tale, but also because she did not come from a family of Zionists. As a youngster she was active in *Zukunft,* the youth wing of the S.C., a Jewish social-democratic party founded in 1897. They opposed Zionism and promoted the Yiddish language and culture, with secular Jewish nationalism. Feigele's schooling was at a Yiddish school where Polish was the second language. However, her younger sister, Henia, had gone to a Polish school and she learnt fluent Polish from her.

She was a teenager when her family were forced into the ghetto in Warsaw in October 1940. Her book *On Both Sides of the Wall,* published in 1948, was one of the first eyewitness accounts of the destruction of Warsaw's Jews. She recalled that even with all the suffering, ghetto life was very rich with clandestine cultural activities. 'Some just refused to commit suicide, continued to educate their children in secret, celebrated their holidays.'

She attended literature classes, remembered 'the atmosphere, the elevation, being together with the people and taking about the writer and the character'. It was, she explained, a way to 'hold on to culture and history so that the spirit should not be crushed'. The subsequent uprising had only been possible, she felt, because of this 'inner preparation to stand up against the enemy'. She watched the 'Great Deportation' between July and September 1942 when between 250,000 and 300,000 ghetto residents were sent to their deaths at Treblinka. They included her mother, 13-year-old brother and married sister. Elie Wiesel, who wrote an introduction to her book, highlighted this passage:

Several wagons went by, loaded with Jews, sitting and standing, hugging sacks that contained whatever pitiful belongings they had managed to gather at the last moment. Some stared straight ahead with vacant eyes, others mourned and wailed, wringing their hands. Women tore their hair or clung to their children, who sat bewildered among the scattered bundles, gazing at the adults in silent fear. Running behind the last van, a lone woman, arms outstretched, screamed: 'My child! Give back my child!' In reply, a small voice called from the van: 'Mama! Mama!'

---

300 Vladka Meed pp.120–21

She also described the Jews being driven to the *Umschlagplatz*. This is the German for 'collection point'. In Warsaw it was a holding area on Stawki Street, near the railway station, where Jews were assembled daily for deportation to the Treblinka extermination camp. There is now a memorial there to the approximately 250,000 Warsaw Jews who were sent to their deaths from there:

> A tremendous churning, black tide ... There were rickshaws carrying invalids; men, women and children, the young and the old, trudging along. Face after face passed below us, faces pathetic, agitated, terrified, some tense, others bereft of hope. We watched intently, searching for a familiar face among the thousands shuffling past. The sight made my head reel. All the faces blended in confusion; only bowed heads and bundles and bent backs, a single wave of humanity. The marchers were silent, the atmosphere stifling, only the sound of footsteps, all sorts of footsteps – the slow and nimble, adults and children ... its cadence pounding a final warning: 'Remember!'

Feigele Peltel survived because of the labour shortage in Warsaw. This meant she was allowed to leave the ghetto to work in a tailor's shop making Nazi uniforms. When the news of the fate of the deported began to arrive she joined ZOB and assumed the personality of Vladka, an ethnic Pole, so she could move freely on the 'Aryan' side of the ghetto. She had light-coloured hair and Aryan features and was able to play that role for almost three years. This was much easier for women because men could always be betrayed by their circumcision.

Vladka spent several months buying black market weapons and ammunition, paying for it with rings, watches and other valuables, which she smuggled into the ghetto: 'I would smuggle dynamite and gasoline for the bombs past the gates. We would wrap it up in greasy paper as if it was meat. Or sometimes we would just bribe a Nazi guard.'

She also wrote: 'At Gesia 13, from the window in the hiding place, I saw the march of the orphanage of Janusz Korczak. The children went silently, carrying blankets, walking hand-in-hand...'

Vladka herself smuggled some Jewish children out to be placed with sympathetic Christian families, but she claimed most ethnic Poles were not sympathetic. In 1973 she said: 'Quite a large number of them were openly anti-Semitic and even, in a way, having satisfaction.'

Vladka watched the uprising from the relative safety outside the ghetto and watched the end of one group of captured Jews; 'At the ghetto wall stood a bearded, kaftaned Hassid and his small son. The guards separated the two, but the boy ran back and clung fiercely to the father. A German raised his carbine [a light rifle] then, smiling, separated the two once more. Again the child darted back, and the German burst into laughter. Then father embraced his child in sheer despair. Several shots rang out – and the two remained together, even in death.'

The fighting lasted 28 days during which the bullets and improvised bombs of the Jews were met by the tools of industrial warfare – machine guns, tanks and flame throwers. It ended with complete destruction of the ghetto. 'People who participated in the armed resistance knew they were going to die. What was important to them was they wanted to choose the way they died.'

The Holocaust historian Michael Berenbaum claims it was Vladka Meed who brought the news that confirmed the worst. The news that the trains filled with Jews returned empty from Treblinka, that no food was going into the camp and that there was an all-pervasive stench of burning and rotting flesh.

Frumka was the first courier to smuggle weapons into the Warsaw Ghetto – she took them in at the bottom of a sack of potatoes, Chavka noted that she and Tema Schneiderman, another *kasharit*, smuggled grenades into the Warsaw ghetto by hiding them in their underwear.

Elie Wiesel commented on the bravery of the women who took on the might of the Third Reich. He particularly praised the courage of Vladka and her colleagues:

> ...And Vladka herself, where did she muster the courage, once on the 'Aryan side' to search for *melinas* [hiding places] for children, to purchase arms for the ghetto fighters, to work as a courier among the Jews in the forest near Czestochowa and the Jews of the concentration camps in Radom?
>
> Is it not harrowing to reflect that the only assistance, the only consolation, that came to the few surviving Jews hidden in caves and cellars was brought, not by emissaries of great governments, or rich Jewish communities, but by a band of frightened, dauntless Jewish girls from Warsaw itself, like Vladka and her handful of friends.[301]

Adina Blady Szwajger (1917–1993) was a young doctor who also acted as a *kasharit*, and described how in the spring before the Ghetto Uprising:

> ...we started to transport guns and ammunition from one place to another, that is from those who sold or provided them, to somewhere near the ghetto, from where someone else would collect them. I was least afraid when I carried a gun, because I knew that I wouldn't let them take me alive. Sometimes before leaving I would drink a glass of vodka on the stairs for Dutch courage and then go out. Tipsy. And in that tipsy state a patrol stopped me on Zelazna street and ordered me to open my bag. Hidden beneath the potatoes was some ammunition. Smiling broadly I opened the bag wide. 'Los' said the German gendarme. And I walked on.[302]

---

301 Elie Wiesel, Introduction to *On Both Sides of The Wall*, p.5
302 P.82

She described how one evening, in autumn 1943, she got off the tram and was accosted by a Pole who stopped her saying '*Jude?*' First she pretended not to understand, but then she dragged him off to the police station on Dluga Street. She complained to the policeman that he had accosted her and his documents should be checked. They checked his and hers but she was not afraid because her documents were real. She later discovered he had followed her some distance because she had been pointed out to him and wanted to earn some money:

> And that is what everyday life was like: people, problems, forever running around – and fear. Already then there was fear. Every familiar face was hostile. The whole town, my town, my own town, that I had grown up in, was strange, hostile, and every corner I turned might be my last. But this fear was subconscious. It was underneath, hiding. It was only because of this fear that we drank so much vodka. In the evenings. Even near the very end, when Marysia moved to Leszno Street, I used to drink on my own. Because it wasn't possible to go through with it any other way.[303]

As well as smuggling arms into the ghettos, the *kashariyot* smuggled Jews out of the ghettos. Both were resistance but getting people out of the ghetto was the only way to save their lives. However, living on the Aryan side was not easy. Accommodation had to be found, false documents and ID acquired and money was needed because people could not work if they feared showing their Jewish faces in public. Adina Blady Szwajger described the burden she found the distribution of funds at the beginning of every month. She divided it into different piles for each *kasharit*. She described one day's events in the autumn of 1943, which started with her collecting one million zlotys from Senatorska Street.

> Not a large sum, but also an enormous package of paper money. One thousand 1000-zloty notes or two thousand 500-zloty notes. I dress appropriately, putting on two layers of clothes. One pair of knickers with an elastic around my thighs underneath my suspender belt, the other pair on top. And two blouses, the one underneath tightly drawn into the waist with a wide belt.
>
> And also a shopping bag with a false bottom. Lots of girls in Warsaw has such bags. These were the bags used by the resistance, messenger girls' bags. The people in the street knew about them, but the Germans never seemed to realize …
>
> Every pile was the only means of support for fifty to a hundred people for a month. Whereas for me these piles of somebody else's money were just pieces of paper. Dangerous pieces of paper at that … We had to get rid of these pieces of paper as soon as possible, because they might cost us our lives …

---

303 ABS p.111

In one flat after another I saw the same thing: pale faces, sad eyes, hands stretched out for those few zlotys, a signature on a small card, and on my way. Then more meetings on the street. Around dusk, a banknote handed over secretively in the entrance to a building. A receipt taken from a shaking hand. Quickly, quickly. Soon it would be curfew. I had managed to give out today's portion, and went off home on the tram.[304]

We have seen how perilous the task was – they had only their

... forged papers and 'good' looks – meaning facial features that didn't give them away as Jews. Some of the couriers bleached their hair blonde; others, including Frumka Plotnicka, had to be convinced to wear makeup to disguise their features. Not all were blonde-haired or blue-eyed. Yes there was one trait that all the couriers required in order to succeed. They all had to have incredible poise and nerves of steel to get them through checkpoints, over borders, into and out of ghettos, and around Europe with illegal documents, weapons and other contraband – in other words to take the risks they took every day. It would be an understatement to say that the missions of these women were fraught with constant danger.[305]

Gusta Draenger, 'Justyna', wrote in her prison diary about the dangers of a Jew trying to pass as an Aryan:

You would reveal your Jewishness in a thousand small ways; every anxiety-filled move; every step taken with a back hunched over from the yoke of slavery; every glance that bespoke the terror of a hunted animal; the entire form, the face on which the ghetto had left its indelible mark. You were nothing more than a Jew, not only because of the color of your eyes, hair, skin, the shape of your nose, the many telltale signs of your race. You were simply and unmistakably a Jew because of your lack of self-assurance, your way of expressing yourself, your behaviour, and God knows what else. You were simply and conspicuously a Jew because everybody outside the ghetto strained to detect your Jewishness, all the people eager to do you harm, who couldn't abide the thought that you might be cheating death. At your every step they would look straight into your eyes – impudently, suspiciously, challengingly – until you would become entirely confused, turn beet red, lower your eyes – and thus show yourself to be undeniably a Jew.

These young teenagers showed great loyalty to their people and enormous courage.

---

304 ABS pp.104–107
305 Ochayon p.5

They are icons of heroism, and they shatter many stereotypes: that the Jews went to their deaths like sheep to the slaughter, that women are less capable than men of resistance. Despite all this, the glorious page of history which is their due has not yet been fully written. It should be. In light of their achievements and their exploits in the nightmare of the Holocaust, we can only be in awe of them.[306]

306 Ochayon p.6

Resistance in the Camps

Franceska Mann (1917–1943)

This story appeared on the internet as an example of resistance in the jaws of death. It is a story which appears in several versions – but there could have been few actual eye-witnesses given where it allegedly took place. I have attempted to use the women's actual words to narrate their stories but that is obviously impossible in this case.

Jerzy Tabau was a non-Jewish medical student who was in Auschwitz. He escaped in late 1943 and wrote a report of the conditions and his experiences, which was known as the 'Polish Major's Report'. He wrote:

> The condemned Jews generally faced their fate calmly, although those arriving in 1943 had a clearer idea of what awaited them. The sporadic attempts at rebellion and mass escape when the freight cars were unloaded upon arrival were bloodily repelled. The special railway siding reserved for the convoys was surrounded by searchlight and machine-gun posts. On one occasion these unfortunate people scored a small success. It must have been during September or October 1943, after a transport of women had arrived. The accompanying SS men had ordered them to undress and were about to drive them into the gas chamber. This moment was always used by the guards as a good opportunity for looting; and rings and wrist watches were torn off women's fingers and arms. In the confusion resulting from one such attack, one woman managed to snatch the pistol of SS Groupleader Schillinger and fire three shots at him. He was seriously wounded and died the next day. This gave the signal for the others to attack the executioners and their henchmen. One SS man had his nose torn off, another was scalped, but unfortunately none of the women were able to escape. Although an attempt was made to keep this incident secret, it resulted in an order being issued whereby SS men were not allowed to remain in camp after 8 p.m.[307]

---

307 Jerzy Tabau, *The Polish Major's Report*, pp.12–13

Franceska Mann. (Courtesy Ghetto Fighters' House)

In his book *Never Again,* Martin Gilbert also described the incident with the heading 'Defiance at Auschwitz':

> When Schillinger ordered one of the women to undress completely, she threw her shoe in his face, seized his revolver and shot him in the stomach. She also wounded SS Sergeant Emmerich. According to some reports she was a dancer from Warsaw, named Horowitz. After her act of defiance, other women began to strike the SS men at the very entrance to the gas chamber, severely injuring two of them. The SS men fled. Shortly afterwards they returned, armed with grenades and machine guns, with the camp commandant, Rudolf Hoess. One by one the women were removed from the gas chamber building and shot.[308]

Kitty Hart-Moxon who was in Auschwitz described it briefly as an occasional 'show of rebellion on an incoming transport' and told me that she heard that it happened at the selection ramp rather than near the gas chambers.[309]

> One of the most remarkable cases was that of a young woman so attractive that the SS officer in charge that day, a man called Schillinger, relaxed his guard and came closer for a better look. She grabbed his revolver, shot him dead.

Naturally these acts of defiance by unarmed women at the gates of the gas chambers aroused my interest. I found a fuller picture on Judi Helt's website

---

308 Martin Gilbert, *Never Again* (New York: Universe, 2000) p.114
309 Kitty Hart-Moxon pp.116–7

'Heroines of the Resistance'.[310] Franceska was born on 4 February 1917 in Poland and had many aliases – Rosenberg-Manheimer, Man and Mannõwna. She studied dancing at the Irena Prusicka school, being placed fourth at an international competition of 125 ballet dancers in Brussels in 1939.

> She was considered one of the most beautiful and promising dancers of her generation in Poland, both in the classical and modern repertoire. At the beginning of WWII she performed at the Melody Palace nightclub...
> On October 23 1943 a transport of around 1,700 Polish Jews arrived on passenger trains at the Auschwitz-Birkenau death camp from Bergen-Belsen. They had been told they were being taken to the Bergau transfer camp near Dresden, from which they would continue on to Switzerland to be exchanged for German POWs. One of the passengers was Franceska Mann...

Filip Müller (1922–2013) was assigned to the Sonderkommando in May 1942, when he was 20. He worked as a *Heizer*, someone who undressed the corpses (when they were clothed), put them into the crematorium, and stirred the fire while they burned. He told Claude Lanzmann for his 1985 film *Shoah*:

> Every day we saw thousands and thousands of innocent people disappear up the chimney. With our own eyes, we could truly fathom what it means to be a human being. There they came, men, women, children, all innocent. They suddenly vanished, and the world said nothing! We felt abandoned. By the world, by humanity. But the situation taught us fully what the possibility of survival meant. For we could gauge the infinite value of human life. And we were convinced that hope lingers in man as long as he lives. Where there's life, hope must never be relinquished. That's why we struggled through our lives of hardship, day after day, week after week, month after month, year after year, hoping against hope to survive, to escape that hell.[311]

Müller wrote his own version, which, apart from telling Franceska Mann's tragic story very fully, also demonstrates the length of the Nazis' mendacity in keeping their wretched victims compliant and calm in their final moments of life. He explained that one of the SS officers, *Obersturmführer* Hössler pretended that he was the representative of the Foreign Ministry and said he would be organising their journey to Switzerland. However the Swiss insisted on them all being disinfected before they crossed border. He continued:

310 Judi Helt, *Franceska Mann (1917–1943)* in 'Heroines of the Resistance' 12 August 2015, accessed 8 September 2017, http://resistanceheroines.blogspot. co.uk/2015/08/franceska-mann–1917–1943.html
311 Filip Müller cited in Richard Brody, 'The Holocaust Is Present', in *The New Yorker*, 10 February 2014.

After your bath, please have your travel documents ready so we can certify that you have been disinfected. Once more, may I point out that the Swiss authorities have declared that nobody will be allowed to cross the frontier without this certificate in his passport. Your special train is waiting at the station. It is scheduled to depart at 7 tomorrow morning and will take you to the frontier. I would therefore ask you in your own interest to follow the instructions of the camp personnel. May I end by wishing you a pleasant journey for tomorrow.[312]

Müller noted that Hössler's words had the desired effect and everyone dutifully left for the underground changing room. Müller and the other *Sonderkommando* men were kept out of the way. 'Perhaps they thought that our presence might make the people hesitant or give us a chance of speaking to them.'

He then said the order for the stoker team to fill the ovens with coke came fifteen minutes later than usual. This was because the yard had to be cleared of people and also because the sound of the coke going into the ovens might have made the crowd suspicious. The 18 men from the *Sommerkommando* were taken down in the lift and waited in the corridor which led to the gas chamber. *Oberscharführer* Voss took them into the mortuary and behind a pile of 'emaciated corpses' there were six hand-painted signboards with the letters A-D, E-H and so on. The men were told to pick them up and go into the changing room and stand facing the people from the transport. Hössler, whom Filip called a 'cunning fox', pointed to the boards and said:

When you have dressed after your bath, kindly queue up at the board with the first letter of your surname where you will be given a certificate confirming that you have been disinfected. Please also remember the number of your hook in the changing room so that the necessary formalities can be dealt with as quickly and as smoothly as possible. And do not regard this disinfection business as something we have thought up to annoy you. It is, let me re-emphasize, the Swiss who insist on it. It is therefore in your own interest to submit to this unavoidable procedure as quickly as possible.

When he finished the people went into huddles and some were speaking Yiddish and some were obviously suspicious, they may well have heard of mass exterminations. They had not been convinced by Hössler's speech and were reluctant to get undressed. The SS took the ones who were undressed towards the gas chamber – they were about half and they were soon behind the great door of the chamber. However the remainder seemed to be playing for time. The SS officers left the changing room one by one and returned with sticks.

---

312 Filip Müller, *Eyewitness Auschwitz* (Chicago: Ivan p. Dee, 1979) pp.84–89

Instead of their earlier marked courtesy and lying talk there were now terse requests of 'Get undressed! Hurry up! Get ready for your baths! Come on, come on!' The people did not respond, but kept standing about, doing nothing. The SS grew nervous. In order to demonstrate that they meant business they shifted their holsters to the front and opened the flaps.

Getting closer to the crowd they began to shout and when this had no effect they began hitting out with the sticks and chaos ensued. People were bleeding from the blows and realising that resistance was pointless, began getting undressed. The SS felt in control again and starting strutting about with a swagger.

Suddenly they stopped in their tracks, attracted by a strikingly handsome woman with blue-black hair who was taking off her right shoe. The woman, as soon as she noticed that the two men were ogling her, launched into what appeared to be a titillating and seductive strip-tease act. She lifted her skirt to allow a glimpse of thigh and suspender. Slowly she undid her stocking and peeled it off her foot. From out of the corner of her eye she carefully observed what was going on around her. The two SS were fascinated by her performance and paid no attention to anything else...

She had taken off her blouse and was standing in front of her lecherous audience in her brassiere. They she steadied herself against a concrete pillar with her left arm and bent down, slightly lifting her foot, in order to take off her shoe. What happened next took place at lightning speed: quick as a flash she grabbed her shoe and slammed its high heel violently against Quackernack's forehead. He winced with pain and covered his face with both hands. At this moment the young woman flung herself at him and made a quick grab for his pistol. There was a shot. Schillinger cried out and fell to the ground. Seconds later there was a second shot aimed at Quackernack which narrowly missed him.

A panic broke out in the changing room. The young woman had disappeared in the crowd. Any moment she might appear somewhere else and aim her pistol at another of her executioners. The SS men realized this danger. One by one they crept outside. The wounded Schillinger was still lying unattended on the floor.

As someone tried to drag him away another shot was fired, catching the SS man who was dragging Schillinger who started to limp. The door was locked and the lights went out so there was a lot of panic. A man asked them where they were from – 'From the death factory,' said one of Muller's companions.

The man was very agitated and demanded loudly: 'I don't understand what this is all about. After all, we have valid entry visas for Paraguay; and what's more, we paid the Gestapo a great deal of money to get our exit permits. I handed over three diamonds worth at least 100,000 zloty;

it was all I had left of my inheritance. And that young dancer, the one who fired the shots a little while ago, she had to pay a lot more.'

Suddenly the door was flung open. I was blinded by the glare of several searchlights. Then I heard Voss shouting: 'All members of the *Sonderkommando*, come out!'

They were very relieved and dashed out, up the stairs and into the yard. Two machine guns had been set up and there was a terrible blood bath for the people caught in the changing room. Meanwhile the Zyklon B had been put into the gas chamber – the trusting had already gone. Next morning they heard Schillinger had died on the way to hospital and his colleague Emmerich was wounded. This brought some satisfaction to the inmates because Schillinger was 'regarded as an extremely brutal and capricious sadist'.

The body of the young dancer was laid out in the dissecting room of crematorium 2. SS men went there to look at her corpse before its incineration. Perhaps the sight of her was to be a warning as well as an illustration of the dire consequences one moment's lack of vigilance might have for an SS man.

As for us, these events had taught us once again that there simply was no chance of escape once a person entered the crematorium: by then it was too late. The promises of the SS, ranging from work inside the camp to emigration to Switzerland, was nothing but barefaced deception, as they had proved to be for these wretched people who had wanted to emigrate to Paraguay.

Though astonishingy Gerda Abraham, her husband and child (see pages 121–24) did get transferred safely from Bergen-Belsen based on their visas for Haiti.

Mala Zimetbaum (1922–1944)

Malka (Mala) Zimetbaum was of Polish Jewish descent. Her family moved to Belgium when she was a child. At school she was very good at maths and languages. In September 1942 she was among Belgian Jews deported to Auschwitz and was sent to the women's camp at Birkenau. She was inmate No.19880 for nearly two years.

Because of her language skills in French, Dutch, German, Polish and Italian, she worked as an interpreter and courier. Whilst this gave her a relatively privileged position, she also worked hard helping other inmates. When they were not fit for hard work she got them easier work. She also got extra food and medicine for people in need, cheered people and encouraged them and was trusted by everyone in the camp – staff and prisoners.

Edward 'Edek' Galinski had planned to escape with his friend Wieslaw Kielar but they fell out when Wieslaw lost a pair of SS guard's uniform trousers they needed as a disguise for their escape. So Edek said he would escape with Mala instead, and afterwards would send the trousers back so Kielar could escape. Mala wanted to escape to tell the world what was happening at Auschwitz and save lives.

They planned that Edek would dress up as an SS guard and escort Mala though the perimeter gate, pretending that he was escorting a prisoner to install a washbasin. Mala would carry a large porcelain washbasin hiding her hair, so no one realised she was a woman. Edek would have a forged pass and Mala would wear overalls over a dress. When they had got away, she would dump the basin and overalls and they would look like an SS guard on a date with a girl in a dress.

They made the escape in June 1944 and succeeded in getting to a nearby town. Mala wanted to buy something, so Edek went into a shop telling Mala to hide somewhere. Someone in the shop became suspicious and called the authorities. When they asked Edek to take off his hat, his shaven head gave him away. When he did not come for her, she gave herself up as they had promised to stay together.

They were taken to Block 11 in the main part of Auschwitz and put in separate cells. A friendly guard passed notes between them and they sometimes whistled to each other down the hall. It is said that when he was outside, Edek would stand outside a window which he thought was Mala's to sing an Italian aria.

They were taken out for execution at the same time in their respective camps. Edek jumped into the noose before the verdict was read, but the guards put him back on the platform. One person told the other prisoners to take their hats off as a sign of respect, which they did, infuriating one particular guard. Meanwhile Mala cut her veins with a razor blade she had hidden.[313]

Mala's story was only made public during the Eichmann Trial in Mrs Raya Kagan's testimony (Session 70 on 8 June 1961). Mrs Kagan was living in Jerusalem and worked in the Ministry of Foreign Affairs. She confirmed that in 1937, she went from Vilna to Paris, to prepare for her studies for a doctorate in history. When the Germans invaded France she was still there. She was detained on 27 April 1942, reaching Auschwitz via Drancy on 24 June. She left on 19 January 1945. She was asked what happened to Mala Zimetbaum.

Raya Kagan said she had known her since the summer of 1942 when she arrived with the Belgian transport. She became a *Laeuferin*, a messenger between blocks and a liaison between the *Blockfuehrerstube*, the *Kapo* and the prisoners:

She was very decent. She was known throughout the camp, since she helped everybody. And her opportunities and the power, as it were, that she possesses were never wrongfully exploited by her, as was often done by the Kapos. She suffered like everybody else. However, she had better conditions – she was able to take a shower in Birkenau.

---

313 Jewish Virtual Library

And suddenly, in the summer of 1944, I heard – I was sitting in the room of my superior –there was a telephone call – I heard them ringing and alerting all the *Kripo* and the *Stapoleitstelle*, all stations of the gendarmerie, and I heard the name of the prisoner, Mala Zimetbaum. She had escaped. The escape was organized. She fled in the uniform of the SS, of an *Aufseherin* (supervisor). The escape occurred on a Saturday afternoon when there was a reduced camp guard. Another Pole escaped with her. They met beyond the camp, on their way to Slovakia. We hoped – we had great hopes – every morning when we got up, that possibly she would succeed.

It is important to note that Mala had many opportunities – she had access to the documents. And it was said that she had stolen documents from the *Blockführerstube* relating to the SD, and that she wanted to publish them abroad. I must remark here that her courage was well-known, but there was also a legend about Mala, and I am not sure whether it is correct that she managed to steal documents, but it was said of her that she was capable of doing so. A fortnight later, we learned that they had been captured, they were caught in a very foolish way, right on the border, by custom officials. Apparently, they had lost their way and asked which way to go. There they had to cross mountains, to pass through the Carpathians. That was when they were captured.

They were sent back to Auschwitz and she knew they were tortured. Mrs Kagan saw Mala one day and asked her how she was. She was in a small hut where people waited to be interrogated.

'Serenely and heroically she said, somewhat ironically: 'I am always well.' The Judge asked what language she used and was told it was German. She said '*Mir geht e simmer wohl.*' When the Judge asked what happened to her in the end, Mrs Kagan said:

Eventually they brought her to Birkenau, they held a major roll-call, and Mandel, the *Schutzlagerfuehrerin* (leader of the protective camp), Marie Mandel, made a speech and demanded a spectacular and exemplary punishment for her. Mala had succeeded in placing a razor blade in her sleeve and, at the time of the roll-call, she cut open her veins. Then the SS man went up to her and began mocking and cursing her. Then, with a hand covered in blood, she slapped his cheek and – again this may be a legend – she said to him: 'I shall die as a heroine and you will die as a dog.' After that, she was taken, in this very terrible state, to the *Revier*, and in the evening she was put on a cart and taken to the crematorium.[314]

---

314 Raya Kagan, *Testimony to Adolf Eichmann Trial*, Session 70 – part 3 of 6, 8 June 1961. 'The Nitzkor Project, http://www.nizkor.org/hweb/people/e/eichmann-adolf/transcripts/Sessions/Session-070-03.html, accessed 24 September 2017

Kitty Hart-Moxon (born 1926) who was in Auschwitz for two years from 1943, recalls being summoned from the 'Kanada' section where she sorted valuables. The news was spreading round the camp:

> There were immediate searches through the camp, savage beatings, wild attempts to pin the blame on scores of innocent inmates. The entire camp was made to pay. But it was worth it. If the two of them could tell the world outside, could somehow get through to the Allies, then surely action could be taken.
>
> Some weeks later, all prisoners were driven out of their blocks, and we in *Kanada* were recalled to the main camp. They wanted us all to see Mala, beaten and bloody. And they wanted to hang her in front of us, as a lesson. The SS leaders, several of whom had liked her and admired her efficiency, were there to watch the ceremony. At the very moment she was to be hanged. Mala suddenly pulled out a razor blade and cut her wrists. An SS man made a grab at her. '*Was machst du, Mala?*'
>
> 'Don't touch me,' she shouted back. 'Filthy dog. Murderer! Murderers!'
>
> She collapsed in a pool of blood. *Oberführerin* Drechsler began to shriek at her. 'You thought you'd get away? Cheat the German Reich? We get everyone in the end – everyone, you see?'
>
> They loaded her on to a hand-cart and ordered some of her friends to push it along the *Lagerstrasse* so that everyone could see. And then she was to go straight to the crematorium. We hoped and prayed she would be dead before she got there. They obviously had every intention of burning her alive. As she went, she managed one last cry,
>
> 'It doesn't matter, your days are numbered. You're going to die, you swine, all of you.'[315]

The difficulties of reporting the Holocaust are demonstrated here. As elsewhere, having written the above, I discovered that Wieslaw Kielar, Edek's original co-escapee, had written his own version of events. He wrote that he was amazed when Edek said he wanted Mala to join them in their escape. He was in love with her and could not leave her behind. Also because of her post she would be able to 'enter the *Blockführer's* office at any time, as she is well known to the SS men. She'll steal the pass without them getting suspicious'. Wieslaw had to admit he had not managed to get the pass they required. However he expressed his concerns:

> With a woman, and what's more with one that is as delicate like Mala, with bouts of malaria, we won't be able to walk far. We shall have to do at least 20 miles, walking very fast. She won't make it. And can one count on people outside helping us once they see she's Jewish?[316]

---

315 Kitty Hart-Moxon, *Return to Auschwitz* (Newark:Quill,2007) pp.166–7
316 Wieslaw Kielar, *Anus Mundi: 5 Years in Auschwitz*, pp.226–229

No one else has mentioned her malaria.

Kielar then rashly wrote to his sister in Zakopane hinting that on her name day, at the end of June, 'she might expect a great and pleasant surprise'. He planned to leave Mala with his sister and her husband, who was a doctor. He and Edek would make contact with the partisans. His letter would be handled by several people to reach his sister. Meanwhile both men avoided having their hair cut, which was not a problem.

On the day in question Kielar was taken to see Mala whose 'russet hair was cropped short'. She was pale and obviously agitated. When she said goodbye to Kielar: 'She gave me her little hand. It was cold and damp and it trembled.' Edek told him they would wait for him at Kozy and picked up his toolbox and eventually Kielar saw Mala carrying a heavy 'lavatory pan'. He watched them leave the camp with Mala in front and Edek a few steps behind her 'casual, normal, as one would often see an SS man escorting a prisoner.'

Watching them Kielar was damp all over:

My knees were weak, my throat was constricted. It took a great deal of courage. No doubt they were by now passing their last obstacle, the barrier at which there was always an SS man on duty. Once they had passed that without being stopped, they were free.

All was quiet – so they had got away.

Revolt of 7 October 1944 at Auschwitz

When I met Kitty Hart-Moxon at her home in June 2013, I raised the issue of why the Germans continued with the 'Final Solution' when they knew they were losing the war. Kitty told me the Jews financed the German war effort through looting as nothing was wasted. Kitty spent eight months in Auschwitz in the Kanada section, sorting men's jackets. She had to break up all seams and she found all sort of valuables – diamonds, gold, various currencies etc. The currency was no good in the camp and was used as toilet paper. Such items were also found sewn into corsets. Kitty took items and buried them so that they could be used to bribe people to get explosives – they blew up the gas chambers on 7 October 1944. She herself was evacuated in October 1944, but all the men and some of the girls were killed after the uprising. She could not be found with anything on her, otherwise she would have been killed. She explained that she buried valuables in a gap behind the toilet hut situated behind her hut and next to Gas Chamber no. 4. She couldn't risk being seen doing it and because of the curfew she couldn't do it at night in the dark. On one occasion she dropped a whole pouch of diamonds into a large container of soup being carried by men which they could later rescue from the soup.[317]

Kitty wrote about the 7 October revolt in her book – she was still working in the Kanada section where they sorted possessions looking for valuables.

---

317 Notes of meeting with Kitty Hart Moxon 19 June 2013.

It was called Kanada 'after that far-off country which for some reason was associated with all the riches the heart could desire.'[318]

Although no further trainloads were entering the camp, there was still a huge backlog of stuff to be sorted. We stood a better chance of staying alive as long as the work was incomplete, so we didn't hurry through the piles. Then, late in the afternoon of 7 October, as we were getting ready for our usual shift, there was a change in the atmosphere. Shots began to rattle from the men's side of the fence. Some of us ran to the windows, some right out of the hut. What a sight! Flames were belching out of Crematorium IV. Within minutes the whole building was on fire. First the roof caved in, then flames began to lick up from the gas chambers. There was an explosion, and a kind of thunder as one huge chimney toppled to the ground. Everywhere there was wild commotion. Was the camp being bombed?

Screams and shouts mingled with the wail of sirens. We couldn't move, not knowing if this was the uprising we'd hardly dared to expect or if we would have to fight with our bare hands or somehow be provided with arms and ammunition. Somebody somewhere had arms – and from the sound of it there were some grenades going off. Then came another mighty explosion. It seemed to come from the direction of Crematorium II.

Fire engines were racing into the camp. SS motorcycles dashed madly all over the place. The cowards looked really frightened, riding or running up and down and shooting at random. Immediate curfew was ordered, and those of us not already safely inside were soon scuttling for cover in our blocks. Once inside we lay on the ground not daring to move. Suddenly a man ran into our hut and crawled underneath a bench, followed by an SS officer who shot him in the head.

As the flames died down, shooting could be heard from within the shattered crematoria. Machine-gun fire echoed across the lawn. And from the direction of the woods came more firing, where another battle seemed to have flared up near the pits. At last the uproar died down. The victorious SS could be seen marching back from their battlefield. There would be no break-out.

In fact this was not what the demonstration had been aimed at. Our stolen valuables had reached the Resistance men all right and had been passed on where they would be most use. Four girls, Róza Robota, Ala Gartner, Regina Safirsztain and Ester Wajcblum, working in the *Krupp Union Werke* ammunition factory had bribed other workers and minor SS so that they could smuggle out explosives. All those slow, spasmodic efforts which I had often thought might be in vain were coming to fulfilment. The Polish Resistance outside had learned through their contacts of the imminent abandonment of Auschwitz by the Germans and the final massacre of the Jews. Men of the *Sonderkommando*,

---

318 P.143 Hart-Moxon

remembering the fate of their immediate predecessors, decided not to wait for their own liquidation but to strike one mighty blow now. It had to be rushed through because their plans were overheard by a 'green' *Kapo,* who they dealt with by throwing him alive into a blazing oven. If that seems hideous, one has only to remember what the usual daily routine of those ovens was.

The destruction of the two crematoria was a wonderful gesture, whatever its other consequences. Bit by bit the details filtered through to us in *Kanada.* In the skirmishes the saboteurs had managed to kill a number of SS men and had thrown another of them into the flames alive. Hidden weapons were dug out of the hiding places and turned against the guards. A handful of men were said to have broken out and escaped from the camp, but we had no idea how far they had got.

Now came an enormous inquiry by the camp police. Women from the ammunition factory squads were tortured and the four girls who had supplied the explosives were soon identified. In spite of even more hideous torture, they refused to give away their contacts, and finally were hanged in full view of the entire camp. After one interminable *Zählappell* we were put on *Sport,* fully expecting it to be followed by a selection for the remaining gas chambers. But apparently we were still of use and had to be kept alive a little longer.[319]

According to USHMM the young Jewish women had been smuggling small quantities of gunpowder from the munitions factory in Auschwitz to the men and women in the Resistance. One of these was Róza Robota, a young Jewish woman who worked in the clothing section at Birkenau. Whilst under constant guard they took small amounts of gunpowder, wrapped it in bits of cloth or paper and then hid it on their person to pass on in the chain of smugglers. Once Robota received the gunpowder she gave it to the *Sommerkommando* who worked in the crematoria. They used this gunpowder to launch the uprising. Nearly 250 prisoners died in the fighting and the guards shot another 200 afterwards.[320]

---

319 Hart-Moxon pp.172–4
320 USSHM, *Prisoner Revolt at Auschwitz-Birkenau, https://www.ushmm.org/ learn/timeline-of-events/1942–1945/auschwitz-revolt* accessed 4 November 2017.

Medical Women

Dr Gisella Perl (1907–1988), Doctor in Auschwitz

Jewish doctors in the Holocaust had a difficult hand dealt to them. Mordechai Lensky, in his memoir about being a doctor in the Warsaw Ghetto wrote about the doctors who gave up hope and used the drugs they could access to commit suicide. He wrote: 'The atmosphere inside the ghetto, the unconcern for the general good and concentration on the individual's well-being centered around the idea that every family, even every single individual was a world in itself.'

The women doctors like Gisella Perl and Adina Szwajger were is a different position – perhaps because they were not with family and concentrated on

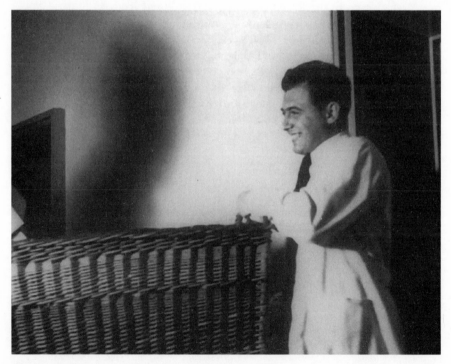

Dr Josef Mengele.

caring for children and women. In both cases they killed children to save them or their mothers from a worse fate. Adina's story is on pages 290–5.

Gisella was born in Sighet in Hungary in 1907, now in Roumania. Aged only 16, Perl graduated first in her secondary school class, becoming the first girl and the only Jew to do so. Her father was reluctant to support her academic aspirations, particularly in medicine, fearing that they would lead her to abandon her faith. She assured him that they would not. Perl later married a surgeon and was working as a gynaecologist in Hungary when the Germans invaded in 1944.

That year, the Nazis sent Perl, her husband, son, parents and extended family to Auschwitz. A young daughter was hidden with a non-Jewish family just before Perl's family was taken from the Hungarian ghetto. Upon arriving at Auschwitz, the Nazis separated Perl from the rest of her family. Her son would die in a gas chamber, and her husband would be beaten to death shortly before the camp was liberated. Gisella Perl was spared, only to become an Auschwitz physician under the notorious Josef Mengele.

On 16 November 1982, Dr. Perl was honoured at a lunch by the Jerusalem Shaare Zedek Medical Center where she had donated her time to its gynaecological clinics. She was 72 at the time. However the past was always in her mind and she remembers her time in Auschwitz where she was called 'Gisi Doctor'. She called herself the Ambassador of the Six Million and talked of the past.

'The greatest crime in Auschwitz was to be pregnant' she said in an interview the other day, recalling the edicts of Josef Mengele. The so-called doctor of death of Auschwitz performed savage medical experiments on prisoners, in particular, women, the physically handicapped and twins, and was in charge of deciding who would go to the gas chambers.

'Dr. Mengele told me that it was my duty to report every pregnant woman to him,' Dr. Perl said. 'He said that they would go to another camp for better nutrition, even for milk. So women began to run directly to him, telling him, "I am pregnant." I learned that they were all taken to the research block to be used as guinea pigs, and then two lives would be thrown into the crematorium. I decided that never again would there be a pregnant woman in Auschwitz.'[321]

She was responsible for all aspects of medicine in Auschwitz:

As one of five doctors and four nurses chosen by Dr. Mengele to operate a hospital ward that had no beds, no bandages, no drugs and no instruments, she tended to every disease-wrought torture, starvation, filth, lice and rats, to every bone broken or head cracked open by

---

321 Nadine Brozan, 'Out of Death, A Zest for Life', *The New York Times* 15 November 1982, accessed 21 February 2017, http://www.nytimes.com/1982/11/15/style/out-of-death-a-zest-for-life.html,

beating. She performed surgery, without anaesthesia, on women whose breasts had been lacerated by whips and become infected.

Gisella wrote her book in 1946, very soon after the experiences she described. She reveals the mendacity of the Nazis yet again. There is a chapter called 'Childbirth in Camp C'. Camp C was a block containing up to 30,000 women at a time. She wrote:

> The poor, young women who were brought to Auschwitz from the various ghettos of Hungary did not know that they would have to pay with their lives and the lives of their unborn children for that last, tender night spent in the arms of their husbands.[322]
>
> A few days after the arrival of a new transport, one of the S.S. chiefs would address the women, encouraging the pregnant ones to step forward, because they would be taken to another camp where living conditions would be better. He also promised them double bread rations so as to be strong and healthy when the hour of delivery came. Group after group of pregnant women left Camp C. Even I was naïve enough, at that time, to believe the Germans, until one day I happened to have an errand near the crematories and saw with my own eyes what was done to these women.
>
> They were surrounded by a group of S.S. men and women, who amused themselves by giving these helpless creatures a taste of hell, after which death was a welcome friend. They were beaten with clubs and whips, torn by dogs, dragged around by the hair and kicked in the stomach with heavy German boots. Then, when they collapsed. They were thrown into the crematory – alive.
>
> I stood rooted to the ground, unable to move, to scream, to run away. But gradually the horror turned into revolt and this revolt shook me out of my lethargy and gave me a new incentive to live. I had to remain alive.
>
> It was up to me to save the life of the mothers, if there was no other way, then by destroying the life of their unborn children. I ran back to the camp and going from block to block told women what I had seen. Never again was anyone to betray their condition. It was to be denied to our last breath, hidden from the S.S., the guards and even the Blockova [*Kapo*], on whose good will our life depended.
>
> On dark nights, when everyone else was sleeping – in dark corners of the camp, in the toilet, on the floor, without a drop of water, I delivered their babies. First I took the nine-month pregnancies, I accelerated the birth by the rupture of membranes, and usually within one or two

322 Dr. Gisella Perl, *I was a Doctor in Auschwitz* (New York: International Universities Press, 1948) pp.80–86. I am grateful to Abby Norman, writer, from Maine, for sending me a pdf of this book, as it is no longer easily available. The link is: https://archive.org/details/IWasADoctorInAuschwitz

days spontaneous birth took place without further intervention. Or I produced dilation with my fingers, inverted the embryo and thus brought it to life. In the dark, always hurried, in the midst of filth and dirt. After the child had been delivered, I quickly bandaged the mother's abdomen and sent her back to work. When possible, I placed her in my hospital, which was in reality a grim joke. She usually went with the diagnosis of pneumonia, which was a safe diagnosis, not one that would send her to the crematory. I delivered women pregnant in the eighth, sixth, fifth month, always in a hurry, always with my five fingers, in the dark, under terrible conditions.

No one will ever know what it meant to me to destroy these babies. After years and years of medical practice, childbirth was still to me the most beautiful, the greatest miracle of nature. I loved those newborn babies not as a doctor but as a mother and it was again and again my own child whom I killed to save the life of a woman. Every time when kneeling down in the mud, dirt and human excrement which covered the floor of the barracks to perform a delivery without instruments, without water, without the most elementary requirements of hygiene, I prayed to God to help me save the mother or I would never touch a pregnant woman again. And if I had not done it, both mother and child would have been cruelly murdered. God was good to me. By a miracle, which to every doctor must sound like a fairy tale, every one of these women recovered and was able to work, which, at least for a while, saved her life.

My first such case was the delivery of a young woman called Yolanda. Yolanda came from my home town. She was the child of an impoverished family and made a living by doing fine embroidery on expensive underwear, handkerchiefs – and baby clothes. To make beautiful baby clothes was the greatest pleasure in her life and, while working on them until late into the night, she would dream about the baby she, herself, would one day have. Then she got married. Month after month she waited and prayed, but Nature refused to grant her most ardent wish. This is when she began coming to me. I treated her for a long time until finally my treatment showed results and Yolanda became pregnant. She was radiant. 'I shall give you the most beautiful present in the world when my baby arrives...' she would tell me every time we met.

In the end it was I who gave her a present – the present of her life – by destroying her passionately desired little boy two days after his birth. Day after day I watched her condition develop, fearing the moment when it could be hidden no longer. I bandaged her abdomen, hid her with my body at roll call and hoped for a miracle which would save her and her baby.

The miracle never came, but one horribly dark, stormy night Yolanda began having birthpains. I was beside her, waiting for the moment when I could take a hand in the delivery, when I saw to my horror, that she fell into convulsive seizures. For two days and nights the spasms shook her poor, emaciated little body and I had to stand by, without drugs, without instruments to help her, listening to her moans, helpless. Around us, in the light of a few candles I could see the thirteen hundred women of her barracks look down upon us from their cages, thirteen hundred death-masks with still enough life left in them to feel pity for Yolanda and to breathe the silent but ever-present question: Why?

The third day Yolanda's little boy was born. I put her into the hospital, saying she had pneumonia – an illness not punishable by death – and hid her child for two days, unable to destroy him. Then I could hide him no longer. I knew that if he were discovered, it would mean death to Yolanda, to myself and to all those pregnant women whom my skill could still save. I took the warm little body in my hands, kissed the smooth face, caressed the long hair – then strangled him and buried his body under a mountain of corpses waiting to be cremated.

Then, one day, Dr. Mengerle [sic] came to the hospital and gave a new order. From now on Jewish women could have their children. They were not going to be killed because of their pregnancy. The children, of course, had to be taken to the crematory by me, personally, but the women would be allowed to live. I was jubilant. Women, who delivered in our so-called hospital, on its clean floor, with the help of a few primitive instruments that had been given to me, had a better chance to come out of this death-camp not only alive but in a condition to have other children – later.

I had two hundred and ninety-two expectant mothers in my ward when Dr. Mengerle changed his mind. He came roaring into the hospital, whip and revolver in hand, and had all the two hundred and ninety-two women loaded on a single truck and tossed – alive – into the flames of the crematory.

In September 1944, Camp C was liquidated to make place for new arrivals. I shall tell later, what this liquidation meant. All I want to say here is that out of thirty thousand women only ten thousand remained alive to be put into other blocks or taken to Germany to work.

As soon as we were installed in Camps F, K and l, a new order came from Berlin. From now on, not only could Jewish mothers have their children in the 'maternity ward' of the hospital but the children were to be permitted to live.

Eva Benedek was eighteen years old. She was a violinist from Budapest, a beautiful, talented young woman who was separated from her husband only a few days after her wedding. Eva Benedek believed with an unconquerable faith that her life and the life of her child would be saved. The child, growing in her womb, was her only comfort, her only pleasure, her only concern. When the S.S. organised an orchestra among the prisoners Eva became the violinist of that orchestra. I bandaged her abdomen and in her formless rags, amidst women whose stomachs were constantly bloated with undernourishment, her condition went unnoticed.

Then came the 'liquidation' of Camp C and Eva Benedek came with me to Camps F, K and L. When the order for the conservation of Jewish children came, nobody was happier than she. Her delivery was only a day or two off and we both believed that the miracle had happened, a miracle of God for the sake of Eva Benedek. She smiles all day and in the evening, in our barracks, she whistled Mozart concertos and Chopin *valses* for us to bring a little beauty into our terror-filled, hopeless lives.

Two days later she had her baby, a little boy, in the 'maternity ward'. But when the baby was born, she turned her back on it, wouldn't hold it in her arms. Tears were streaming down her cheeks incessantly, terrible silent tears, but she wouldn't speak to me. Finally I succeeded in making her tell what was on her mind.

'I dare not take my son in my arms, Doctor' she said. 'I dare not look at him, I dare not kiss him, I dare not get attached to him. I feel it, I know, that somehow they are going to take him away from me...'

And she was right. Twenty four hours after Eva Benedek had her son, a new order came, depriving Jewish mothers of additional food, a thin, milky soup mixed with flour, which swelled their breasts and enabled them to feed their babies. For eight days Eva Benedek had to look on while her son starved slowly to death.

His fine, white skin turned yellow and blotched, his smooth face got wrinkled and shrivelled and on the eighth day I had to take him out and throw him on a heap of rotting corpses.

In her book she also described her encounters with Irma Greze. She described Irma:

She was one of the most beautiful women I have ever seen. Her body was perfect in every line, her face clear and angelic and her blue eyes the gayest, the most innocent eyes one can imagine. And yet, Irma Greze was the most depraved, cruel, imaginative sexual pervert I ever came across. She was the highest tanking S.S. woman in Auschwitz and it was my bad luck to be under her eyes during my entire camp life.[323]

She described how Grese seemed sexually aroused by watching Perl operate on women's infected breasts. She only had a knife which she sharpened on a stone and no anaesthetic and so the women screamed in pain throughout. She described Grese's response:

Irma Greze put down her whip, the handle of which was inlaid with colored beads, sat down on the corner of the bench which served as an operating table and watched me plunge my knife into the infected breast which spurted blood and pus in every direction.

I happened to look up and encountered the most horrible sight I have ever seen, the memory of which will haunt me for the rest of my life.

---

323 Perl p.61

Irma Greze was enjoying the sight of this human suffering. Her tense body swung back and forth in a revealing, rhythmical motion. Her cheeks were flushed and her wide-open eyes had the rigid, staring look of complete sexual paroxysm.

From that day on she went around the camp, her bejewelled whip poised, picked out the most beautiful young women and slashed their breasts open with the braided wire end of her whip. Subsequently those breasts got infected by the lice and dirt which invaded every nook and corner of the camp. They had to be cut open, if the patient was to be saved. Irma Greze invariably arrived to watch the operation, kicking the victim if her screams interfered with her pleasure and giving herself completely to the orgastic spasms which shook her entire body and made saliva run down from the corner of her mouth.[324]

She also described how Grese insisted that Dr Perl perform an abortion on her, arriving with a case of sterilized instruments and a gun. Dr Perl was convinced she would be killed as soon as she finished the procedure. Instead afterwards Grese said:

'You are a good doctor,' she said. 'What a pity you have to die. Germany needs good doctors...' I said nothing. 'I am going to give you a coat,' she continued. 'And I don't have to tell you to keep quiet about this. If you ever open your mouth, I'll find you, wherever you are, and kill you...'

By the time Dr. Perl's book was published, Grese had been hanged by the British following due process: a luxury denied her victims.[325]

In all that time as a doctor in Auschwitz, Dr Perl told the *New York Times* she only had one palliative: the spoken word.

I treated patients with my voice, telling them beautiful stories, telling them that one day we would have birthdays again, that one day we would sing again. I didn't know when it was Rosh ha-Shanah, but I had a sense of it when the weather turned cool. So I made a party with the bread, margarine and dirty pieces of sausage we received for meals. I said tonight will be the New Year, tomorrow a better year will come.[326]

One of her first tasks was to persuade the women to give their blood for the wounded German soldiers. She wrote what she saw in Block VII:

...six hundred panic-stricken, trembling young women were looking at us with silent pleading in their eyes. The other hundred were lying on the ground, pale, faint, bleeding. Their pulse was almost inaudible, their breathing strained and deep rivers of blood were flowing round

---

324 Perl p.62
325 Perl pp.63–5
326 Brozan

their bodies. Big strong SS men were going from one to another sticking tremendous needles into their veins and robbing their undernourished, emaciated bodies of their last drop of blood. The German army needed blood plasma! The guinea pigs of Auschwitz were just the people to furnish the plasma. *Rassenschande* or contamination with 'inferior Jewish blood' was forgotten. We were too 'inferior' to live, but not too inferior to keep the German army alive with our blood.[327]

Dr Perl spent the last months of the war in Bergen-Belsen, which she described as 'the supreme fulfilment of German sadism and bestiality'.[328] She was liberated on 15 April 1945 by the British Army. She left to look for her family and learned her husband had been beaten to death just before liberation. He and her parents had died in camps. She was so desperate she tried to poison herself but was saved by a priest, Abbé Brand who took her to a convent to recuperate and she stayed there for several weeks.[329]

She went to New York in 1947 and ironically was interrogated as she was suspected of helping the SS. There was a particular suspicion that she had assisted Dr Mengele in his experiments.

In 1979 she moved to Israel to be with her daughter. It was a fulfilment of a vow she made with her husband in 1944: 'After four days in the cattle car that took us to Auschwitz, suddenly the S.S. officers opened the door, and prisoners in striped pyjamas threw us out. My father and husband both embraced me, saying "Swear we will never go back, we will meet someday in Jerusalem."'

She lived in Herzliya with her daughter Gabriella Krauss Blattman, who was hidden by a non-Jewish family and there was a grandson. She died in 1988 aged 81.

Bertha Zilverberg (1914–1997), Nurse

I came across Bertha Zilverberg in Ad van Liempt's remarkable book about how Jews were hunted for money in Holland during the Holocaust. In Dutch the book is called Kopgeld *and the English version is* Hitler's Bounty Hunters. *Bertha's behaviour aroused my interest and I wanted to know more about her story.*

Van Liempt stated Eddy Moerberg was a 'bounty-hunter' who was paid for rounding up Amsterdam Jews for deportation.

[Moerberg's biggest haul] took place on August 4, 1944, exactly the same day that the Frank family were picked up at 263 Prinsengracht in Amsterdam. Moerberg had to go all the way to Oss, in the southern

327 Perl p.74
328 Perl p.166
329 Perl p.188–9

province of North Brabant. By order of Otto Kempin, the chief of police, he was to pick up a group of Jews there, who were not only staying at private homes but also at a sort of 'secret rest home'.

Kempin must have been tipped off about the rest home in Oss by Bernard Joseph, a 'half-Jewish' young man, who worked for the Amsterdam SD as a *V-Mann* (informant). Joseph had a friend in Oss, a certain Günter Blanken, who spent a lot of time with a Jewish woman, Bertha Zilverberg (30). Bertha worked as a nurse at the rest home and would sometimes tell Joseph, whom she trusted completely, about her work there. Blanken and Joseph were Germans, but Bertha was not the least bit suspicious.

On August 4, 1944, two men from the SD turned up at Bertha's door in Oss, Eddy Moerberg and his partner Krikke. Bertha was placed under arrest and forced to accompany them to the rest home. The people there were arrested, but they had to wait for transportation. Bertha was allowed to go out and get food for the patients, for the trip. Seventeen people were registered as living at the rest home, twelve adults and five children. Some of them spent most of their time at home, but their addresses were known, so it was not difficult to find them. The only reason we know so much about the course of events that day was because, by some miracle, Bertha Zilverberg managed to survive the war. In a post-war interrogation she said: 'The SD knew about everything.' Moerberg...asked her there in Oss to become a *V-Frau*. 'Come work for the SD. Otherwise you're going to Poland, and you'll never come back.' Moerberg had said, according to Bertha in her testimony before the Special Court. Moerberg had it all worked out: she would live together with Bernard Joseph and they would work together as a team ... 'Then I understood it was Bernard Joseph who sold us out. I grabbed him by the throat and called him every name I could think of.' He also proposed working together, 'since otherwise I'd never come back from Poland,' Bertha said to the judges in Moerberg's trial.

In the meantime a truck had been chartered from the *Wehrmacht,* and all the people who were on the list had been rounded up. The procession departed for Amsterdam. Bertha went to Amsterdam by train with two guards, a man from the SD and a number of children. She continued to reject any offers to cooperate; she chose to care for her patients, first in Amsterdam prison and later in Auschwitz. In 1945 she was the only one of the whole group to return. She could only assume the others were gassed, as most of them were elderly and sick. She was herself liberated by the Russians, During her interview with the police, she gave investigators a list of the names of the seventeen dead. For the rest of her life (she died in 1997) she would have to bear the burden of this unimaginable experience, which had never been recorded anywhere, save in the transcript of Eddy Moerberg's trial.[330]

---

330 Van Liempt, *Hitler's Bounty Hunters*, pp.131–2

Later in the book Van Liempt repeats Eddy Moerberg's threat to Bertha. In addition, he states 'there is also testimony from a Jewish barber who had to supply Moerberg with addresses where Jews were hiding: 'If you give me the addresses of Jews you can go home, otherwise you're going to Poland too, and you know you won't be coming back.'[331]

I wrote to Ad van Liempt to try to get more information and he told me 'I remember that I was very moved indeed when, in 2001, reading about the behaviour of Bertha Zilverberg'. He told me he got the information from the files of the court case and 'it is a huge bunch of paper'. It is all in Dutch and only accessible in the National Archive in The Hague.[332]

Bertha was born on 30 April 1914 in Oss. She was the second of four children. Maurits (Max) was born on 30 October 1912. Isidoor was born on 16 August 1916 and Henri Wilhelm was born on 26 April 1919. Max married Wilhelmina on 2 September 1936. After their mother's death on 16 February 1932, their father Abraham married Henriette Schaap. Abraham died after 13 months.

Subsequently Henriette had a guest house with a dining area. During the war she had permission to run a guest house for Jews and non-Jews were not allowed to stay. Henri was a cabinet maker but it is not known what the other sons did. In October 1942 Henri and Isidoor were rounded up and deported to Auschwitz and were killed before 31 March 1944. Their stepmother had been gassed on 14 May 1943 at Sobibor. When the others were deported, their home was appropriated and new occupants placed there. Bertha was permitted to rent a room there.

After the war Bertha came back and her brother Maurits also survived. Willy van der Welden (a resident of Oss) said that Bertha worked with him at the office of the Zwanenberg company. He said she was a very clever girl. She kept her Jewish star in her bag so no one knew she was Jewish.[333]

I then approached an old colleague Ed van Rijswijk, who has helped me in a number of ways over the years. His grandparents, Jacob and Hendrika Klerk, hid a little Jewish girl Suze, and Ed and I have been in touch ever since. I visited Suze's daughter Arleen in Providence, Rhode Island, in 2010. Ed sent me a great deal of information about Berthe and, as ever, I am extremely grateful to him.

Bertha lived together with her brothers and step-mother Henriette Schaap at her parents' house at the Kruisstraat in the village of Oss. Her mother (Elisa Bertha Leviticus) had died in 1930 and her father (Abraham Zilverberg) died in 1934, just 13 months after he had married Henriette Schaap.

Bertha worked as a nurse in a retirement home at the Spoorstraat in Oss. Later on in the war another retirement home was opened up in the

331 Van Liempt p.169
332 Ad van Liempt, email to author 2 February 2017.
333 Petra de Ruitjer, email to author 3 July 2017.

house of Isaac Elsbach at Monsterstraat 6 in Oss, just 5 minutes walk from the house where Bertha lived.

Johanna Geisel…also worked as a nurse at the Spoorstraat. On 8 August 1944 she was deported to Camp Westerbork and from there to Auschwitz on 3 September. At arrival at Auschwitz on 6 September 1944 she was killed. Rosina Fresco was also a nurse which worked at the Spoorstraat but later also at Monsterstraat 6. Like Joanna she was also deported to Auschwitz on the 3rd and killed upon arrival on the 6 September 1944.

Bertha and Rosina also took care of the Hes family on Heuvel 79 because with this family there was an outbreak of scarlet fever, according to a declaration drawn up by the doctor Margaritha Denby. She was also in charge of the retirement home at the Spoorstraat. Other nurses were Sophie Toncman and a niece of the Hes family, Roodje Hes. Sophie's family lived at the Kruisstraat 27, so very close to where Bertha lived.

On 4 August 1944, this family was betrayed to the 'Jewhunters' led by Eddy Moerberg. The whole family, including all the nurses were arrested to Camp Westerbork to be shipped to Auschwitz on the 3 of September 1944. The last train leaving Westerbork Only Bertha Zilverberg survived. All others were killed on the 6th of September.

Ed explained that he got this information from a little book published in connection with the placing of *Stolpersteine* (Stumbling Stones) in Oss. Sophie Toncman also survived and died in 2009. He commented that it was remarkable that the whole family and all these nurses were still walking freely in Oss when all the Jews in the Netherlands had already been deported to the East a year earlier. He sent this additional information from the Jewish Monument (www.joodsmonument.nl).

In the spring of 1943 it became known that all the Jews of Oss had to go to Camp Westerbork or Camp Vught in a short period of time. Hugo Hes managed to get postponed for some time. In consultation with a general practitioner (GP) from Oss, he decided to hang a sign on the door of his house, which was read in large letters, that someone had scarlet fever. On April 5, 1943, the same GP issued a medical certificate confirming that Hugo's daughter, Mia Hes, had scarlet fever. Because there was a risk of infection, she had to be nursed at home. Both the sign on the door and the medical statement convinced the head of the municipal police in Oss, which allowed Hugo Hes and his family to live longer in Oss. Hugo Hes could further extend his stay because he was the local representative of the Jewish Council [*Judenrät*]. On Friday, August 4 1944, however, an end came to the stay of the last Jews in Oss. After arrest, they were taken to Camp Westerbork.[334]

---

334 Ed van Rijswijk, information sent to author 30 April 2017.

Ed points out that the last members of the Amsterdam Jewish Council were arrested in September 1943 – they included the co-chairmen David Cohen and Abraham Asscher.

Henri Obstfeld (whose parents' story is on pp. 260–3) found the following information about the nurses, which he translated for me:

> The young ladies whose task it was to care for these people were Rosina Fresco, 18 years and Bertha Zilverberg who was a few years older.
>
> None of these girls had received an education as a carer. Nevertheless, they accepted the responsibility of the difficult tasks of looking after these vulnerable people. At an age at which life should have provided totally different perspectives these girls were condemned to a dangerous existence and a very uncertain future. Who is not affected by that?
>
> To stress their role and position with respect to the world surrounding them, these 'surrogate' nurses had acquired an appropriate uniform consisting of a white apron. They hoped that this would provide them with recognition of their status, but their main thought was that this would provide them with some protection.[335]

Berthe was liberated on May 1945 from Liebau camp (Lubawka in Polish) on 9 May 1945, the Russians having arrived on 7 May. Liebau was previously used as a training and recreational centre for the Hitler Youth. It appears the Liebau labour camp was a sub-camp of KZ Gross-Rosen.[336] and the first transport of 200 Hungarian Jewish women was sent on 19 September 1944. Those women were given numbers 59,801 to 60,000. They were divided into three groups and allocated to work for three local companies. Prisoners 59801 to 59850 went to the Kurt Laske furniture factory where they made ammunition crates; numbers 59851 to 59900 were sent to the Heinz Wendt machine factory where they made aircraft parts; and 59901 to 60000 worked at Nordland GmbH making tank treads.

In mid-October 1944 another 300 women arrived, this time they were Polish, Hungarian, French, Belgian and Dutch. They were given numbers 74101 to 74393 and were allocated to the same companies. We can assume they included Bertha Zilverberg, although another group of 50 women came later, their nationality is not specified. These 550 women worked in shifts as the works continued 24 hours a day. The conditions were not too bad but the supplies of clothing were inadequate and sometimes the guards shared their clothes with the prisoners, which was not allowed. The food was very poor – mostly watery soup twice a day. The camp existed for eight months until liberation. Ten women died through illness and were buried in coffins near the Catholic cemetery.[337]

---

335 Henri Obstfeld to author – received 17 March 2017, http://struikelstenenoss. blogspot.co.uk/p/boek-opdat-zij-niet-vergeten-worden.html

336 Jeff Overste, of *Joods Monument*, emails to author 2 February 2017.

337 USHMM, *Encyclopedia of Camps and Ghettos 1933–1945*, Vol. 1 Part A (Bloomington: Indiana UP) pp.761–2

After the war Bertha married Bernhard Benjamin de Vries on 25 June 1950 and they had a daughter Marion Elizabeth who was born on 30 July 1952. Her husband Brent Richheimer told Ed that Bertha had to work in various work camps after she was sent to Auschwitz. After liberation she walked to Prague where a local family took care of her. He had a photo of the coin Bertha carried with her all the time she was in the camps.[338]

Her husband died on 30 November 1974 and Bertha on 19 October 1997. Her daughter died on 24 July 2005 in Knokke, Belgium.

Adina Blady Szwajger (1917–1993), Medical Student

We have already mentioned Adina in other sections. I came across Adina's book when I was researching Holocaust rescuers. I read her piece about the merry-to-round operating just outside the Warsaw Ghetto walls with blaring music and laughing children, whilst Jews were dying in burning buildings.

Adina was born in 1917 in Poland and went to the University of Warsaw to study medicine.

When war broke out on 1 September 1939 Adina was 22 years old and in the sixteenth term at the Faculty of Medicine at Warsaw University. She had been married for six weeks. They had married in a hurry because she wanted her married name on her degree and doctor's licence she was due to receive in the academic year 1939–1940. To get the doctor's licence you had to prove your citizenship. Adina's father was a refugee from Russia with a *Nansen* passport which could present problems, so being married to a Pole would avoid such complications. *Nansen* passports were issued after World War I to stateless people by the League of Nations, named after a Norwegian, Fridtjof Nansen (1861–1930), who was the League of Nation's High Commissioner for Refugees from 1920 until 1922. He won the Nobel Peace Prize in 1922.

It was forty years after the Holocaust that she wrote her book. When she was in her 70s and ill in a Warsaw hospital, the memories came flooding back:

> I had to speak out. But still I hung back. Still I resisted. Until another fear came over me. That I wouldn't make it in time. That I wouldn't repay the debt I owed to those times…And I started to hurry. There on a hospital bed, I started to write. Quickly. To win the race against time. To make it in time. Even if incompletely, fragmentarily, through the prism of my own incomplete memories.[339]

On 1 September 1939 Adina woke to the sound of an air raid, however she managed to get to the Hospital of the Bonifrater Fathers, a psychiatric clinic,

---

338 Ed van Rijswijk, email to author, 25 June 2017.
339 Adina Blady Szwajger, *I Remember Nothing More*, Collins Harvill (1990) pp.3–4

to begin her training. Already half the boys were missing having been called up. The professor took the classes through various air raids until 4 September. At the end of the day the professor said 'As from tomorrow the hospital is under military control. I dismiss you and consider the classes as credited. Leave your registration books to be signed, and see you after the war.'[340]

When Warsaw could no longer defend itself on 28 September: 'I stood amongst the crowds on Krakowskie Przedmiescie and watched the Germans march in. The crowds were so quiet you could hear the buzzing of a fly. Pale, drawn faces. And silent tears. The night of occupation had begun.'[341]

Early in October she went back to the faculty offices with two colleagues. The new Dean, appointed by the Germans, 'their' Professor Lauber, told them: 'What for you is the invader is for me the fatherland. And don't even think of passing exams. We won't be needing Polish, let alone Jewish doctors.'

There were rumours that the Jan Kazimierz University in Lvov was still open and they thought they could finish their degrees there. She spent some months there studying and doing exams. She remembers 'meagre provisions' and lots of fugitives. She left when a Ukrainian whispered: 'Go – I've seen your name on the list of deportees.' She didn't go back to her accommodation with her cousin and her son, but straight to the station. She tried to persuade her cousin to leave too but she didn't believe the rumour, so Adina went alone. 'The next day, the cousin and her one-and-a-half-year-old child were taken away. Miraculously they survived in the far north.'[342]

It took her five days to get back to Warsaw and return to her mother. Her husband turned up and there was more food than in Lvov – 'milk, cheese and meat coming in from the country'. However, Adina became ill with a terrible abscess and remained so until the end of February 1940. As money lost its value you had to barter to get food. The fall of France was very discouraging but Adina still wanted to be a paediatrician and through a friend's daughter who was a nurse, she went to the Bersohn and Bauman Hospital.

Dr. Skonieczny, whom she was sent to see, asked her if she was a trainee nurse. She admitted she looked eighteen, and told him she had come to be an intern on the Ward for Internal Diseases. It was 11 March 1940 and the ward was an ordinary one for children with normal diseases. They were able to give those needing it better nourishment, even getting extra eggs and cocoa. It was a marvellous hospital with a great tradition – 'a hospital for all children regardless of their faith, truly a Hospital for the Children of Warsaw.'

When she first started the children were priority and sometimes they died:

> …later there were the grotesquely bloated little bodies, swollen from hunger, to which skinny arms and legs had been attached like sticks to a badly made puppet. These we sometimes managed to save with glucose and vitamin C, a little powdered milk, a few grams of margarine, the

---

340 P.6
341 P.7
342 Pp.8–10

remaining drops of watered down milk. But those times, too, had not yet come. In the spring of 1940, there was even room for hope.[343]

The hospital was closed by the German authorities with a claim of an outbreak of typhus in the building:

No one was allowed to enter or leave. At night, we slept side by side in the great library hall on the ground floor, under the portraits of the hospital's founders, the Bersohns and the Baumans. We ate in the canteen, meals which consisted of a plateful of watery soup. We took baths in the washroom in the hall, the so-called 'bath on the catafalque' (before the war, this had been the admissions room – the bath stood high up). And we became one family. That dreadful move of the German authorities – to close people off in quarantine, to separate them from families and home, to subject them to hunger and discomfort – brought the entire staff together to form a tightly knit unit which nothing would be able to tear apart.

The staff all met for a communal breakfast at ten o'clock in the lab:

And these 'breakfasts', our basic meal of the day, served on Meissen china and 'drunk' from crystal glasses, consisted of one hundred grams of rationed bread, cut into wafer this slices, and ten grams of beet marmalade or five grams of 'monkey lard'. This was followed by one – literally one – twenty-five gram glass of pure, undiluted spirits which we drank in one neat gulp. This one glass didn't make us tipsy, but it did help us to work. We only discovered its calorific value later, during periods of extreme hunger when none of our group was swollen. Two hundred extra calories certainly proved vital. And after the closure of the ghetto, spirits were our only salvation. With a superb lack of consistency, the invader, while depriving us of food, provided doctors with spirit rations.[344]

By the time the ghetto was closed in November 1940, everything was changing both on the streets and in the hospital.

Jews transported from other cities and towns were pouring into Warsaw. On the streets, there were more and more starved, ragged paupers begging for a crust of bread. In the hospital, more and more flea-ridden, lice-infested, fungus-diseased children. More children emaciated from hunger with the eyes of adults; more and more tuberculosis [TB].

Things became worse:

---

343 P.25
344 P.27

We already knew that there was less and less we could do to save lives; that instead we were becoming more and more bestowers of quiet death. In search of the mercy of such quiet death, one cold autumn day, a ragged homeless child stripped naked in front of the hospital gates and howled like a wounded puppy, to be taken in because he was alone, hungry and cold. And when I was leaving the hospital one evening, I stepped on something soft: a baby's corpse, swollen, covered with newspapers.[345]

Hungry children were filling the Ward for Internal Diseases until they took up all the beds. No one gave in to despair:

> ...not the orderlies, who moved around with difficulty on swollen legs (after all, starvation did not spare them either), nor the nurses, who worked ten to twelve hours regardless of their schedules. We, the doctors, also made our way, carrying not only the meagre medicines which we injected intravenously into swollen arms, but also the equally meagre rations provided...half a powdered egg, ten grams of margarine – treasures which we couldn't entrust to the orderlies, who were dying of hunger, not because they weren't honest but because we couldn't expose them to the tortures of temptation.
>
> Hunger is a terrible thing. And this was real hunger, the kind that kills.[346]

Adina had a serious bout of typhus in July with a very high temperature but managed to recover. Some weeks later when recovered she went back to the hospital to the typhoid ward where the children weren't dying but there weren't enough beds.

The ghetto streets were full of 'snatchers' who grabbed parcels of food from people walking past or broke pieces off someone's loaf. 'Once on Leszno Street, a little pauper snatched a bunch of violets from my hand and ate it.' One day she heard a child say:

> Oh, when my sister died, Papa said it didn't matter where they buried her because we wouldn't live long enough to visit her grave anyway. And Papa wrapped her up in paper and took her out into the street, but Mamma cried and wanted to snatch her away but she wasn't strong enough.[347]

In the autumn of 1941 there seemed to be only helplessness. Now there were four children in a bed and if a child got better there was often no one to collect him or her from the hospital. The work became harder and food

---

345 P.3
346 P.31
347 P.36

shortages more frequent – even the starvation rations were affected. 'One day, on the 'older children's' ward, the famished skeletons threw themselves at the soup pot, overturned it as they pushed the nurse away, then lapped up the spilt slops from the floor, tearing bits of rotten swede away from each other.'[348]

A new Children's Hospital was created out of an old school in October 1941:

> So there, in those enormous wards, on wooden bunks, on paper mattresses with no sheets, lay children covered with the same paper mattresses. And in the corner of the room stood tin buckets because there weren't any bedpans or chamber pots and those children were suffering from *Durchfall* – the bloody diarrhoea of starvation – and couldn't get as far as the lavatory. So, in the morning, when you went in, those buckets were overflowing and slopping all over the floor – there was a terrible stench of blood, pus and faeces.
>
> On the bunks lay skeletons of children or swollen lumps. Only their eyes were alive. Until you've seen such eyes, the face of a starving child with its gaping black hole for a mouth and its wrinkled, parchment-like skin, you don't know what life can be like.[349]

Adina discovered a stock of morphine and with a colleague, Dr. Margolis, they took a spoon and went to the infants' room:

> And just as, during those two years of real work in the hospital, I had bent over the little beds, so now I poured this last medicine into those tiny mouths. Only Dr Margolis was with me. And downstairs, there was screaming because the Szaulis and the Germans were already there, taking the sick from the wards to the cattle trucks.
>
> After that we went in to the older children and told them that this medicine was going to make their pain disappear. They believed us and drank the required amount from the glass. So they lay down and after a few minutes – I don't know how many – but the next time I went into that room, they were asleep. And I don't know what happened after that.[350]

On 25 January 1943, Adina went to the Aryan side and started her life as a *kasharit* (see pages 262–3). She later reflected on what had happened:

> But not even a single fragment remains of the wall which separated one third of the residents from the rest; not a vestige of the stone desert which they made of the place where people lived, fought and died – people who had been there for a thousand years. Not a single

---

348 P.39
349 P.42
350 P.57

burnt-down house from whose windows mothers had thrown their children and jumped after them.

Sometimes I walk though that new, modern neighbourhood, along pavements which cover the bones of those who were burnt there. I look up at the sky, there where my house and all the other houses once stood.

Adina died of pancreatic cancer on 18 February 1993 in Lodz. Her first husband, Stefan, was tricked by the Nazis and killed. She married again later and had two daughters Hanna and Alina, four grandchildren and two great-grandchildren, all in Poland.

Elisabeth Sommer-Lefkovits (1904–1994), Pharmacist

I am grateful to Antony Rudolf for telling me about Elisabeth Sommer-Lefkovits and sending me her memoir Are You in This Hell Too? Memories of Troubled Times 1944–1945. *Her son gave her a computer on her 85th birthday and after her initial doubts about mastering it, she completed her memoir in 1994. 'I simply wrote my memoirs as a final gesture in order to honour the memory of those members of my family who did not survive persecution'.*[351]

The memoir starts in September 1944 in Presov, Slovakia:

It is a beautiful, warm summer's day.

I am trying to prepare myself to cope with all the heavy duties I have to undertake. I am Jewish, with a diploma in pharmacy, which puts me in a 'reserved occupation', and I am employed at the Pfeiler Pharmacy in Prešov. Apart from me, there are two other colleagues who hold diplomas, and two technicians. We are very busy, because, apart from the clientele from the town, we also have another very important and nerve-wracking duty to perform.

Even before the national uprising against the Nazi regime in Slovakia in August 1944, we had begun to supply the partisans with medication, bandages and disinfectants in ever greater quantities. However, this had to be done very carefully and in the greatest secrecy, so that neither partisans nor we pharmacists put ourselves in danger. At that time even the smallest assistance to the partisans was punishable by death.

The order was brought secretly into the pharmacy in an envelope by an unknown member of the resistance, mostly when several customers were present, so it was difficult to see who had put it there. The completed order was then collected unobtrusively. Even we, the members of staff, were hardly aware of when and by whom the order had been collected. In the event of any of us being arrested and questioned, none of us could betray another.

---

351 P.76

That's how things were till 11 September 1944.

A few weeks later, as I lay on the straw-covered cement floor of the Gestapo prison, I had all day and night to mull over whether our dangerous aid to the partisans, carried out so meticulously and carefully, had been known to the Gestapo all the time.

One sunny morning, Mrs. Kissoczy, wife of the well-known and respected Presov doctor, came into the crowded pharmacy. She came straight to my counter and asked me in a calm, quiet tone for aspirin. It was unusual for a relative of the doctor, in whose practice hundreds of different medicines were stored, to come into a pharmacy and buy aspirin.

As I handed her the small packet of aspirin, as requested, she bent her head as if talking to her purse, and whispered 'Disappear right away; the Gestapo are now arresting all the Jewish doctors and pharmacists who are still here,' and she quietly left the shop.

With a calm movement I put my fountain pen into its usual holder (we didn't have ballpoint pens in those days), went to the back to take off my overall, and made to leave the shop by the main door. At that very moment, two men from the Gestapo, accompanied by a Hlinka guardsman, entered the pharmacy. In a loud and vigorous voice one of them shouted 'Heil Hitler! We are looking for the Jewess, Elisabeth Lefkovits.'

My colleagues did not betray that the Jewess they were looking for had just left the pharmacy with the lie 'I'll be back in a minute.'

I kept sufficient presence of mind to warn the vet, Dr. Benedek, who I happened to meet in the street at that moment, of imminent danger. Thanks to my warning, the Benedek family were able to escape.

So began seven frightening weeks of a life in hiding for me and my children.[352]

She explains the background to her situation:

This 'final purge' by the Gestapo, after the Slovak national uprising, caught us unawares. Since the main deportation in 1942, we had over-estimated the apparent state of peace and taken our relatively comfortable existence as Jews 'necessary to the economy' too much for granted. The Russians seemed to be making such victorious headway, that we never imagined at the time that another round of deportations was on the cards, and had made no preparations for a life on the run.

So when she left the pharmacy on that sunny day, she had no idea where to go and feeling 'like a hunted animal' she only knew she couldn't go back to her flat. Fate seemed to take her to where Katica Svaton lived. She was 'a very dear, "Aryan", unmarried dressmaker. She was loved by all the families in

---

352 Pp.17–18. Hlinka Guard was the militia of the pro-Nazi Slovak party, named after Andrej Hlinka who died in 1938.

whose houses she worked.' Fortunately she was at home but when Elisabeth told her tale, they were both at a loss as to where she could find shelter. Mrs Svaton fed her and said she would put her up overnight – she put her in bed, leaving the blinds open 'so that the neighbours don't get suspicious about me hiding anyone. I'll put food at the end of the bed. Don't get out of bed all day.'[353]

Sleep did not come easily, in spite of her exhaustion, but eventually she slept. She was worried about her children, Paul and Ivan were in an orphanage in Presov just a few hundred feet from her. 'My husband lay in a hospital bed in far-off Budapest, but hospitals offered a certain safety, or so I thought. No-one would be deported from there. Hospitals, with their white cross on the roof, are even spared in the bombing.'

Mrs Svaton told her the Gestapo had been back to the pharmacy several times looking for her. On the fourth day, through the half-open window, she heard two neighbours chatting: 'One said to the other in excited tones: "The Gestapo are looking for Mrs. Lefkovits and her children." "Yes, I heard that too," answered the other indifferently. "The boys are in the orphanage in Jarkova Street, aren't they? They'll find them sooner or later." That went to my heart.'

On the eighth day, Prešov suffered massive bomb damage and she heard on the radio that the orphanage had been hit. 'Muffled in a black headscarf and a dark coat borrowed from Katica, I ran like a mad woman to the orphanage. Thank God, I found my children there, safe and sound.' The Principal told her they were evacuating the whole orphanage to the country and would take little Ivan but 14-year-old Paul would have to be hidden elsewhere. She was distraught at the boys being separated.

After a great deal of thought Katica and Elisabeth decided that Katica would go to see Ivan's godfather, Josef Stracensky, and seek his advice. She returned beaming 'He'll take both boys to the country with his own family.' Neither Ivan nor his mother can recall how they got to Lipovec safely, but they did.

Elizabeth moved to another hiding place where she joined four other people in a small flat on Hinkova Street. Meanwhile a paediatrician friend of hers, Dr Friedmann-Mayer, who rescued many Jewish children, arranged for Ivan to be smuggled illegally on false papers to safety in Hungary in March 1944; unfortunate timing because the Germans invaded Hungary on 19 March 1944. A friend of hers Mrs Olga R., was to take Ivan aged 7 and a 14-year-old girl. Both children were disguised as being of the opposite sex. The examination of documents at the Slovakian/Hungarian border was stressful and lengthy as both nation's border police had inspections. They were extremely fortunate because 7-year-old Ivan, confused by the questions, revealed his real name was Ivan. The policeman was taken aback and sent his colleagues on to the next compartment:

He bent over the child and said in a very low and serious tone: 'Do you know what would happen to all of you if I was a bad man? You would

---

all three go straight to a concentration camp. Don't ever, anywhere, tell anyone what you have just told me. I didn't hear anything.' Then he left the compartment.

All three of them were in a terrible state and poor Ivan kept asking them to forgive him. 'Mrs Olga R. had helped refugees before this journey and continued to do so afterwards, but she said that this journey to Budapest was probably the one that was most nerve-wracking and, perhaps, the most dangerous.'[354] Ivan too told her about it much later.

He was left with Dr Odon Propper, a dentist, who was a distant relative. It was planned that Ivan would stay there until she, Paul and her husband were re-united in Budapest. Unfortunately her husband was suffering from kidney failure and was taken to the Jewish Hospital by taxi on 12 March 1944. His first visitor was Ivan. Elisabeth and Paul were to be smuggled into Hungary on 20 March but just beforehand she received an anonymous telegram saying 'Don't come; stay where you are.' She didn't understand until she heard on a neighbour's radio that the Germans had occupied Hungary. Jews were not allowed to own radio sets.

Things were more peaceful in Tiso-Slovakia so she had the children returned to her and managed to get them accommodated in a Catholic orphanage in Kremnica. However Paul wrote desperate letters to her and wrote he did not want to be saved without her. Both of them absconded in September 1944 and after travelling on various trains and buses they turned up in Prešov. She managed to get them into the local orphanage thanks to Father Titus. He had also baptised the family after weeks of preparation.

This was the situation when Elisabeth had to flee the pharmacy. Josef, who took the boys with him to Lipovec, was a dental technician whose family owned a flat there. He had learnt his trade from Elisabeth's husband creating a father-son relationship. Although he joined the Hlinka party, he kept them informed. All was well until her eldest son, who was a good footballer, was recognised by a fellow player. They could not endanger the family who had helped them, so the boys came back to Prešov.[355]

The two boys joined the five already hiding with Madame Elise, who had been a hairdresser and who lived there with her sick, elderly mother. A neighbour prepared their food out of kindness. The Slovak authorities agreed to the Germans offering a reward of 500 crowns to anyone leading them to hiding Jews. Concealing Jews was punishable by death.

On 22 November, Madame Elise burst into the room full of fear saying the Gestapo were searching the house and they all rushed to the hiding place. One of Ivan's slippers fell off in the rush and was found by a guard. Madame Elise, with great presence of mind, said her cat played with it. However, they returned in the night, when they were all in bed and caught them all, including poor Madame Elise. They were taken from the prison

---

354 Pp.22–24
355 Pp.25–30

on 26 November and herded into freezing cattle trucks late at night in great secrecy when the citizens of Prešov were in bed.

> On the transport there were doctors, pharmacists, medical personnel and people who, until a month ago, had been Jews in 'reserved occupations'. Their exceptional status and work permits had been withdrawn from them. They were arrested and given one hour in which to pack a few necessities.[356]

It was desperately cold and as their watches had been taken they only knew by their hunger and thirst how time was passing. At the first stop they were forced out and given a warm liquid and some water. When the train finally stopped there were 17 corpses in their wagon alone. They had arrived at Ravensbrück.

On arrival all the men and boys over 14 were taken away to the men's camp. Elisabeth was desolate when 14-year-old Paul was sent with the men, as she was already separated from her husband who was so ill in a Budapest hospital. She and Ivan were in the 'Mother and Child' hut, barrack number 12. She did receive a message on a greasy bit of paper from her good friend Dr Bela Rosenberg in the men's camp. 'Zsuzsa, don't worry about Paul. We will look after him.'[357] That piece of paper was with her all the time and she read it hundreds of times. She always remembered Dr Rosenberg with gratitude and prayed for him.

Early in the morning and evening they had a lukewarm brown liquid, coffee substitute with a sedative, probably bromide. Bread ration came in the morning and had to last all day. It was difficult because there was nowhere to put it down or keep it, yet something was needed to eat in the evening. The only warm meal was soup in the evening. One way of improving their diet was volunteering to work outside, which she often did to ensure Ivan had enough calories.

They became unsightly within a day – unkempt, apathetic beings, dressed in rags. Their hair wasn't cut, they looked awful and didn't recognise each other. Washing was a struggle at a long cement trough in limited time before the tap was switched off. Diarrhoea was a danger to everyone and they couldn't always wash their hands. Roll-call was at five in the morning and usually lasted for four to four-and-a-half hours. If someone was late or did not turn up, everyone was punished with another two hours standing in the freezing cold. Their clothing was inadequate because their warm clothing was taken away and replaced with summer dresses. The clothes were handed out regardless of size and shoes were also ill-fitting.

They were given typhoid injections, which were terribly painful because the needles were blunt. They also used too large a dose, which gave people high fever and back pain – she was a pharmacist after all.

---

356 P.35
357 P.39–41

After roll-call she was sent to a labour group to carry five- or six-metre-long telegraph poles between two of them from one place to another. After a while she was really struggling. She was in pain and had a high temperature. She couldn't carry on and told her partner, a strong young Hungarian 'Juliska, I'm going to put the pole down.' 'Dear God, please don't do that, they'll shoot us on the spot.'

Just then the overseer went by and she told him she was sick and couldn't carry on. He asked her what she had done in civilian life. 'I was a pharmacist.' He said 'Leave it there' and carried on. They just went back to the assembly point. On the way Juliska told her she had just arrived from Budapest and miraculously was able to tell Elisabeth that her mother, Anna Strauss, was still alive.

The outside duty for extra soup was very hard:

The duty consisted of us pushing a wheelbarrow laden with newly dug earth to a distant spot from somewhere, emptying it out, pushing the empty barrow back from whence we had come, filling it up once more and emptying it out again on to the growing heap. Since we were poorly nourished and scantily clad, it was only a question of time before we collapsed from exhaustion. Only a few were able to hold out.

Two merciless women overseers had the job of supervising the intermittent work of the prisoners. They were accompanied by two superbly trained German Shepherd dogs, who were so amazingly well drilled that, if anyone remained standing or stopped work for too long, the two furious dogs would leap barking shrilly on to the 'striking' women and tear the clothes from their backs.

Filled with dreadful fear and terror, the women would move off again. The overseers fell about laughing, and the dogs knew they had done their duty. They immediately stopped tearing the clothing and return to their 'mistresses'.

Since then I have never been able to look at a German Shepherd dog without fear and trembling.

Ravensbrück was basically a women's camp but from 1944 they provided the huts for 'mothers and children'. There is no knowing how many were there as some died every day. There was so little food and not enough water. The children begged for food and water but the mothers could do nothing. When Ivan had terrible pain in his ears and a high temperature, a young Belgian doctor gave her an aspirin substitute and told her to put a poultice on. He would probably be deaf in both ears. He could not hear properly but after a few days his ears healed one after another. The poultice she made by soaking a cloth in warm coffee worked and his hearing was unimpaired.

They got weaker and weaker but one morning they were moved to a different block. There were no bunks, just long rows of straw-filled sacks – it was a real tower of Babel with several languages but in her block Ukrainian was the most common. The Italians suffered most with the cold. There was a young teacher from Padua and Elisabeth warned her to put everything she owned under her head at night. Nocturnal stealing was happening all the time with groups of women stealing anything they could find, clothes, bread. The poor Italian woman lost her coat and standing in the roll-call without it gave her fever and three days later she was dead. It nearly happened to her one night but she shouted out loud and other women came to her and the gang went off to find a weaker victim.[358]

They were isolated from the outside world and had no idea what was happening. One day an old soldier came with a message: 'Hold out! Don't despair. It's nearly over – we will survive!' The note had a miraculous effect. They made plans and talked about what they would cook or bake. 'We were already swapping recipes, while our stomachs were still rumbling with hunger.'

The discipline was not imposed in the same way and overseers and 'trusties' disappeared. The food, if possible, became worse and less. They heard aeroplanes overhead and nightly air-raids. In March 1945 they were told they were moving on – a week-long 'death march'. Ivan was already weak because of the poor diet and his ear infection. In addition his boots were much too small for him. She tried to carry him on her back but she couldn't do it all the time. Klari Fischer took it in turns with her. There were bodies of the dead or exhausted at the roadside.

They stopped in barns at night and if there were animals they provided warmth. Sometimes elderly women would bring bread and/or milk which helped their rumbling stomachs and also their spirits. They slept on the straw and then were roused by the SS men. Each morning fewer women got up. Finally they arrived at Bergen-Belsen. Her faith was challenged by the atrocities she experienced and witnessed.[359]

They arrived in dire distress and misery and had to line up by a long wooden house and waited for hours. It was bitterly cold and they were weak from hunger and fatigue. They were told they could have a bath and every now and then 15–20 women and a few children went in but never came out. They were fearful that they were gas chambers – but there were none at Belsen, where Jews died of hunger and cruelty. They had amazing showers with wonderful hot water and were then pushed naked into the cold to collect clothes from a table with disinfected piles.

Again there were 'mothers and children' huts and Ivan and Elisabeth were in one. It was more crowded than Ravensbrück but she was pleased to meet old friends and acquaintances and they all huddled together. There were lots of bodies everywhere, which they were used to seeing. However in Ravensbrück they had been shot or had thrown themselves at the barbed wire. In Belsen the bodies were skeletons.

They received a piece of bread and a portion of soup. They were surprised there was no roll-call. Mrs G from Brünn said 'We don't have a roll-call, this is a rest-camp not a work-camp.' There were toilets in their block, but you

---

358 Pp.48–50
359 P.51–3

had to queue. Water was in short supply, there was dysentery and then a typhoid epidemic and then TB began to spread.

There were hardly any SS. Mrs G. warned that the Germans knew they had lost and did not want to leave any witnesses so no one would survive. Mrs G. warned her about Josef Kramer and Irma Grese (see pages 364–5). Then lice became prevalent, even though they tried to control them. Elisabeth and Ivan both caught typhoid.[360]

By April 1945 the camp had run out of water. Those who were still mobile dragged themselves around looking for relatives and friends. Someone called out 'Zsuzsa! I think I saw your sister Ilka somewhere.' She grabbed Ivan's little hand and went searching. She called out 'I'm looking for Ilka Diamant, my sister, from Bratislava!' but there was no reply. On her way back to her block feeling dejected she saw a figure on a top bunk.

She was almost completely bald and her face was etched by disease and suffering. She looked down and called out in tears: 'Zsuzsa, are you in this hell, too?' I hardly recognised my sister, just her voice. Was it really my sister? I couldn't reply, but we threw our arms round each other, sobbing and wordless.

Much later she heard Ilka's story. She and her husband, Dr Nikolaus Diamant, were transferred from the ghetto in Bratislava to a holding camp in Sered. They lived there in awful conditions with other families they knew. When the camp was closed, they tried to hide in the country with other people from Sered. They were arrested and Ilka was sent to Gross-Rosen and her husband to Oranienburg. She managed to get Ilka moved in with her and Ivan where the conditions were marginally better. On that first day they still got a bowl of soup but that was the last.

From now onwards there would be nothing at all, not to eat nor to drink. No liquid, no calories. Ilka lay there in total apathy and we were dying of thirst. Our legs were swollen and we slept for most of the time.

We used the latrines less and less, since we had nothing to evacuate. It rained once or twice, and when it did we managed to collect a little water and to dampen our fevered faces and cool them down. The swelling of Ivan's stomach went down, we were dehydrated and had difficulty breathing. Ivan's pulse, when I felt it from time and time, was irregular – sometimes fast and sometimes hardly discernible.

There was absolutely nothing to eat. The guards were only in the watchtower. They had no strength to look for food but an old soldier came into their block and brought them beetroot which they ate ravenously. They were so weak they lay surrounded by the bodies of their friends.[361]

---

360 Pp.54–7
361 Pp.58–59

On 15 April someone told them there was a white flag. She dragged herself to the door and saw the flag. Nothing changed and they were still locked in but the electric fence was switched off. The real liberation happened on 17 April. 'By this time I could only crawl on all fours and weighed nine kilograms.'

The first thing the British Army Medical Corps brought were huge cisterns of water. They gave them food – sardines, peas, beans, ham and eggs, all sorts of canned fish, dried figs and 'lots of other goodies'.

The starving people seized on all this food and couldn't stop eating. However, their shrunken stomachs could not cope with this unaccustomed nourishment and, having been reduced to skin and bone, they died by the hundreds in unbearable pain and cramps through perforated stomachs.

The liberators had meant so well giving us these generous rations, but they had no experience of dealing with such starvation. How could they guess that the excellent food and generous quantities might have such a disastrous effect on starving people.

Elisabeth did not eat all the food they were given, because she hoarded some 'just in case'. She was unaware of the British taking control, apart from the arrival of the water – 'It was the tankers of drinking water which embodied and symbolised liberation for us.'

The British quickly sent for specialists to deal with the victims of starvation, they distributed the 'Bengal Famine Diet' which was a fluid containing molasses and included glucose and salt. It had been successful in Bengal years before and saved thousands of the Nazis' wretched victims at Belsen. In spite of all this relief, 'People were still dying around us all the time.'[362]

All the SS men and women except for Josef Kramer and Irma Grese were ordered by the British to deal with the bodies, which were put into communal graves. The SS had the same conditions and calories as their former victims. Each grave held 5000. Gradually the British had a new enemy, the typhoid epidemic, and the burials were speeded up. The English chaplain rushed from grave to grave.

Communication between the British and the prisoners was difficult. Elisabeth's English helped her find out what was happening. They turned the SS officer school, off-site, into a hospital with thousands of beds. Gradually prisoners were moved by ambulance but it was slow because they could only take four at a time. The ambulances had to drive slowly as well, so that contaminated dust was not disturbed. She and Ivan held hands as they saw Belsen disappear through the ambulance window.[363]

After being washed twice, they were put to bed, exhausted but happy.

362 Pp.60–63
363 64–8

We awoke in soft, clean beds, in surroundings which looked human again. Outside, just a few kilometres away, the dying was continuing. Here in the hospital, every human life was worth something; we were looked after, cared for, human beings once again.

But she had lost Ivan in the hospital – when she asked for him the nurses thought she was delirious, her temperature was over 40 degrees with fever. She found one of the orderlies spoke Hungarian. She asked him to ask the children – there were very few – if anyone was called 'Ivanko' As the days passed, she just cried. 'Suddenly my door opened and what did I see? Wearing a sky-blue nightshirt, which I still see in my mind's eye, there was my little, very pale Ivan in the arms of that wonderful Hungarian nurse.' Then they both sobbed with joy.

Towards the end of June 1945 we informed the authorities that we felt fit to travel and wanted to go home. We left Bergen-Belsen with light hearts and travelled back through a bombed-out and destroyed Germany to Czechoslovakia. Our arrival in Prešov was much more distressing than we had imagined. Seventeen of our closest relatives were missing, including my husband, my eldest son, Paul and my mother.

Nearly fifty years have passed since then, but the loss of my dearest ones is a wound that never heals. I shall remember those events till my dying day. I cannot – and do not want to – ever forget them.[364]

---

364 P.71

Diarists

Rosina Sorani (1895–1945)

I wrote about Rosina Sorani in the chapter about books in Who Betrayed the Jews? *She was a secretary in the Rome Synagogue when the Nazis looted it in October 1943 and kept a diary of the time. She was threatened by the Nazis and was extremely courageous. Keith Posner kindly translated the diary into English.*

Rosina was born on 2 June 1895 and died on 9 May 1945. She never married and was retired at the time of her death. I have been unable to establish any more about her life or the cause of death. She has been described as 'a very brave woman and one of the most interesting figures...of the nazi-fascist occupation'.[365] Her brother was born in 1899 and married his cousin Lina Sorani who was a good artist. They had no children and moved to Florence where he was secretary of the Jewish community until he died. Their grandfather was Rabbi Mosè Sorani, the Chief Rabbi of Cuneo (Cento) around 1880. His son Giustino was their father. Their mother was Elisa Sorani. The Sorani family originated in Sorano, near Pitigliano in the south of Tuscany.[366] Pitigliano (known as *La Piccola Gerusalemme* or Little Jerusalem) was first settled by Jews in the sixteenth century. Sorani studied there with Rabbi Jacob Maroni who later became the Chief Rabbi of Florence.[367]

Rosina's brother Settimio Sorani also worked in the Rome synagogue for a charity, Delasem (Committee for Aid to Jewish Emigrants). As a result Settimao and Renzo Levi, the President of Delasem, learnt the horrors of the Holocaust from both the Red Cross and the Vatican. Both men protected themselves by obtaining non-Jewish identities and went into hiding on 8 September with their families. Unfortunately, most Jews did not believe what they were told including the President of the community, Ugo Foà. Foà later wrote his view was based on considering that the 'excesses to which the

---

365 Gabriella Yael Franzone, Dept. of Culture, Jewish Community of Rome, email to author 8 May 2017.
366 Franzone emails to author 9 and 10 May 2017.
367 Henry Samuel Morais, *Eminent Israelites of The Nineteenth Century* (Philadelphia, Edward Stone & Co, 1880) p.326

brethren in faith had fallen victim in other lands invaded by German armies would not be repeated in Rome.' He believed that the Jews of Rome would be protected because there were relatively few of them. The 'Eternal City' would be respected by the occupiers and the community was making 'every effort in order not to give any pretext for persecutions'. Eventually, when he was in hiding, he concluded 'Not even Italy was immune'.[368]

Rosina's diary was later published by the community, who first removed entries that portrayed the community negatively. It appears that Foà accused Rosina of giving the SS his home address, which upset her because it was the community's executive secretary, Fortunato Piperno, who had done so. This is one of the pieces that was later removed:

> Since the Signor Presidente had not yet arrived, they demanded that I turn over the keys to the safe and the desks. When I said I didn't have them, they threatened me, saying that if I didn't give them the President's telephone number or his home address, I would have to pay with my life. But with all their threats I didn't tell them either one.
>
> ...Then the Germans, who could get nothing out of me, went to the other members of staff and especially to *Commendatore* Piperno...who on the first demand and the first threat immediately gave in and told both the telephone number and the address of the Signor Presidente.

These events took place on the eve of the Jewish New Year 5704, on 30 September 1943.[369] It is because of Rosina's diary that so much detail is available to us 70 years after these events. About 20 officials searched the synagogue premises and as Rosina noted, they paid particular attention to the two libraries – the *Biblioteca Comunale* and *Biblioteca del Collegio Rabbinico*. These libraries were the communal centres of both spiritual and secular life. The next day, 1 October 1943, two men from the ERR came and introduced themselves to Ugo Foà as Orientalists. One of them, in a captain's uniform, claimed to be a specialist in Hebrew from Berlin. Permission was sought to examine the community's libraries.

It must be remembered that the Jewish community in Rome was the oldest in Europe having existed since 161 BC when Judah Maccabee sent delegates. Consequently the libraries were not typical synagogue libraries and held amazing treasures:

> The *Biblioteca Comunale* had a magnificent collection, one of the richest in Europe, not only for the study of Judaica, but also of early Christianity. A heritage of 2,000 years of Jewish presence in Rome, the library contained vast treasures that had not yet been catalogued... Among the known material were the only copies of books and manuscripts dating from before the birth of Christ, from the time of

---

368 Robert Katz, *The Battle for Rome* (New York: Simon & Schuster, 2003) p.64
369 Robert Katz, *Black Sabbath: A Journey Through a Crime Against Humanity* (Toronto: Macmillan, 1969) p.109

the Caesars, the emperors, and the early popes. There were engravings from the Middle Ages, books from the earliest printers and papers and documents handed down through the ages.[370]

The arrival of Jews expelled from Spain considerably enlarged the collection in 1492. However, research was difficult as the catalogue was based on the date of acquisition. Undeterred, the ERR officers told Foà to hand over the catalogues. A few days later a lieutenant arrived, claiming to be a palaeographer (student of ancient writing) and a specialist in Semitic philology. His men rifled through the libraries whilst the witness watched the Nazi intellectual and described what she saw:

> ...the officer, with artful and meticulous hands like fine embroidery, touched softly, caressed, fondled the papyrus and incunabula; he turned the pages of manuscripts and rare editions and leafed through membranaceous codices and palimpsests. The varying attention of his touch, the differing artfulness of his gestures were at once proportionate to the volume's worth. Those works, for the most part, were written on obscure alphabets. But in opening their pages, the officer's eyes would fix on them, widening and brightening, in the same way that some readers who are particularly familiar with a subject know where to find the desired part, the revealing passage. In those elegant hands, as if under keen and bloodless torture, a kind of very subtle sadism, the ancient books had spoken.[371]

Rosina Sorani was present when the officer telephoned an international shipping company and arranged for the books to be transported out of Rome. She was threatened by the Germans and recorded the events in her diary on 11 October 1943. and told Foà, who contacted the President of the Union of Jewish Communities, Dante Almansi. The two men drafted a letter sent to four of the regime's offices. Not surprisingly, none of the fascist officials were willing to intercede, especially Guido Buffarini-Guidi who ran three of the offices. He was a notorious anti-Semite and war criminal and was busy drafting further anti-Jewish legislation, far fiercer than that of 1938.

On 13 October two large freight containers pulled up in front of the synagogue. Foà and Almansi were frantic and were especially worried about priceless gold and silver religious items they held. However a genius decided to use the *Mikva*, which was drained and a workman was brought in to hide precious items within the walls. Some books were hidden in a nearby municipal library, *Biblioteca Vallicelliana*.

Promptly at 8.30am the next day the ERR officials came back with transport – it was 14 October, the first day of the festival of Succoth. It took all day to load the contents of the two libraries, whilst the workman continued hiding valuables in the Mikva walls. Later large pieces were hidden

---

370 Robert Katz, *Black Sabbath* (Arthur Barker, 1969) p.120
371 Giacomo Debenedetti, '16 Ottobre 1943' cited in *Black Sabbath* p.123

in gardens and homes all over Rome. The remaining items were collected on 22 December – this time it was the first day of Chanukah. The Nazis had confiscated 10,000 books.

These activities rightly caused panic amongst Rome's Jews who were less protected than their books, most of which returned after the war. Most of the Jews did not. By the autumn of 1943 the diplomats, the military and the Vatican, including Pius XII, knew the Germans were preparing to deport the Jews. The SS commander in Rome, Herbert Kappler, received orders from Berlin to seize Rome's eight thousand Jews and transport them to northern Italy, 'where they are to be liquidated'. It is claimed this is the only Nazi document that makes direct reference to 'liquidating' the Jews rather than 'special handling'. Two days after the book raid, on 16 October 1943, early on the Sabbath over a thousand Jews were seized in the ghetto and held over the weekend very close to the Vatican, but the Pope did not interfere. One poor woman, Marcella, captured with two children, gave birth overnight in the courtyard; the Germans refused to let her go to hospital. On Monday morning the Jews were herded onto the railway for their terrible journey to Auschwitz. They arrived on the evening of 22 October but because several other trains were already there they had to wait until the following morning for their fate.

The *Auschwitz Chronicle* for 23 October 1943 records:

1,035 Jewish men, women and children arrive with an RSHA transport from Rome. After the selection 149 men and 47 women are admitted to the camp and receive Nos. 158491–158639 and 66172–66218. The remaining 839 people are killed in the gas chambers.[372]

Presumably Marcella and her three little ones would not be suitable as workers. Of the 1,041 Jews deported that day, only fifteen returned to Rome after the war.

From the diary of Rosina Sorani, secretary of the Jewish Community of Rome during the period of the German occupation of Italy:

Sunday, 26 September 1943
This morning, the head of the Department of Race within the Italian Ministry of the Interior, Dr. Cappa, came to the office of the Jewish Community to summon Ugo Foà, President of the Jewish Community to the German Embassy this evening at 6:00 p.m. where an urgent message was awaiting him. He was summoned together with His Excellency, Dante Almansi, President of the Union of Italian Jewish Communities. They arrived at the German Embassy promptly at 6:00 p.m., where they were ordered by SS Captain Kappler to deliver over 50 kg of gold to the German authorities within 36 hours. If the demand was not met within the specified time, 200 Roman Jews, chosen by lottery, would be arrested and deported to Germany.

---

372 Danuta Czech, *Auschwitz Chronicle*, p.512. RSHA transports were organised by Eichmann's office.

Monday, 27 September 1943
Early this morning I received a phone call from the President of the Community Foà asking me to telephone all of the counselors and important members of the Community and invite them to an urgent meeting at 10:00 a.m. in the Community offices. I telephoned them all immediately, and they arrived promptly at 10:00 a.m. At 10:30 a.m. the President arrived and convened an official meeting of the counselors, including in the meeting some of the most influential members of the Community. His Excellency Almansi was also in attendance. The President told them about the demand made by the German Embassy: the specified amount of gold had to be delivered by 12 noon on 28 September 1943.

Monday to Tuesday, 27–28 September 1943
Great commotion this morning. Collection of gold in progress. Lots of people coming and going, especially the ordinary members of the community. There were three people dedicated to weighing and testing the gold; the female clerks employed to give receipts for the gold, together with me, took all the gold into safekeeping. All of this took place in the Council Room.

Tuesday, 28 September 1943
By about 11:30 a.m. the required amount of gold had not yet been collected, so the President went to the German Embassy to see if they could give us more time, given that the 12 noon deadline was imminent. After much insistence, an agreement was reached whereby the deadline would be moved forward to 4:00 p.m. that same day. At the request of the President I stood watch in his office for the entire period that the gold was being weighed and placed into boxes for subsequent transport. In addition to the gold, 2,021,540 Italian Lire in cash was also collected. Once the required amount had been collected, the office of the President was locked, and a city police officer was stationed at the door for the entire time that the gold remained in the office. I did not leave the Community offices all day. With me was Renzo Levi. At 4:00 p.m. precisely the President went to the Embassy to deliver the gold, accompanied by His Excellency Almansi, Dr Cappa, head of the Department of Race within the Italian Ministry of the Interior, two policemen and Angelo Anticolo, the person in charge of weighing the gold.

Wednesday, 29 September 1943
Eve of Rosh Hashana
This morning everyone was in the office working as usual when all of a sudden we were raided by German soldiers. There were approximately 40, including officers, regular troops, and interpreters. The soldiers were armed with machine guns and on the street they had brought machine gun trucks and two big tanks intended to knock down the main front door, if they had found it locked. None of the employees were allowed to leave the premises until they had gone. The other employees were permitted to leave at about 1:00 p.m., except for me. I was required to follow the proceedings between

the President and the German officers all the time that they remained in the office.

Thursday, 30 September 1943
First day of Rosh Hashana
This morning two German officers came to inspect the offices on the second and third floors, and they paid particular attention to the two libraries.

Friday, 1 October 1943
Second day of Rosh Hashana
The two German officers returned to inspect the various volumes in the two libraries. Together with them were other Germans who conversed with the President in a room on the third floor. They demanded information that the President did not provide, despite repeated threats against him.

Saturday, 2 October 1943
This morning I was in the house of Chief Rabbi Israele Zolli. I was accompanied by a builder, who had to force the front door open, as the house was empty due to the Rabbi having fled as soon as the Germans entered Rome. They took away several volumes in Hebrew, and some documents of limited value.

Monday, 11 October 1943
This morning I went to the office as usual to see if anything new had occurred. As it happens, after a short time two German officers arrived. I was alone in the office. After inspecting the library yet again, one of the officers picked up the telephone and called the company Otto and Rosoni to find out when they could send a truck to load up the books. Once they found out that the truck would only come in a few days, they turned to me and told me that they had made a thorough inspection, knew how many books the library contained, and the way in which the books were ordered, and they therefore declared that the two libraries were under an expropriation order. In a few days they would come back to take away the books and they expected to find everything as they had left it. If this was not the case, then I would pay with my life. I reported all the details of this conversation to the President when he came to the office later that morning. He instructed me to lock up everything immediately and not to give the keys to anyone for whatever reason, not even to him.

Wednesday, 13 October 1943
Eve of Sukkot
This morning a man from the company *Otto and Rosoni* appeared in the office and told me that they had a truck in the street outside the main entrance, ready to load up material that they had to take away immediately. I made it clear that I did not know what this was about. At that point the man called his company office, who told me that the truck was there to take

away the library books, and that I should wait because a German officer would be arriving.

Thursday, 14 October 1943
First day of Sukkot
As expected, the usual German officer arrived this morning at 8:30 a.m. With him was an employee from the transport company and several porters who had moved all of the books from the Jewish Community Library on the second floor, apart from those that were in the office of the Chief Rabbi and a part of the books from the Library of the Rabbinical College on the third floor, near the large room. With regard to the other books, they were unable to tell me when they would return to collect them, perhaps the following week. In the end the German officer thanked me and said "Well done!" I answered that I would have happily done without his congratulations.

Saturday, 16 October 1943
Third day of Sukkot
Hundreds of Jews in various districts of Rome, especially in the Ghetto, were seized by the Germans. From midnight on Friday they started watching the main entrances of the apartment buildings of the people they intended to seize, and on Saturday morning at 6:00 a.m. they started the roundup, which lasted for several hours. On leaving home, as usual, to go to see the caretaker of the Synagogue to see if there was any news, I was told by a girl that I should not leave my house because they were seizing the Jews. I did not want to believe this and continued walking, but once I reached the flower seller on Garibaldi Bridge, I was told by a Jewish man that I should not go to the office because there was a danger of being seized. Unconvinced by this, I continued on my way, but that same Jewish man who was nearby the flower seller called me back and implored me not to go any further because the black-covered trucks that were taking the Jews away were still going past; in fact I saw one fully loaded with men, women, and children. So I stood there for a few moments, uncertain what to do. In the end I decided to phone the President, I told him that I had an urgent need to speak to him regarding a very serious matter. He told me that I should wait and that he would come immediately to the Community offices. I told him that that was absolutely impossible, that I would have to come immediately to his house. I went to his house before 8:00 a.m. to make him aware of what was happening and to try to advise him to get away from his home immediately. I phoned my brother and asked him to find me accommodation. He sent me to the Hotel Milan, where I stayed until Monday and from here I went to Mrs. Lallai, a very kind old lady in Via Cremona 71.

The Germans forced any Jews that they found at home to follow them. They gave the Jews leaflets with the following instructions; in some cases they had the Jews read the instructions but did not give them the leaflets.

You will be deported together with your family and with other Jews who live in your building.

You must take the following items with you: foodstuffs for at least eight days, ration cards, identity card, and cups.

You may take one suitcase, with personal effects, underwear, blankets, etc., money and jewelry.

Lock your apartment and take your keys with you.

Sick people, even those very seriously ill, cannot remain behind for any reason. Nurses will be available on site.

Your family must be ready twenty minutes after receiving this leaflet.

Tuesday, 26 October 1943
In the hotel where I was staying, *Commendatore* Piperno distributed an advance of the salary payments for October and November with an addition of 100 Lire for October, as had been done for September.

Thursday, 28 October 1943
This morning the Germans seized my brother.

Saturday, 6 November 1943
Today was a very happy day for me; my brother was finally freed, Thank G-d, after ten days of imprisonment at the German Embassy in Via Tasso, where he had suffered greatly and had been starved of food. For me these were ten days of agony. I did nothing but pray to G-d day and night that he would be freed, that anything could happen to me but that he should be saved. I sincerely thank the good Lord who answered my prayers and gave me back my brother safe and sound.

Tuesday, 16 November 1943
Tonight, finally, and after much insistence, exactly one month after the first roundup, the President moved away from his house and went to stay with Miss Bonci in Via Catania, 21.

Saturday, 27 November 1943
This morning, in the presence of the President, the lawyers Roccas and Calò, and the *shamash* of the Synagogue Giorgio Sierra, all the objects deposited at the Banco di Napoli, were withdrawn. These objects consisted of holy gold and silver ornaments from the Synagogue. These objects were then delivered to the Bollinger company, a shipping agent in Piazza di Spagna, for safekeeping, until better times. I returned from the shipping agent together with Giorgio Sierra after lunch, and everything was packed up in nine very well packaged boxes.

Tuesday, 14 December 1943
The exact same officers who came exactly two months ago, returned today to see the libraries, and they were astonished that I was not there and that

the Community offices were closed. The caretaker told them that since 16 October no one had gone to the offices. As they did not have the keys, they forced entry.

Tuesday, 21 December 1943
The Germans returned to take away the books from the Library of the Rabbinic College. They waited for the truck but the company Otto and Rosoni told them that they could not come that day because they did not have petrol. They had to ask permission in order to obtain petrol.

Wednesday, 22 December 1943
First day of Chanukah
Having received petrol the truck arrived. They began to load up the books.

Sunday, 2 January 1944
They removed all the telephones, both from the Community offices and from the Rabbinic Office.

Monday, 10 January 1944
In the presence of the President, *Commendatore* Piperno, Mr. Camapgnano, the Synagogue *shamash* Giorgio Sierra, the caretaker Edmondo Contardi, and myself, silver objects that had remained in the Synagogue were hidden in the walls of the ritual bath. Two gold keys and a gold pen which had been placed with the precious objects at the Banco di Napoli were given to me for safekeeping by the President. During the entire period of persecution, I kept these items in the lining of a suitcase that I had with me, at great personal risk and danger of discovery.

Wednesday, 2 February 1944
The Chief Superintendent of Police of Rome issued a command to all the Rome police chiefs to seize all of the Jews of pure race in Rome for deportation to Germany. As soon as I heard this news from my brother in Piazza Porta Pia, I reported it to the President, who sent me to the Ghetto square to warn my fellow Jews so that they could escape. But none of them believed this warning, and many Jews were seized because they did not want to leave their homes. Some of them even went to the Campitelli police station to find out if the warning was true, where they were told to go away immediately otherwise the police would be forced to arrest them. Despite all of this, these Jews continued to stay in the Ghetto.

Wednesday, 9 February 1944
Jewish New Year of the Trees
On the order of the Prefecture, they sealed up the Community offices, the Rabbinic Office, the Synagogue, and the basement rooms, stating that everything had been expropriated and was from now on part of the property of the state.

Sunday to Monday, 20 – 21 February 1944
In the Ghetto, more Jews were seized.

Tuesday, 22 February 1944
The seals were checked by the new head of the Campitelli police station Mondelli and by marshal of the *Carabinieri* Ansuini. I was also present, and I accompanied them to each room. The marshal asked me if I was Jewish. When I answered no, he told me that in that case I could also stay because if I was Jewish, he would have been required to arrest me. We also performed the checks in the Synagogue. After they had found that everything was in order, they closed up and went away.

Thursday, 24 February 1944
The person in charge of expropriation went to take the inventory of objects in the various offices of the Community.

Thursday, Friday, Saturday, 9 – 11 March 1944
9 March – Purim, 10 March – Shushan Purim
During these several evacuees, under the orders of the Police headquarters of Rome, entered the empty Jewish shops and houses as if they were entering their own houses.

Wednesday, 21 March 1944
In the Ghetto square and surroundings, many more Jews were seized.

Tuesday, 23 May 1944
Today, as usual, I went round to Gemma,[373] to find out what was new, and I found the main entrance closed; I became alarmed. I tried to find out from passers-by why the entrance was closed, but no one was able to tell me anything. So after a lot of pointless waiting and asking, I saw the wife of the *shamash* Gino Moscati, and after some consideration I went with her to see Edmondo's sister. She told us that Edmondo had been seized by fascists, and his wife was doing everything possible to get him freed. Back at home very late, I told everything to the President, who was very distressed about this, both because of concern for Edmondo himself, and because of the fact that the caretaker of the Synagogue had been arrested. That evening the President decided that if Gemma was unable to do anything, he would do everything he could to get Edmondo freed.

Wednesday, 24 May 1944
This morning I went to the Synagogue with the President to see what Gemma had been able to achieve. Instead of Gemma I saw the caretaker coming towards me. Together we walked towards the President who was waiting nearby. The President was very happy.

---

373 Gemma Fazi, wife of the caretaker of the Synagogue, Edmondo Contardi. Both of them were Catholics.

Saturday, 3 June 1944

At last, after nine months of indescribable suffering, tonight the Germans left Rome.

Sunday, 4 June 1944

Everyone stayed up most of the night watching the advance of the Allied troops, who have finally reached Rome, and have therefore thank G-d liberated us from the tyrannical German domination, during which we suffered so.

Sylvia Guttmannova (1929–1942)

I came across Sylvia's story when someone tweeted about it. The diaries of young girls in the Holocaust are a rich source of information. It is remarkable how these very young women coped with their horrible predicament. Sylvia wrote her diary from 1941–42 and included little drawings. I am grateful to the Ghetto Fighters' House in Israel for providing me with an unedited English transcript.[374]

Sylvia was born on 7 April 1929 in Prague. She had an older sister, Zuzana, who was born on 4 August 1925. Her father was Simon (born 1888) and mother Stepanka (born 1895). Simon had at some time tried to get a US visa. Sylvie was only nine when Germany annexed the Sudetenland region and she was ten when the Nazis occupied Czechoslavakia's entire territory. The diary was given to Sylvia by her grandmother, Maherova, who wrote the following in it: 'After so many years, when you open this diary, in which you wrote down your experiences, your eyes will shine and your heart will rejoice.'

Sylvia's first entry:

My diary, Sylvia Guttmannova, September 9, 1941

The day before yesterday was wonderful. First of all, I came back from the hospital, where I spent six weeks because of scarlet fever. Also, I got this diary and three books. And thirdly, I got 100 crowns from my father to buy a bicycle. I've been saving so much in my piggy bank and also in an envelope too…Before I got sick, I used to ride on my cousin Jerzy's bike, but I can't do that now I can barely stand on my feet and for 14 days I can't see other kids. It's so stupid. I can't go to school or to Hagibor[375] and in the evening I can't sit in the kitchen, because Jerzy,

---

374 Sylvia's diary is accessible from GFH – Catalogue No: 38160, accessed 17 July 2017, http://www.infocenters.co.il/gfh/notebook_ext.asp?item=147074&site=gfh&lang=ENG&menu=1

375 Hagibor was an area of Prague where there was a Jewish Sports Hall. It was the last place Jewish youngsters could meet when they were no longer allowed to go to school, use playgrounds and parks, or public transport. In 1944 it was turned into a labour camp where mica was processed.

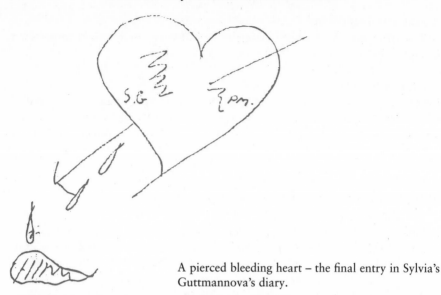

A pierced bleeding heart – the final entry in Sylvia's Guttmannova's diary.

Petr and Edita are there. We lived in a rented apartment with Uncle Aula, of whom I used to be really scared. I like it here, because the entire family is at home together. One year ago I went to school with two other girls and four boys. I was so afraid of the final exams, but I got good grades. I passed the tests at the Jewish school, where I also caught the scarlet fever. In the *Na Bulovce* hospital I lay in a room with three girls, all of whom I already knew. Two them were in religious classes with me and the other one took an exam with me. It is raining, so I can't go outside. Grandma's idea to buy me a diary was brilliant, especially one that locks. My sister is keeping a diary, but in a notebook which she locks in a box. Petr recently opened the box using the gramophone key. If he's that nosy, I should be more careful. I have to end now. I'll add more text time.

September 16 – today is exactly one week since I last wrote in my diary. I keep postponing it – either I don't have time or I don't know what to write...

Actually, we meet every Monday with the girls that were in the hospital with me, but today I couldn't go. Instead I could go with my mother to Vinohrady [a district of Prague]. In front of our house we ran into Ms. Kronbergrova, my teacher, who smiled at me fondly. She said I was quite pale. Next week I'll be back in school. I look forward to it, especially since Vera A., whom I met today, told me that many nice girls would go with me. Gretka, the one who was lying next to me at the hospital, is already going happily to Hagibor. I'm very jealous of her, because I can't go there until my punishment is over. I very much look forward to it, although I don't know if Jirka hasn't forgotten me in the meantime. At the hospital I got a letter from Honza Liban. One year ago I would've jumped for joy, but now it doesn't matter anymore. Eva and Greta are both seeing someone. Only I'm not. We are expected to be marked as Jews soon. So I'm already curious.

October 2 – This week I was sick again. I'm healthy now, and tomorrow I'm going back to school. Before my illness I was at school twice and I got two bad behaviour remarks in the notebook. I was sent outside, to stand behind the door. Father signed it peacefully. I've been given markings for a long time, and so it's not so bad. Before I fell ill, I used to go to Hagibor every day, and Edita (she's my friends, who goes to school with me, not my cousin Edita) told me that Jirka asked about me several times and then he started going out with her, while I was sick again (lie!). She didn't want to take a walk with him, so he was offended and stopped talking to her. Before that I cried a lot, but now it doesn't matter anymore, because I'm crazy about – should I write this? Petr Herzog, Peter Mahrer's friend, but it's hopeless, because he already has a girlfriend. But I don't mind. Just as long as I can talk to him when he's with Piti. I think I have a crush on Petr's other friend, Karel Knina. He asked me how old I was. Petr told me that he was probably offended, because I didn't say hello. I don't care about that either. I want Petr. I was at the hairdresser's today and now I have curls. Everyone says it's pretty. Only Edita said it was silly. I have to go to bed. School is calling!

November 4 – Since my last entry, many things changed [deletion] – we now carry signs that we're Jewish – Yellowish stars. Many people are now going to Poland, and we will eventually go as well. I don't even remember being at the hospital anymore. Yesterday I was there visiting a teacher who had a caecum [pouch connecting large and small intestines] operation. Our class has now joined another one, to which Edita Morgensternova is also going. Today we studied natural science. Helga and I have books, so we don't need to write it down. We chatted, and the teacher sent me home with a stupid note in my copybook... Now I have a class, but I don't know anything, I'll use the transports to Poland as an excuse.

November 17 – I'm writing in my diary again. I'm visiting the Mahrers' room again, because ours is cold and I have a bit of a temperature. Jerzy is here and he's nagging me to write something about him. So I'm writing about him, that he's stupid...Yesterday I walked alone because Edita was at school. I just walked round the city. Walked around the city. I walked into a shop or two and tried stuff on. When I came back home it was after Jewish shopping hours. On Melantrich, old ladies sell lemons that are usually hard to come by. (And now I'll write with less pathos or theatrics or whatever it's called). Well, the old ladies offered lemons to the passers-by. I saw a bearded Jew who stopped a few steps before the lady selling the lemons. He stood there for a few minutes and looked at her. Then he suddenly moved closer to her, but immediately changed his mind, looked at his watch and left with a sad look on his face, so I started crying, I thought that maybe he has a sick child at home who can't live without lemons, and now he can't buy the lemons. When I came home I calmed down a bit, but if someone would dare say something bad to me, I would immediately burst into tears again …

December 12 or 13, 1941 (don't know for sure) It's been a while since I last wrote in my diary. I'm so lazy and forgetful. Much has changed in the meantime. The transports to Poland keep going, actually now they are to Terezín. Zusa's boyfriend left and even before that she and Bedia were always crying in her apartment, but now it's okay. Tomorrow Edita Mahrer will go. Her mother and father, grandma (who gave me this diary) and grandpa and also Edita Morgensternova. I'm completely shocked. Meanwhile, while I wasn't keeping my diary, I and Edita Mahrerova fooled around.

Monday January 23, 1942 – it's been a long time since I last wrote (a very long time). Just one thing worth writing about happened. But I won't write about it now…

April 13, 1942

Nothing new. School started. It's disgusting. There's some test tomorrow. I don't care about it all. I'll flunk, well – crap and nothing will happen, transports are leaving again. This thing is completely hopeless. I'm terribly in love with Petr, and at the same time jealous of Zuza and Lia. That Petr likes Lia – I knew that long ago, but today Zuza told me it was mutual. I'm so unlucky. Zuza started liking Jirka again…When Lia is here, he only pays attention to her. If she's not here, he moves to Zuza and dances with her. Similarly, if none of them is here, only then does he notice that I'm there. But hardly. Mom recently complimented me. I don't remember what for, but Petr said: 'You did that very well' and hugged me (sarcastically of course). He tut-tutted and sent a kiss near me, as if missing me. I blushed and started hitting him – it was very unpleasant. Today I was with Lia at the seamstress on Blererdi Street, and she wasn't there. I'm very upset, and nothing cheers me up. I'd like to go out with a guy. I was hoping it will happen in Hagibor, except the girls from the class come here, and they're a thousand times prettier than me. I disappear. 'So Sylvia, don't fool around, alright?' I'd like to stop being preoccupied with Petr, but it's not working! So, bye bye!!!

That was the last written entry but after two blank pages there a drawing of a pierced heart. Inside the heart are initials SG on the left and PM on the right (see page 316).

Sylvia was deported to Terezín on 7 May 1942 with her parents and sister. Sylvia was 13 and Zuzana was 16. On 13 June they were sent to Sobibor where they were murdered.

The diary was donated to GFH in January 2017 by Zuzana Helinsky from Sweden. Her mother, Eva Benesova was born on 13 March 1925 and was a classmate of Sylvia's sister at the Krasnohorska school. Anat Bratman-Elhalel, who is in charge of the GFH's archive defined the diary's impact: 'It mostly demonstrates how the girl tries to maintain the old order, to keep up with her routine social life on the backdrop of the difficult events taking place around her, which barely infiltrate the world she is describing.'[376]

Sylvia's diary is remarkable for many things. A very young girl wrote about the privations of life after the Nazis, her ill-health, her friends, school, her romances both real and imaginary and even the old man looking at the lemons; she wrote about them all with the same matter-of-fact approach. One and a half million children were murdered by the Nazis in the Holocaust.

Rachel Liebeschuetz (1894–1993)

I came across Professor Wolfgang Liebeschuetz when I read an article he had written about life at my old school, Sutton High School (SHS), during the war. His late sister Lizzie had died and so her chums had invited him to make a contribution in her name to the booklet they were creating about their wartime experiences at the school. In his piece her referred to his mother's memoir. I tracked him down and asked about his mother, Dr Rachel Liebeschuetz, and the memoir she had written of the years 1932–38 when they lived in Hamburg. He kindly sent me a copy in February 2017 and the following is based on that memoir. I think the insights she gives on Hitler's rise to power and their acquaintances' responses are of particular interest.

In the memoir Wolfgang wrote for SHS he explained that in 1938 he was attending a small school in Dockenhuden, where they lived, run by Fräulein Arndt in two rooms of their grandmother's house. Jewish children were no longer allowed to attend the ordinary schools. Also at the school was Gloria Mangold, who lives very close to me in London, and went to SHS. Her brother Tom Mangold became a famous reporter for BBC television. One of Wolf's cousins, Annelies, also attended SHS. Wolf and his sisters left Germany on 13 December and all the other children got out of Germany. Fräulein Arndt was deported and murdered and the parents of one of the boys committed suicide. As they crossed the German border their passports marked with a red 'J' were examined by an official. He explained to the compartment at large 'these are Jewish children.'[377]

The 1980 memoir opens with a description of the difference in attitude to Jews between the lower and upper classes. Workers were normally social democrats who opposed antisemitism and had many Jewish leaders, but outside politics the Jews and Gentiles did not mix – Jews were regarded as strangers and not workmates. The opposite was the case amongst the upper classes, there were friendships. There was an opinion that Jewish influence

---

376 Ahiya Raved, *We'll be labelled as Jews soon, and I'm quite curious about it,* Ynetnews.com Magazine 24 April 2017, Accessed 17 July 2017, https://www. ynetnews.com/articles/0,7340,L–4953028,00.htm

377 Professor Wolfgang Liebeschuetz, *How We Came to England,* unpublished anthology of wartime memories of SHS, written around 2000. Kindly lent to me in 2016 by Gloria Randall née Mangold.

should be resisted. However Rachel felt that particularly in Hamburg, where they lived, there was considerable tolerance.

When the First World War started it was assumed that differences would disappear in the face of the common enemy but Jews and Gentiles had different experiences. 'It was well known that in some units of the army Jewish soldiers could have a bad time, that under some conditions they might have more to fear from their comrades than from the enemy.[378] Many Jews nevertheless did volunteer.

After the war, the returning defeated soldiers were resentful of those who had stayed at home and achieved success at work, whilst the soldiers still had to establish themselves – this applied to all faiths – but envy of the outsiders was greater. This was aggravated by the role played by Jewish leaders in the revolutions, first in Russia, then in Austria, Hungary and Germany.

In Germany when democracy was re-established the right-wing re-organized itself under the banner of antisemitism, because they knew from the 1880s that only this ideology would bring the working classes to join the conservatives who had created the *Deutschnationale Volkspartei* (National German People's Party). Rachel refers to the influence of Adolf Stöcker 1835–1909.

They wanted the pre-war situation with a fiercer racist rather than religious anti-Jewish leaning. There was also a development of smaller parties calling themselves '*voelkisch*'.

Rachel wrote she first heard of Hitler in 1922. She felt that the hostility to Jews was strengthened by the high inflation in 1923 and when Hitler and Ludendorff staged their Munich rebellion unsuccessfully. After he was released from prison in 1928 his appeal increased.

It was caused by the economic recession, unemployment, despair at the exorbitant reparation payments to the Allies, at the continuing occupation of the Rhineland, where the presence of black soldiers was bitterly resented. In Hamburg Hitler's following came mainly from the lower middle class. Still it was a complete surprise when his party won 130 seats at the parliamentary election of 1930. From this moment his participation in the government of the 'Reich' became a possibility and a menace.[379]

In January 1931, when her son Wolfgang was four she was disturbed to see a large Nazi demonstration partly because of 'all the overwhelming numbers of demonstrators, but even more the applause given by solid, middle class onlookers to what was generally considered as a movement of the

---

378 Dr. Rachel Liebeschuetz, *My Memories of the Times When Hitler was Dictator of Germany,* Unpublished memoir 1980, I am grateful to Professor Wolfgang Liebeschuetz for send me a bound copy in January 2017. P.1
379 P.3

uneducated, the violent and the dangerous elements in the country, and this was happening not in Munich or Thuringia but in our Hamburg'.[380]

A holiday in Mussolini's Italy in 1931 made them aware of the differences in the fascism in the two countries – partly because women did not seem involved in Italy and the influence of the Church was so great.

Hans was a lecturer in Medieval Literature at Hamburg University and also taught Latin and *Kulturkunde* (Literature, History and Religious Studies combined) at an experimental school in Hamburg. Rachel was a lecturer in Physiology but she had two boys aged four and two and was expecting a third so she was limited to discussing nutrition with girls studying Domestic Science.

Hans had a wide circle of friends. He belonged to lots of clubs, which was common in Hamburg – some of which included wives. He was also keep to keep in contact with the Jewish community. Rachel too had a wide circle of friends, two from her time at Eppendorf Hospital. A close friend was Elisabeth Marcks née Tietgens whom she met at grammar school. Her husband Erich was one of the men responsible for ending the Weimar Republic and he was later well known as one of Hitler's generals. He went to Freiburg University and Rachel's brother Hubert met him and told her that Marcks and Heidegger were 'the shining lights' of the course. After two years, he had a nervous breakdown and was advised to undertake a year of military service before he went back to his studies. After a year, he decided to make his career with the military. His brother was killed early on in the 1914–18 war and Erich too was severely wounded in the face. After recovering he was quickly promoted and before the end of the war he was seconded as a lieutenant on the Supreme Commander's staff.[381]

In 1931 he stated that Germany's position was better than all the other European countries because the Communists and National Socialists neutralized each other. Later, in 1932 Rachel was shocked to find their contacts and friends were supporting Hitler. Even her old school friend Erna Axien told her: 'Hitler is horrible, but he will lift Germany up again.'

During the winter of 1931/32 the country was preparing for the presidential election in March 1932. Everyone right of the Democrats, including Chancellor Brüning, was secretly negotiating with the Nazis. They all thought they would tame Hitler by letting him participate in government:

> ...there was no doubt that a deterioration in the position of the Jews would be part of any agreement. What the Nazis had in store for us was partly revealed in a circular which Heinrich Landhal of the Democrats in Hamburg had sent to all members of the Jewish community. Murder was not mentioned. Jews were going to be deprived of their positions and their money; they would be excluded from all occupations except for hard manual labour, such as draining of marsh land.[382]

---

380 P.4
381 P.10
382 P.13

The Jewish community felt more should be done to counter the Nazi propaganda. Her brother Hubert and his wife Ilse produced their own leaflet, which Rachel thought was well written and they sent it to various prominent people. Rachel, at their request, provided a list, which included Erich Marcks and Kurt Woermann. However she did not know that the former was busy working for a coalition with Hitler and the latter was already a fully-fledged Nazi.

She described the line-up for the election as paradoxical. Hindenburg, originally the candidate of the Right was now supported by the Left – from the Social Democrats to the Left of Centre party. Only the Communists had a candidate of their own. The Right had abandoned their hero Hindenburg but were divided. The Nazis and the followers of Hugenberg – 'The Harzburger Front' – wanted Hitler to be president. The conservatives who thought Hitler too radical wanted Stahlhelm, who was the vice-chairman of the war veterans' society.

> The election campaign was fought with passion, with noisy demonstrations, singing, street fights and hanging out of flags. In residential areas the overwhelming majority of flags were swastikas; in the working-class streets the houses were almost covered with red floats and flags with hammer and sickle. The result of the first poll was inconclusive: Hindenburg's majority was not absolute. In the second poll on April 10 he was re-elected and Hitler, who had now stood against him alone, was defeated. It was a success of the Chancellor Brüning, who had vigorously campaigned for his chief. However, in this as well as in the following local elections, the Nazi vote was larger than ever. It was the time of the world-wide recession. Yet we had a glorious spring. In these days I wrote into my diary: 'the cherries and peaches are in bloom and here there is an idyllic calm, while general depression and unrest prevail in the world. Shall we be able to keep this beautiful possession?' (meaning our garden).[383]

Brüning resigned on 30 May, which was a shock to them. Apparently it had been Hindenburg's intention to replace the existing cabinet by one that was exclusively conservative and possibly included Hitler. Brüning had anticipated that if this happened, he would have to go. Hindenburg's plan was supported both by the army and his son, whose influence was expanding.

Meanwhile their son Hugo had appendicitis and they were expecting the birth of another child. Hugo first fell ill on 6 June but it took 12 days before the diagnosis was confirmed. Their daughter Elizabeth was born on 13 June at her mother's house and Hugo had his operation on 18 June. The family re-united on 12 July.

Previously on 1 June her friend Elisabeth Marcks came to Hamburg for her father's birthday. As usual they spoke about politics and Elisabeth told her the background of Brüning's fall.[384]

---

383 P.14
384 P.15

General von Schleicher had been working for a long time to get Brüning out. He believed that a coalition with Hitler was unavoidable and that it ought to be achieved as soon as possible. Schleicher foresaw a financial catastrophe in the autumn. If Hitler was called into the government after the crash it would be much more difficult to contain him than now...The real ruler would not now by Herr von Papen but Schleicher, her husband's chief. He was going to avoid the financial debacle by a devaluation of the German currency by 40%...Politicians belonging to the Social Democratic party and the left wing of the Centre party would be removed from all positions of power. Regarding Hitler's personality, von Schleicher did not think much of him, nor did Erich Marcks; but they needed him. Elisabeth added that she did not like Herr von Schleicher very much either. He was abrupt, *'schnodderig'* and a friend of beautiful ladies. (*Schnodderig* means speaking with a swanking Berlin accent.)

Later, after Elizabeth had gone home, Rachel received a long type-written letter from Erich himself, replying to her criticisms – mainly an indictment of Brüning. He had apparently tried to counter the Nazi movement by 'increasingly repressive prohibitions and restrictions' and was also accused of 'servility to President Hindenburg' and other character defects. They tried to keep the letter but it was lost somehow. She believed she was not the only recipient as Erich had been appointed Press Officer for the *Reichswehr* ('Realm Defence' – German militia permitted by the Versailles Treaty, 1919–1935, replaced by the *Wehrmacht*). When Franz von Papen became Chancellor on 31 May 1932, Erich was offered the post of *Reichspressechef* – the Government PR officer, but he chose the lesser role 'to avoid any appearance of military rule'. A few months later, when von Papen was replaced by von Schleicher, Marcks became *Reichspressechef,* after all. His dismissal was to be one of Hitler's first acts as chancellor.

Initially von Papen's government had some success and in July 1932 the Lausanne Conference reduced the reparations owed by Germany and its allies. However, at home, there was still fighting in the streets between Nazis and Communists and murderous attacks on left-wing politicians. In August a parliamentary election resulted in a record number of Nazi seats and the Communists increased their share too. Rachel noticed the non-Jewish middle classes were having second thoughts about Hitler:

His behaviour in the notorious 'Beuthen murder' case, when he addressed the murderers as 'comrades', did harm to his reputation in these circles. But it was also a sign that the Führer was now strong enough to do without middle class approval. In the *Klassentag* [class reunion] the members of *Stahlhelm* [paramilitary group] were now definitely against Hitler. They were indignant at the treatment their own youth group suffered in the streets from the Nazi youth.[385]

---

385 P.17

In the summer of 1932 she was busy with the new baby but after the holidays Hans expressed the view that their children's future in Germany looked bleak and it was time for them to learn English. The tutor they engaged stayed for two years, leaving in November 1934. Rachel did not remember why she left 'But at the time I was not unhappy about a change as I had the impression that she was increasingly sympathising with the regime.'[386] Various other tutors followed.

The November elections were better than expected as the Nazis lost votes and Papen had more support.

> But it was not enough and it was too late. Hitler had already become too strong. V. Papen resigned on November 18th. Negotiations between the President and the party leaders followed. The nomination of Hitler as Papen's successor was possible. One knew that he had once demanded three days of 'free streets' for the S.A.; would this request now be granted? Hans and I were discussing how to send our children to safety. I wrote into my diary: 'Hitler ante portas' [Hitler is at the gates]. In fact the worst was averted once more: v. Schleicher was appointed Chancellor and Hitler remained in opposition.[387]

On 15 December the *Klassentag* met at their house, following 'a rather bloody encounter of Hitler youth and young Stahlhelmers' in Berlin. They were in favour of Schleicher and anti-Hitler. She noted:

> Reinhard, a prominent sportsman in the 'Stahlhelm', and the judge Adolph Freidag condemned the Nazis in terms which we could have hardly surpassed, but, alas, for the last time. In spite of the uncertainty of the future we had the same kind of comfortable family Xmas as every year. And so to New Year's Eve and 1933.

Early in 1933 there was a staff meeting at the University. Rachel went with Hans and heard Dr. Rein speak about the 'political university', which would 'select the material offered from the point of view of its relevance for the nation, in other words from a political point of view'. There was considerable opposition expressed: 'academic freedom of research and of speech was in danger.' Two weeks later Hitler was Chancellor and a few weeks after that Dr Rein was Rector Magnificus of Hamburg University.

On 30 January von Schleicher was forced to abdicate and Hitler was appointed Chancellor. He started with a coalition government in which the Nazis were in second place but 'Within five weeks we had a Dictatorship.'[388]

Early in February Hans discovered that Griphan had been a member of the 'Party' for quite a long time. Immediately Hans wrote to Walter and told

---

386 P.20

387 P.21

388 Kurt von Schleicher was a victim of Hitler's 'Night of the Long Knives'. He was murdered in his Berlin flat on 30 June 1934.

him their friendship could not continue. 'Griphan was hurt.' But he wrote to their parents to complain about Hans' 'unprovoked' action. Griphan was promoted. In 1938 after the Anschluss he became the Chief of Police in Vienna as by then he was a fierce Nazi. He and his wife joined a Germanic cult and 'were not ashamed of acquiring furniture from intimidated Austrian Jews'.

At the next meeting of the *Klassentag* on 5 March 1933 – the day of *Machtergreifung*, seizure of power, everybody was for Hitler. Hans raised questions about the Western democracies' reaction. 'The English,' said Reinhardt, 'do not object at all to Hitler; they quite agree with what he is doing.' That evening Hans wrote he would no longer attend the meetings. [389]

Rachel and her family were fortunate to get to England in time to escape their intended fate in the Holocaust. Her memoir is a fascinating description of the life in pre-war Germany. She was a well-educated women and her son described her as 'remarkable'[390] – a very successful physician. Perhaps this memoir can be published and reach the wider audience it deserves.

Helga Weiss (1929–)

I was attracted to Helga's story by her drawings of the horrors of life in Terezín. As no one was permitted to take photos, her drawings have become an important part of her testimony. Of the 15,000 Jewish children aged under 15 deported to Terezín, only around 100 returned to Prague.

Helga was born in Prague in 1929, the same year as Anne Frank. The diary she wrote was described by Nicholas Shakespeare in 2013 as 'the most moving child's eye testimony since the diary of Anne Frank'.[391]

She is now Helga Hosková-Weissová – a survivor of Terezín, Auschwitz, Freiberg and Mauthausen. It was on 4 December 1941 that they were taken to Terezín from the Prague flat where she still lives. She told Shakespeare about the hunger she experienced in Terezín. It was not a death camp but people did die of starvation there.

> Hunger drove her to hide cabbages and lettuce in her underwear, but she had to be alert in case the Germans searched her, ready to throw the food away or gulp it down. 'Once it happened to me that I was walking under a plum tree and I took a plum and shared it and some worker saw me – because we were watched by the Jews too. And after that we were

389 Pp.23–4

390 Email to author, 20 September 2017.

391 Nicholas Shakespeare, 'Helga Weiss: an interview with a Holocaust survivor', *Telegraph*, 19 February 2013, accessed 14 November, http://www.telegraph. co.uk/culture/books/9873580/Helga-Weiss-an-interview-with-a-holocaust-survivor.html

going to be included in a transport, until my father managed to stop it. For one plum, you could pay with your life.'

In the following passage she describes arriving at Auschwitz from Terezín which they left on 4 October 1944. Their father had been taken away on 1 October to build a new ghetto they were told – he was never seen again:

It's getting light out. Where are we now? We've just passed through a station. Katowice. My God, that's the Polish border. Where are they taking us? The front's in Poland now. Could it be Birkenau?...

We've been travelling for twenty-four hours. Where, only God knows. We're all starting to get nervous. People were saying all sorts; listen to them and the front must be far behind us, and yet we've been travelling across Poland for half a day now and there's no sign of it. The train has started to slow. Could we finally be there? I don't want to believe it – I'd started to think this trip would never end. We're getting close, definitely – you can see buildings over there. And so many of them – it's a huge camp. I can see people, but what are they wearing? It looks like pyjamas, and they've all got the same ones.

My God, those are prisoners' clothes! Where have they taken us?! This is a concentration camp! There are some men working over there, stacking boards. Why is that man beating them so hard? It must hurt horribly, he took a cudgel to them. How can he be so cruel? He isn't even a German – he's also in a striped jumper, but he's got a band on his arm.

I must have been wrong; we can't be stopping here. Why would they take us to a concentration camp? It's not as if we've done anything. It's horrible how they treat people here. I can't watch; it makes me ill. He's walloped another one, an old man. What a stinker, he's barely twenty. Shame on him; that man could be his father and to treat him that way. He kicked him again till the old man staggered.

So that's what a concentration camp looks like; I could never imagine it. People have been living this way for several years. And we complained about Terezín. That was an absolute paradise compared to this.

What's this? The train has stopped. A whole group of striped people is running towards us. Is there anyone among them from Terezín? Maybe they've come to help with our baggage. Perhaps Dad's among them. But no, they've probably just come to see what sort of train this is. We're not getting off here surely? Or – why didn't it occur to me earlier? – this is Auschwitz, of course. Birkenau is nearby, maybe the trains don't go there, so we'll have to walk that bit. Definitely, that's the way it is. This is Auschwitz, the concentration camp.

The carriage next to us is already alighting. Why so much noise over there? They're banging on our door. I suppose it's our turn now. Why are there so many SS men outside? Are they all here to guard us? Where would we run to? It would be pointless anyway. We're in it; there's no helping us.

'Everyone out! Leave your luggage where it is! *Alle heraus schneller!!!*' Leave everything here, hand luggage too? Why are they shouting so much, what's with the spiteful smiles? They're grabbing everyone by the wrist; what are they looking for, watches? If only they wouldn't yell so much, and what do the grimaces and comments mean? They're treating us as if we belong in that concentration camp. One woman just got a slap for trying to take a loaf of bread with her. Is this Birkenau?

Why is my throat so scratchy? I don't want them to know how I feel. Stupid eyes – why are they smarting? I mustn't cry! For all the world, not now!! *'Alles da lassen!'* – 'Leave everything as is!!' – *'Schneller, heraus!!!'*

They sort us into two groups. One – older women and mothers with young children – goes to the left; the other goes to the right. 'Sick people shouldn't say anything,' hushed voices repeat; 'you're all healthy,' one of the ones in prisoner's clothes whispers in Czech just behind me. A Czech, then. The queues in front of us move; soon it will be our turn. As long as they leave me and Mum together. Surely they can't separate us if I say we belong together. Or will it be better not to say we're together? Probably; maybe they deliberately wouldn't let us stay together if they knew how much it mattered to us.

They're even taking mothers away from their children. I know that girl there; she's going to the right and her mum's going left. But the mum's quite old; she's got grey hair. My mum still looks young. But… maybe I look too much like a child? Maybe they'll ask me how old I am. Should I tell the truth? Fifteen; no, that's too little – they'd send me left and separate me from Mum. I'd better say I'm older, maybe eighteen. Do I look it? Sure, maybe they'll believe me.

The queue is getting shorter; the group of five in front of has gone. Oh Lord, I pray to you, leave me and Mum together. Don't let them send us each a different way.

Two more people and it's our turn. For God's sake, what if he asks me what year I was born? Quickly: 1929 and I'm fifteen, so if I'm eighteen… 29, 28, 27, that makes 1926. Mum is standing in front of the SS man, he's sent her to the right. Lord, let us stay together! *'Rechts!'* the SS snarled at me and pointed the way with his finger. Praise be, we're both on the same side. Thank you, God, a thousand thanks for making it work out.

First they led us to the baths, where they took from us everything we still had. Quite literally there wasn't even a hair left. I've sort of got used to the shaven heads, but the first impression was horrid. I didn't even recognize my own mother till I heard her voice. But so what, hair will grow back, it's not such a tragedy, as long as we survive. I don't hold out much hope.[392]

---

392 Diary pp.118–121

Her pessimism was misplaced as she did survive. She and her mother were only in Auschwitz for 10 days and her number 54391 was not tattooed. They were moved to Freiburg with 500 women where they worked in an aeroplane factory, later they were in Mauthausen. On 5 May 1945 she recalled 'Up until then, we were watched from all sides and corners. But on that morning they ran away, threw off their uniforms, dressed in civilian clothes and ran.'

She and her mother returned to Prague and eventually got their apartment back. In July 1945 her Uncle Josef turned up with Helga's drawings of Terezín and two yellow notebooks of her diaries. 'Entrusted with them on the eve of her transportation to Auschwitz, he had bricked the whole lot into a wall in his barracks at Terezín.' Her father did not return.

With her diaries returned, after reading the entries, she continued writing from where she had left off. 'I needed to get it out of me. It was still inside me. That's why I wrote it in the present…It is still present.' As is her father: 'I am still in touch with him. In many situations, I ask him what he would say, what he would do, and I remember his words, everything he taught.' At the end of the interview she smiled at Shakespeare: 'At this moment, I am happy. Isn't it a wonder, after all, to have been granted to a few of us the chance of giving birth? And our children are now older than our parents were, and I'm a great-grandmother. [393]

She told Neil Bermel on 1 December 2011, that she started to write her diary aged twelve. She said she was quite politically aware because her parents had a lot of political debates in their flat and she felt she understood what was happening.

> I was writing only for myself, and I don't think that I had any special plans beyond that. Well maybe I did, maybe I didn't; I don't know. But I drew as well. I drew for myself, although maybe I was also thinking – just a little bit …about the fact that this needed to be recorded.
>
> In Terezín loads of children kept diaries; and not only children, adults as well, because people needed to come to terms with the situation and so they started to write. They wrote poems as well – people who had never done so before and wanted to take part in the cultural life [of the camp]. So there a number of these diaries around.[394]

When asked why someone should read yet another Holocaust diary, she replied: 'Mostly because it's truthful. I've put my own sentiments into it as well, but those sentiments themselves are emotional, moving and most of all truthful. And maybe because it's narrated in that half-childish way, it's accessible and expressive, and I think it will help people to understand those times.'[395]

---

393 *Telegraph*
394 P.187
395 P.205

Artists and Musicians

Tova Berlinski/Gusta Wolff (1915–)

I had been writing about terminating Jewish pregnancies as a result of Nazi policies when I saw a headline in the New York Times: *'"Born in Auschwitz", Israeli Artist, 102'.[396] I was curious and reading further was rather crestfallen to find the NYT had been somewhat mischievous with its headline.*

Tova was born into a Hasidic family in 1915. She was the eldest of six children born to Samuel and Gizela Wolf in the Polish town of Oświęcim. She recalled that her parents had good relations with their Polish Christian neighbours. The town's population of 12,000 was half-Jewish. Although her father had a furniture shop, he was not a good businessman and accordingly as a young woman she spent 1933–1936 in Paris. She lived with her uncle and his family because her parents could not afford to pay for her education. When she returned her parents were in Krakow and they then moved to Sosnovicz. However, the economy was not good there and there was strong anti-semitism. She met her husband, Eliyahu Berlinski (Elijah Berlin), in the Betar Youth Movement in Sosnovicz and in 1938 they emigrated to Palestine. They had no children.

In 2008 she was interviewed by *The Jerusalem Post* when she held a joint exhibition with one of her pupils, Rina Peled. She recalled

> …leaving behind her hometown of Oświęcim locked in her memory as a small garden village splashed with colourful flowers and friendly relations between Jewish and Christian and German and Polish neighbors. Unlike most of the local survivors, Berlinski never saw the Auschwitz camp going up a kilometre away from the town or her neighbors being transported there. She never encountered the Nazi guards, and never saw or smelled the acrid smoke spilling across the sky. Leaving Poland before the war not only saved her life, she says, but has

---

396 Isabel Kershner, 'Born in Auschwitz, Israeli Artist, 102, Harnesses the Dark and the Light', 14 October 2017, accessed 14 November 2017, https://www.nytimes.com/2017/10/14/world/middleeast/israel-tova-berlinski-auschwitz.html

largely defined who she is as an artist, captivated by disparate images of beauty and pain.

Flowers are what she remembers of her hometown, which would later become a concentration camp, where her parents and four of her siblings were killed. History and death are entwined in her memory with images of color and growth. She is struggling to make sense of it. 'The flowers are angry.'

After seven visits to Poland since 1984, what haunts her is that there are no graves for the loved ones she left behind, and nowhere for her to leave memorial flowers. 'The colors express my pain; my rage,' she says. In the 1990s, Berlinski spent several years painting flowers as memorials and commentary, including her black period of solitary flowers, scratched aggressively in black and gray pencil and chalk on paper, one of which was donated in 2006 to the museum at Auschwitz.[397]

In 1995 she had a solo exhibition at the Israel Museum in Jerusalem called 'Black Flowers' – a peak in her long career. It was only later in her painting career that she tackled family portraits:

A painting of the artist's father shows him looking quiet, while part of his face fades into a geometric pattern. The portrait of her middle brother is further abstracted, with the face fading in and out of geometric fields and patterns. Her mother, she says, was the hardest and most emotional to paint. A young and petite, but stylish and independent-looking woman in a dress stares elusively forward, while she fades in and out of focus, as if trying to escape a desert mirage.

Even though she was 2,400 miles from Auschwitz when she was in Jerusalem, she is motivated by what happened.

The burden of keeping one's family legacy alive, one that was wiped out in the Holocaust, while living in Jerusalem, a city that is the center of the world for so many people, in culture, religion and anguish, is a tall order. For artist Tova Berlinski, it is a mandate.[398]
...'Recently I began to paint portraits, but even when I painted in my abstract periods there were portraits hidden in my work. I painted without faces. All of my abstract work has figures and tells stories. My paintings are my biography.'

Speaking about her family, she told Issacson that her parents were 'Hasidic, yet Bohemian'. Both had beautiful voices. 'My mother decorated gothic

397 Lauren Gelfond Feldinger, 'The 'grande dame' of Jerusalem', *Jerusalem Post*, 29 May 2008, accessed 15 October 2017, http://www.jpost.com/Arts-and-Culture/Arts/The-grande-dame-of-Jerusalem

398 Judy Issacson, 'Berlinski', @*The Source*, Issue 29, 22 February 2006, accessed 15 November 2017, http://thesourceisrael.com/issue29/portrait_article/

letters, while my sister was family artist. I always thought that I'd go into the theater.'

According to Yad Vashem, the Jews of Oświęcim were rounded up in 1941, their property having already been confiscated. They were deported to ghettos and then sent to death camps. Only one sibling of Tova's survived. She went to Germany and then to Israel. She was the person who told Tova of the family's fate. Tova said 'I felt great pain. That pain I feel to this day'.[399]

There is considerable irony in the fact that Jews used to refer to Oświęcim as *Oshpitzin*. The word comes from the Aramaic word for guest, *ushpizin*. This is the name of a traditional *Sukkot* prayer that welcomes guests. Never have guests been made less welcome anywhere. The first Jews arrived in the mid-16th century and a Polish nobleman gave them land for a synagogue and a cemetery. Seventy-seven Jews returned home after the war but most had left in the 1960s as life was difficult under the Communists. Szymon Kluger, who died in 2000, was the last Jew of Oświęcim.[400]

Issacson concluded:

Tova Berlinski's paintings tell her life story. They serve to illustrate for both the painter and the viewer the images and personalities of her childhood. The complicated emotions of seeing family members in both a subjective and objective manner come into play with Berlinski's images.

The memories of her complex relationships with both her parents and her siblings are expressed in the portraits she paints. The viewer is given the rare opportunity to meet and become acquainted with a part of a family that was destroyed in the Holocaust.

Her home in Jerusalem holds many interesting items. One is a framed letter in Polish. It was signed by the Mayor of Oświęcim, congratulating her on reaching the age of 100. He wrote 'On this extraordinary day, I extend to you greetings from the heart, from the city of your birth, Oświęcim.'

Tova is a unique woman. She had happy memories of the town where she grew up. The Nazis transformed that pretty town of Oświęcim into the nightmare that was Auschwitz and murdered her family there, whilst she was far away.

Alice Herz-Sommer (1903–2014)

In September 2008 I gave a talk in Didsbury, Manchester and they gave me a book about Alice as a thank you. In 2014 I read the obituary in The Times *when Alice died aged 110, then the oldest Holocaust survivor. In August*

399 *NYT* 14 Oct. 2017
400 Anna Goldenberg, 'When Auschwitz Was a Jewish Town', in *Forward*, 21 May 2014, accessed 15 November 2017, http://forward.com/culture/198520/when-auschwitz-was-a-jewish-town/

2017 Yisrael Kristal died aged 113, both the oldest Holocaust survivor and the oldest man in the world.

Alice Herz-Sommer was born in Prague in 1903 with a twin sister Marianne (Mizzi). She had three older siblings. She was a child prodigy and had a successful career as a pianist. Mizzi left Prague on the last train out in 1939 and went to Palestine, Alice saw Hitler in Wenceslas Square on 16 March 1939 when the Germans had invaded. Her 72-year-old mother was deported in 1942, never to return. Her husband Leopold was roped into the *Judenrät* and had to draw up the lists for the 'transports'. In July 1943 the list included him, Alice and their baby son. 'Even before they were out of the door their neighbours and former friends were taking their pictures, carpets and furniture.'

She played in over a hundred concerts in Theresienstadt and three times a year they played for the Red Cross – 'It was propaganda.' She recalled being summoned in Terezín by a Nazi officer and fearing the worst, he said: 'I can hear your concert from the window. I come from a musical family and understand music. I thank you from the bottom of my heart.' Her son had a part in *Brundibár* – an opera for children by Hans Krása. After the liberation a concert she gave on Czech radio was heard in Jerusalem and that was how Mizzi knew she was still alive; but only Alice and her son had returned. Leopold was sent to Dachau where he died of typhus in 1944. Anti-Semitism was still around in Prague and in 1949 she joined her relatives in Israel. After many happy years, she became isolated and went to London in 1986 to be near her son.[401]

In 2007 she wrote the foreword to a biography about her:

Life gave me the talent to play the piano and to inspire happiness in people through music; and I am just as grateful that it gave me a love of music. Music makes us humans rich. It is the revelation of the divine. It takes us to paradise.

Since my childhood music has been my real home. It provided me with security when I had to confront my first inner torments and through it I found support, when death robbed me of my loved ones. Its meditative power provided me with the determination to cope first with the fascist and then the communist dictatorships that declared me and others like me subhuman.

When, in the early summer of 1942, my seventy-two-year-old mother was issued with a deportation order and I had to go to the assembly point and say goodbye to her for the last time, I was out of my mind. How was it possible to tear an old lady away from her world with nothing more than a rucksack on her back and send her to a concentration camp? Even to this day I can clearly hear the inner voice that spoke to me: 'Practise the Chopin Études, they will save you.'

---

401 Obituary in the *Telegraph*, 24 February 2014, accessed 19 November 2017, http://www.telegraph.co.uk/news/obituaries/10657632/Alice-Herz-Sommer-obituary.html

Although Chopin's Études are among the most difficult pieces ever written for the repertoire, I began to learn them immediately...Every day for a year, I knuckled down to this seemingly insuperable task and mastered all twenty-four of them before I myself, my husband and our then six-year-old son were also deported to Theresienstadt. There I gave more than a hundred concerts for my fellow prisoners, and at more than twenty of them I played the Études.

Music gave heart to many of the prisoners, if only temporarily. In retrospect I am certain that it was music that strengthened my innate optimism and saved my life and that of my son. It was our food; and it protected us from hate and literally nourished our souls. There in the darkest corners of the world it removed our fears and reminded us of the beauty around us. Music supported me as I turned my back on my home town of Prague for the last time and to think of learning new languages, and I am thankful for it too, at my great age, when I spend many hours alone. It hardly matters where I am: I am not prone to loneliness. Although I no longer travel any more, through music I can see the world.

Music has been a great friend to me. Even today I receive visits almost every day. Many friends come regularly and every Saturday afternoon I receive a call from Zdenka Fantlová, who was in Theresienstadt at the same time I was. And every Sunday afternoon at around five the cellist Anita Lasker-Walfisch pays a call; she only survived Auschwitz because she played in a girls' orchestra for Josef Mengele and the SS.[402] Above all I thank music for the privilege, even today, at the age of 103, for the ability to speak to and laugh with people all over the world. That makes me happy.

A few years ago the love of music brought me into contact with Reinhard Piechocki, himself a great music-lover. He rang me from his home on the island of Rügen and asked me a question no one had asked me since my liberation from Theresienstadt: where had I found the strength and inspiration to perform Frédéric Chopin's uncommonly difficult 24 Études in the concentration camp? I told him that playing them was – albeit transitory – liberation. He visited me in London soon afterwards and it was the beginning of a wonderful friendship. We became close, we laughed together, and since then we talk almost daily on the telephone. We don't just talk about music; we talk about God, philosophy and the world.

When he suggested writing a book about my life, I immediately said no thank you...Reinhard Piechocki finally managed to convince me to agree to this book, because it was to be a book about the power of music and love, a book about a person for whom others were more important than she was to herself...

The following was written by Alice's son, Raphael, a successful cellist, who died suddenly from a heart attack whilst in a concert tour in Israel in 2001. This was written some time before.

---

402 Read about Anita Lasker-Walfisch in *Who Betrayed the Jews?* pp.214–6

The Story of a Miracle

This is a true story. I can swear to that because I lived it myself. Even in the darkest days of the twentieth century miracles occurred. In the middle of hell, my mother created a Garden of Eden for me. She built a strong wall around me out of love and gave me such security that I could not find anything extraordinary in our lives, and in retrospect I can say with good conscience that my childhood was wonderfully happy. How my mother managed it I cannot say. She says it was the obvious thing to do. For me it remains a miracle.

My mother has a gift which, I believe, is given above all to Jewish and central and eastern European women. Without any self-pity they make their own requirements secondary to those of their families. I lived under the protecting veil of my mother and so cannot describe the darker side of our lives in the concentration camp. I was a child and I understood events as they seemed to me; I naturally believed everything my mother told me. Not once did she allow me to see the humiliations and insults she had to suffer. With inner strength and inexhaustible reserves of love she concentrated on just that: me, her beloved son and the creation of a joyful and 'normal' environment around me that had little to do with the reality in which we lived. With her attentive care my mother managed to shift the terror away from my gaze and provide me with the most valuable of gifts – a happy childhood. That this was possible behind the wire of a National Socialist concentration camp must, in all truth be called a miracle.

In Theresienstadt I shared a bunk with my mother. I was so close to her that I never actually felt frightened. During the day, my mother had to work in the factory, I played in the kindergarten. I was so little aware that our lives were in any way unnatural that I also have no recollection of our concern when my father, together with 3,000 other men, was sent away and never returned.

A single trauma lodged itself like a splinter in my heart and is still there, and to this day the scar is not fully healed: my mother was forced to work. I screamed, I dropped my guard and my fever raged. My mother and I clung to one another and we went from one building to the next to find someone who was prepared to look after me. The nagging uncertainty that took hold of me on that day I shall never forget. Children's worries are abiding worries and, although I got my courage back after my mother had told me that she was only going to be transferred from the factory to the laundry, my childish trust was temporarily shaken. For all that my early childhood, which for all those close to me seemed to be horror and nightmare, seemed to me happy and utterly normal. For this I thank my mother – she performed miracles.[403]

---

403 Alice Herz-Sommer and Raphael Sommer, in *A Garden of Eden in Hell* by Müller and Piechocki (London: Macmillan, 2007) pp. ix–xiv

Zuzana Ruzickova (1927–2017)

Zuzana Ruzickova was already on my list of women to be included as I had read about her as she celebrated her 90th birthday and was featured in the press. She died on 26 September 2017 and I saw her charming face in the media again.

Her cousin Frank Vogl wrote about her on 12 April 2015, just before the 70th anniversary of the liberation of Bergen-Belsen on 15 April.[404] His cousin was there with her mother Poldi for four months. She says she survived because: 'The spirit of Bach was always with me and kept me alive.' She told *The Times* that Bach was the constant in her life.[405] She grew up in Pilsen in the 1930s in a Czech-Jewish family. She was a sickly child and aged nine she was recovering from TB when she asked for piano lessons as a reward. Her teacher realised she was a fast learning pupil and knew that Bach was better on a harpsichord. She therefore encouraged her to go to Paris to study with the world's top harpsichordist, Wanda Landowska. Hitler had other ideas. 'I had no experience of antisemitism until Hitler came, but I was so flabbergasted by being something 'different' that I immediately started to read everything about Zionism. I would argue with my father's friends – assimilation is not possible!' She and her parents were among the first to be deported to Terezín concentration camp. She was fifteen.

Zusana's father died in Terezín. She was reluctant to talk about the privations, instead she spoke of her first boyfriend Hans. 'We both wanted to study Hebrew and Latin and a very famous professor from Vienna agreed to teach us for half a bread ration each.' She did well with the professor: 'By the time I went to Auschwitz I had already read the book of Samuel and Caesar's *Gallic Wars*.'

She practised on an old piano and sang in the children's opera *Brundibár*, composed by Hans Krása before he and most of the performers were sent to Auschwitz and gassed. Then she and her mother were sent to a so-called family camp in Birkenau in December 1943. In March 1944 those who had arrived in September 1943 were gassed, exactly six months after they arrived. 'And of course we knew we would go the same way.' Instead, in July 1944 she and her mother were chosen by Dr Mengele to join 1,000 healthy women to go to Hamburg to repair damage caused by Allied bombing.

She was sustained by music. She would sing opera arias to her fellow prisoners. 'I'd tell them what the operas were about and sing and they felt it helped them.' Once when hired as slave labour for a private company, she spoke about having soup in the canteen and hearing Chopin on the radio. 'I fainted. It was so fantastic that somewhere in the world somebody was playing Chopin.'

---

404 Frank Vogl, 'The Liberation of Bergen-Belsen: A Survivor Remembers', 12 April 2015, https://www.theglobalist.com/the-liberation-of-bergen-belsen-a-survivor-remembers/ accessed 19 December 2016.

405 Neil Fisher, 'The harpsichordist who survived the Holocaust', *The Times* 18 October 2016.

She remembers writing down a small section of Bach's English Suite No. 5 in E minor on a scrap of paper when she left Terezín in a cattle truck bound for Auschwitz. 'I wanted to have a piece of Bach with me as a sort of talisman because I didn't know what was awaiting us.' What beckoned was more hardship. Her camp number at Auschwitz, 72389, which was tattooed on her arm, has faded now, but she has not forgotten it. She can also remember how 'terribly frightened' she was. Although she was only a teenager, she wishes she had been tougher. 'Seeing the gas chambers, the smoke every day. I'll never forgive myself that I always went in the evening to my mother and I wept and I said, "I want to live, I don't want to die." '[406]

Her language skills got her through the last, desperate stage when in February 1945 they were sent to Bergen-Belsen.

> If Auschwitz was hell, Bergen-Belsen was another hell – this was the lowest part of hell. Nobody wanted us to survive. The weak and ill prisoners were not supposed to survive. But we did somehow. We were housed in military barracks – maybe 500 or even 700 people in one barrack – so it was not possible to lie down. If you wanted to sleep, you had to be like sardines and lie in the lap of another person. There were already masses of dead bodies lying around. There was nobody giving us any food or drink. There were heaps and heaps of dead bodies. The Germans already probably thought the end of the war was coming, so they made pyres of those dead bodies and burned them. And if you volunteered to get the dead bodies to the pyres, you got a cup of soup. My mother was too weak at that time, but I volunteered and I sometimes got the soup for her and for myself. But then even that stopped and we were starving.[407]

She managed to hang on until the British arrived in April. 'There were about 30,000 dead when the English came and most of us were infected with the plague.' They got medical attention and she acted as an interpreter for the British Army. She was full of praise for the British and the way they organised everything.

When they got home finally, her music teacher looked at her hands – she was now eighteen years old. They were badly damaged by years of hauling bricks. 'She started to weep. Then she said, 'Well, anyway, you're back, you're wonderful with languages, so back to school and university.' Zuzana replied 'I can't live without music.'

She got hold of a piano from an ethnic German family who fled Czechoslovakia and practised twelve hours a day to make up for lost time. She went back to music school and was in a class with teenagers, 'But every three months I went up a year. It went rather quickly.' Finally in 1947, aged

406 Rebecca Jones, 'The "miraculous" life of Zuzana Ruzickova', *BBC News*,19 December 2016, accessed 19 December 2016, http://www.bbc.co.uk/news/magazine–38340648

407 Frank Vogl, 'The Liberation of Bergen-Belsen: A Survivor Remembers', 12 April 2015, https://www.theglobalist.com/the-liberation-of-bergen-belsen-a-survivor-remembers/ accessed 19 December 2016.

20, she was admitted to the Academy of Performing Arts and in the third year she opted for a course on the harpsichord – at last. Meanwhile she met Viltor Kalabis and they married in 1952.

Some people were not enthusiastic about introducing the harpsichord into her piano recitals. 'One of the leading critics in Prague said it was like using a *fiaker* [horse and carriage] when I could have a car.' She entered the ARD International Music Competition in Munich in 1956. However, there were problems when the Czech conductor, Rafael Kubelik, who was a political exile in Germany, refused to conduct the Bavarian Radio Symphony Orchestra in the final if there was a Czech artist who represented communist Czechoslovakia. 'So I gave my last ten Deutschmarks to the porter of the hall, he let me in at six in the morning and I learnt the orchestral part of the first two movements of my concerto.' She played both the solo and orchestral passages of Benda's concerto for keyboard and won first prize.

Finally, an international music career was open to her. An early event was the Bach Festival in Ansbach in Bavaria, but she wasn't comfortable with going back to Germany. 'I was afraid. I was afraid of meeting someone from the camps, from the SS.' She shuddered later when she read Rudolf Hess had attended. Yet her husband told her she had a duty to play in Germany. 'He said, 'Play Bach to make them realise that there is another Germany, that Hitler didn't destroy all the great culture.'

'The effect of the Nazi atrocities…was that musicians became afraid of big gestures or of emotionally freighted performances, particularly if the titans of German culture were involved: Bach, Beethoven, Schubert. The whole early music movement was actually trying to avoid the pathos of Beethoven, to reduce it to original small orchestras. We are still afraid of believing in something "great".'

Rusicková influenced generations of early music practitioners. She officially retired in 2006 when she was 79. This was also the year her husband died. 'Better for people to say it's a pity that she doesn't play any more than it's a pity she still plays.' She listened to the 20 CDs of Bach's Complete Keyboard Works that were re-issued for her 90th birthday in January 2017. She was the first person to record all Bach's works. She died aged 90 on 28 September 2017.

When my father was dying (in Terezín camp in 1943) my mother said to him, 'I hate all the Germans and I will get revenge for your life.' My father said, 'Don't hate. Hate is something that poisons your soul. Leave the revenge to God'. Zuzana added. 'I still feel that hating somebody is really poisoning yourself. Hate is a negative thing. You ought to avoid hate. Sometimes I really felt a little characterless for not hating the Germans as much as I maybe should. But hating is a very negative emotion.

I was very often asked whether I could forgive a German, and I said first of all he would have to ask forgiveness. And then I could consider whether I had the strength to forgive. But maybe I could forgive sometimes. But not forget, never forget.[408]

---

408 Vogl p.2

Non-Jewish Women

Margarita Ferrer – The Wedding in Auschwitz

This story was written by Iga Bunalska who is a full-time researcher at Auschwitz for the Auschwitz Study Group. It caught my eye because a wedding at Auschwitz was unlikely and as proved, this was a unique event.

The only official wedding in the history of Auschwitz took place on 18 March 1944. Margarita Ferrer and Rudolf Friemel got married in the camp.

Rudolf Friemel was born in 1907 in Vienna and he was a car mechanic. He met Margarita when he was fighting in Spain and she was the love of his life. They got married in Spain according to the law there. When he was deported to France, Margarita followed him. She gave birth to their son in 1941 in Vienna, where she lived with Rudolf's father.

Rudolf Friemel was then arrested and deported. In the beginning of 1942, he was sent to Auschwitz, where he was registered as prisoner number 25173.

The Friemels. (Courtesy Iga Bunalska, Auschwitz Study Group)

His father and Margarita were doing anything they could to make sure the Nazis would allow them to get married again as – according to the law in the Third Reich – their marriage was illegal. They sent a special letter to Heinrich Himmler who gave his permission.

Rudolf's father and brother, Margarita and her son Edi were allowed to come to Auschwitz for the wedding. Rudolf was allowed to grow his hair for the ceremony, and the camp administration gave him a suit, shirt, tie and new shoes as a wedding gift. They came from the SS warehouses.

On the day the wedding guests (the prisoners of the camp and Rudolf's family) and the couple went to the council, where they got married. The ceremony was accompanied by music from the Prisoners' Orchestra. Margarita and Rudolf were allowed to spend the wedding night together. She left the camp the following morning. Hermann Langbein, an inmate reported, 'That was the single instance of a camp prisoner getting married. On the day of the wedding he got his civilian clothes and the couple was escorted to the Auschwitz Civil Registry. After the wedding they were brought back to the camp and lodged on the upper floor of Block 24, which was the site of the brothel. The day before the regular occupants had been moved from their apartments.'[409] Photographs were taken by the camp *Erkennungdienst,* the department for taking photos of incoming prisoners.

On 27th October 1944 the prisoner resistance in the camp prepared a very special escape. Five top members of the resistance were to take part in it. One of them was Bernard Świerczyna who worked in the warehouses in the camp and he was able to go to the laundry in Bielsko very often – the laundry was washing and sorting the clothes from the camp. He thought he could hide with other prisoners in the truck filled with the dirty clothes. They bribed the SS-man who drove the truck – his name was *Rottenführer* Johann Roth. What's more, the prisoners informed the civil resistance in the camp about the planned escape. It was essential as the information about that very escape soon reached London and foreign radios all over the world.

Johann Roth turned out to be a traitor and he took the truck (with the prisoners who wanted to escape hiding in the back of it), and pulled by Block 11 in Auschwitz I. The prisoners tried to kill themselves by eating the poison they had prepared in case the escape was unsuccessful. Two of them died (Zbigniew Raynoach and Czesław Duzel), whilst three of them, Świerczyna, Piotr Piątry and an Austrian man Ernst Burger were put in the bunker of Block 11. Soon the SS arrested other prisoners, suspected to be taking part in the preparation of that escape. Their names were Ludwig Vesely and Rudolf Friemel. More prisoners were arrested as the Gestapo was investigating the case.

The five prisoners were hanged in the public execution that took place on 30th December 1944. The other prisoners had to watch the

---

409 Herman Langbein, *People in Auschwitz* (University of North Carolina Press, 2004) p.289

execution. The gallows were put in front of the camp kitchen. Just by the gallows there was a Christmas tree, decorated with some lights.

Rudolf was killed in the very last execution that took place in Auschwitz I. He was hanged in his white wedding shirt. The female prisoners embroidered roses on his shirt to make it even prettier for the wedding. The camp was liberated less than a month after.

Two weeks before he died, Rudolf sent a message to his wife:

My love, my lovely Margo, I hold you so tightly and I wish you Merry Christmas. I am forever yours. Please, keep me informed about our little stubborn boy. Write me lots about him. I kiss you both.

Margarita and Edi survived the war.

Jane Haining (1897–1944)

I was privileged to be present at Number 10 when the Prime Minister Gordon Brown recognised several Britons as British Heroes of the Holocaust in March 2010, because Bertha Bracey and Henk Huffener who featured in my first book were honoured. Jane Haining was also honoured for her courage. In 1997 she was honoured as Righteous Among the Nations, the only Scot to date.

Jane was born in 1897 in Dunscore near Dumfries in Scotland. In 1932 she was appointed Matron of the Girls' Home of the Scottish Mission in Budapest. She liked Budapest and quickly became fluent in Hungarian. She spent the next 12 years teaching and caring for mostly Jewish girls. The school was next to the Girls' Home. She was responsible for 400 children aged six to sixteen. She was loved and respected both by the children and her colleagues, who thought she was the best matron they had ever had.

In 1940, with the worsening situation in Europe, the missionaries from Scotland were ordered to go back home but Jane refused to leave because 'her' girls needed her in those days of 'darkness'. With the occupation from 19 March 1944, deportations of Jews from the regions began. Haining stood by the students with great courage but on 25 April 1944 two Gestapo came to the Mission. They searched her office and gave her 15 minutes to get her things together. She was taken to Foutca prison for questioning. Eight charges were presented including working with Jews, visiting British POWs and listening to the BBC. She was deported to Auschwitz and was prisoner No. 79467. She had to do hard labour and her last message to friends was a postcard asking for food. She ended it by writing 'There is not much to report here on the way to heaven.' She succumbed to starvation and the awful conditions in Auschwitz and probably died on 17 July 1944, aged 47.[410]

---

410 Yad Vashem, 'Jane Haining', accessed 17 November 2017, http://www.yadvashem.org/righteous/stories/haining

Jane was the half-sister of Agnes O'Brien whose daughters are Deirdre McDowell and Jane McIvor. They live in Londonderry and have spoken about their 'extraordinary' and 'inspirational' aunt. Jane was apparently betrayed by the school cook's son-in-law. Apparently she had caught him eating from the scarce supply of food intended for the pupils. A former pupil said that Jane's last words to the sobbing children were 'Don't worry, I'll be back for lunch.'

Deirdre said:

> She was such a courageous woman, very determined, considerate and kind. She followed the Christian example by looking after and caring for vulnerable children. Our family is honoured by Jane's actions. Her story is an example to us all and must continue to be told to benefit the next generation because the world should never forget the Holocaust.

Her sister Jane added:

> Jane was amazing woman and did such tremendous work at the Scottish Mission in Budapest. She lived a life of faith and was a loving person who put everyone else first. I was named after Jane Haining, so I consider her a guide and mentor in my life. If we can do anything, in any small measure that Jane did, our world would be a different and much better place.

A gold and red garnet ring that belonged to her was featured in a special Holocaust edition of the BBC's *Antiques Roadshow* where all the items belonged to victims and survivors of the Holocaust. It was broadcast for Holocaust Memorial Day 2017. The Rev. Ian Alexander of the Church of Scotland said: 'Jane Haining's story is one of heroism and personal sacrifice. She was a woman who was simultaneously ordinary and extraordinary.'[411]

Irmgard Conti Powell (1932–2017)

Frau Nanna Conti was made the Chief Midwife under the Nazis in 1933. Her second son Leonardo was born in 1900 and was a prominent Nazi leader in the health and euthanasia areas. Who Betrayed the Jews? *contains a piece about the different attitudes of the sons of two major Nazi leaders, Hans Frank and Otto von Wächter. I was naturally interested to find Frau Conti's granddaughter, Irmgard Powell, had written a memoir of growing up in a Nazi home.*

---

411 Adrian Rutherford, 'Northern Ireland sisters reveal moving story of Aunt', *Belfast Telegraph* 14 January 2017, accessed 14 January 2017, https://www. belfasttelegraph.co.uk/news/northern-ireland/northern-ireland-sisters-reveal-moving-story-of-aunt-sent-to-die-in-auschwitz-for-saving-jewish-kids-from-nazis–35367005.htm

Irmgard died on 12 November 2017 and I am writing this the day before her funeral on 17 November.

She was the daughter of Leonardo and was born in April 1932 in Berlin. They lived in an apartment on the second floor over some shops. Her father had an office in the apartment. She was looked after by a Nanny Emmi.[412] As a small girl she liked to play in the playground near their flat, which had a sandpit. She loved going there and all the local children met there. Irmgard wrote:

> There was one playmate with whom I liked to play, particularly in her home. She lived in an apartment around the corner from us, and her room had so many things that the room shared by my sister and I did not. There was a little child-size table and chairs and tea set. Her mother fixed us hot chocolate and we would have a tea party with our dolls. It was so cosy and so much fun, her mother sometimes pretended to be a 'guest' at our party. It was something my mother never did.
>
> Then one day, Mutti took me aside and told me I could no longer go there to play. I protested loudly. I must have been only four or five years old...I asked her why and she said my father would explain it to me, which he did. He told me the girl's mother was Jewish. When I told him how nice she was, he answered patiently that there were nice Jewish people, but when it came to do what was best for the German fatherland, they most often chose to think of themselves.
>
> What is a child to make of that? And so I obeyed my father. I always obeyed. I did not go to play with her anymore. I am sorry that I cannot even remember her name. In time I forgot, never saw her again, and do not know what happened to her or her family. Now, fearing for what might have been their fate, I grieve for them and for all of us.[413]

When her parents were newlyweds, they scraped their finances together and bought a tiny summer house in Mellensee, a village by a lake south of Berlin, in the late 1920s. It was primitive with no indoor plumbing but they all loved going there and spending the summer away from the city. Imgard recalled that:

> In the summer of 1944 some family silver was buried there, for fear it would get lost in the battle of Berlin. After 1945, the East German government gave the place to what was called a 'deserving citizen'. For all I know, the silver might still be there in the ground. I have never been back.[414]

---

412 Irmgard Powell, *Don't Let Them See You Cry* (Wilmington: Orange Frazier, 2008) p.17.

413 Powell pp.21–2

414 Powell p.31

The Germans were doing what the Jews had been doing some years earlier and probably for many previous centuries!

> My father gave up his private practice sometime before Hitler came to power in 1933. As head of the Public Health Department in Berlin from 1934 on, he was in charge of medical care for all participating athletes during the 1936 Berlin Olympics.

She writes of him meeting local 'Madams' of the brothels in Berlin and warning them to report to the Public Health Department if they had contact with a VD-infected customer. She also recalls running about at the Olympics to do somersaults on the metal rails that encircled where Hitler was sitting. When her mother went to get her back Hitler smiled at her. She also remembers watching Jesse Owens winning a race, to applause from the audience:

> Whereupon I asked my mother, *Der Schwartze wieder?* (The black one again?) I had not seen a black man before, but this was merely my way of pointing him out. It was not his color I found striking; it was how wonderfully he ran and jumped! He was doing something I loved to do, and he kept winning. I do not recall if there was any reply from my mother.[415]
> ...My father was appointed *Reichsgesundheitsfuehrer* (Reich Health Leader) in April of 1939 and in August of the same year was made State Secretary for Public Health in the Ministry of the Interior. We still lived in the apartment in the Landauerstrasse 9, and I do not recall much about it, other than seeing many more visitors coming to our house and hearing their impressive sounding titles. Politics and health issues had been table talk in our family for as long as I could remember, so this did not seem like anything out of the ordinary to me.[416]

She was seven when the war started and she recalled the adults talking about the atrocities in Poland against the Germans:

> The Poles attacked a German radio station on the Polish border, the infamous 'Gleiwitz incident' that began the war. In actuality, Hitler staged the incident using German criminals dressed in Polish uniforms. These men were killed and left as 'Polish casualties', proof that Germany's border had been violated. The German people, caught deep in Hitler's propaganda, accepted this event as the truth. A lifetime later, I would come to see it as the rhetoric that precedes war throughout history.

---

415 Powell pp.32–3
416 Powell p.34

She talks about the rationing and how there was never enough meat. She also referred to a car accident her father had, which fractured both sides of her father's jaw. When she went through her mother's papers in 1998 she found some papers which reminded her of the accident:

> ...I remembered how strange all that seemed to me as a child. There had been a lot of talk going on at home that I did not understand. But now I see that my mother suspected at the time that the car crash might not have been an accident. I have no idea if there was ever an inquest or even if a visit by Rudolf Hess – a family friend – had anything to do with my mother's fear for my father's safety.[417]

She saw less of her father and they went away without him. On one occasion 'on the way back to Berlin I caught head lice from the upholstered cushions in our first class compartment'. Her mother treated it with kerosene-smelling stuff.

> One day there was a knock on the door. I opened it with the evil-smelling towel on my head, facing my teacher who had come to the house to see how I was doing. My mother became red in the face and asked her to come in. That's when I found out that she had made up some phony excuse for my absence from school, and now she had to beg the teacher not to let it be known that the daughter of the Reichshealth Minister had head lice.[418]

In 1942 they moved from the apartment of her early childhood into a large house in Berlin-Grunewald. One day she saw a prisoner working in the garden:

> He wore the black and white striped clothing that I had seen in newspaper pictures on concentration camp inmates but I do not know if he came from a KZ or a regular jail. I kept my distance. He ate lunch in the kitchen with Emmi and I assumed that he could not be a Jewish inmate since my parents would not have allowed him to be in the house...
>
> It was not until 1998, when I cleaned out my mother's apartment and took a photo out of its frame, that I discovered this was not our house. My parents had rented it from the city of Berlin. It had been previously owned by a Jewish banker. This came as a shock to me and once again as a reminder: in my childhood many things were not what they seemed to be.
>
> We lived only three years in this house and it horrifies me to think there could have been Jewish children before me and what might have befallen them. Sometimes, when in church here in America, I look at my

---

417 Powell p.37–8
418 Powell p.41

two young grandsons and I am unable to separate my love and joy from the horror experienced by parents whose children were jeopardized.[419]

Sometime in early 1943, her father asked her 'What would you think if we left Berlin and moved to Munich and I would work there as a family doctor again?' Irmgard was not impressed with this idea and protested loudly. Nothing more was said. Years later her mother told her that around that time her father had written to Hitler, asking to be released from his post so he could return to private life. She claimed the letter was held up by Martin Bormann who was Hitler's secretary and saw all the Führer's post. He only passed it on after the defeat at Stalingrad. By then Hitler had declared *totaler Krieg* (total war) and his response was that he would gladly release him once the war was won but 'until then every German was duty bound to remain in the Fatherland's service'.[420]

His secretary Fraulein M., told Irmgard at her mother's funeral in March 2002 that she remembered typing the letter on 'the special large font typewriter that had to be used for any correspondence that went to the Führer's headquarters'. She herself was interrogated several times and was held prisoner for over three years without being accused of anything and then released.

The last time they were all together was Christmas 1944 when she was twelve. After the bombing of Dresden on 13 February 1945, she was sent to a children's home in Bavaria the following month. The last time she saw her father was at the railway station. After Germany surrendered on 9 May 1945 the home was told that it would be dangerous if the Americans found someone like her there and so she was moved to another home. She had to sign the official change of residence form (*Abmeldeschein*). She was given an old bicycle and accompanied by a 16-year-old girl who was 'simple-minded' set off for Munich.[421]

Food shortages were serious but she refers to food coupons supplying 'meagre rations of not much more than 1000 calories a day', which sounds positively luxurious compared with the Jews' rations in the Warsaw Ghetto.[422]

They heard on 14 January 1946 that her fsther had committed suicide on 6 October 1945. The family struggled to get information about the circumstances of the suicide. Only in 1998 did Irmgard see the translation of his suicide note which said 'he was going out of this life because he had lied under oath about the typhus experiments conducted on inmates'. She wrote: 'Even then, as a grown woman, I did not wish to acknowledge anything but his love for me.'[423]

In 1959 she married American soldier Mark Powell and in 1960 they went to the US.

---

419 Powell pp.47–48

420 Powell p.53

421 Powell p.71

422 Powell p.75

423 Powell p.93

She had a son and a daughter and is survived by four grandchildren and a great-grandchild. Writing her memoir was a very important event in her life. Her obituary mentions that she was a Tupperware saleswoman – such a banal fact about such an extraordinary family. Later she became an international telephone operator.[424]

In the Epilogue to her book written in 2008, she wrote:

Like many children of prominent Nazis, I, too, grew into adulthood after 1945, harboring feelings of disbelief, guilt, and shame over the horrible things that had taken place during Hitler's regime. Although I told myself that I was innocent of the crimes committed by my parents' generation, that truth did not help me overcome these feelings.

I was one of those idealistic children who could not imagine anything evil going on in a government in which my father participated and held a position of responsibility. Other officials maybe, but not him...

As I started my new life in the United States of America, time went by and friends began asking me many serious questions, things I had never thought about before or did not want to think about. It was time to take the blinds from my eyes. The bitter truth is that my father was actively, rampantly anti-Semitic, and he helped a terrible regime to flower. My mother and father, my Oma, all fell under the heavy blanket of anti-Jewish propaganda that was spread over the country in the years after Germany's defeat in the First World War. My father's political associations led to his death...

But my father was also another man, my gentle Vati, whom I shall always love. Even the reading of the documentation of his part in Hitler's euthanasia program made me feel *Zwiespalt* – an inner discord. I felt as if merely by my contemplation I was betraying him.

We were so close, and when he worked at his desk, I sat quietly underneath, content to be merely be near him. As a small child, I waited for him to arrive; he was the sun in my life. Finally, I am able to say: *Oh, Vati, how could this happen?* The insanity of those times will forever remain a mystery to me. But what I am now able to recognize is this: my father was two men. One of them was a man I loved; the other was a man I did not know.[425]

The 'man she did not know' worked in partnership with his mother (Oma). He had been a Nazi from an early age. Although he was *Reichsärzteführer* (leader of physicians in the Third Reich) from 1939 he failed to retain his influence and was outmanoeuvred by Hitler's personal doctor, Karl Brandt (1906–48) in the 1940s.

---

424 Newcomer Family Obituaries, Imgard J. Powell, 1932–2017, accessed 16 November 2017, http://www.newcomerdayton.com/Obituary/149873/ Irmgard-Powell/Dayton-Ohio

425 Powell pp.172–3

In 1939, when the first meetings with Hitler about the 'euthanasia' program took place, Leonardo belonged to the select circle of men who discussed the plans for the 'mercy killing' of the incurable sick. Hitler himself was very keen on this topic but left the details to his subordinates. However, when Leonardo did not make progress, Brandt, with the assistance of Göring, Himmler, and Frick, used his chance to plot against him and also against Martin Bormann, the head of Hitler's secretariat, both of whom they wanted to exclude from this influential task. In the end, Brandt, together with Philipp Bouhlar (1899–1945), the head of chancery in Hitler's personal office, became responsible for the 'euthanasia' program. Still Leonardo was involved in the planning. In December 1939 or January 1940, the first experimental killings of adults took place. Testimonies from the Nuremberg trials indicate that Brandt and Leonardo gave the first lethal injections themselves and also watched a group of patients being killed by gas. As Leonardo was Conti's favourite son and they were close companions, it is difficult to imagine that he didn't tell his mother about those 'mercy killings' – maybe not the details, but at least the purpose behind the registration of 'inferior' babies.[426]

Olga Watkins

When Olga's 20-year-old fiancé Julius Koreny was arrested she set off to look for him.

Born in 1923 in Sisak, Yugoslavia (now Croatia), when she was 18 Olga met Julius who worked at the Hungarian consulate. They fell in love and on days out visited her Jewish step-aunt, although neither Olga nor Julius was Jewish. Soon after Julius was arrested whilst visiting his native Budapest and disappeared. Without a thought Olga packed a bag and without papers or a passport set off to find him. Whilst visiting Julius' family in Budapest she was arrested and taken to the interrogation centre at 60 Andrassy Avenue which is now the House of Terror Museum. The authorities deported her back to the border at Osijek.

She did not give up and smuggled herself onto a train to Austria. She found out that Koreny had been sent to Komarom. She managed to see him and talk to him through a barbed wire fence before he was put on a train to Dachau. Olga managed to get herself to Dachau but could not find out what had happened to Julius. She was sitting on a bench in the town of Dachau watching a bombing raid when a pretty young woman in a pink dress came and sat next to her. They got chatting and the girl said she was called Helga, was from Holland and worked in a concentration camp. Helga said to Olga

---

426 Lisner & Peters, 'German Midwifery in the Third Reich', in *Nurses and Midwives in Nazi Germany: the euthanasia program*, Eds. Benedict & Shields (London: Routledge, 2014) p.188.

'Can you type? My boyfriend has a good position in the concentration camp; maybe he can give you a job. I'm not sure, but we'll try when the alarm is over.'[427]

Olga was of course ambivalent about this offer. The thought of working for the Germans in the concentration camp worried her and then she remembered she had no documents. Helga nevertheless took her into the camp to see her boyfriend, who gave her a job on the spot without any question of her producing any documents. She was provided with accommodation in a room with Helga and two other girls who chatted whilst they made up her bed:

> They all seemed perfectly normal. Nothing in their manner or conversation suggested that they worked in one of the most infamous concentration camps in the Third Reich. To them it was just a job.
>
> That night, lying in bed in the darkness listening to the shouts of the guards whilst the other girls slept, I said to myself: 'I'm in a concentration camp and going to begin work tomorrow. So help me God.'[428]

When she woke the next morning she could hear the camp 'resuming its grim daily routine'. Her office was just outside the main gate in the SS camp, just next to the railway line where the prisoners arrived and were then marched into camp.

> As we walked, I was amazed by how many prisoners there were. The camp was built for 6,000 inmates in 1933 and now, in April 1945, there were 32,000 crammed in. Many prisoners died through disease and starvation; epidemics would sweep through the overcrowded huts, decimating the camp population.
>
> Executions happened almost every day, with shootings carried out by SS guards, often against a wall just outside the Bunker. Hangings were conducted by a fellow prisoner forced to act as executioner. Prisoners were often paraded past the body of their comrades, still hanging from the gallows.
>
> The greatest cruelty was the medical experiments in which prisoners were literally frozen to death or where they were starved of oxygen to recreate conditions at high altitude.
>
> Everyone in the camp lived in constant fear. If they were sent to another camp there was every chance they would die on the way. It was hardly surprising that suicide was common.
>
> Helga kept talking as we walked, seemingly oblivious to the horror around her. It was as if she were introducing a new girl at work in any office anywhere in the world.[429]

---

427 Olga Watkins, *A Greater Love* (Droxford: Splendid Books, 2011) pp.175–6.
428 Watkins p.178
429 Watkins pp.179–189

Olga found the place terrifying – so much worse than the prison in Komarom and the cells of Andrassy Utca where she had been held.

Here in Dachau the entire camp lay under a stifling atmosphere of terror, the air heavy with the stink of death. The prisoners – horribly malnourished and skeletal – shuffled rather than walked, as if every step might be their last. Their eyes flicked nervously away from eye contact with anyone – even us girls who worked in the offices.

In a bleak, cheerless location amid a clutch of buildings and empty horizons, this great mass of humanity struggled every day just to survive.

In the office Olga was shown a card index in long blue boxes and she had to update the system according to who had died or moved elsewhere. She was anxious to look in the box marked 'K' to see what had happened to Julius but had to choose her moment. At midday Helga came to take her for lunch, where they sat at a long table with SS officers and other staff.

It struck me as bizarre and frightening to be sitting down with SS men and listening to the buzz of everyday lunchtime conversation in the heart of one of Germany's worst concentration camps.

No one talked about the camp nor mentioned that the Americans were just days away. It was as if everyone had decided they would talk only of the most trivial matters, to keep the horrors at bay.

Prisoners who worked in the camp kitchens served our food. Two men, wearing the red badges used to identify political prisoners, brought out large tureens of soup. We all helped ourselves – the food was very good. The soup was followed by a main course of meat and vegetables. None of the others seemed surprised by the quality of the meal but I was amazed. After so long of never having enough to eat and needing ration coupons for the most meagre meal, the food in Dachau was a luxury. Clearly the Germans looked after their camp staff very well.

Olga was given a pass, in her false Hungarian name, Kovach, which allowed her to use all four entrances to the camp. Another SS man said he had something to show her and they went to a large locked building:

Here we are, there's plenty in here for a pretty girl like you...

On our right was a flat table upon which was arranged a glittering display of jewellery: rings, bracelets, necklaces, watches – all gold or silver, all very expensive and of the highest quality.

The SS guard picked up a gold chain and held it up to the light. 'Look,' he said 'isn't it beautiful? It would look good on you.'

I was speechless. The room reminded me of the grand department stores that my aunt Alice and I visited in Zagreb before the war. On one side were the men's clothes: racks of suits all neatly pressed, a shelf of bowler hats, another for trilbys and homburgs. Opposite were women's dresses, fur coats, skirts, blouses and lingerie. On a high shelf to one side lay stacks of human hair.

'Choose anything you like and take it,' the SS guard said.

Some new clothes would have been useful after losing so many during my travels but these clothes and jewellery could only have come from prisoners, some of whom would now be dead. I couldn't possibly take them.

When she refused the SS guard was puzzled saying 'All the girls working in the camp offices come here for their clothes.'

I learnt later that when prisoners arrived they were taken first to the *schubraum* (shunt room) in the main block where they were stripped of all clothes and belongings and issued with the infamous blue-striped pyjama uniform. No wonder there were so many clothes in the store room...

For civilian staff the working day began at eight o'clock, lunch was called at noon then there was a break until four o'clock. The work finished at seven in the evening.

There were bars and dining rooms in the SS camp and the office girls were in great demand as there were hardly any female guards in the camp. Relationships were frequent – Helga was by no means the first to find a boyfriend amongst the SS men. I was invited to join them in the evening but said I was too tired and went back to our room, grateful to escape.

I lay on my bunk as darkness settled over the camp. Outside the shouting seemed to become louder. Somewhere, among all those prisoners, were some who had spent their last day alive. Whenever a new day dawned at Dachau, there were those who had not survived the night. This night would be no different. Yet, not far from me was a group of young women – just like myself – singing and dancing with the SS. What had happened to us all?

The next day the Allies dropped leaflets saying the Americans would arrive soon. The leaflets were destroyed and life in the camp carried on as usual. More prisoners arrived because as the Germans retreated they took their prisoners with them – some camps had already been liberated. Olga carried on with her work and saw a train arrive:

The guards threw open the doors of the cattle trucks and I expected to see people jumping down from them. Instead, there was a pause and then bodies fell out onto the dusty ground. Other desperately emaciated men and women were pulled out of the trucks more dead than alive. As soon as those able to stand were marched away to the *schubraum*, working parties of prisoners were sent into the cattle trucks to clean out the remainder of the bodies.

It was a gruesome, dreadful scene – and one that I've never forgotten. It was only when I saw that train arrive that I fully realised what went on in Dachau.

I was turning away from the window when a lorry delivering food pulled up near the administration block. The driver had failed to fasten the tailgate properly and some carrots slipped out onto the dirty ground. I watched, horribly fascinated, as a prisoner so starved he could no longer walk (known in the camps as a musselman) began crawling towards the dropped vegetables.

Just as his fingers reached out to grab the food, an SS guard brought the butt of his rifle crashing down on the prisoner's head. I heard the crack of his skull and he collapsed in the dirt, his arm stretched out. Shortly afterwards, his body was dragged away.

Olga was curious about the large chimney she saw

...in the distance, always sending up a pall of black smoke into the sky.

I said to Helga how surprised I was that the prisoners' food was so bad, as the kitchen chimney always seemed to be working. She looked at me in amazement.

'Those aren't the kitchens,' she said. 'That's the crematorium where they take the bodies. Don't go there. It's best avoided.'

Death was so routine that it was no wonder the crematorium chimneys kept pumping out smoke, sending the smell of death across the camp.

I felt foolish and naïve for not realising but it made me more determined to find out what had become of Julius and then to get out of the camp as quickly as possible. I had to act fast.

Olga was working on the blue boxes marked C and D. Another girl had the box marked K. Olga had to wait until the girl went for a break. She found Julius' card but was dismayed by the information that he had arrived from Hungary on 21 December 1944 but was sent to another camp, Ohrdruf, on 20 January 1945. She found that camp was part of the Buchenwald network:

I was gripped by despair – I was in the wrong place and had been all along. Julius had been brought to Dachau after I saw him in Komarom but his letter had taken so long to reach me he had been sent on to another camp before I even began my journey.

I sat at the table in silent anguish. How could fate be so cruel? The trip to Dachau, the hardship and the suffering, all for what? Nothing at all. It had been a journey of the utmost futility.

Tears sprang to my eyes but I couldn't let my fellow workers see me cry. I looked at the card again. Ohrdruf was another camp – but I didn't even know where...

Now that I had discovered what had become of Julius one thing was certain: I had no reason to stay any longer in this dreadful place. It was only a twist of fate that brought me here, my only reason being to find the man I loved. I had no desire to help the Germans in any way.

As that day's work drew to a close, I gathered up what belongings I had with me in the office and, leaving everything else back in my bedroom, walked to the main camp gate. I showed my pass, stepped past the *Arbeit Macht Frei* sign and turned my back on the camp with its armed watchtowers, starving prisoners and smoking crematorium.

I walked to the town in the warm spring sunshine, determined to forget the horror I had seen in Dachau.

I never have. It haunts me to this day.

Olga wrote those words in her eighties and died in December 2016 aged 93.

Ohrdruf was the first camp to be liberated by the American troops and was visited by General Eisenhower, Supreme Commander of the Allied Forces in Europe on 12 April 1945, with Generals Patton and Bradley. He reported to General George Marshall:

> ...the most interesting – although horrible – sight that I encountered during the trip was a visit to a German internment camp near Gotha. The things I saw beggar description. While I was touring the camp I encountered three men who had been inmates and by one ruse or another had made their escape. I interviewed them through an interpreter. The visual evidence and the verbal testimony of starvation, cruelty and bestiality were so overpowering as to leave me a bit sick. In one room, where they up twenty or thirty naked men, killed by starvation. George Patton would not even enter. He said he would get sick if he did so. I made the visit deliberately, in order to be in a position to give first-hand evidence of these things if ever, in the future, there develops a tendency to charge these allegations merely to 'propaganda'.[430]

Olga's fiancé was eventually tracked down in Buchenwald itself, where he had been sent on a forced march. Fearing he was not there, she was about to leave when she discovered him close to death in a typhus ward. She nursed him back to health and they married in Weimar — and returned to Buchenwald for their honeymoon.

After the war they went to Budapest but lifelong happiness was not to be. On 18 May 1948, Olga was summoned home to Zagreb to visit her seriously sick father. When she was ready to go home, her stepmother begged her to stay longer and she reluctantly agreed. On 28 June, the Kremlin sealed the eastern borders and she was unable to get a visa to return to Julius in Budapest. Post was disrupted and the phone lines were cut. Olga and Julius

---

430 USHMM, Ohrdruf, https://www.ushmm.org/wlc/en/article.
php?ModuleId=10006131, accessed 31 July 2017.

could not communicate in any way. She was unable to find a job with her Hungarian connections and finally the marriage was dissolved under communist legislation in 1950. She kept her married name.[431] Olga went to Paris and then in 1954 to London, where she worked as a dressmaker for Hardy Amies, Liberty and Jaeger. In 1963 she met her second husband Gerry Watkins, a civil servant. They married in 1964 and were together until he died in 2013.

In her eighties, she wrote her story in *A Greater Love*. She had a reunion with Julius in Vienna in 1985 – 40 years after their honeymoon in Buchenwald they toasted each other and shared their memories before going their separate ways. She had travelled 2,000 miles to find him during the war. 'It was the end of one of the Second World War's most unusual love affairs.'[432]

431 Watkins pp.262–8
432 Olga Watkins, *Times* obituary, 14 February 2017.

Witnesses to the Post-War Trials

This chapter covers three young girls who found themselves in Germany towards the end and after the war. Patsy Crampton was a translator at the Nuremberg trials, Alma Soller documented the Nuremberg trials and Norma Falk was a Red Cross nurse who looked after the women defendants at the Belsen trials. Norma was Jewish and Alma and Patsy were not. Patsy and Norma both worked for a while as VAD nurses. Alma was American. Whilst none of these girls were victims of the Holocaust they witnessed the evidence of the Nazis' crimes. They were all very young at the time; Alma was born in 1919, Norma in 1924 and Patsy in 1925. I knew Norma from when I lived in Sheffield but only heard about Patsy Crampton when I read her obituary in *The Times* on 8 December 2016. I was interested to read that she had been a translator at the Nuremberg Trials. Her mother's parting advice as she left for Nuremberg was 'You will come straight back, won't you darling, if there's anything nasty?'

Norma has written about her experiences but although Patsy spent her life translating over 200 children's books, I could not find anything she had written about her own experiences. However, I did find she had been interviewed by the Imperial War Museum (IWM) in 1997. Although there was no transcript, the IWM agreed to provide one. I am extremely grateful to the IWM and Jenny Byers who prepared the transcript for me in May 2017.[433]

Patsy Crampton

Patsy Cardew Wood (1925–2016) was born in India. The family returned to England in 1930. These are her words, mostly verbatim:

CW: Did you specialise in languages when you were at school?
PC: Well, one hadn't very much choice. I delighted in them; my first school [High March in Beaconsfield] started French straight away so

---

433 The interview is Accession No: 17426 (4 reels). The interviewer was Conrad Wood (CW).

I was very lucky there. No other school in England, that I know of, did that. So when I went to my public school I was quite advanced in French. And then immediately started German, which I absolutely loved. I remember rushing home and saying to my mother, 'Couldn't you start learning German too? Because it's so exciting, it's wonderful.' And my poor mother, who had effectively, with her sister, ousted German governess after German governess when she was a child, was not keen on the idea. And then, they were very careless at my school, my mother didn't really know much about that kind of thing, announcing, when she took me along to see my future headmistress, 'And Pat will be going to Oxford.' She didn't know you didn't just say that, but the headmistress took it very well. However, they forgot that that meant I had to take my Latin exam effectively in matric, before I went out, before I could go up, and they thought of that only two years before I was due to take my entrance exam for Oxford. And I loved that too, it was great...

CW: What was the special attraction of the German language for you?

PC: I couldn't possibly tell you. Though I did French from a very early age, I never liked it as much. I don't know, I just thought the whole way it worked and everything was fascinating. And later I used to spend lots of private time translating German poetry, certainly not French. And I suppose that's why I went for the Scandinavian languages as well later, instead of the Latin languages.

...Well, when the war was over I was obviously, if one was reading Languages at Oxford, Modern Languages, one would normally have been sent on, I think they were called 'reading tours', or something like that, which people did before the war, in order to get your language up to date and fluent and so on, but clearly that wasn't possible. So, when the war was over and I came down when I was twenty, I said 'Well, now I must go abroad,' to my father. And he said 'Well, you can't go to France or Germany, and unfortunately, you're not twenty-one, and I say where you can go, and they're too dangerous, they're too war-torn.' I don't think he knew anything about it, actually, his war service was all in, well no, it wasn't all in India, stationed here and there. But that's what he thought anyway. So I said, 'Well I'll go to Sweden'. And he said 'Well, you must have a family to invite you'. How he thought I could do that, I mean travel between countries just then wasn't very, not the way it is now at all, and certainly Swedes weren't hopping to and fro. But by great good fortune, a small Swedish delegation, Swedish army, in fact, though they of course didn't take any part in the war, actively, came over to Oxford...I have no idea why they were there, nor have I any idea why I met them, but I did. And I told one of them it would be very kind if he would write a letter and in fact I wouldn't be any nuisance to them and I wanted to come to Sweden, and if, when he got back he would write a letter inviting me that would be very kind. And he didn't, I subsequently discovered why. So I wrote myself a letter, my father was rather easily taken in. I jumped up and down with excitement, didn't present the envelope, but presented this letter in rather odd English, inviting me to stay. And went off on the SS *Saga*, fourth class, my father didn't believe in one's being spoilt in any way...

CW: So you felt you were helping the war effort?

PC: I certainly did feel I was, hoped I was, and I went off and became a very junior VAD after I got my Oxford entrance when I left school...

CW: What exactly did you have to do as a VAD?

PC: I went to a place which is, I forget what it is now, I think it might be some national sports training place, called Bisham Abbey, which is in Berks, isn't it, near Marlow, somewhere along there. And it was a nursing home and convalescent home for nurses who had, who were suffering from what we would now called stress, I don't know what we would, nervous breakdowns, I suppose it was called at the time. So it wasn't anything at all glamorous, I don't think I wanted to do anything glamorous to do with nursing, I don't think I would have been very good at it. And I wasn't very good at it; I did what I could, taking temperatures and things. Mostly, I think, I was a skivvy, dusting, sweeping, washing up, you know?

...As it happened, two girls had come to the school, actually, as evacuees from London, but their family were refugees, and I imagine they'd come over early. As you know, people started coming over in '33, especially if they were particularly at risk, and these two girls, Jewish girls, I don't think they had any German accent left, so their families probably had come over at a very early age, and they probably always had been to English schools, so, of course they didn't. But at the same time, it brought that aspect of the war home to one very strongly. And I of course read *Deuces*, which my parents had on their shelves. It was one of the books I wasn't supposed to read, but I read every single book they had, so, after all, they were not there a lot of the time. And that made a great impression on me, so that there was some direction of that kind also in the choice.

And we had to sit an exam, a Foreign Office exam. And I know from subsequent chit-chat in Nuremberg that my father's job, he had quite a lot of connection with MI5 as well, as the experimental research station that he ran, and then his work in India, helped me to get in.

CW: Perhaps you can paint a word picture now, or what your impressions were? [of Nuremberg]

PC: Well, I hadn't, of course, realised that there wasn't one street, probably not one building complete, left standing. The streets were piles of rubble, neatly cleared away to each side for the minimal traffic, mainly American, that went along them. The Grand Hotel had been rebuilt and was our sort of centre, where we ate and were some of the very senior people lived. Otherwise we were all dispersed right out to the outskirts, more or less in country, to houses out there. So one saw a city that was not, in any respect, a town, that was simply rubble. I think I've got photographs somewhere, the tiny photographs one had in those days, black and white. And the first thing they rebuilt, bless their hearts, was the opera house, for the sake of their morale. There were cellars; people came out of cellars in the morning, from the exits they'd devised, well, long since, really, by the time I got there. I didn't go out until nearly 1947. And it was still in a state of the kind of post-war ruin in every way that no English city had been reduced to. I think only Coventry even came near it, as far as I know. I didn't see northern towns; some of them may have been much worse hit. But London, of course, was a great deal of London standing, in spite of the intensity of the bombing.

...In the different sections in the Palace of Justice, there were, of course, quite a number of refugees from Germany, Jewish refugees from Germany, and especially among the Americans, and the kind of rigorous testing that, I think it's still true now, that English people are accustomed to, hadn't been applied to them, so they weren't the best of translators or interpreters, though there were some brilliant ones among them, But it was very difficult in spite of one's intense sympathy, the way they expressed, some of them, a few of them, the way they expressed their bitterness was, even in view of the material we were translating, curiously distasteful. I mean, there's a way of hating what's happened to your people, and there's a way of letting it turn you rather bad. But that happened, it hadn't happened to anybody in the English section, at all, and I gathered we'd been vetted very much for background and what these days we'd call 'attitude' and so on, as well as linguistic ability. Mind you, my eighteenth-century German was much better than my contemporary German at that time. And I remember taking a taxi from the little airfield, I addressed the taxi driver, much to his surprise, in sort of 'Goethe German', knowing no better, really.

What would you like to know? There was a very curious induction process which I was trying to remember, but I couldn't really, and that, that I expect would have been in the early letters. I hadn't the faintest idea what I was doing, or what was expected of me, or anything. And I was taken in hand by an absolutely darling man, who remained my great friend till his death about five years ago. He was, his family had been patrons of Richard Strauss and, you know, all the great musicians of the time. He let them down completely, they were Jewish and they'd got out thanks to workers on their estate. That's what I mean about the ordinary Germans, they valued the people who had been very good superiors to them, and always treated them well, and they sheltered them and enabled them to get out.

... And we had good friends among the British interpreters, who weren't necessarily British in origin, and the one that I also failed to marry, but that's a different story, anyway, the one I took up with, was someone called Wolfgang Hildesheimer, who later became a very distinguished German, first artist, and then painter and writer. Very, very popular, very quirky. He was an interpreter and he had been got out early because his grandfather was Grand Rabbi of all Germany, for which he didn't give a damn because he was not a practising

Jew. But his father was a director of Unilever, and Unilever behaved magnificently. They got all their German staff who had any background problem, which they, of course, had, out in '33, and he was sent to St Christopher's Letchworth, which was one of the few co-educational schools in the country, and then was in intelligence in our forces in Palestine. So, anybody who was connected with Unilever was safe, right from the very start of what was to come.

...Incidentally, one of the very benevolent rules that we were not to eat at German restaurants, not because of not fraternising, in the British zone it would have been not fraternising, because I went to the British zone to see my uncle a lot, and gosh, did I get into trouble chatting with Germans. But in the French zone there was no non-fraternisation either, the French don't go in for that, they mix, completely. But we weren't supposed to go into German restaurants as they gradually came into being again, in order not to take their rations when we were more than adequately fed, so actually we didn't get a lot of fresh food because all our food was American, shipped over, that wasn't terribly good for us, as a matter of fact, all this tinned stuff, and so on. There you are. But, owing to a growing circle of friends in Munich and Heidelberg, we ate a lot of German rations. But of course we were able to supply whiskey and all the, well, above all, the currency, which is cigarettes.

That was quite extraordinary, there was nothing you couldn't buy with cigarettes, and you knew the price of everything that wasn't at the American PX, in cigarettes. You could buy your train fare, anything, petrol, I bought a Jeep, was 7 pence a gallon, equivalent of, everything was, I suppose, pretty easy for us. But in any case, it was my first job and England hadn't been easy, and something else that struck me when I looked at the letters when my mother did begin to keep them, was something I'd completely forgotten, which is saying something about England, not about Nuremberg at all, really; almost every letter is 'Some marvellous material has come into the PX, would you like coat material, would you like material for Jenny,' that was my little sister...'how about shoes? I'll send chocolate, but I wouldn't like you to think it's all for Jenny, you must have some too.'

... In England, by then, everyone had been reduced to this revolting 'utility' china, thick horrible stuff, and I could take whole services for my mother and aunt and grandmother and so on, because, in the British zone, typical, isn't it, each zone was absolutely typical of its country of occupation, they didn't go in for anything like that at all...Imagine, I was able to adopt the New Look, I was able to have my clothes made by a German dressmaker in the New Look. Of course I wore nylons, navy blue nylons, black nylons, oh, the excitement. But quite nice, I thought, I thought this as a reaction now, then it was obviously something one did automatically...

CW: You were just saying about the work that you were doing, you were comparing the 'IG Farben Trial' with the 'Doctors' Trial'.

PC: Yes. Well, the Doctors' Trial, of course, by now, so much of this is known, but I think in those days there was nobody in the ordinary world who knew anything about the experiments that were conducted. And, of course, the trouble with that kind of thing, when it's taking place, as it inevitably was, in close proximity to, or even within, a concentration camp, is that, however vile the doctors were, particularly vile considering that their profession was to heal, in conducting the experiments they did, being also located in connection with camps, there were other people who were allowed to abuse, who just did it for fun, and this was the unbelievable aspect which one never, probably, got over. I think in a sense I live with it every day, even though it's 50 years ago. As I say, all this material, and worse from people's minds, even now, is more or less taken for granted, but then, it was unimaginable. I don't know if you actually want me to mention the kind of things, because it's quite difficult to do so.

But I think the first, the very first that I came across, was nothing to do with any kind of medical research, was the insertion of mice into the vagina of women prisoners, and things like the repeated breakings of legs, of children and adults, to assess the different healing properties and capacities of different ages. I don't know if I can really go on about this. But there were no lengths without even the faintest excuse of research to which people wouldn't go. And yet, I can remember my cousin John Chaplin asking me, when I got back, he was the only person who did ask me, no one else wanted to know, 'Well, what do you think of the Germans now? We're beginning to hear all about it.' And I remember that I said, and obviously believed it very strongly, 'There but for the grace of God.' And he said, 'You can't mean that.' Because you also discovered the other people who'd been involved, they weren't just Nazis, members of the Party, Germans, what we would call trustees were involved, people from all over defeated, occupied, Eastern Europe. And they were saving their own skins by being involved, to some extent, but at least you knew that there were human beings from anywhere you like who would do anything they liked.

CW: So, these were depositions which you were translating?

PC: People who had come out alive, and in some cases, of course, with the experiments, were all fully annotated, and although the Germans did their very best to get rid of all records, as the Allies came in, they of course didn't entirely succeed.

CW: So you felt these were reliable reports.

PC: Oh yes, yes. Heavens. And if you had seen some of the witnesses in the court, you couldn't doubt their word for one second. But the others, I mean, they were perfectly ordinary records kept by the medical services, the German medical services, of what had been done, in quite cold blood.

CW: So your work as a translator actually took you into court sometimes?

PC: Well, it, your work didn't, any of us could go into the courtroom, and we on the whole didn't. But occasionally, we would be told that some particularly extraordinary event was happening. For instance, there was a man called Oswald Pohl, who was head of the *Einsatzgruppen*, and we all went into court when he was there, because he'd been making a fool of the judges throughout his trial, in every possible way, and sentence was due to be pronounced. And there was no one in my section who would go to court for the pleasure of seeing sentence pronounced on any of these people. There were some who did, and as I say, you can't really blame them at all, but for him, the judge was foolish enough on that last day to ask him to raise his hand, I remember, again, to take the oath, for whatever good that did. And how he sneered, of course, because he was manacled, as the judge knew perfectly well, but just wasn't thinking. You know, 'Raise your hand,' and he raised his feet after sentence was pronounced. He claimed to have been personally responsible for the, what would you call it? Signing the documents, really, which led to the deaths of six million people, and he said he would do it again. And the irony of his vow to the judge, which you could only interpret as 'you next', it had that whole kind of look about it.

There were some very horrific people, but don't forget, I didn't mention, although the dates would make it clear, that the trials started almost immediately after the war, and were international, to begin with, and all people like Göring and, the known names, the big names, were tried then. The ones I was involved with were the people who were being tried who came from the American zone, Bavaria and around, and the same could be said of the British trials and the French trials. I was asked to go to Berlin afterwards, where, I don't know who they were, whether they were people who specifically belonged there, or whether perhaps all the remainder of the trials were pushed up there, in the end, but I didn't want to stay on in '49. And those were the kind of things, of course, that we never talked about.

What we did talk about was sort of mild amusement in those circumstances, was the missed day during the trial, the Krupps, they were involved too, of course, when the Krupp defence team walked out because the judge had told the leader of the team to stop talking and get on with it, and they all walked out. So the next day the Krupp team was back, on trial for contempt of court. A sort of lighter side of. But I can't help wishing that I had, in fact, recorded much more, because now it would be interesting. At the time one didn't want anything more to do with it when the day's work was over. And we worked, we often worked through weekends too. It was very hard work, was both demanding and had very long hours, and we'd go off particularly joyfully on, when we got a weekend off, or even a day off. I remember being so entranced by the countryside, which showed me why, Brueghel was, Brueghel showed me so much about the background.

CW: I'm surprised, coming back to Pohl, that he was defiant.

PC: Absolutely, right to the end.

CW: Any other incidents you remember from court proceedings that you attended?

PC: Not of that rather dramatic nature, no. I didn't go in often, you see? It was, again, slightly, it sounds awfully prudish, slightly a point of honour not to be in among the people who went in licking their lips over the sentences. It may sound silly now, it seemed to matter then, not to get oneself twisted, you know? I don't know.

CW: Were you happy with the way in which the trials were conducted?

PC: I think it seemed an extraordinary, it seemed an extraordinary thing, and a good thing, to try. They tried desperately, I mean, the Pohl trial; I seem to remember there was a lengthy set-back where they said something had technically gone wrong. He thought it was a great joke. So they had to do it all again. I thought it was extraordinarily fair and an extraordinary thing to do, and a lot of people must just have wanted to murder these fellows out of hand.

CW: So, all the big names had been dealt with by the time you arrived?

PC: Yes. And I think those were the only two major trials that I was concerned with. But I remember a mass of documents, which must have been, in fact, I think they must have been for some sort of use later on, documents about uranium and things like that, which probably came in very handy for some of the later commercial uses. I seem also to remember being involved in translations of some of the stuff on Peenemünde [where the V2 rocket production was based from 1941] where the V-weapons came from, but not directly. Not, what I'm saying is, I'm sorry this isn't at all clear, not as material for the trials. So although one was working all the time for the Office for Chief of Counsel for War Crimes, I think, looking back, that a lot of the documents we worked on later, at the end of '48, were of interest, but no longer actually concerned with people who were being tried. That's what I'd say.

CW: You were telling me earlier, off the record, that you, about the reaction in Britain to the fact that you had done this job at Nuremberg, and the degree of interest, or lack of interest, that was shown. Could you repeat what you were saying to me earlier, please?

PC: Yes, well, considering now, that I go all over the world, speaking on extremely innocuous subjects like copyright and the importance of children in deprived countries having books which are not school books, all those kind of things, perfectly acceptable subjects, and at that time I'd done that job, I remember only once being invited to speak, and that was by my old school, about it. And I'm quite sure that they wished that they hadn't asked me, because I would have been, I expect I was fairly careful, but I would have been more ready to discuss the kind of things that you actually find more and more difficult as you get older. And no one else wanted to hear anything about it at all. I don't think they thought it was a very proper thing for me to have done. And in a strange way I think, this is perhaps a funny use of the word lucky, but I think I was lucky in my parents, because they would have thought as I did, that it was a very important thing that should be done, and in spite of my mother's very innocent remark, they wouldn't have dreamed of trying to stop me.

CW: So, in Britain there was a 'head in the sands' attitude towards it.

PC: Absolutely it was too, too awful. I mean, the Germans that I met were well aware of all the repression, were well aware that Jews had had to leave or else, but they didn't begin to be aware of the atrocities, and I know that for certain. But I also know that on the uneducated level, propaganda had been totally successful, more or less totally. My dressmaker, when she'd seen quite a lot of me, she was very uncommunicative at first, not from stubbornness or Naziness, but from not knowing really whether a member of the occupying power was going to be savage or brutal or something extraordinary. But when she realised I was just an ordinary young woman she started to open up, and she told me how somebody who had employed her, I remember the angle from which she was telling me this story, before the war, had left, and had filled many, many, they wouldn't have been plastic sacks in those days, but sacks, with the stuff they'd left behind, and had said to her, if there's anything there that you want, please take it. And how she had found that a lot of the stuff was things like almost-empty toothpaste tubes and so on, and she said this with great indignation and added, '*Sie war nur eine Jude.*'[She was just a Jew] And I let go, then.

CW: How did she react to your letting go?

PC: Absolutely, '*Ah, die Fraulein weint, die junge Fraulein weint.*' [Oh, the lady is crying, the young lady is crying.] And she had never, nobody, you see would have been, she wouldn't have talked to people who would have said, 'But that was an appalling, those were appalling things that we were asked to believe'. Nobody. Who would have? In her particular ambience. Who would have said to her, you know, 'That wicked Goebbels'? It's just they lost the war.

Norma Falk (1924–)

Norma's parents were Esther Rabinovitch, born in London in 1900, and Hyman Wolfson, born Zemel in Lithuania in 1894. Hyman Wolfson came to Sheffield to join his family including uncles and aunts, brother and sister, around 1911. He changed his name to Goldstone from Wolfson. He fought in WW1 and stayed in Sheffield. He met Norma's mother in 1923 when she was living in Manchester.[434]

Norma was born in Sheffield and was still at school when war was declared. As a young woman she decided she wanted to be a nurse and she trained at the Sheffield Infirmary. In 2010 she had an article published about her experiences as a Red Cross nurse at the 1945 Belsen War Trials.[435]

I must have been about fifteen when Sheffield was blitzed. One night I was in the YWCA in Sheffield at a drama class when the sirens went.

---

434 Nigel Grizzard, emails to author, 25 April 2017
435 Norma Falk, *Belsen War Trials*, in 'Everyone's War: The Journal of the Second World War Experience Centre', No. 21, Summer 2010

Norma Falk as a Red Cross nurse, probably taken in 1944.

There must have been 200 girls at all the different classes and none of us could go home. We were taken down the stairs where they made us porridge and we sang to pass the time.

After the 'All Clear' we came out to find the cinema, just a few yards away, was completely on fire. The whole of The Moor (a main street) was burning and we had to walk home. It was very frightening. We were very young. We didn't realise the enormity of it until that first blitz. I remember wondering how the First World War lasted four years, and I was sure this war would be over very soon. We couldn't comprehend the enormity of it. Daddy probably did; his parents were shot in Lithuania with my aunts and uncles. My Daddy never saw his parents after he left Russia at nineteen but he was terribly worried about them. We heard from them regularly until the war started but then the letters stopped.

I badly wanted to nurse and did my Red Cross training, and in 1943 I volunteered to join up and my father was very worried. He didn't like the idea of my going away and the thought of me nursing. However I volunteered and joined up but there was a waiting list. I did eight months in a mining hospital near Doncaster. It was a wonderful experience because there were just four Red Cross girls, two nurses who had been there for years and a matron. I had some wonderful training there. Then my call-up papers came through and I was sent to York Military Hospital, a receiving station, and I spent a month there on night duty. I was transferred to a camp reception station which was awful, just a large house where we gave gargles and treated very minor things, so when a notice came round asking for people to volunteer for theatre work and blood transfusion a friend and I decided to volunteer. The theatre course was full but we were accepted for the blood transfusion work and we did the Army blood transfusion course at Bristol College.

My first post, in May 1944, was the hospital at Lüneburg. It was a barracks, really, and a lot of the patients were war-wounded. I nursed on heavy surgical wards and one day I was asked by Matron to go on duty at the first war trials in the courthouse in Lüneburg. These were those who were guilty of or were being indicted for atrocities in Belsen. Those on trial included Kramer, the camp Commandant and Klein, the camp doctor, who were accused of terrible atrocities, Irma Grese, a really dreadful wardress, and another woman called Bauman who used to walk around setting her dogs on people. There were others, but those stand out in my mind because they were so appalling.

My duties began in the morning when the defendants arrived. A lot of them had headaches. They were being fed on soups and not very much else and they complained of tummy aches, headaches, spots or cuts, and we would dispense some aspirin and perhaps put a plaster on a cut, that sort of thing. Then I would go into the courtroom and sit with the Military Police until the questioning of the female prisoners when I actually escorted them and sat at the side of their box as they were questioned and then afterwards, I had to escort them back again. I was there in case the female defendants fainted or something, just as a nurse. Even when I treated them they never spoke a word, although I didn't really speak any German at the time and they didn't speak any English. They simply sat there looking very sullen. They didn't try and communicate at all. They were just brought in each morning, sat in their rows and were taken out after the trial was over for the day.

The trials took quite a long time because Colonel Backhorse, the Chief Prosecutor, and most of the council didn't speak German, so the questions were put to the witnesses and defendants in English, translated into German and Polish (because a lot of them only spoke Polish), and then the answers were translated back into English, so each question took some time. I must just say, I thought it spoke very highly for British justice because all the defence counsel were British and, although they knew the people they were defending were guilty, I felt they were given a fair trial.

It must have been very hard for the defence counsel; whatever questions they were asked, the accused would reply with, 'That is not true' and 'I never saw it' and those were the only answers they gave to whatever questions they were asked. It was all they said right through the trial. It was extraordinary. Kramer sat writing copious notes; I don't know what he thought he was going to do with them. Klein, the doctor, was a very thin, drawn sort of man and he was accused of conducting terrible experiments in the camp. I was just twenty-one at the time and I found it very harrowing listening to the evidence, but what I found so extraordinary was seeing them all sitting there, so very passive, with no sign of emotion at all.

One of the witnesses would stand up and say, 'I saw a man beaten to death because he had stolen something.' The barrister acting for the accused would say, 'Are you sure you saw this? Have you remembered this correctly? Are you sure it's not in your imagination?' I felt terribly sorry for some witnesses because it seemed as though they were being put through the 'third degree'; making out that they had forgotten what they had seen, and I am quite sure they hadn't. That was their main way of defending the accused, trying to prove that the witnesses were, perhaps, not reliable.

I remember Irma Grese very clearly, she had this long blond hair and tossed her hair the whole time. No sign of emotion. When I heard some of things Irma Grese did, like bashing children against a wall, she was twenty-one years old, my age, as I sat there I just couldn't believe it. It sounded so far-fetched, these horrific atrocities that they had perpetrated. I remember one particular witness, a female doctor called Dr. Bimko, who spoke extremely well. She had helped treat some of the patients who had suffered at the hands of the accused.

A lot of the Belsen staff, the uneducated workers who were following orders, got away with prison sentences, but I was actually there when the death sentences were pronounced. Colonel Backhouse put on his black cap, I remember, and after the sentence was passed they just walked out of the court showing no emotion whatsoever. I think they must have known this was going to happen.

Before I went on duty at the courthouse, and I was working in the theatre at the hospital, we had German orderlies, young girls working as cleaners. The Colonel would not allow us to give any leftover food from the mess to our German orderlies because he was so incensed at what he had seen at Belsen. We used to feel a bit sorry for these girls, and sometimes used to take something across for them, against strict orders not to, but they were hungry and we felt sorry for them, but I must be very honest, I didn't feel the same way after I had heard about the terrible things that happened in Germany at the trial.

My responsibilities at the trials ended once the verdict had been given and we were taken to Belsen, to the camp which had been emptied by then. I did visit the hospital in Bergen-Belsen, and I remember thinking, how could the patients here smile at us? They had just been released and they were in a terrible state and yet they managed to smile.

I stayed in Germany after the trial for twenty-two months. The hospital at Lüneburg closed. It had been very hard nursing there because, being a barracks, there was no hot water and we slept in big empty barrack rooms. We were transferred to a proper hospital in Hamburg which had been completely destroyed, from the hospital to the town was just rubble, and I nursed there for seventeen months.

Eventually Norma returned to Sheffield and married Dr Joseph Falk in 1948/9. Norma has two sons and still lives in Sheffield.

Norma referred to Irma Grese and people are often shocked to find that women guards were so sadistic. Irma was known as 'The Beast of Belsen'. At the 1945 trial she was one of the 'most sinister and hated figures' and witnesses claimed she beat women until they collapsed. These cruel women who became such 'sadists' and beasts' had led ordinary lives. Elisabeth Volkenrath, chief female overseer in Auschwitz and Bergen-Belsen, sentenced to death in 1945, was an unskilled labourer prior to becoming a guard. Ruth Closius, also sentenced to death for her exceptional cruelty, had dreamed of becoming a nurse but, since she left school too early, became a saleswoman in a textiles warehouse. The notorious Irma Grese worked at a dairy farm after leaving home at 15 years of age.

Unlike the men, most women were not fervent Nazis but attracted to a well-paid job with a uniform and accommodation. However the Nazis had to resort to conscription because so many female guards were needed with the increasing number of female prisoners. Grese claimed it was the labour exchange that sent her to Ravensbrück where the female guards were trained and brutalised within days. 'One prisoner noted how it took one guard just four days.'

Many of these women were never brought to trial and were able to return to their pre-war, ordinary lives. For those who were brought to trial, however, such as Irma Grese, their ordinary life became a distant prospect to which they were never able to return. Seventy years after the liberation of the camps, it is important to remember that women were not the only victims, mothers or wives; they too were active in sustaining the terrors experiences by millions during the Holocaust.[436]

Alma Soller (1919–2017)

Alma was the last surviving participant of the Nuremberg Trials, where she worked for Robert H. Jackson who was a member of the US Supreme Court. She was 25 when she starting working on the case against the German war criminals in the Justice Department. Little did she know then that she would work in this field for many years. After the trials were completed, Jackson asked her to pull the record together so that history could make its own judgement.

Over the next four years, long after the trial had been completed, Soller, who was a warm, good-hearted woman, worked on the grimmest account of criminality, atrocity and sadism in the history of jurisprudence.

Eventually she produced ten volumes, each 1,000 pages long, known as the Nuremberg Red Series, which historians and lawyers dealing with the period have come to regard as the unvarnished truth.[437]

I found a brief memoir by Alma from 2005 in which she described working for Robert Jackson. She wrote he 'will undoubtedly be remembered in history as a founder of International Law. I will always remember him as a kind, gentle man with twinkling eyes.'[438]

---

436 Lauren Willmott, 'The Real "Beast of Belsen"? Irma Grese and Female Concentration Camp Guards', *History Today*, 1 June 2015, accessed 20 July 2017. http://www.historytoday.com/lauren-willmott/real-beast-belsen-irma-grese-and-female-concentration-camp-guards
437 Alma Soller, obituary, *The Times*, 8 May 2017.
438 Alma Soller McLay, 'That Twinkle in His Eyes', McLay (Final) DOC, 1 September 2005. Accessed 21 June 2017, https://www.roberthjackson.org/wp-content/uploads/2015/08/That-Twinkle-in-his-Eyes-McLay.pdf

She was appointed very quickly and with seventeen other people prepared to leave on 18 June 1945. On the Sunday before they left, Jackson hosted a lunch at his home. She noticed swings in the garden and asked him about grandchildren. He told her with a twinkle 'the swings are for me...that's where I do my thinking.' When they were in London, he took the whole team to meet the US Ambassador John Winant at the US Embassy, which was very unusual. 'Justice Jackson treated everyone alike, whether you were an attorney, secretary or diplomat.'

The trial had advanced technology for the times. 'Testimony, questions, answers and even evidence was rapidly translated into four languages, which lawyers and others could listen to on headphones. A team of interpreters were housed in a soundproof glass box in the courtroom to handle the translations.'

Jackson stated that 'The facts in this circumstance are so horrific, no one would believe the facts unless they had access to the documents.'[439] Alma Soller explained how it took four years, after the trial, of work in the Pentagon to compile the documents into the ten volumes. She was acknowledged in the preface of the first volume. Afterwards she was asked to help 'record the negotiations among England, France, the Soviet Union and the United States, that had resulted in an agreement on how to try the Nazi War Criminals'. At a lunch with Jackson, he told her the State Department wanted to publish a book about the four power conferences held in England. He told her he was counting on her to be his representative in the work. As they discussed the details of how the work would be done, he added,

> ...with that twinkle in his eyes, 'there's one small box full of shorthand notebooks, it's never been transcribed.' And so for many weeks I had the privilege of working in his office and I succeeded in transcribing the contents of the four power conferences, which centered on written submissions by each country.

Alma met her husband in the 1950s. He was Stanley McLay, an Air Force colonel. They moved to Los Angeles, where she continued to work in government departments until she retired in 1984. They had three children and three grandchildren. Stanley died in 1991 and Alma died on 5 April 2017, aged 97.

Interviewed in 2004, Soller recalled with pride at the age of 84, that Justice Felix Frankfurter, who was a colleague of Jackson's, used to stop and ask her how she was. He was from a Viennese Jewish family and said 'You are doing such a service for our country. We should all be thankful. The whole world should be thankful.'[440]

---

439 Steve Marble, 'Alma McLay, last surviving member of US team that prosecuted Nazi War Criminals at Nuremberg, dies at 97'. *LA Times* 10 April 2017, accessed 21 June 2017, http://www.latimes.com/local/obituaries/la-me-alma-mclay-20170410-story.html

440 *Times* obituary

Afterword

Leona Grunwald (1913–1991)

I feel the stories of the women that I have presented speak for themselves. I didn't think some trite remarks from me about their bravery and courage were required. I therefore decided to conclude with my own mother's story. To be honest, it has been in my mind all through the research. It has inevitably been a profound influence on my own life and my motivation in the work I have done on the Holocaust. It is, of course, my own story as well.

Leona Grunwald née Klein was born in 1913 to an assimilated Jewish family in Budapest. The family did not keep a kosher home, but always lit the Friday night candles to welcome the Sabbath. She was the eldest of four girls – a fifth child, a boy, was stillborn. Her father, Armin Klein, had an ironmongery business. My mother said the Depression and his ill-health,

Leona and Philipp Grunwald with the author in Budapest, January 1946.

which meant he spent considerable time in hospital, resulted in him going bankrupt. My mother had wanted to be a concert pianist, but at 16 she had to leave school and go out to work to support the family. She worked for a Jewish man who bought up forests and then sold the trees as timber. She worked for him for 13 years until the Holocaust disrupted both their lives.

She told me how on a Friday afternoon she could see her father waiting outside for her to exit with her wages so that they could buy the food for the family. I know my mother resented the responsibility and the sacrifice of her dreams. However, it must have been humiliating for him. The man who I believe was the love of my mother's life had a widowed mother, she told me, and he wouldn't leave her to marry. He died in a concentration camp. My mother told me, later, when she was pushing me in my pram, she met his mother. His mother looked into the pram. She didn't say anything, but the look on her face suggested she was thinking that if they had married she would at least have had a grandchild.

My parents were married in Budapest in March 1942 when Hungary was not involved in the war. The future was, however, uncertain and she told me they weren't thinking of the long-term. The Hungarians had introduced their own anti-Jewish legislation and in 1943, my father was rounded up for forced labour along with 50,000 other Jewish men. Bizarrely he was allowed home on leave and that was when I was conceived, my mother told me. He was taken to Poland and worked on disposing of mines and building airfields 'Over 40,000 died, emaciated by hunger or succumbed to disease, the harsh Russian cold winter, the risky removal of landmines, or the bad treatment by their non-Jewish Hungarian commanders.'[441] Very few came back; but my father returned in March 1945. The only thing he ever told me about the war was that mulberries saved his life when others were dying of dysentery. He was very embittered and wouldn't have more children after the war. He committed suicide in 1955 when I was ten, leaving my mother to bring me up alone and to provide for us.

After my father was taken away, my mother continued living in the flat that my parents had rented on Kaplar Utca. Then 'Mrs. Leona Grünwald, nee Klein (wife of Philipp (Fülöp) Grünwald) ... obliged to wear the star of David, was forced to leave her apartment flat at II. Kaplar Street No. 8 in the second part of June 1944 and she moved to V. Josef Katona Street No. 31.' As I understand it, this was accommodation designated for Jewish women – my mother called it a 'Star of David house'.

From there when I was on the way, in mid-July, she went to a clinic at 68 Varos Major, Budapest XII because as a Jew the normal Maternity Hospital was closed to her. She had a long and difficult labour with no pain relief. After three days I was born on 14 July. The documents that my parents obtained from the Representative Organization of Budapest Jewry on 9 September 1946 were a translation of documents in German. Presumably these were obtained to assist their aim to leave for England. One states:

441 Mordecai Paldiel, *Saving One's Own: Jewish Rescuers* (Philadelphia: Jewish Pub. Society, 2017) p.139.

> After she had given birth to her daughter Agnes in July 14th 1944 she went to live with her child at her mother-in-law's apartment, Frau Grünwald, wife of Emil Grunwald, at V, Waitzner Street, No.4.11.10, on July 29th 1944 because her baby was not liked at the former address.

I'm not sure what I could have done at that age to upset the other residents. I assume that there was an issue about a baby being there and the translation is awkward.

At some point between my birth and November when we were sent to the Budapest Ghetto, my mother was told to report the next day to a particular place. I don't know what she knew about what was happening but she was fearful enough to try to leave me with her mother-in-law, as her mother had died in 1941. My grandmother said she could not feed me as my mother was breastfeeding me, so the next day my mother reported with me in her arms. My mother was fairly enigmatic and all she told me was 'the man in charge sent back the women with children.' I have no idea who the 'man' was – he could have been a Nazi German or Hungarian, a policeman, a civil servant or even a Jew – a member of the *Judenrät*. The Nazis were adept at getting the Jews to do their dirty work for them. I always thought we had have been put on the train to Auschwitz like most of the Hungarian Jews. However, only months ago I was told that the trains to Auschwitz stopped around the time I was born, so I don't know what our intended destination was. But for the 'man' we would have been off to a, no doubt, more dangerous place.

We were sent to the Budapest Ghetto on 28 November 1944, to No. 35, Wesselenyi Street Utca. It was not a good place to be as there was very little food but I was fortunate that my mother could breast-feed me even when she had very little to eat. It was extremely cold, with no fuel available except, perhaps, furniture that could be burnt. The Hungarian fascists liked to take shots at the Jews in the Ghetto so many people died. My mother's cousin, Pali, told me he found my mother in the Ghetto when it was liberated. She was sitting on some steps holding me, surrounded by dead bodies.

She returned to her flat and the Russian soldiers who had liberated Budapest were marauding around. She was not tall but she had authority and whilst rape and mayhem surrounded her in the block of flats, the Russians in her flat merely asked for food. She didn't have any and they disappeared, returning some time later with a frozen animal. They cut it up and somehow she cooked it and they all ate it. She told me she thought it was a dog. They went to sleep on the floor and left the next morning. The rest of our story is for my family memoir, yet to be written.

My mother, like all the women in this book, coped with situations she could never have envisaged before 1933. She kept us both safe and alive, to bring me to England in 1947. So many millions of Jews were not so fortunate.

Glossary

Aeltestenraete	Council of Elders (imposed by the Nazis)
AFO	Anti-Fascist Fighting Organization
Aktion (*Aktionen* plural)	Operation involving the mass assembly, deportation, and murder of Jews by the Nazis
Aliyah (Hebrew)	Immigration to Israel
AJR	Association of Jewish Refugees (in London)
Aramaic	Semitic language
Aufseherin (plural *Aufseherinnen*)	Female guards in concentration camps
Battue (French)	Driving game towards hunters by beaters
Bauernfuehrer	Farmers' Leaders were party appointees, not necessarily members of the Nazi party, who were to represent local farmers to the administration such as the *Bürgermeister* (the Mayor)
Blockova	Another word for *Kapo* – used particularly in Ravensbrück, but also used by Dr Perl in Auschwitz
Commissar	Political leader of a military unit
CV	*Centralverein deutscher Staatsbürger jüdischen Glaubens* was founded by German Jewish intellectuals on 26 March 1893 in Berlin, with the intention of opposing the rise of antisemitism in the German Empire. Closed down by the Nazis in 1938
Eretz Israel	The Land of Israel
ERR	Einsatzab Reichsleiter Rosenberg – Nazi organisation dedicated to appropriating cultural property
Geehrte	Esteemed
Gatow	Luftwaffe's Technical Academy at Gatow airbase at Lake Wannsee
Gräfin	Countess (male *Graf* – Count)
Gymnasium	A grammar school in Europe – not a gym

371

Hashomer Hatsair	The Young Guard – Zionist youth group
Hauptsturmführer	Head Storm Leader – Nazi paramilitary rank
Hlinka Guard	Slovak militia established by the pro-Nazi Slovak party in 1938 after the Munich Conference. Named after a Slovak nationalist Andrej Hlinka
Hochdeutsch	Literally High German
ITS	International Tracing Service based in Bad Arolsen. Provides information on the fate of victims of the Nazis and returns personal effects
JDC (the Joint)	American Jewish Joint Distribution Committee and Refugee Aid
JHI	Jewish Historical Institute in Warsaw
Judenrät (plural *Judenräte*)	Jewish Council (imposed by the Nazis)
Judenrein/Judenfrei	Free of Jews (Nazi term)
Kashariyot (singular *kasharit*), Hebrew	Female underground couriers
Kibbutz – kibbutznik	A communal settlement in Israel, typically a farm. Someone who lives on a kibbutz.
Ladino	A type of ancient Spanish spoken by Sephardi Jews
Magen David (Hebrew)	The Star of David
Melinas - Polish	Hiding places
Mikvah	Ritual bath
Praktikant	Farm worker
Protective Custody	The arrest – without judicial review – of real and potential opponents of the regime under the Nazis.
Revier	Concentration camp hospital
RV	*Reichsvertretung der Juden* in Deutschland: an umbrella organisation for German Jews
Scarlet Fever	An infectious disease which was very dangerous before the development of antibiotics
Shabbos (Hebrew)	The Sabbath (Saturday)
Shema Yisroel	The most important Jewish prayer that a Jew should recite as he dies. 'Hear O Israel the Lord my God is One'
Shiva	Hebrew Prayers for the dead at home, for seven days after the funeral
SS Schutzstaffel	'Protection squadron', paramilitary group that took over from *SA*

SS Haftlingsentgelte	Collected payments for work by slave labourers from the companies that used them
SS WVHA	*Wirtschafts-und-Verwaltunghauptamt.* Main Economic and Administrative Office of the SS
Szaulis	Lithuanians in the service of the Germans
VAD nurse	Voluntary Aid Detachment members. Established by the UK War Office in 1909 when volunteers were recruited and trained in first aid and nursing. They proved invaluable nursing support in both world wars
UNNRA	United Nations Relief and Rehabilitation Administration 1943–46
USHMM	United States Holocaust Memorial Museum in Washington
USC	University of Southern California
Vilna (Polish)	Polish name of Lithuanian city of Vilnius in the inter-war period, when it was held by Poland
Volljuden	Full Jew
Volkssturm	People's militia – at end of war
Yeshiva (Hebrew)	Jewish educational institution that focuses on the study of traditional religious texts, primarily the Talmud and Torah
YIVO	A Jewish history institution based in New York. Founded in Vilna in 1925 as the *Yidisher Visnshaftlekher Institut*
Yom Kippur (Hebrew)	The Day of Atonement, the most solemn day in the Jewish Calendar – a fast day usually in September or October
Żegota	Council for Aid to Jews, *Rada Pomocy Żydom* (RPŻ)
ZOB	Jewish Fighting Organization (*Zydowska Organizacja Bojowa*)

Bibliography

Bauer, Yehuda, *Jews for Sale? Nazi-Jewish Negotiations, 1933–1945* (New Haven: Yale UP, 1994)

Benedict, Susan & Shields, Linda, eds, *Nurses and Midwives in Nazi Germany: the euthanasia program* (London: Routledge, 2014)

Blady, Adina Szwajger, *I Remember Nothing More: The Warsaw Children's Hospital and the Jewish Resistance,* translators Tasja Darowska and Danusia Stok (London: Collins Harvill, 1990)

Child Survivors Assoc. of UK, *We Remember: Child Survivors of the Holocaust Speak* (Leicester: Matador, 2011)

Clare, George, *Last Waltz in Vienna* (Basingstoke: Pan Books, 2007)

Dublon-Knebel, Irith, ed, *A Holocaust Crossroads: Jewish Women and Children in Ravensbrück* (London: Vallentine Mitchell, 2010)

Erbrich, Edith with Peter Holle, *Ich hab' das Lachen nicht verlent* (Neu-Isenberg: Edition Momos, 2014)

Felstiner, Mary Lowenthal, *To Paint her Name: Charlotte Salomon in the Nazi Era* (New York: Harper Collins, 1994)

Ferencz, Benjamin B., *Less Than Slaves* (Cambridge Mass.: Harvard UP, 1979)

Fulbrook, Mary, *A Small Town Near Auschwitz: Ordinary Nazis and the Holocaust* (Oxford: OUP, 2012)

Ginaite-Rubinson, Sara, *Resistance and Survival: The Jewish Community in Kaunas 1941–1944* (Oakville, ON: Mosaic Press, 2015)

Grunwald-Spier, Agnes, *The Other Schindlers* (Stroud: The History Press, 2011) *Who Betrayed the Jews?* (Stroud: Amberley Books, 2017)

Hart-Moxon, Kitty, *Return to Auschwitz* (Newark: Quill, 2007)

Holden, Wendy, *Born Survivors* (London: Sphere, 2015)

Huberband, Shimon, *Kiddush Hashem: Jewish Religious and Cultural Life in Poland During the Holocaust,* Gurock and Hirt, eds, translator David Fishman (Hoboken NJ, Ktav,1987)

Kaplan, Marion A., *Between Dignity and Despair: Jewish Life in Nazi Germany* (New York: OUP, 1998)

Kassow, Samuel D., *Who Will Write Our History?* (Bloomington: Indiana University Press, 2007)

Kolonomos, Jamila Andjela, *Monastir Without Jews: Recollections of a Jewish Partisan in Macedonia,* Robert Bedford ed, translators I. Nehama and B. Berman (New York: FASSAC, 2008)

Liebeschuetz, Rachel Dr, *My Memories of the Time When Hitler Was Dictator of Germany,* unpublished memoir, 1980

Lubetkin, Zivia, *In the Days of Destruction and Revolt,* translator Ishai Tubbin (Israel: Ghetto Fighters' House, 1981)

Bibliography

MacGregor, Neil, *Germany: Memories of a Nation* (London: Penguin, 2016)

Müller, Filip, *Eyewitness Auschwitz* (Chicago: Ivan P. Dee, 1979)

Mulley, Claire, *The Women Who Flew for Hitler; The True Story of Hitler's Valkyries* (London: Macmillan, 2017)

Neumann, Yirmeyahu Oscar, *Gisi Fleischmann: The Story of a Heroic Woman*, translator Karen Gershon (Tel Aviv: WIZO, 1970)

Paldiel, Mordecai, *Saving One's Own: Jewish Rescuers During the Holocaust* (Lincoln: University of Nebraska Press, 2017)

Perl, Gisella Dr, *I was a Doctor in Auschwitz* (New York: International Universities Press, 1948)

Powell, Irmgard, *Don't Let Them See You Cry: Overcoming a Nazi Childhood* (Wilmington: Orange Frazer Press, 2008)

Rudolf, Anthony, ed, *Jerzyk: Diaries, Texts and Testimonies of the Urman Family*, translator Antonia Lloyd-Jones (Bristol: Shearsman Books, 2016)

Sachs, Andrew, *I Know Nothing* (London: The Robson Press, 2015)

Senesh, Hannah, *Her Life and Diary*, translator Nigel Marsh (New York: Schocken Books, 1989)

Sokolow, Reha and Al, *Defying the Tide* (Jerusalem: Gefen Publishing, 2013). Original memoir by Ruth Abraham.

Sommer-Lefkovits, Elisabeth, *Are you here in the hell too? Memories of Troubled Times 1944–45*, translator Marjorie Harris (London: The Menard Press, 1995)

Stessel, Zahava Szasz, *Snow Flowers: Hungarian Jewish Women in an Airplane Factory, Markkleeberg, Germany* (Lanham: Rowman & Littlefield Publishing, 2013)

van Liempt, Ad, *Hitler's Bounty Hunters: The Betrayal of the Jews*, translator S.J. Leinbach (Oxford: Berg Publishers, 2005)

Vitis-Shomron, Aliza, *Youth in Flames: A Teenager's Resistance and Her Fight for Survival in the Warsaw Ghetto* (Omaha: Tell the Story Publishing, 2015)

Temkin-Berman, Basia, *City Within a City*, Emmanuel Berman, ed, translator Jerzy Michalowicz (New York: IP Books, 2012)

Watkins, Olga, *A Greater Love* (Droxford: Splendid Books, 2011)

Weiss, Helga, *Helga's Diary: A Young Girl's Account of Life in a Concentration Camp*, translator Neil Bermel (London: Viking, 2013)

Wünschmann, Kim, *Before Auschwitz: Jewish Prisoners in the Prewar Concentration Camps* (Cambridge: Harvard UP, 2015)

Yahil, Leni, *The Holocaust: The Fate of European Jewry, 1932-1945*, translators Friedman & Galai (Oxford: OUP, 1991)

Zuckerman, Yitzhak, *A Surplus of Memory: Chronicle of the Warsaw Ghetto Uprising* (Berkeley: University of California Press, 1993)

Index

Note: women's names in **bold** have their stories given in detail